Y0-CBU-419

trial manual 5
for the defense
of criminal cases

Volume 1: Proceedings Through
Arraignment

American Law Institute American Bar Association Committee on Continuing Professional Education

As of June 22, 1988

trial manual 5 for the defense of criminal cases

Volume 1: Proceedings Through Arraignment

ANTHONY G. AMSTERDAM
of New York University School of Law
Reporter

A JOINT PROJECT OF THE

American College of Trial Lawyers

National Defender Project of the
National Legal Aid and Defender Association

ALI-ABA Committee on
Continuing Professional Education

AMERICAN LAW INSTITUTE-AMERICAN BAR ASSOCIATION
COMMITTEE ON CONTINUING PROFESSIONAL EDUCATION
4025 CHESTNUT STREET • PHILADELPHIA • PENNSYLVANIA 19104

Library of Congress Catalog Number: 88-71176

© 1988 by The American Law Institute. All rights reserved

First Edition 1967. Fifth Edition 1988

Printed in the United States of America

ISBN: 0-8318-0582-X

James D. Maugans of the ALI-ABA staff
supervised the production of this book.

FOREWORD

Twenty-four years ago, the American College of Trial Lawyers and the ALI-ABA Joint Committee on Continuing Legal Education, known as ALI-ABA, undertook the preparation of publications and the conduct of courses for lawyers in elementary and advanced civil and criminal trial practice.

The President at the time of the American College of Trial Lawyers, Bernard G. Segal of Philadelphia, appointed a Committee on Professional Education in Trial and Appellate Practice, with the late Hicks Epton of Wewoka, Oklahoma, as Chairman, to oversee the project on behalf of the College.

Because of the urgent national need for lawyers to defend criminal cases, the project was initially oriented to the trial of a criminal case. The National Defender Project of the Legal Aid and Defender Association, the American College of Trial Lawyers, and ALI-ABA furnished the financing.

The sponsors were fortunate to obtain for the preparation of the *Trial Manual for the Defense of Criminal Cases* the brilliant and inspired services of Professor Anthony G. Amsterdam, then a member of the faculty of the Law School of the University of Pennsylvania, as Chief Reporter for the project. They were fortunate, too, in the fact that Professor Amsterdam engaged as Associate Reporters for the *Manual* Messrs. Bernard L. Segal, formerly the First Assistant Defender, Defender Association of Philadelphia, and Martin K. Miller, of the Philadelphia bar, whose zeal and expert contributions added immeasurably to the final product.

In addition to the Committees of the sponsors, the Reporters were assisted in their original endeavor by an able advisory committee[1] and by a national panel of consultants.[2]

---

[1]Lawrence A. Aschenbrenner, *Public Defender for the State of Oregon,* Portland, Oregon; John J. Cleary, *Deputy Director of the National Defender Project,* Chicago, Illinois; Edward Cleary, *University of Illinois College of Law,* Champaign, Illinois; Daniel Freed, *Acting Director, Office of Criminal Justice of the Department of Justice,* Washington, D.C.; Gerald S. Gold, Cleveland, Ohio; Richard A. Green, *Project Director, American Bar Association Project on Minimum Standards for Criminal Justice,* New York, New York; David Hall, *County Attorney,*

The first edition of the *Trial Manual for the Defense of Criminal Cases* appeared in 1967, and a second edition followed in 1971. In 1972, Professor Amsterdam undertook continuing responsibility for keeping the *Manual* current and produced the third edition, published in 1974 and supplemented in 1975, 1977, and 1978; and the fourth edition, published in 1984, which grew to two volumes.

Although there is no empirical data to measure the degree to which the *Trial Manual for the Defense of Criminal Cases* has advanced the competence of lawyers to defend criminal cases, the pervasive influence of this work is evidenced by the more than 27,000 copies of the various editions that have been purchased since the work first appeared. Without a doubt it has contributed immeasurably to advancing the cause of criminal trial advocacy in the United States.

Tulsa, Oklahoma; Thomas S. Jackson, Washington, D.C.; C. Paul Jones, *Public Defender, State of Minnesota,* Minneapolis, Minnesota; Joseph Sloane, *President Judge, Court of Common Pleas No. 7,* Philadelphia, Pennsylvania; Roszel C. Thomsen, *Chief Judge, United States District Court,* Baltimore, Maryland; William F. Walsh, Houston, Texas.

Ex officio: The President and the Committee on Professional Education in Trial and Appellate Practice of the American College of Trial Lawyers; The ALI-ABA Joint Committee on Continuing Legal Education and Its Director; Association of Continuing Legal Education Administrators represented by: Eli Jarmel, *Administrator, Institute for Continuing Legal Education, Rutgers School of Law,* Newark, New Jersey; Douglas Lanford, *Director, Continuing Legal Education, University of Alabama, Extension Division,* University, Alabama; Peter C. Manson, *Director, J.C.C.L.E., Virginia State Bar and Virginia Bar Association,* Charlottesville, Virginia; Justin Reid, *Director, Pennsylvania Bar Institute,* Harrisburg, Pennsylvania.

[2]Lawrence A. Aschenbrenner, *Public Defender for the State of Oregon,* Portland, Oregon; James J. Doherty, *Chief Assistant to the Public for Cook County,* Chicago, Illinois; Donald Chapman, *Public Defender for Santa Clara County,* San Jose, California; Sam D. Johnson, *Director, Houston Legal Foundation,* Houston, Texas; Robert Nicco, *Chief Deputy Public Defender of the City and County of San Francisco,* San Francisco, California; Sam Robertson, *Chief, Criminal Division Houston Legal Foundation,* Houston, Texas; William J. Shaw, *Public Defender of St. Louis County,* Clayton, Missouri; Hugh Stanton, *Public Defender of Shelby County,* Memphis, Tennessee; William F. Walsh, Houston, Texas.

This new edition, the fifth, has been divided into three volumes, each of which can stand alone, for those attorneys looking for coverage of particular portions of criminal defense process; as a set, the three volumes will provide a complete manual for all phases of the criminal defense.

This first volume deals with all proceedings from initial client contact through arraignment. The second volume will deal with pretrial motions, preparation, and proceedings; and the third volume will cover all proceedings from the election or waiver of a jury trial through appeal and post-conviction proceedings. Each volume will have its own table of cases and subject index. The size of these individual volumes makes them more manageable and, therefore, more easily transported than the large binders used in the previous edition. The remaining volumes will be published later this year.

This fifth edition incorporates the numerous changes in the law and developments in trial tactics since the publication of the previous editions. A field as fluid and as essential to society as the criminal justice process requires periodic updating through new editions. ALI-ABA is most fortunate that Professor Amsterdam has remained at the helm of this project, thus assuring completeness of coverage and timeliness of the contents.

PAUL A. WOLKIN
Executive Director
American Law Institute-
American Bar Association Committee
on Continuing Professional Education

May 12, 1988

PREFACE

Bernard L. Segal and Martin K. Miller collaborated with me in the first edition of this book. Much of what remains useful in the present edition is the product of their insights and their efforts. My debt to Bernie and Marty continues undiminished. I have so frequently and thoroughly revised the text since 1967, however, that they cannot justly be held responsible for its errors.

Morton S. Freeman was the editor of the early editions and updates; James D. Maugans has edited the more recent ones. To both Mort and Jim, I owe all that any writer can owe to fine, intelligent, sensitive editing. That is a great deal.

Without the encouragement, understanding, and support of Paul A. Wolkin, neither the *Trial Manual* nor the project that produced it would have been possible. Thanks again, Paul.

My other debts would wear upon the reader unjustifiably. I feel them deeply but honor them in silence.

ANTHONY G. AMSTERDAM

CONTENTS

CONTENTS

I. INTRODUCTION

[1] The Nature of the Trial Manual for the Defense of Criminal Cases. The TRIAL MANUAL is a how-to-do-it handbook of basic criminal procedure for the practitioner. It provides a compact guide through the stages of an ordinary criminal case, from arrest and investigation to appeal. Its focus is upon the key points at which decisions must be made and actions taken by defense counsel. Options and factors to be considered in each decision and steps that can be taken to assert the defendant's rights and protect the defendant's interests at each stage are delineated.

[2] Caveat—the uniqueness of cases. Of course, no criminal case is "ordinary" in any but a highly artificial sense. Every criminal charge is intensely personal to the accused. Every accused is a complex and unique individual. Every prosecution of an accused is unique in facts and in law and makes unique demands on the skills of the defense attorney. Every defense attorney has his or her own style. There is no such thing as conducting a criminal defense generally. What is right in one case is wrong in another. The most important attribute of the good criminal lawyer is perceptive selectivity—the ability to determine the precise requirements of each case and to respond to them in a highly specific manner.

[3] Same. No book can capture or instill that quality. All that is attempted here is a listing of available options for the lawyer, an identification of the major strategic considerations that may affect choice among the options, an introductory description of the prevailing legal principles and potential legal arguments, procedures, and practical techniques that defense counsel may encounter or may wish to employ, some warnings about common problems, and some suggestions of ways to avoid them or to cope with them. Counsel will have to cull all

1

these things according to his or her own lights and the needs of the particular case in making the ultimate, lonely decisions what to actually do.

[4] A second caveat—the need for a pro. The MANUAL should communicate enough information to dispel the edge of uneasiness that a lawyer without much criminal experience naturally feels when s/he is retained or appointed in a criminal matter. Having at least a general notion of what is coming and what can be done about it rightly inspires some confidence, and confidence is no less important in dealing with a criminal defendant than with any client. Confidence should not get out of hand, however. Criminal practice *is* a specialty, and the lawyer with relatively little specialized experience must be careful not to bite off more than s/he can chew. In difficult matters s/he should consider the practicability of consulting (formally or informally and on a limited or extended basis), associating with, or withdrawing in favor of, a more experienced criminal practitioner.

II. OUTLINE AND FLOW-CHART
OF A CRIMINAL CASE

[5] **Different procedures for offenses of differing seriousness.** Most jurisdictions have two or more distinct sets of criminal procedures to govern charges of differing degrees of gravity. The jurisdictions vary regarding the number of sets of procedures employed (usually two or three), the charges governed by each set, and the particular courts, stages, and practices involved in each set. Local statutes, rules, and customs must be consulted. (In federal practice, for example, criminal prosecutions in the United States District Courts are governed by the Federal Rules of Criminal Procedure; there is a separate set of Rules of Procedure for the Trial of Misdemeanors Before United States Magistrates.) What follows in paragraphs [6]-[22-A] *infra* is a brief description of the typical stages in each set of procedures in a three-set jurisdiction. In such a jurisdiction, *summary procedure* is used for petty state charges and for most municipal ordinance violations when ordinance violations are conceived as being criminal rather than civil matters. *Misdemeanor procedure* is used for charges of middling seriousness, and *felony procedure* for serious charges. From *summary* through *misdemeanor* to *felony procedure* (the terms are used artificially here, since the line between the second and third categories in many jurisdictions does not correspond exactly to the technical felony-misdemeanor line), procedure becomes increasingly elaborate and increasingly protracted. A summary defendant may be tried, convicted, and sentenced within hours of arrest. A felony defendant is often not formally charged in the court having jurisdiction to try the charge (that is, s/he is not indicted) for months after arrest. It is meaningless to generalize about the duration of "ordinary" cases of the three types; the variations within each type are extreme. Counsel principally familiar with civil litigation will notice, however, that the pace of criminal litigation is generally far more rapid: The early stages (through bind-over) are usually

3

completed within days or weeks, and (except when the defendant is serving a sentence on another conviction) there is nothing like the years of pretrial delay common in civil cases.

[6] Summary Procedure—complaint and warrant or summons. (A) Summary cases ordinarily begin with the filing of a complaint against the defendant before a member of the minor judiciary [hereafter called, generically, a magistrate]. The complainant, who may be a private citizen or a police officer, appears *ex parte* before the magistrate and signs and swears to a written (often printed-form) document, called the complaint, which describes what the defendant did (often in the conclusory language of the criminal statute) and characterizes it as an offense. If the magistrate is satisfied that an offense is legally stated, s/he issues a warrant authorizing the arrest of the defendant, or in many jurisdictions s/he may issue a summons or notice ordering the defendant to appear before the magistrate on a designated date. This procedure, in the jargon, is called the swearing out of a warrant by the complainant.

(B) It should be noted that the complaint ordinarily has two discrete functions in summary procedure: (1) It constitutes the charging paper or initial pleading against the defendant in the court having jurisdiction to try the charge, and (2) it serves as the basis for the issuance of an arrest warrant. In the former aspect its technical sufficiency is governed by state law; but in the latter aspect it must also satisfy the Fourth Amendment to the Constitution of the United States (see paragraphs [227], [229]-[231] *infra*), which requires that arrest warrants be supported by a sworn statement of facts in sufficient detail to permit the issuing magistrate to make an independent determination whether there is probable cause to believe that the defendant has committed the offense charged (see paragraphs [236](C)(2), [241] *infra*). Conclusory forms of complaint that are commonly used may be sufficient as pleadings under state law, but they are assailable under the Fourth Amendment (see paragraph [241](B)(3) *infra*) insofar as the validity of an arrest or detention subsequently comes into issue (*cf. In re Walters*, 15 Cal. 3d 738, 751, 543 P.2d 607, 616-17, 126 Cal. Rptr. 239,

248-49 (1975))—for example, in connection with a motion to suppress illegally obtained evidence (see paragraphs [223], [236](A) *infra*) or in connection with a motion to dismiss the prosecution in those states in which the magistrate's jurisdiction depends upon a valid arrest (see paragraph [136] *infra*; *cf. Welsh v. Wisconsin*, 466 U.S. 740 (1984)).

[7] Same—arrest. In a limited number of cases (principally involving offenses that constitute breaches of the peace), police are authorized to make arrests for summary offenses without a warrant. When a defendant is arrested without a warrant, the officer brings him or her before a magistrate and immediately files the complaint or has a private complainant file it. Practice varies on whether in these cases the magistrate then issues a *pro forma* warrant. Even when they are authorized by law to arrest without a warrant, police will often refuse to do so in summary cases but will require the private complainant to swear out a warrant.

[8] Same—station house bail. Police who have made an arrest for a summary offense with or without a warrant are ordinarily authorized to release the defendant on bail for his or her appearance before the magistrate on a designated date. The amount of this "station house" bail is sometimes subject to police discretion and sometimes regulated by a bail schedule prescribed by a statute or court rule, setting the bail for specified offenses. When police discretion is allowed, the police often have their own more or less inflexible bail schedule.

[9] Same—trial. When the defendant is brought before the magistrate or appears pursuant to summons or to a bail obligation, trial is often had on the spot. If a recently arrested defendant requests a continuance to obtain a lawyer, a continuance is usually granted for a few days. Brief continuances may also be granted the prosecution or the defense because of the unavailability of witnesses or the requirements of adequate preparation. The complaint (or, in some jurisdictions, the warrant) constitutes the charging paper. The defendant is asked to plead to it. If s/he pleads guilty, the magistrate proceeds to sentence. If s/he pleads not guilty, an evidentiary trial is had. In theory, the prosecution presents its evidence first, and the charge should be dismissed if the prosecution's evidence is insufficient, without requiring the defendant to testify or to present defensive evidence. In practice, however, magistrates frequently begin the trial by simply reading the police report or asking the officer to state under oath that it is true and then asking the defendant to tell his or her side of the story. This shortcut procedure is neither authorized by law nor is it constitutional; but if the prosecution's case is relatively simple and easily provable or if the defendant has a good defensive story, the better course for the defense is usually to go along with the magistrate's chosen practice and not to rock the boat by raising legal or constitutional objections to the manner in which the magistrate wishes to proceed. Summary trials before magistrates are ordinarily very informal, and since the magistrate will sometimes acquit a technically guilty defendant on the basis of mitigating circumstances that appeal to his or her sense of fairness, it is helpful to keep on the magistrate's good side. Nevertheless, in appropriate cases— particularly (1) when the complainant or the arresting officer does not appear in court or (2) when there is doubt that the prosecution's evidence will establish the elements of any offense or (3) when the defendant does not wish to testify or has no believable exonerating story to tell or would be assisted in testifying by the prior testimony of prosecution witnesses or (4) when, on the whole, the defendant appears unlikely to attract the magistrate's sympathies—the defendant can, and should, insist upon a procedurally proper trial. The constitutional presumption of innocence gives every criminal defendant a right to require that the prosecution prove the facts establishing guilt "by probative evidence and beyond a reasonable doubt." *Estelle v. Williams*, 425 U.S. 501, 503 (1976) (dictum); see paragraph [385] *infra*. This means that "one accused of a crime is entitled to have his guilt or innocence determined solely on the basis of the evidence introduced at trial, and not on grounds of official suspicion, indictment, continued custody, or other circumstances not adduced as proof at trial." *Taylor v. Kentucky*, 436 U.S. 478, 485 (1978);

Holbrook v. Flynn, 106 S. Ct. 1340, 1345 (1986)(dictum). Thus the prosecution must produce legally admissible evidence, subject to cross-examination, *see Brookhart v. Janis*, 384 U.S. 1 (1966); *cf. Moore v. United States*, 429 U.S. 20 (1976) (per curiam), that is sufficient "to convince a trier of fact beyond a reasonable doubt of the existence of every element of the offense." *Jackson v. Virginia*, 443 U.S. 307, 316 (1979); *see also Pilon v. Bordenkircher*, 444 U.S. 1, 2 (1979)(per curiam). This fundamental constitutional model of a criminal trial is not dispensable merely because the offense or the penality is minor. *See, e.g., Thompson v. City of Louisville*, 362 U.S. 199 (1960); *Johnson v. Florida*, 391 U.S. 596, 598 (1968) (per curiam); *Vachon v. New Hampshire*, 414 U.S. 478, 480 (1974) (per curiam); *cf. Berkemer v. McCarty*, 468 U.S. 420 (1984). In every criminal prosecution the Fifth Amendment privilege against self-incrimination gives the defendant a right not to testify if s/he chooses to remain silent. *Griffin v. California*, 380 U.S. 609 (1965); *Carter v. Kentucky*, 450 U.S. 288 (1981); *and see Baxter v. Palmigiano*, 425 U.S. 308, 317, 318-19 (1976) (dictum); *Jenkins v. Anderson*, 447 U.S. 231, 235 (1980)(dictum). S/he, therefore, plainly cannot be called upon to make a defense before the prosecution has presented and proved its case in open court. *Cf. Brooks v. Tennessee*, 406 U.S. 605 (1972). Defense counsel will often have to bear the primary burden of reminding the magistrate (as tactfully as possible) of these basic principles and of other applicable rules of law in summary trials because, except in some metropolitan areas, the state is seldom represented by a law-trained prosecutor. The arresting policeman or a ranking police officer usually conducts the prosecution, and the district attorney's office is rarely involved. In many localities, indeed, the magistrate is not a lawyer: The Supreme Court of the United States has rejected the contention that law-trained judges are constitutionally required for the trial of minor offenses, at least if a trial *de novo* by a law-trained judge is available as a matter of right on appeal (see paragraph [10] *infra*). *North v. Russell*, 427 U.S. 328 (1976). Because of the hurried, assembly-line atmosphere and carelessness or even ignorance of legal procedures that pervade summary trials, defense counsel who wants procedural regularity may have to demand it explicitly and tenaciously.

[10] **Same—disposition and review.** The magistrate has jurisdiction to dispose of summary cases finally; that is, s/he may acquit the defendant or convict and sentence the defendant. Review of the conviction and sentence, usually by a trial court of record—the court of general jurisdiction of the locality—is frequently but not invariably allowed. This review may take the form of a technical "appeal" (available either as of right or on the discretionary allowance of an appeal by the court of record), or it may take the form of a prerogative writ proceeding, commonly *certiorari*. In some jurisdictions both appeal and *certiorari* may lie. Counsel should be aware that the time for filing an appeal typically is short, sometimes only five days or so; periods for filing *certiorari* tend to be somewhat longer. Local statutes should be checked and often appeal papers prepared in anticipation of conviction. Appeal commonly is for trial *de novo*; that is, once an appeal is filed, the defendant stands as a person accused in the court of record, which tries the case by hearing evidence exactly as though the proceeding had begun in that court. The prosecution (now, generally by a law-trained prosecutor) presents its evidence, the defendant may present evidence, the court acquits or convicts, and upon conviction the court sentences the defendant afresh. This means, of course, that when the magistrate has not imposed the statutory maximum sentence, a defendant who appeals for trial *de novo* risks a harsher sentence on the appeal. *See Colten v. Kentucky*, 407 U.S. 104 (1972); *Ludwig v. Massachusetts*, 427 U.S. 618, 627 (1976). S/he may be able to avoid this risk by using other forms of appeal proceedings or *certiorari* proceedings that involve more limited review, raising only questions of the jurisdiction of the magistrate, the constitutionality and construction of the underlying criminal statute, or other issues of "law" not requiring factual determination and not occasioning an entire trial *de novo* and resentencing. The defendant *is* constitutionally protected, to some extent, against the prosecutor's "upping the ante" by filing new and

more serious charges in the court of record in retaliation for the defendant's appeal. *Blackledge v. Perry*, 417 U.S. 21, 28 (1974); *Thigpen v. Roberts*, 468 U.S. 27 (1984); *and see Borden-kircher v. Hayes*, 434 U.S. 357, 362-63 (1978) (dictum); *United States v. Goodwin*, 457 U.S. 368, 372-77 (1982) (dictum); *Wasman v. United States*, 468 U.S. 559, 565-66 (1984) (plurality opinion) (dictum). Appeal, and in some cases *certiorari*, may lie, even though the defendant has pleaded guilty in the magistrate's court. This plea is inadmissible against the defendant in a *de novo* trial on appeal, since it is rightly regarded simply as a procedural device for kicking the case upstairs. Methods of taking appeal or petitioning for a prerogative writ vary. Ordinarily the defendant must file both an appearance (bail) bond and a cost bond (or a single bond covering both appearance and costs) as the condition of appeal; part or all of this may be waived under state procedure (and the cost bond, at least, must be waived as a matter of federal constitutional law, see paragraph [299] *infra*) for indigents. After disposition in the court of record, appeal on questions of law (or on particular questions of law specified by statute) may lie to an appellate court.

[11] Misdemeanor Procedure—complaint and warrant or summons. Like summary cases, misdemeanor cases frequently begin with a complainant's filing a complaint (sometimes called a criminal arrest complaint or an affidavit for an arrest warrant) before a magistrate. Upon the magistrate's *ex parte* consideration of the complaint, s/he may issue an arrest warrant or, in some cases in some jurisdictions, a summons. In a few localities (principally large cities), there is an administrative practice of having an assistant district attorney examine the complaint before it is filed. Police present their complaints to that assistant as a matter of routine, and a private citizen who goes before a magistrate will be referred by the magistrate to the district attorney's office. Where this practice prevails, the assistant district attorney checks the complaint for substance and form and attaches a paper (sometimes called a buck slip) indicating that s/he has cleared the complaint.

[12] **Same—arrest and bail.** More frequently than in summary cases, arrests are made without a warrant. In most jurisdictions, police are authorized to make warrantless arrests on probable cause for misdemeanors involving a breach of the peace and for any misdemeanor committed in their presence (so-called *on view* or *sight* arrests). Following an arrest with or without a warrant, the police bring the defendant in front of a magistrate. There, in the case of a warrantless arrest, a complaint is filed, and in some jurisdictions a warrant is issued. Police are often authorized to admit arrested persons to bail in misdemeanor cases. A misdemeanor arrest warrant will frequently carry an endorsement by the issuing magistrate setting the amount of bail. If it does not or if arrest is made without a warrant, the police set station house bail in an amount governed by their discretion or by bail schedules prescribed by legislation, court rule, or police administration; and the defendant may also apply to a magistrate or a court of record for bail.

[13] **Same—first court appearance: the preliminary hearing.** Shortly after arrest the defendant is brought, or after the defendant's release on station house bail or after service of a summons s/he appears, before a magistrate for a preliminary hearing. The term *preliminary hearing* is used confusingly to mean sometimes one, sometimes another, or sometimes both of two proceedings, more clearly differentiated by the names *preliminary arraignment* (see paragraph [14] *infra*) and *preliminary examination* (or PX, for short) (see paragraph [15] *infra*). When a preliminary hearing includes both these proceedings, the magistrate reads the complaint or charging paper to the defendant and advises the defendant of the rights to have or waive counsel and to have a preliminary examination. The magistrate appoints counsel if the defendant is entitled to, and does not waive, the appointment of counsel, asks the defendant how s/he pleads, and—upon a plea of not guilty—hears prosecution evidence (usually presented by a law-trained prosecutor) to determine whether there is sufficient proof (described in technical language as "probable cause" or a "*prima facie* case") to justify detaining the defendant pending

the filing of charges and a trial in a court of record. Upon a plea of guilty the magistrate simply commits the defendant (that is, orders the defendant detained for trial) without further examination. In either case, the magistrate sets the amount of bail upon which a defendant who has been ordered detained will be released pending appearance in the trial court; or if station house bail has previously been set, s/he may continue the defendant on that same bail. (In some jurisdictions the defendant is not asked to plead to the complaint; s/he is simply informed that s/he has a right to a preliminary examination and asked whether s/he elects or waives the examination. This is the current federal practice. *See* FED. R. CRIM. P. 5(c).) The preliminary hearing in a misdemeanor case, unlike the magistrate's hearing in a summary case, is not a dispositive proceeding. The magistrate cannot convict the defendant; s/he can only commit the defendant ("bind the defendant over") for proceedings in the court of record, which alone has jurisdiction to try the prosecution on the merits. Similarly, the magistrate cannot acquit a defendant; s/he can only discharge the defendant from custody on the ground that a *prima facie* case has not been made out. Such a discharge does not bar the defendant's rearrest and subsequent bind-over by the same or another magistrate on a fresh record. In some jurisdictions discharge does—and in some it does not—preclude the prosecutor from proceeding without rearrest to charge the defendant in a court of record by filing an information (see paragraph [16] *infra*) and thus requiring the defendant to go to trial on the merits of the offense for which s/he was discharged. When the prosecutor is permitted to proceed in this fashion following a magistrate's discharge, the sole effect of the discharge is to allow the defendant to remain at liberty prior to conviction. In felony cases (see paragraph [20] *infra*) and in misdemeanor cases in jurisdictions permitting grand jury indictments for misdemeanors, discharge by the magistrate usually does not preclude the grand jury from indicting the defendant and thereby forcing the defendant to trial. Practice varies with regard to whether defendants indicted after a magistrate's discharge will remain at large throughout the trial or may be arrested on a bench warrant issued by the criminal court upon the indictment (see paragraph [21] *infra*).

[14] **Same—preliminary arraignment.** (A) In some jurisdictions misdemeanor defendants are not entitled to the full preliminary hearing described in paragraph [13]; they receive only a preliminary arraignment. This means that they are brought or appear before a magistrate; the charges are read to them; they are advised of their rights to counsel, to bail, and to trial; counsel is appointed for them, if appropriate; they are sometimes asked to plead to the charges; bail is set by the magistrate; and unless bail has already been posted in a sufficient amount (see paragraph [12] *supra*) or is posted forthwith, they are remanded into custody pending their first appearance in a court of record or until they post bail for that appearance. (In the wake of *Gerstein v. Pugh*, 420 U.S. 103 (1975), discussed in paragraph [127] *infra*, a defendant who has been arrested without a warrant is constitutionally entitled to some form of judicial determination of probable cause before s/he can be committed to jail or required to post bail for trial. As construed in *Gerstein*, "the Fourth Amendment requires the States to provide a fair and reliable determination of probable cause as a condition for any significant pretrial restraint of liberty." *Baker v. McCollan*, 443 U.S. 137, 142 (1979) (dictum). Jurisdictions that do not provide a full preliminary hearing must, therefore, modify their preliminary arraignment procedures to supply a method for making this determination—for example, by requiring that the magistrate review the sworn complaint or affidavits to assure that they disclose sufficiently incriminating facts, in sufficiently concrete detail, to establish probable cause. *See In re Walters*, 15 Cal. 3d 738, 543 P.2d 607, 126 Cal. Rptr. 239 (1975).) If the defendant pleads not guilty or if no plea is required at this kind of preliminary arraignment, the defendant may be given a date for his or her first appearance in the court of record (that is, for a formal arraignment), or the case may be referred to the calendaring officer of the court of record ("the trial court"). The prosecutor will thereafter file an information against the

defendant in the trial court (see paragraph [16] *infra*), and the defendant's next trip to court will be his or her formal arraignment in the trial court upon that information (see paragraphs [16], [188]-[200] *infra*). If the defendant pleads guilty at the preliminary arraignment, the case is ordinarily calendared or referred to be calendared for a single appearance in the trial court, at which the defendant will be arraigned upon an information (which may be filed in open court on the date of this appearance), and the defendant will be expected to plead guilty before the trial judge, who will often impose sentence forthwith. (See paragraph [135] (A) *infra*.) (The reason for requiring the defendant to plead at the preliminary arraignment in some jurisdictions that do not provide for a full preliminary hearing is to facilitate the setting of an early date for these proceedings at arraignment in the trial court in cases in which the defendant is not contesting guilt. See paragraph [305] *infra*.)

(B) In other jurisdictions the defendant is entitled to a full preliminary hearing—both the preliminary arraignment just described and the preliminary examination described in paragraph [15] *infra*—but, as a matter of general practice or of practicability in particular cases, only the preliminary arraignment is held at the time of the defendant's first appearance before the magistrate. Frequently the defendant has no lawyer at that time. So, after the charges have been read and the defendant has been advised of the rights to counsel, to bail, and to a preliminary examination, the proceeding is adjourned to a later date to permit the defendant to retain counsel. When the defendant is indigent and does not waive counsel, the magistrate may appoint counsel to appear for him or her at the delayed preliminary hearing date or, under the clumsy system in effect in some localities, may refer the case to the trial court for the appointment of counsel. Appointment of counsel for indigent defendants is constitutionally required in all criminal prosecutions, whether classified as felony, misdemeanor, or summary prosecutions, in which any term of imprisonment is going to be imposed as a result of conviction (*Argersinger v. Hamlin*, 407 U.S. 25 (1972); *Scott v. Illinois*, 440 U.S. 367 (1979); *Baldasar v. Illinois*, 446 U.S. 222 (1980)); and

it is likely that this right to appointment of counsel, which the
Supreme Court has already held applicable at the preliminary
arraignment and preliminary examination stages of felony
prosecutions, *see White v. Maryland,* 373 U.S. 59 (1963) (per
curiam); *Coleman v. Alabama,* 399 U.S. 1 (1970); *Moore v. Illinois,*
434 U.S. 220 (1977); *cf. Gerstein v. Pugh, supra,* 420 U.S. at 122-
23, is also applicable at the parallel stages of misdemeanor
prosecutions. When the preliminary hearing is set over either
because the defendant is unrepresented or because local practice routinely requires a second separate appearance for preliminary examination after the preliminary arraignment, the
magistrate may commit the defendant pending the preliminary
examination and may set new bail for the defendant's appearance at that examination or may continue the defendant's
release on whatever bail s/he has previously posted. The preliminary examination can be waived by a defendant, and many
magistrates accept or even coerce these waivers from uncounseled accuseds at their first appearance. Coercion, and perhaps
even acceptance, of a waiver of preliminary examination by a
defendant who is not represented by a lawyer is unconstitutional (see paragraph [130] *infra*); remedies for the deprivation
of preliminary examination will be discussed in paragraphs
[129]-[134] *infra*.

[15] **Same—preliminary examination.** At the preliminary
examination ordinarily the prosecution may amend the complaint or charging paper to charge additional or other offenses
relating to the episode for which the defendant was arrested
or summoned. The prosecution presents its evidence; but since
it is required to make only a *prima facie* case at this stage, it
frequently discloses only a part of what it will ultimately present
against the defendant at trial. In some jurisdictions or localities
magistrates will receive, and base a bind-over upon, hearsay
evidence; where this is permitted, the prosecutor frequently
calls only the investigating police officer. Cross-examination
by defense counsel is permitted (although it is frequently un-
conscionably limited by the magistrate, again on the theory
that only a *prima facie* showing, not guilt, is at issue); and the
defendant may, although s/he usually does not, present ex-

culpatory evidence. At the conclusion of the hearing the magistrate may discharge the defendant or bind the defendant over for trial on specified charges. In many jurisdictions these may be any charges on which there is sufficient evidence in the magistrate's record to constitute probable cause; they need not be limited to the charges made in the complaint. (If, however, the complaint failed to give the defendant fair notice of the charges on which s/he is subsequently bound over, so that s/he was denied the opportunity to defend against those charges—or at least to decide advisedly whether to attempt to defend against them—at the preliminary examination, this practice is subject to serious constitutional challenge. See paragraph [146] *infra*.) The magistrate now sets bail for the defendant who is bound over; frequently, but not invariably, s/he will continue the amount of station house bail previously set.

[16] Same—information and arraignment. The misdemeanor defendant is tried in a court of record. Prosecution in that court begins with the filing of an information, which is a sworn statement by the prosecuting attorney describing what the defendant did (often in conclusionary terms that track the statutory definition of the offense charged) and characterizing it as criminal. In some jurisdictions the prosecutor may charge in an information only offenses for which the defendant has been previously bound over; in others s/he may charge a bound-over defendant with any related offenses (or sometimes any offenses at all) of which there is evidence in the magistrate's transcript, whether or not the magistrate held the defendant for those offenses; in still others the prosecutor (sometimes as a matter of right, sometimes by leave of court) may charge a bound-over defendant with offenses that go beyond the magistrate's transcript and may also file an information against a defendant who has been entirely discharged by the magistrate or who has never been arrested and brought before a magistrate. The defendant is arraigned on the information; that is, it is read or handed to the defendant in open court, and s/he is required to plead to the charges in it. Ordinarily s/he has had advance notice of the arraignment date, and frequently the case proceeds to trial immediately following a plea of not guilty at arraignment or to sentence immediately following a plea of guilty or *nolo contendere*. If trial or sentencing is not immediate, a trial date or sentencing date is usually set following the entry of the defendant's plea. Special pleas (for example, double jeopardy) and motions and objections attacking the information (for failure to charge an offense or on other grounds) or the propriety of the proceedings at the preliminary hearing or any other anterior stage are—depending upon local practice—required to be made by the defendant either before arraignment or before entering one of the general pleas (not guilty; guilty; *nolo contendere*) or before the start of trial.

[17] **Same—trial; disposition; review.** Most jurisdictions give the defendant a right to trial by jury for the majority of misdemeanor offenses; all are required by the federal Constitution to recognize the right to jury trial for "serious" misdemeanors—a category that includes, at the least, any misdemeanor for which a sentence of more than six months' imprisonment is authorized. See paragraph [315] *infra*. Misdemeanor defendants, however, frequently waive a jury and elect a bench trial. Evidentiary trial is had in the usual fashion: The prosecution presents its case in chief first; the defendant (following the customary motion for acquittal on the prosecution's proof or "demurrer to the evidence," as it is sometimes called) may present defensive evidence; the prosecution (relatively infrequently in misdemeanor cases) may present rebuttal. The defendant renews the motion for acquittal; if it is denied, counsel make their closing arguments to the jury or the bench; then, in a jury-trial case, comes the judge's charge. The jury or judge returns a verdict or finding of acquittal or conviction; and, in the event of conviction, the judge often imposes sentence without more ado. In some jurisdictions the convicted defendant has a right to a postponement of several days before sentence is pronounced (called, in the jargon, demanding his or her time), but deferred sentencing hearings and presentence reports are not commonplace in misdemeanor cases. Following the entry of a formal judgment of conviction

and commitment (or sentence to a fine), the defendant may appeal for review of the ordinary sort by an appellate court. Bail pending appeal is usually allowed in the discretion of the trial judge, reviewable for abuse. In some jurisdictions bail pending appeal is allowed as a matter of right in misdemeanor cases; in others it is a right in any case in which the sentence does not include a term of imprisonment.

[18] Felony procedure—arrest and bail. Felony procedure is generally similar to misdemeanor procedure through the stage of the magistrate's bind-over. A few significant differences deserve note. Ordinarily police are authorized to arrest without a warrant when they have probable cause to believe that a suspect has committed a felony; most felony arrests are, in fact, made without warrants. Magistrates usually have little or no power to issue summonses in lieu of arrest warrants in felony cases, and they sparingly exercise what little power they have. As a result, felony prosecutions almost invariably involve an arrest, and it is quite usual for the complaint to be filed after arrest. Station house bail is also much less frequently authorized in felony than in misdemeanor cases, and in some jurisdictions magistrates themselves are powerless to admit an arrested person to bail on some or all serious but bailable felony charges. In these cases bail-setting must be sought by *habeas corpus* or by a motion or other statutorily prescribed procedure in a court of record. This means that most defendants get at least a short taste of jail at the beginning of a felony case.

[19] Same—preliminary hearing; the role of the prosecutor. A law-trained prosecutor is more frequently involved in the drafting of felony complaints than of misdemeanor complaints, and s/he sometimes participates with the police in postarrest interrogation of a defendant. Prosecutors, therefore, tend to know more about felony cases earlier in the process and to undertake early responsibility for deciding whether and what to charge. They also tend to prepare more carefully for the preliminary examination, which in felony cases is almost never left solely to the police. Magistrates are generally more willing in felony than in misdemeanor matters to grant the prosecution or the defense time to prepare for the examination, and prosecutors will often ask for and secure a continuance for the purpose of entirely defeating the defendant's right to a preliminary examination by the device described in paragraphs [21], [129]-[131] *infra*. In any event, more in felony cases than in misdemeanor cases do preliminary arraignment and preliminary examination assume the aspect of two distinct procedural stages, often separated by a few days or longer unless, of course, the defendant at preliminary arraignment waives a preliminary examination and is immediately bound over.

[20] **Same—the grand jury.** The principal difference between misdemeanor and felony procedure involves the intervention of the grand jury in felony cases. In many jurisdictions felony defendants may be prosecuted only by indictment. An indictment is a charging paper (in content similar to an information) returned by a grand jury. A grand jury is a body of citizens, usually 15 to 23 in number, ordinarily chosen from the general venire of jurors for a term of court, who meet in secret to hear the prosecutor's presentation of evidence (or, in theory, any other witnesses that the grand jury may call) in support of written charges drafted by the prosecutor, called bills (or, in theory, any other charges that the grand jury may want to consider). Grand jury proceedings are not attended by a judge; the grand jury takes its legal instructions from the prosecutor; neither defendant nor defense counsel is present during its evidentiary hearings; defendant and defense witnesses may be called to testify by the grand jury in its discretion (subject to any valid claim of the privilege against self-incrimination). If a majority of grand jurors is satisfied that there is probable clause to believe that the defendant named in a bill is guilty or that there is *prima facie* evidence of the defendant's guilt or that the evidence against the defendant would warrant conviction by a trial jury if unrebutted and believed (the standards are differently phrased in different jurisdictions but differ little in substance), the grand jury "returns" (that is, reports out to the court) the bill endorsed as a "true bill." This is the

indictment that requires the defendant to go to trial. If a majority of the jurors is unwilling to return a true bill, the jurors "ignore" the bill ("no-bill" or "*ignoramus*" the case), a disposition that precludes the prosecutor from proceeding to trial at this juncture but does not bar the prosecutor from resubmitting the bill to the same or another grand jury at any time within the statute of limitations. (In some jurisdictions, a resubmission may be made only with leave of court.) It should be noted that a felony defendant's right to prosecution only by indictment of a grand jury may be waived: On a written waiver of the right, the case is prosecuted by information (as in misdemeanor procedure), or in some jurisdictions the grand jury returns an indictment based solely upon the bill and written waiver, without hearing evidence. A number of jurisdictions permit felony charges (or some subclass of less serious felony charges) to be prosecuted by information; in these jurisdictions the grand jury procedure is available but not required; the prosecutor has the option to proceed by indictment or by information.

[21] Same—relation of the grand jury to preliminary hearing. In theory (and in most cases in actuality) the grand jury does not act on a defendant's case until after s/he has had a full preliminary hearing and been bound over (the style in felony cases is "bound over to the grand jury"). But the grand jury is legally empowered to indict any person without an antecedent bind-over, preliminary hearing, or even arrest; and once its indictment has been returned, a judge of the criminal court may, without further inquiry, issue a "bench warrant" authorizing the defendant's arrest and detention pending trial. Using these two legal authorities, a prosecutor who does not want to expose the prosecution's case at preliminary examination will frequently—often as a matter of routine practice in some types of cases, such as sex and narcotics cases—(a) request the magistrate at preliminary arraignment to continue the preliminary hearing of an arrested accused, (b) submit the case to the grand jury during the period of the continuance, (c) obtain an indictment and a bench warrant, and (d) thus obviating the need for a bind-over to justify holding the defendant for trial, effectively circumvent the defendant's right to a preliminary examination. (The possibilities for defeating this prosecutorial tactic are discussed in paragraph [130] *infra*.) When a bench warrant is issued, the issuing judge will ordinarily set bail by endorsement on the warrant. If s/he does not, a motion for bail may be made to any judge of the court. If the bail endorsed on the warrant is too high, a motion to reduce it is appropriate.

[22] **Same—arraignment; trial; disposition; review.** The indictment, like an information, serves as the accusatory pleading on which the defendant is tried. S/he is arraigned by being read the indictment in open court and asked how s/he pleads to it. Ordinarily s/he will plead not guilty, guilty, or *nolo contendere* (for present purposes, the equivalent of a guilty plea) or request a continuance to permit adequate preparation before pleading. As in misdemeanor practice (see paragraph [16] *supra*), special pleas, motions, and objections attacking the indictment, the grand jury proceedings, or other preliminary proceedings are required to be filed—depending on the jurisdiction—prior to arraignment, to the entry of the pleas of not guilty, guilty, or *nolo contendere*, or to trial. On a guilty plea the defendant may be sentenced forthwith, ordinarily following argument of counsel, and sometimes following a brief evidentiary hearing on the question of sentence. Alternatively, sentencing may be deferred pending a presentence investigation by the probation officer of the court or a fuller evidentiary hearing or both. More frequently than in misdemeanor procedure, a convicted felony defendant has a right to "demand [his] [her] time" and thereby secure a delayed sentencing proceeding. In murder cases (and, less often, in the case of other offenses divided into degrees), a defendant is sometimes permitted to plead guilty only to the offense generally, following which plea a judge or jury hears evidence to determine the degree of the offense and to set the sentence. Similarly, a jury may be impaneled to fix sentence on a plea of guilty to any felony for which the applicable statutes authorize or require jury sentencing. After a plea of not guilty to a felony, the case seldom proceeds to trial immediately following arraignment;

usually at that time it is assigned a future trial date. The case is heard by a jury unless the defendant waives jury trial. Trial practice is similar to that in misdemeanor cases but with a host of minor differences: Rules governing joinder of offenses and defendants may be different, more time and greater *voir dire* questioning of prospective jurors is generally allowed in selecting a felony jury, more peremptory challenges to jurors are generally permitted in felony trials, and so forth. Following conviction, greater use is made of the practices of deferred sentencing, presentence investigation, and evidentiary hearings on sentence than in misdemeanor cases. Appeal lies from the final judgment to an appellate court for consideration of claims of trial error within the ordinary scope of appellate review; bail pending appeal is allowed in the discretion of the trial court, subject to appellate revision for abuse.

[22-A] Flow-chart of summary, misdemeanor, and felony procedures. There follows a flow-chart of the three sorts of procedures described in paragraphs [5]-[22] *supra*:

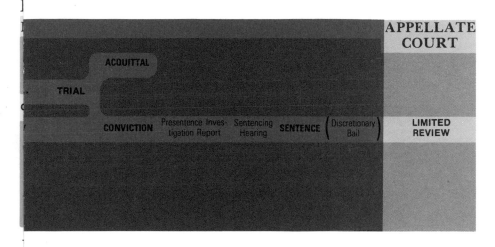

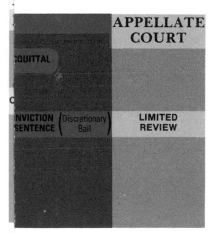

III. THE LAWYER'S ENTRANCE INTO THE CASE—FIRST STEPS

[23] **The stage of entry.** Defense counsel may have occasion to enter a criminal case at almost any of the stages just described. In the early stages, at least, the critical ingredients for beginning to provide proper representation of the client are essentially the same. The major differences in the jobs that confront counsel at the different stages principally involve the order in which various initial steps are required to be taken and the amount of time available to familiarize oneself with the situation and its demands and to make decisions. The lawyer who has some general knowledge of the interests of the client that need to be protected at a given stage can usually begin to function adequately, notwithstanding both a lack of detailed information concerning the intricacies of local practice and procedure and a lack of opportunity to prepare completely on technical matters. S/he will have to learn the details and the technical points rapidly as s/he proceeds with the work of providing representation. Here, as elsewhere, counsel's preparation and research should be as thorough as is practicable. Knowledge of the individual case and client and of the local procedures and functionaries can spell the difference between wise choices of action and foolish ones. But at the outset of a criminal case particularly, a tradeoff does exist between the virtues of time-consuming preparation and the importance of getting started quickly to protect the client's interests when they may be irreparably damaged by fast-breaking events that will not wait for counsel to make a consummately prepared appearance.

[24] **The request for help.** Three common situations in which a lawyer enters a criminal case are discussed in the following sections, paragraphs [25]-[53] *infra*. Best characterized by reference to the circumstances in which the lawyer finds the client, they involve: (a) a telephone call for help from, or on behalf of, a client in custody soon after arrest; (b)

25

a call for help for a client at large who is, or may be, wanted by the police; and (c) an appointment or a retainer to represent a client making a first court appearance at preliminary arraignment. These situations have been selected for treatment both because they are innately important—in view of the frequency of their occurrence and the urgency for quick action that they present—and because discussion of them develops considerations that must be taken into account by the lawyer who enters a case under other and varying conditions at different stages. In each case the focus in this chapter is on the immediate needs generated by the client's circumstances and the practical things that the lawyer should do to meet those needs. Legal procedures and doctrines that are implicated will be discussed in more detail in subsequent chapters.

A. The client in custody shortly after arrest

[25] **Summary.** Counsel called on behalf of a recently arrested defendant who is being held in custody must:

(1) In talking to the caller,

(a) Take the caller's name (with spelling), address, telephone number, and relationship to the defendant;

(b) Take the defendant's name (with spelling);

(c) Ask where the police took the defendant, if the caller knows;

(d) Ask where the arrest was made; whether made by uniformed or plain-clothes officers; and whether the officers were of any special squad (if the caller knows) or were otherwise identifiable by the caller;

(e) Ask what the defendant was arrested for and what the officers said s/he was charged with, if the caller knows;

(f) Ask whether, if counsel can arrange bail, the caller or the defendant's family (and who specifically) can put up bail money and how much bail money they can make available and how soon;

(g) Ask how the caller can be reached during the next several hours and tell the caller how to reach counsel during that time;

(h) Get the caller's authorization to represent the defendant;

(i) If counsel will handle the case at this stage, tell the caller so.

[If the caller can and will put up sufficient funds to cover any bail that is realistically likely to be set (or to pay the necessary bond premium) and if the location of the defendant's detention is known with certainty at this time, counsel should also arrange to have the caller meet counsel at the police station or court where bail will be posted (or at a bondsman's office) at a designated time.]

(2) Locate the client by telephoning the police quarters where s/he is likely to be (see paragraphs [27]-[28], [32] *infra*).

(3) Speak to the client by phone if possible and:

(a) Tell the client that counsel is a lawyer and that [caller] has asked counsel to represent the client and to give the client whatever help counsel can;

(b) Ask the client whether s/he wants counsel to represent him or her; explain that counsel is willing to represent the client if s/he wishes, just for now and for the immediate future, until they can get together and talk about whether the client wants counsel to continue with the case; and obtain an explicit statement by the client that s/he wants counsel to represent him or her;

(c) Tell the client that counsel is now representing the client and that counsel is coming down to see the client immediately (or as soon as counsel judges that s/he can get there);

(d) Tell the client to say nothing at all to the police until counsel arrives; to say nothing to anybody—cellmates, persons arrested with the client, their lawyers, reporters, or anyone else—until counsel arrives; to refuse politely to answer any questions, saying that s/he is refusing on advice of counsel, who has told the client that s/he should speak to no one until s/he has first talked with counsel; to say no to any requests by police or anyone else to search the client's home or car or any other place or thing; to say no to any requests by police or anyone else to accompany them to any place and to tell them that s/he wants to stay where s/he is because counsel is coming; if the client is taken to any place, to remain absolutely silent and not to point out anything or go through any motions that the police or anyone may request the client to make or to help them in any way; not to sign any papers or forms of any sort; and, if anyone tries to talk with the client about anything—or if anyone accuses the client of anything or gives any evidence against the client or says anything against the client—to tell them that a lawyer has asked the client not to talk to anyone or to say anything until the lawyer gets there;

(e) Tell the client to refuse politely, on advice of counsel, to appear in any lineup or to be shown to any person for identification in counsel's absence; to object to any lineup or identification that the police may want to stage and to ask to phone counsel; not to resist physically if the police insist on putting the client in a lineup or displaying the client for identification and not to try to cover his or her face or to make faces but to observe all of the people and everything that happens at the lineup (see paragraph [36] *infra*) and to remember them until s/he has a chance to write them down *after* the lineup is concluded;

(f) Tell the client to object to any physical examination, inspection of the client's body, taking of hair or blood samples, or any other police investigation in which s/he is used in any way in the absence of counsel but not to resist physically; and to refuse on advice of counsel any request to take a lie detector test;

(g) Tell the client that if news photographers try to photograph the client, s/he should not duck, hide his or her face, or make faces but just remain calm;

(h) Ask the client exactly where s/he is now (by precinct station number or street address or by description of the building and its location) and where *within* the building s/he is; ask whether s/he knows of any plans by the police to move him or her elsewhere; if so, ask where and when;

(i) Ask the client whether the police are mistreating the client in any way; whether s/he is hurt or injured or needs any sort of medical attention;

(j) Ask the client what the police have said that the client is charged with (being sure to ask, "Is that all of the charges that they have told you?"); whether the police said anything about possibly adding any other charges or about the client's being involved in any other criminal matters, and specifically what;

(k) Ask the client whether s/he has been told (and, if not, ask the client to ask the police now) whether bail has been set for the client and how much;

(l) Ask the client who should be called (spouse, family, friend, employer) to put up bail money or pay the bond premium (unless, of course, counsel has already arranged for bail money in speaking to the original caller and is sure that the original caller will come through) and take the person's name (with spelling) and phone number or other contact information;

(m) Give the client the telephone number at which counsel can be reached unless counsel is leaving immediately for the police station; and

(n) Instruct the client to tell a police officer, while counsel is still on the phone to hear this said, that the client does not want to talk with the police or prosecuting authorities in counsel's absence but wants to conduct all future communications with the authorities through counsel as his or her attorney.

(4) Speak to the investigating officer by telephone and:

(a) Tell the officer that counsel is an attorney and is representing the client;

(b) Ask the officer where the client now is (including location within the building); whether there are any plans to move the client elsewhere and, if so, where and when (adding a request to hold the client where s/he is if that seems best to counsel);

(c) Ask the officer what specific charges are now placed against the client (being sure to ask, "Is that all the charges now?"); whether other charges are being considered; and, if so, what they are;

(d) Ask the officer whether bail has been set for the client; if so, how much; if not, whether station house bail is ordinarily fixed for charges such as those against the client and how much; and if the officer has indicated a possibility that additional charges may be placed against the client, ask what the bail on those charges will be;

(e) Tell the officer that counsel is requesting the officer not to interrogate the client or to ask the client any questions until counsel arrives; not to ask for the client's consent to conduct any search or investigation; not to remove the client from the station for any purpose (except for medical treatment if the client has indicated that s/he needs medical treatment); and not to place the client in a lineup or exhibit the client for identification or make any physical or mental examination, body inspection, or test of any sort until counsel arrives (expressing the hope that counsel will be able to cooperate with the officer as soon as s/he arrives but saying that s/he really must ask the officer not to deal any further with the client at this time until counsel has had a chance to confer with the client and to find out what this matter is all about);

(f) Tell the officer to take the client to the hospital if the client has indicated that s/he needs medical treatment; and ask to what hospital the client will be taken, so that counsel can meet them there;

(g) Tell the officer that counsel has instructed the client to say nothing, to answer no questions, to give no consents, and to participate in no investigative procedures until counsel arrives;

(h) Tell the officer that counsel will be there as soon as s/he possibly can; and

(i) Take the officer's name (with spelling), rank, and number; and ask the officer where s/he will be and how counsel can contact him or her during the next few hours.

(5) Telephone a bail bondsman if one is to be used; confirm that s/he will write bail for the client; ask the amount of the premium, whether any collateral will be required, and in what form s/he wants the premium and any collateral; and arrange to have the bondsman's agent meet counsel at the police station or wherever bail must be posted, stating its location.

(6) Telephone the person identified by the client or the original caller as the one who will post bail or pay the bond premium; tell the person how much money or security is re-

quired and in what form; and arrange with the person to bring it to the bondsman or to meet counsel and the bondsman's agent at the police station or wherever bail must be posted, stating its location.

(7) Go to the station where the client is being detained, taking some identification as an attorney. Ask to see the client, interview the client (see paragraphs [51], [76]-[90] *infra*), and arrange the client's release on bail (see paragraphs [38]-[41], [54]-[71] *infra*).

[26] **Same.** These various steps are discussed in more detail in the paragraphs that follow. Understanding of the necessity for them and appreciation of the needs of a client in custody shortly after arrest require some initial knowledge of postarrest police practices. See the next four paragraphs. One general point respecting police organization should be made at the outset. Each police station or headquarters has (a) a commanding officer on duty and (b) a "desk" officer who handles inquiries from the public, including counsel's. When phoning or arriving at the station, counsel should first seek information from the desk officer relating to the client: the room or cell where s/he is being held, the charges on which s/he has been booked or that are under investigation, and the names of the investigating officers. Complaints about mistreatment of the client or about police practices in the case should be directed to the commanding officer. When talking to an officer, counsel should always take the officer's name (with spelling), rank, and number.

[27] **Police practices following arrest—logging in.** Following an arrest, the arrested person (hereafter called defendant) is usually taken to the police station or headquarters for the division or precinct in which the arrest took place. The defendant's arrival there is ordinarily, but not invariably, noted in a police log, which indicates in order of appearance before the log officer the names and log-in times of all persons arrested and brought to the station. Practice here varies widely. Some police conceive this logging-in as a part of the "booking" or "slating" process described in paragraph [30] *infra*. They

maintain a single blotter or arrestbook in which is recorded (a dozen defendants or so to the page) not merely the name and the time of logging but also the time and the place of arrest, some identifying characteristics of the defendant, such as sex and race, and the charge. Some police conceive logging-in as a recording routine unrelated to "booking" and maintain two books—the log and the blotter. Under this latter practice all persons brought in may be logged in on arrival, and those against whom it is decided to lodge charges may later be noted on the blotter. Or persons brought in against whom it is clear that charges will be lodged may be noted immediately on the blotter, whereas persons brought in "for investigation" or "on suspicion" may be noted in the log (sometimes called the "small book"). In any event, police generally feel no obligation to make an immediate log or blotter entry when investigative reasons exist not to do so, for example, when interrogation is in progress or when there is fear that a defendant's relatives or lawyer may be looking for the defendant, eager to obtain the defendant's release on bail or on *habeas corpus*.

[28] Same—interrogation and other investigative procedures. (A) Whatever the logging-in practice, the defendant is ordinarily subjected to some interrogation by the investigating officers prior to the full, official recording of his or her arrest, called booking or slating. If the arrest charge is at all serious, a rank officer, detective, special deputy, criminal investigator, or other specialized investigative agent (depending, of course, on the size and the organization of the police force) assumes responsibility for the case from the outset and conducts the interrogation. In a metropolitan police department the interrogation is normally handled by detectives in their own headquarters in the precinct station house. When officers from special squads, such as narcotics or vice, are involved, the defendant may be taken—either immediately from the place of arrest or from the station where s/he was initially brought by arresting officers—to the central headquarters of the special squad. The interrogation is designed to secure the defendant's admission or confession of the offense for which s/he was arrested, the defendant's implication of any other persons involved in the offense, and the defendant's admission or confession of other "uncleared" offenses that s/he may have committed. In particular cases, such as those involving the arrest of persons known or believed to be youth-gang members, the police may also seek, through interrogation, to learn general information about recent developments in the neighborhood or the gang or about its other members, which information they believe to be useful for intelligence or crime control.

(B) In addition to interrogation a defendant may be subjected to other investigative procedures before or immediately after booking. S/he may be exhibited to witnesses in a lineup or showup. S/he may be taken to the scene of the crime to "reenact" or demonstrate what happened. S/he may be taken home or elsewhere to assist the police in finding secreted or discarded weapons, loot, or evidence and, in this connection, may be asked to give consent to warrantless police searches that, without this consent, would require a search warrant. See paragraphs [229]-[231], [240]-[248] *infra*. Specimens of the defendant's hair or blood, swabs, washes, or body scrapings may be taken for laboratory analysis. Each of these proceedings may develop incriminating evidence. A defendant may have rights not to be subjected to some of these procedures and not to be subjected to others in the absence of his or her attorney. See paragraphs [227]-[249], [363], [374] *infra*. But these rights can be waived—and they often will be waived unless counsel takes adequate steps to insure their protection.

[29] Defendant's rights of communication. A defendant's right to make a telephone call (or two) after arrest is recognized by some state statutes and police department regulations. These may not explicitly require that the defendant be permitted to make the telephone call prior to the conclusion of interrogation and other investigative procedures. The constitutional requirements announced in *Miranda v. Arizona*, 384 U.S. 436 (1966), however, supplant these local regulations and require that a defendant undergoing interrogation be permitted to make a call to obtain counsel at any point after arrest. *Miranda* expressly requires that any in-custody interrogation be preceded by warnings to the suspect (a) that s/he has the right to remain silent; (b) that anything s/he says may be used against him or her in court; (c) that s/he has a right to the presence of an attorney during interrogation; and (d) that, if s/he cannot afford an attorney, s/he has a right to the appointment of counsel without cost prior to any interrogation. See paragraph [363](E) *infra*. "[A] person taken into custody [must] be advised immediately" of these rights, *Doyle v. Ohio*, 426 U.S. 610, 617 (1976) (dictum); *see, e.g.*, *Berkemer v. McCarty*, 468 U.S. 420 (1984), and "the police [must] respect the accused's decision to exercise the rights outlined in the warnings." *Moran v. Burbine*, 106 S. Ct. 1135, 1141 (1986) (dictum); *see, e.g.*, *Smith v. Illinois*, 469 U.S. 91 (1984) (per curiam).

[30] **Booking or slating and fingerprinting.** Following the interrogation period and the decision of the police to formally charge a defendant with an offense, the charges are noted on police records. This is the booking or slating process, which involves making a record of the name of the defendant and of some identifying information about him or her, of the time and place of the arrest, and of the offenses charged. These items are noted in summary form on a police blotter and, in more detail, on arrest cards, on file forms, or on both maintained for the individual case. Detailed and sometimes extended printed forms may be filled out that require the defendant to be questioned about his or her vital statistics and some of the circumstances of the arrest. In particular cases (narcotics arrests, for example), additional forms may be used that require the defendant to be questioned about his or her background and criminal record. The defendant's fingerprints and photograph are almost invariably taken as a part of the booking process. Upon completion of the process, the defendant is incarcerated pending preliminary arraignment or release on bail.

[31] **Answering a call and locating the client.** If the call requesting the attorney to represent a defendant in police custody comes from someone other than the defendant, it is important to obtain the name, address, and telephone number

of that person and his or her relationship to the defendant. The police may require that the attorney furnish this information in order to establish the attorney's right to visit the defendant for an initial interview. The caller should be asked to spell the caller's own name and the defendant's. (If Mr. Fish's name is spelled Physch, counsel will avoid a lot of subsequent trouble by this detail). If the caller has no telephone, counsel should ask for the number of a nearby telephone (neighbor, local drugstore, or bar if these are open) and the name of a person at that number who can find the caller. It is also wise to ask the caller where s/he will be during the next several hours, in the event more information is needed. Counsel can often save much delay and effort in securing the client's release on bail if s/he asks the caller at this time whether the caller can and will put up bail for the defendant, how much the caller can put up, and if the caller is not going to provide bail money, who can. In any case, the caller should be asked where the defendant was taken by the arresting officers. Even if the caller thinks s/he knows the answer to this question, the attorney should ask the following additional questions to assist in locating the defendant: where (by precise street location) the arrest took place; whether it was made by uniformed police or detectives; whether the caller knows any of the arresting officers by name, number, or by the officer's usual beat; and whether the arresting officers appeared to be from any special squad (such as the highway patrol, the tactical patrol, the narcotics or the vice squad). See paragraph [32] *infra*. The caller should also be asked to describe, if s/he knows, the circumstances of the arrest and what the police said that the defendant was charged with.

[32] **Same.** The most effective way to locate the defendant is usually a series of trial-and-error telephone calls. The order of the calls depends in part upon the time elapsed since the arrest, but the first call should ordinarily go to the desk officer of the police station for the precinct where the arrest occurred, and the second call should ordinarily go to the detectives who are likely to be interrogating the defendant, that is, unless a special squad is known to be involved, the detective head-

quarters in the arrest precinct. See paragraphs [27]-[28] *supra*. (Remember that the desk officer and other uniformed police at a station house will have no communicable knowledge of the presence of a defendant until s/he has been turned over to them by the interrogating detectives for booking.) If counsel fails to obtain information of the defendant's whereabouts from the precinct-station desk or detectives, calls should next be made to the headquarters of special squads and then to the commanding officer on duty in the arrest precinct. If the commanding officer claims ignorance, counsel should ask for the name and phone number of the highest ranking official of the police department then on duty and should call this official to confront him or her with the fact that counsel's client has disappeared since being taken into police custody. Finally, a call to a member of the prosecutor's staff objecting to the incommunicado detention of the defendant may produce information. All else failing, counsel should call a judge of the court of record of the county and ask to appear before the judge at the earliest possible opportunity to present a petition for a writ of *habeas corpus* directed to the chief of police, the prosecutor, or both, charging them with illegal detention of the defendant. See paragraph [68] *infra*.

[33] **Keeping records of calls.** Counsel should keep a record of the times at which s/he made telephone calls to locate the defendant and the names (correctly spelled), ranks, and numbers of all officers to whom s/he spoke.

[34] **Calls from the client.** An arrested person who calls the attorney directly while in police custody should be asked to identify his or her whereabouts by precinct or headquarters' name and street address or, if these are unknown, by general location and building description. S/he should be asked whether s/he has heard or seen anything suggesting that s/he might be taken by the police to any other location; if so, where and when. As a failsafe s/he should also be asked the street location where s/he was arrested, the charge, and whatever s/he knows about the identity of the arresting and investigating officers. It is a good idea to ask the client where

the telephone s/he is using is located (detectives' room? pay telephone in the corridor?) and whether any officer is listening to the call. The client should be instructed to answer this last question yes or no. (See the following paragraph.) Counsel should also speak to the investigating officer and cover the matters indicated in paragraph [25](4) *supra.*

[35] Advising the client—protecting the client against interrogation. (A) The first and most emphatic advice to give a client reached by telephone is not to talk to the police until the client and counsel have had a chance to meet privately and discuss the case. It is not sufficient to tell the client, "Don't make any statements to the police." Many people think a "statement" means a signed confession. Tell the client, "Say nothing at all to any officer except that your lawyer told you to say nothing. If the police ask you any questions or try to talk to you about anything, tell them your lawyer told you not to talk. If they say anything about having evidence against you or if they tell you what the evidence is or if they bring in someone else who says something against you, they are just trying to get you to talk. Don't fall for it. Whatever they say, tell them your lawyer told you not to talk."

(B) Ordinarily, the client should be instructed to respond to all police questioning and to all accusations by saying *explicitly* "My lawyer told me not to say anything until the lawyer gets here." This is preferable to advising the client simply to keep quiet for several reasons. Being more concrete, it is easier for most clients to understand. It gives the client something affirmative to say instead of having to suffer the discomfort of remaining silent in the face of questions or accusations. And it avoids the risk that the client's complete silence may later be used against the client as a "tacit admission" (see paragraph [367-A] *infra*) or as evidence to impeach a later exculpatory story as a "recent fabrication" (see paragraph [390] (I) *infra*).

(C) The client should also be told not to talk to *anybody*— cellmates, codefendants, reporters, even visitors whom the client knows—until counsel gets there. Cellmates may be snitches; codefendants may be turncoats; reporters may be police cronies; and the police may eavesdrop or bug supposedly private conversations between the client and visitors. Police may also wiretap, listen on extension phones, or simply stand within earshot while an arrested person is talking on a station house telephone. For these reasons it is wise to advise the client (1) to make and receive no phone calls until counsel's arrival except calls to and from counsel and calls that have to be made immediately and urgently (such as calls to arrange bail money or calls to close family members to assure them that the client is all right) and (2) during the latter calls to say nothing unnecessary and certainly nothing about the client's doings before s/he was arrested. For the same reasons counsel should keep his or her own phone conversation with the client circumspect and should not go into the events leading to the client's arrest or let the client tell his or her "story" over a station house phone. It is best to stick exclusively to the matters itemized in paragraph [25] (3) *supra*.

(D) Before ending the conversation, counsel should instruct the client to get the attention of a police officer and tell the officer, while counsel listens on the phone, that the client does not wish to talk further with the police in the absence of counsel and that the client wants all further dealings with the police to be conducted by counsel on the client's behalf. Once the client has made a statement of this sort, with counsel in a position to testify that s/he heard it made, the client has obtained the fullest possible protection against police interrogation while in custody, short of counsel's physical presence. For under the rule of *Edwards v. Arizona*, 451 U.S. 477 (1981), the police may not thereafter question the client, even with full *Miranda* warnings and waivers, "unless the [client] . . . himself [or herself] initiates further communication, exchanges, or conversations with the police." *Id*. at 485; *see also Smith v. Illinois*, 469 U.S. 91, 95 (1984) (per curiam); *Shea v. Louisiana*, 470 U.S. 51, 54-55 (1985); *Michigan v. Jackson*, 106 S. Ct. 1404, 1405 (1986) (dictum).

(E) Counsel should next ask to speak to the investigating officers and (a) should ask them what charges have been placed against the client; whether and what additional charges are being considered; whether and what amount of bail has been set, and what the bail will be in the event that additional contemplated charges are made; and the officer's name, rank, and number; and (b) should tell them that counsel has advised the client to remain silent and to answer no questions until counsel has talked with the client; that counsel has advised the client to consent to no seaches or investigations, to waive no rights, and to sign no forms, until counsel arrives; and (c) should direct them, politely but specifically, not to question or deal further with the client, not to exhibit the client for identification by any witness, not to ask the client for any consents or waivers of the client's rights, and not to conduct any examinations or tests involving the client, until counsel arrives. See paragraph [25] (4) *supra*.

(F) If the whereabouts of the client has been determined but the police say that counsel cannot speak with the client on the telephone, counsel should ask to talk to the investigating officers and should tell them (or the desk officer if the investigating officers are also said to be unavailable to talk) that counsel insists on speaking to the client immediately. If counsel is still not put through to the client, s/he should ask whether s/he will be permitted to see the client if s/he comes to the place of detention in person. If the answer is yes, s/he should go there as soon as possible. See paragraph [37-A] *infra*. If the answer is no or noncommital, s/he should call the commanding officer in the arrest precinct and proceed up the line of authority outlined in paragraph [32] *supra*, complaining that the investigating officers are denying counsel access to the client. (In either event, before terminating the initial call, s/he should ask for the name, rank, and number of the officer to whom s/he is talking and should cover with the officer items (a) through (e) in paragraph [25](4) *supra*.) It is important that counsel speak directly to the client and arrange to have the client personally assert the right to communicate with the authorities only through a lawyer, in the manner described in subparagraph (D) *supra*. Until this is done, counsel's own instructions to the police not to interrogate the client are ordinarily unenforceable except to the extent that local law requires the police to obey them. See the discussion of *Moran v. Burbine*, 106 S. Ct. 1135 (1986), in paragraph [233] (A) (2) *infra*.

[36] Same—protection against lineups and showups. (A) A defendant in police custody is in danger not only of being interrogated but also of being exhibited to possible eyewitnesses for the purpose of identification as the perpetrator of the crime for which s/he was arrested or of other crimes. Counsel who reaches an in-custody client by telephone must advise the client how to respond to lineup or other identification procedures. It is presently unclear to what extent the police can lawfully compel an unwilling accused to submit to identification confrontations in the absence of counsel. See paragraphs [233], [237] (A) (3), [374] *infra.* The client should accordingly be advised to object to any lineup, showup, or confrontation for identification being held in the absence of counsel and to tell the police, if they say anything about showing the client to any witness for possible identification, that the client wants to have his or her lawyer present and s/he is asking the police either to phone the lawyer (giving them the lawyer's number) or to let the client phone the lawyer, so that the lawyer can come down to the station and represent the client during any identification procedure. The client should also be instructed that if the police do place the client in a lineup or do display the client to any person for identification, the client should not speak any words or answer any questions—including his or her name—during the procedure. S/he should not, however, physically resist being exhibited; and if the police insist on going ahead with the exhibition after s/he has told them that s/he objects to it, the client should follow whatever orders the police may give with regard to the client's going up onto a lineup stage or stepping forward or walking about. S/he should never attempt to hide his or her face or to make faces. These tactics or a failure to obey instructions to step forward or walk about will only direct attention to the client and enhance the likelihood of a positive identification; they may also be used against the client as evidence of guilt; and physical resistance to the officers may result in a beating or the lodging of assault-upon-an-officer charges or both. If the client is told that s/he is being taken to a lineup or identification room, s/he should orally object to the absence of counsel but should not sit down or physically refuse to go, since this action will often result in the witnesses' being brought back to view the client in the cellblock—a far more suggestive form of confrontation than the lineup itself. If s/he is told s/he is being taken anywhere to be shown to witnesses, s/he should insist, *first*, that s/he be given a chance to phone his or her lawyer and to have the lawyer present and, *second*, that s/he not be shown to witnesses except in a lineup with other people who resemble the client. Once in a lineup or identification confrontation, s/he should observe and re-member everthing about it that s/he can, particularly (a) how many other persons were in the lineup, how they were dressed, and what they looked like (getting their names, before the lineup if that is possible without attracting attention to the client, or afterwards if the client sees these persons again while s/he is in custody); (b) how many witnesses were asked for identifications, what they said, what the officers said to them, their names if mentioned, and what they looked like; (c) how many police officers were present and their names, numbers, and descriptions; and (d) the time and place of the lineup. See paragraph [374] *infra*. The client should not attempt to take notes during the lineup or in any place where s/he may be observed by the witnesses to the lineup; but s/he should write down everthing that s/he can remember as soon as s/he returns to the cell.

(B) Counsel should also specifically demand, when speaking to the investigating officers, that the client not be shown in a lineup or exposed for identification in counsel's absence and should ask the officers (a) whether there is any plan to hold a lineup or identification with the client; (b) if so, when and where; and (c) if not, to telephone counsel if the police later decide to hold a lineup or identification exhibition of any sort. Should the police indicate that they may proceed to conduct an identification confrontation in counsel's absence despite counsel's objection, counsel should insist, *first*, that the client not be displayed except in a lineup of persons resembling the client and, *second*, that the names of all subjects in the lineup, all witnesses brought to observe it, and all officers present at the lineup or who bring witnesses or subjects to it be recorded and preserved, together with sufficient information to enable these people to be located.

(C) The most effective protection against station house identifications, of course, is for counsel to secure the client's release as rapidly as possible. In most cases, this means getting bail set and posted promptly (see paragraphs [38] - [41] *infra*) or making prompt arrangements for relase on recognizance (R.O.R.) (see paragraphs [56], [61], [65] *infra*). Procedures for negotiating these or other forms of conditional release (see paragraph [56] *infra*) are discussed in paragraphs [62] - [72] *infra*. Less commonly, there may be grounds for obtaining the client's unconditional release ("discharge") from custody by *habeas corpus* proceedings. (See paragraph [38] *infra*.) If *habeas* is unavailable and some form of conditional release cannot be quickly arranged in a case in which the police appear likely to try to have the client identified by witnesses, counsel is well advised to go to the police station and to stay there with the client so as to be present during any identification procedures. (See paragraph [37-A] *infra*.)

[37] Same—protection against other investigative procedures and against news reporters. (A) The client should be instructed that if anyone asks for permission to go to the client's house or car or to any other place in order to search for evidence or weapons or pieces of clothing or anything else, s/he should say, "No," and add, "My lawyer told me to say 'No,' " whether or not s/he thinks that the things the police are looking for will be found or that the search will prove the client innocent. S/he should be instructed to give the same answers if the police ask the client to lead them to any place or thing or to act out or demonstrate any action; and to object to being taken from the cell area for any reason, saying that s/he wants to stay there and wait for an attorney who is coming. S/he should be instructed not to sign any forms or papers and not to write anything down for the police. Again, the answer is, "My lawyer told me to say 'No,' until s/he gets here." The client should be instructed that if anyone attempts to inspect or examine his or her body, to take swabs or washes or scrapings from it, to cut nails or take hair samples, the client should tell them, "My attorney said to wait until s/he got here"; but if they go ahead anyway, the client should not try to fight them off. Finally, the client should be advised not to talk to reporters or newspeople and, if asked questions by them, to tell them that the lawyer has insisted that s/he say nothing at all to anyone until the lawyer gets there. If news photographers or television camera operators start taking pictures, the client should not attempt to duck or dodge, cover his or her face, or make faces but should just stand still and remain calm. If s/he has time to ask the police to stop a camera person from taking pictures before the camera is aimed, s/he should do so; but s/he should not attempt to call out or signal an officer after the camera person has the camera aimed. Photographs of dodging, menacing, or shouting defendants tend to make them look guilty; publication of these photographs can be exceedingly prejudicial.

(B) In talking to the investigating officer, counsel should mention that s/he has instructed the client not to participate in any investigative procedures, examinations, or tests and not to give any waivers or consents in the absence of counsel. The officer should be asked to postpone all these procedures and all requests for waivers or consents until counsel arrives at the station and should be asked also not to admit any news reporters or photographers to see the client prior to counsel's arrival.

[37-A] After counsel's arrival at the station house. (A) At the station house, counsel should show the desk officer some written evidence that identifies counsel as an attorney. S/he should say that s/he is representing the defendant (or has been asked to represent the defendant) and should ask to see the defendant immediately. If a delay of more than a few minutes occurs, s/he should repeat this request and ask, alternatively, to see the commanding officer. Obstructionism on the part of the commanding officer can be handled as indicated in paragraphs [67]-[68] *infra*. Obviously, if counsel is told that the defendant is making a statement, is being exhibited in a lineup, is undergoing any testing, or is being booked, counsel should insist that these procedures stop until counsel has had a chance to confer with the defendant.

(B) Once counsel reaches the defendant, s/he should request the use of a room in which the two can consult privately, and s/he should conduct as thorough an initial interview as is practicable under the circumstances. See paragraphs [50]-[51], [76]-[90] *infra*. As those paragraphs suggest, counsel should conclude the interview by instructing the defendant categorically not to talk to the police or anyone else; not to sign or write any papers for the police or anyone else; not to waive any rights or consent to any searches or examinations; not to agree to leave the cell area or to go with the police to any other place except to court (or to jail if arrestees are routinely transported to another facility for precourt detention); and to ask that counsel be called and be present if the defendant is exhibited to any witnesses or subjected to any sort of bodily examination. Paragraph [51](C) *infra* sets out the form of a card that counsel can leave with the defendant to assist the defendant in asserting and preserving the defendant's rights while in custody.

(C) Counsel should ask the investigating officers whether the defendant has made any written or oral statements; and if s/he has, counsel should request to see them or (in the case of oral statements) to be told of their contents immediately. Counsel should ask whether the defendant has been exhibited to any possible witnesses for identification purposes and whether any tests or examinations have been conducted on the defendant. If so, s/he should ask the nature of the identification proceedings or tests, who conducted them, what they showed, and the names of all persons present during the identification or testing procedures. S/he should ask whether any future identification or testing procedures are anticipated and when; and s/he should ask and arrange to be present when they are conducted. S/he should tell the investigating officers that s/he has instructed the defendant not to talk to anyone and not to give any consents or waivers in counsel's absence; and s/he should ask the officers not to question or talk with the defendant unless counsel is present and not to take any consents or waivers from the defendant without counsel's prior approval.

(D) Counsel can claim no right to prevent the police from exhibiting a legally arrested defendant for identification or to stop them from taking a legally arrested defendant's fingerprints, photographs, or handwriting and voice exemplars. See paragraphs [232], [237](A), [238] *infra*. Only to a limited and uncertain extent can counsel plausibly object to the form of an identification confrontation on the ground that it is improperly suggestive (*compare Moore v. Illinois*, 434 U.S. 220, 230-31 n.5 (1977), *with Manson v. Brathwaite*, 432 U.S. 98 (1977); and see paragraph [374] *infra*) or to the methods used in conducting bodily examinations of the defendant on the grounds that they are unreliable, brutal, or demeaning (see paragraphs [228]-[231], [237](A), [238] *infra*). Indeed, counsel's right to insist on being present at any of these procedures is presently subject to considerable confusion. See paragraphs [97], [233] *infra*. But at least until the law in these areas is clarified, counsel should take the positions: (1) that no identification or investigative procedures requiring the defendant's presence and active cooperation may be conducted unless counsel is permitted to attend and advise the defendant, see paragraph [233] *infra*, or is permitted, at the least, to consult with the defendant before the defendant makes the decision whether to cooperate, *cf. Estelle v. Smith*, 451 U.S. 454, 469-71 (1981); (2) that no bodily examinations of the defendant may be conducted without a search warrant, see paragraph [238] *infra*; (3) that no such bodily examinations may be conducted (a) if they involve significant discomfort or risk of injury to the defendant or are demeaning or (b) in any case, other than by qualified, medically trained personnel, see paragraphs [228], [238] *infra*; and (4) that no identification confrontations or bodily examinations may be conducted in a manner that is likely to produce unreliable evidence of guilt, see paragraphs [228], [374] *infra*. When examination or testing procedures require technical proficiency, counsel should also take the position (5) that they may not be conducted in the absence of a defense expert; and counsel should ask for the opportunity to secure the presence of such an expert. See paragraph [270] (H) *infra*.

(E) Defense counsel who obtains permission to attend identification or examination procedures should ordinarily act as unobtrusively as possible. S/he should not attempt to interfere with them in any way or to play any part beyond making suggestions for improvement of their reliability and fairness — for example, suggestions about the form of lineup that should be conducted (see subparagraph (F) *infra*; *United States v. Wade*, 388 U.S. 218, 236-37 n.26 (1967); *cf. Moore v. Illinois*, subparagraph (D) *supra*). Counsel's primary role is that of an observer. S/he should watch and take notes on everything that happens, be sure to get the names of all persons present, and ask questions both before and afterwards about anything s/he does not understand. If it appears that the procedures will involve the defendant's performing any kind of action — for example, giving a voice exemplar or walking about on a lineup stage — counsel should ask to be told in advance what that action will be and should request the opportunity to confer privately with the defendant before the procedures begin, so that s/he will not have to interrupt them for the purpose of giving the defendant advice.

(F) At a lineup or a showup, counsel should ask to speak to the possible identifying witnesses *before* the defendant is exhibited to them; and s/he should ask them (1) to describe in detail the person who they think committed the offense; (2) to describe the circumstances under which they observed that person; (3) how sure they are that they could recognize the person if they saw the person again; (4) by what characteristics they would recognize the person; (5) what description of the person they have given the police; (6) whether they have previously been asked by the police to attempt to identify anyone, either in the flesh or by photograph, and whether they made any identifications on these occasions; and (7) what they have been told by the officers who brought them, or asked them to come, to the station today. Counsel should request the police to exhibit the defendant in a lineup, not individually; counsel should ask that the lineup be composed of at least six persons who resemble the defendant in general characteristics —

height, weight, body type, age, skin color, hair style, clothing, and accessories; and counsel should ask that all subjects be exhibited in street clothes, not jail garb. If more than one witness is to view the lineup, the witnesses should not be present during one another's viewings; the positions of all subjects in the lineup should be changed between witnesses; and the witnesses should not be assembled where they can talk together either before, or after the conclusion of, the proceedings. At the lineup counsel should record the descriptions, names, and means of later contacting all the subjects. S/he should record the names and means of later contacting all witnesses who are present to view the lineup (whether or not they attempt or make any identifications), what is said to them, and what they say. S/he should record the manner in which the lineup is conducted, including distances, lighting, any directions to the subjects to walk, move, gesture, or speak, what they do, and when in the course of these proceedings any identification is made. S/he should also note the names, ranks, and numbers of all officers present and of those who brought witnesses to the lineup. Similar interviews, observations, and notes should be made of showups, to the extent applicable.

(G) In the case of other testing procedures, counsel should record the names of all technicians and officers present and the means of contacting them and should ask them to describe for counsel what procedures, materials, substances, chemicals, and so forth, they are using as they proceed. If possible, s/he should get them to describe *before* any testing is done what indicators or results they believe will demonstrate positive and negative findings. S/he should also ask them whether their testing procedures will affect the substances being tested, and, if so, request that they leave a sufficient amount of the substances untouched for subsequent defense testing. See paragraph [270] (H) *infra*. Any refusals of the technicians or officers to cooperate in these regards or to explain what they are doing should be noted.

(H) Before leaving a client in custody, counsel should have the client inform an officer, in counsel's presence, that the client does not wish thereafter to talk or deal with the police or prosecuting authorities without counsel but wants to communicate with them only through counsel. See paragraph [35] (D), (F) *supra*. Counsel should give the officer counsel's professional card and also give one to the desk officer on the way out.

[38] **Securing the client's release by habeas corpus or on bail.** The importance of securing the client's release from custody is made evident by the preceding paragraphs. As long as a defendant remains in the hands of the police, they can conveniently conduct any number of investigative procedures that may produce incriminating evidence. Ordinarily, too, getting out of custody is what the client most wants at this stage. If the client has been arrested illegally (that is, arrested without probable cause or otherwise in violation of constitutional or statutory restrictions on the arrest power, see paragraph [236] (C) *infra*) or is being detained too long without a preliminary arraignment or without a judicial determination of probable cause (see paragraph [127] *infra*), then the client's confinement is illegal and should be challenged immediately by a writ of *habeas corpus* directed to the chief of police and the prosecutor. See paragraphs [67]-[68] *infra*; and see paragraph [71] *infra* with regard to *habeas corpus* in a federal district court. *Habeas corpus* may also be available if the client is being subjected to illegal or abusive methods of investigation while in custody, although in such a case the writ would not order the client's outright release but would order only that the client be released unless the improper investigative techniques are discontinued. (In *Bell v. Wolfish*, 441 U.S. 520, 527 n.6 (1979), the Supreme Court raised and reserved "the question of the propriety of using a writ of habeas corpus to obtain review of the conditions of confinement, as distinct from the fact or length of the confinement itself." This means that insofar as *federal* judicial relief may be required, counsel would do best to caption the initial federal pleading in the alternative, as a petition for a writ of habeas corpus under 28 U.S.C. §2241(c)(3) and as a civil complaint for injunctive relief under 28 U.S.C. §1343(3) and 42 U.S.C. §1983. *Cf. Hutto v. Finney*, 437 U.S. 678 (1978); *Winston v. Lee*, 470 U.S. 753 (1985). State law, of course, determines whether the appropriate *state*-court

remedy would be an injunction or a conditional writ of *habeas corpus* or both.) If the client's detention is lawful, unconditional release is out of the picture; but the client's relase on bail or recognizance (see generally paragraphs [54]-[75] *infra*) can ordinarily be arranged in one or more of the following ways.

[39] **Station house bail.** The police may have statutory authority (most commonly in summary and misdemeanor cases) to release defendants on bail immediately after booking. This is usually called *station house bail*. The amount of bail is ordinarily set according to a fixed schedule and depends entirely on the offense charged. In some localities, however, the police exercise a limited discretion in setting the amount. A number of jurisdictions also allow the release of defendants in minor cases through the issuance of a police citation or summons to appear without the requirement that bail be posted.

[40] **Bail-setting by a magistrate or court.** If station house bail is not available, is refused, or is fixed in an amount that the client cannot make or deems excessive, an application may be submitted for the setting or reduction of bail or for release on the client's own recognizance to a magistrate or a judge of the court having jurisdiction over the offense with which the defendant is charged. A procedure used in some jurisdictions is for counsel to obtain a written stipulation from the prosecuting attorney of the amount of bail and to have this sum allowed by a judge. Procedures for securing the client's release on recognizance, for getting bail set by a magistrate or judge, and for posting bail once set are considered in paragraphs [62]-[72] *infra*. It is important to keep in mind that these procedures are ordinarily cumulative; that is, a lawyer whose client is refused bail, or reasonable bail, by the police can go next to a magistrate, then to a judge of a court of record, then to an appellate court or judge. Similarly, if one bail-setting authority is unavailable, the lawyer on a representation or affidivit to this effect may proceed up the ladder to the next.

[41] Same—factors relevant to amount. Notwithstanding the legal doctrines relating to bail, see paragraphs [55]-[61] *infra*, the conventional approach of lower courts and prosecutors in setting the amount of bail is to pay attention first to the nature of the offense charged and then to the prior criminal record of the defendant. Particularly ugly or aggravating facts in the circumstances of the crime can be counted upon to increase the amount of bail. Conversely, defense counsel wants to concentrate on mitigating the facts of the offense and the defendant's record. As counsel moves up the line of courts to those in which legal doctrine is likely to be important, however, s/he will also want increasingly to take account of the statutory and constitutional principles of bail discussed in paragraphs [55]-[61]. These focus on the amount of security required to assure the defendant's appearance at trial, and therefore, they permit consideration of the question whether the defendant has sufficient stability of residence, employment, and family contacts to indicate that s/he is a good risk for release without financial security or for release on a smaller amount of bail than would ordinarily be demanded of one charged with the offense for which the defendant is held. In attempting to show this to a court, counsel should not rely merely upon the client's story about his or her background or even the client's sworn statement (see paragraph [60] *infra*) but should verify the client's story independently and obtain supporting affidavits if time permits. A Bail Project or R.O.R. Project should be brought in immediately if one exists in the area. See paragraph [61] *infra*.

B. The "wanted" client

[42] Making inquiries of police and prosecutor. A client ordinarily becomes aware that s/he is wanted for arrest because of police efforts to locate the client or because of news reports or because s/he learns of the arrest of companions. Of course, s/he may be wrong in believing that s/he is wanted, and counsel acting on behalf of a supposedly wanted client should be careful when making inquiries of the authorities not to give them any ideas or information that they do not already have. Before calling them, counsel should conduct a preliminary interview with the client (see paragraphs [44], [52] *infra*) and should ascertain as much as possible about the circumstances which have led the client to think that the police are seeking him or her. Counsel should then consider how much of this information can be revealed to the authorities without suggesting that the client feels or is guilty of some offense and ought to be wanted by the police if s/he is not yet. Forearmed with a plausible, nonincriminating reason for the inquiry, counsel should phone the police concerned with the client's arrest (those who are said to be looking for the client or the desk officer in the precinct station for the district of the client's residence) or the prosecutor's office (if, in this locality, the prosecutor's office customarily gets involved in prearrest investigations and charging decisions). Counsel should identify himself or herself as an attorney, say that s/he has been informed that the police may be looking for the client, and ask whether this is so. If it is, s/he should ask whether an arrest warrant for the client has been issued, what the charges are, and whether the warrant specifies a bail figure. If there is no warrant or if the warrant does not specify a bail figure, counsel should ask whether the police are authorized to set bail on the charges and what the amount of bail will be. Particularly in cases in which no warrant has been issued but in which the police are seeking the client for a warrantless arrest (see paragraphs [12], [18] *supra*), the precinct desk officer may have little information to give counsel and may refer counsel to the investigating officers. In any event, on the basis of the information s/he does receive from the desk officer, counsel should consider whether s/he wants to ask affirmatively to speak with the investigating officers in order to ask them about the nature of the charges, bail, and the circumstances of the supposed offense or offenses. This will depend on whether counsel believes that s/he can get more information than s/he will be giving out in such a conversation. As indicated in paragraphs [8], [12], [18] and [39] *supra*, the police may have (or may claim that they have) little discretion in setting the amount of bail because it is governed by a bail schedule. Nevertheless, in some jurisdictions they do have a range of *de jure* discretion even in regard to station house bail; and they—or the prosecutor—can always exercise *de facto* discretion either by (1) changing the nature of the charges (unless a warrant has been issued) in order to change the applicable bail-schedule figure or (2) agreeing to go jointly with counsel to a magistrate or judge (who is not bound by the bail schedule) and to recommend that bail be set in an amount different from the bail-schedule figure. Counsel's offer to arrange the surrender of a wanted client can, therefore, be used as leverage to bargain about the amount of bail on which the client will subsequently be released. But in some cases the police will refuse to make any concessions on bail in return for the client's surrender because they feel that they do not have discretion to make them or because they are confident that they can soon and easily arrest the client anyway or because they prefer to maintain high bail in order to further their in-custody investigations of the client (see paragraphs [27]-[30], [35]-[37-A], [38] *supra*) or to keep the client "off the street" following his or her apprehension. If the police stonewall, counsel should phone the prosecutor's office and attempt to negotiate a surrender and the setting of reasonable bail directly with a prosecuting attorney.

[43] Arranging surrender. The client is not, of course, obliged to surrender once the fact that s/he is wanted for arrest has been confirmed; nor is counsel obliged to surrender the client or facilitate the client's arrest by telling the authorities where s/he can be found. (The client's communications to counsel, including the client's whereabouts, are privileged.) Counsel will, however, ordinarily wish to advise a wanted client to surrender voluntarily because the potential harms of an arrest to the client (*inter alia*, inconvenience and embarrassment, the risk of physical injury, subjection to postarrest custodial interrogation and investigation) are substantially greater than those of a voluntary surrender made under circumstances that counsel can partially control. In negotiating a voluntary surrender with the authorities, counsel should insist upon securing their assurances that the client will not be interrogated, exhibited to witnesses for identification, or subjected to searches or examinations while in custody prior to making bail. A time and place for surrender should be agreed upon, and counsel should accompany the client to assure that the agreements which s/he has made with the police or prosecutor are carried out. If the police and prosecutor are both unwilling to make satisfactory agreements or if counsel suspects that the agreements which they have made against interrogation and other postarrest investigative procedures or their agreements to release the client immediately on a specified amount of bail will not be faithfully honored, s/he should phone a magistrate, explain the problem, and request a time when s/he can surrender the client in open court, make bail, and have the client released forthwith. When bail in a reasonable amount has not been previously set by an arrest warrant or by a station house bail schedule or through counsel's negotiations with the authorities, counsel should appear before a magistrate or judge to have bail set, in the manner indicated in paragraph [40] *supra* and in paragraphs [62]-[72] *infra*, or to have an arrest warrant setting bail issued *before* the surrender of the client. Arrangements should also be made in advance, either with a professional bondsman or by getting the requisite cash, securities, or property deed in hand, to have the necessary security for posting bail available at the time of surrender. An attorney seeking to avoid harmful publicity arising from the surrender of a client of notoriety should consider picking a time and place inconvenient or inaccessible to the press and radio-television media. Once reporters have obtained facts about a case or photographs of the defendant, it is virtually impossible to restrain their subsequent dissemination, notwithstanding its prejudicial impact on the defendant or the defendant's ability to get a fair trial. *See Oklahoma Publishing Co. v. District Court*, 430 U.S. 308 (1977); *Smith v. Daily Mail Publishing Co.*, 443 U.S. 97, 103 (1979).

[44] **Anticipatory advocacy and bargaining.** Paragraph [42] *supra* suggested that counsel conduct at least a preliminary interview with the "wanted" client *before* phoning the authorities to make inquiries. Although focusing on the reasons the

client believes that s/he is wanted, this preliminary interview should also cover (1) what the client knows about the nature of the charges; (2) what the client knows about the events underlying the charges; (3) whether the client appears to be in danger of immediate arrest before counsel can discuss with the authorities the possibility of a voluntary surrender; (4) the advisability of a voluntary surrender if the client *is* wanted; and (5) the sources and amount of the client's resources for making bail. After talking with the authorities, counsel will want to confer again with the client, to discuss the client's feelings about surrendering and to advise the client concerning the wisdom of that course in general as well as the specifics of any agreements that counsel thinks s/he can negotiate with the authorities and the mechanics of a surrender if one is arranged. Then prior to the client's actual surrender, counsel should do a further, full-scale interview of the client (see paragraphs [52], [76]-[90] *infra*) or as much of one as practicable. Here, counsel should focus upon exploring with the client factual information and tactical considerations that will enable counsel and the client to decide whether before, at, or immediately after, the client's surrender, (a) the client should make an oral or written statement to the police, propose a lineup, or otherwise co-operate with police investigative procedures (see paragraph [87] (B) *infra*); (b) counsel should begin discussing the facts of the case with the police or prosecutor in an effort to per-suade them to drop the charges (see paragraphs [91]-[105] *infra*); or (c) counsel should begin to engage in plea bargaining with the prosecutor (see paragraphs [206]-[219] *infra*), in-cluding in the bargaining package an agreement on the fixing of a reasonable bail.

C. Appointment or retainer at preliminary arraignment

[45] **Preliminary arraignment.** The preliminary arraign-ment is usually the first proceeding following arrest at which the defendant is taken before a judicial officer (ordinarily a magistrate, justice of the peace, or judge of some other minor

court). In many instances it is also the first time that the defendant has an opportunity to see a lawyer. Counsel is often appointed, particularly in felony cases, at the preliminary arraignment. In some instances just about the only function performed at the preliminary arraignment is the appointment of counsel. But in some jurisdictions the defendant may be called upon to plead to the charges, and frequently s/he is required to decide whether to insist upon, or waive the right to, a preliminary examination—that is, a hearing before the magistrate at which the prosecution will have to establish probable cause to hold the defendant for trial. See paragraphs [13]-[15] *supra*; [125]-[126], [135], [137] *infra*.

[46] **Insistence on adequate time.** It is absolutely essential that a newly appointed or newly retained attorney not act precipitously in making decisions at the preliminary arraignment. Often the magistrate, anxious to push cases along, pressures defendant's counsel to make immediate elections. Elections made in haste at the preliminary arraignment—to enter or not to enter a plea, to waive or to demand a preliminary examination, to insist upon or to waive the time limits for preliminary examination—may prejudice the defendant's rights or preclude the raising of vital defenses at a later stage. Counsel must, therefore, insist upon a reasonable opportunity to interview the client and to weigh alternative courses of action. Allowance of five or ten minutes to do these things, as magistrates will suggest in some instances, seldom provides sufficient time to make critical decisions. Counsel who is forced to proceed under these circumstances ought (a) to object strenuously, asserting that s/he is not prepared to go ahead, stating the circumstances of counsel's recent entry into the case, and invoking the client's Sixth Amendment right to effective representation by counsel, see paragraph [53] *infra*; (b) to enter no plea; and (c) to waive no subsequent procedures, such as preliminary examination or indictment.

[47] **Preliminary examination.** When the defendant at the preliminary arraignment is offered an opportunity to ask for a preliminary examination, s/he should ordinarily request the

examination. This is frequently an important opportunity, perhaps the only one, to get discovery of the prosecution's case. Waiver of preliminary examination ought to be the exception rather than the rule. There are, however, some cases in which waiver of an examination would be well advised. See paragraphs [137], [305] *infra*. For this reason, counsel should insist on *time to decide one way or the other* whether s/he wants an examination and should resist the magistrate's blandishments to "go on with the examination now, since you won't lose anything that way." If the magistrate insists on going on, counsel should formally ask for a continuance, again citing the Sixth Amendment. If this is denied, it is generally wise to let the examination go on rather than to waive it. See generally paragraphs [124]-[147] *infra*.

[48] **Pleas.** When a defendant is asked to enter a plea to the charges, counsel should consider entering a guilty plea only if some very distinct advantage accrues to the defendant from doing so. Sometimes the prosecutor will agree to accept a plea to a less serious charge than that for which the defendant is being held or agree to a favorable fine or sentencing disposition at this stage. The final choice of alternatives, between accepting a prosecution offer to dispose of the case at the preliminary arraignment and going on to the criminal court, should be left to the client, for s/he must live with the outcome. When in doubt, counsel should advise against a guilty plea, since a not guilty plea can generally be switched later to a guilty plea with greater freedom and with fewer possible adverse consequences than attend attempts to switch the other way. In all events, counsel should exercise care before recommending disposition of a case at preliminary arraignment. Although in most instances a favorable offer from the prosecutor is motivated by the desire to avoid cluttering up the criminal trial dockets with cases that the prosecutor does not consider important, sometimes it is indicative that the prosecutor thinks s/he may not be able ultimately to prove any case against the defendant. See generally paragraphs [201]-[219] *infra*.

[49] **Bail.** The preliminary arraignment is also an opportunity to have bail set or reduced, or R.O.R. allowed, for a client who has not previously been released on bail. Counsel will need to be prepared with facts concerning the defendant's background to support requests for R.O.R. or for a favorable bail setting or for a bail reduction. When it appears likely that the difference in the amount of bail set will justify the inconvenience of the intervening detention to the defendant, it may be better for counsel who first comes into a case at preliminary arraignment to ask that the case be passed for a few hours or even for a day in order to obtain verified information about a client rather than to proceed with only the information that the client can provide on the spur of the moment without supporting investigation. See generally paragraphs [54]-[75-A] *infra*.

D. Considerations relating to the first interview with the client

[50] **Pressures on the first interview.** Counsel's first interview with a client accused of a crime is discussed in detail in paragraphs [76]-[90] *infra*. A lawyer who enters a criminal case in some of the pressing situations just discussed—with a client in custody or wanted for arrest or already before the court—may not be able to conduct the full initial interview that is recommended in those paragraphs. Of course, the scope of the initial interview with a client and the amount of knowledge that counsel will have to obtain beforehand in order to prepare for the interview vary, depending on the particular client's circumstances and immediate needs at the stage of the case at which the attorney is called in. The concerns of thorough preparation will sometimes have to be sacrificed to a need for speed in seeing the client and obtaining from the client some limited information required for an immediate purpose, such as getting bail set. But although it is frequently essential that counsel act quickly on first entering a case, the value of quick action may well be negated if counsel proceeds

in ignorance. The first interview with the client is psychologically critical, quite out of proportion to its other functions in
the case. The defendant who senses ignorance or disorgani-
zation as the characteristic of a previously unknown lawyer,
particularly a court-appointed lawyer, is going to have enormous difficulties in ever establishing an adequate attorney-
client relationship. It is, therefore, essential for counsel to plan
in advance—even if necessarily hurriedly—to deal with the
significant questions and decisions s/he is going to be faced
with when s/he meets the client for the first time.

[51] **Client in custody.** (A) The major concern of the client
who is in custody shortly after arrest ordinarily is to obtain
release on bail quickly. S/he will ask counsel whether and how
arrangements can be made to have the client bailed out. Counsel should know as much as possible about the answers to these
questions before the initial interview. If counsel is not already
familiar with the law and practice of bail in the jurisdiction
(see paragraphs [54]-[75-A] *infra*), s/he should quickly do
the necessary research and make inquiries of an experienced
local criminal attorney, a reliable bondsman, or a staffer of an
available R.O.R. Project. If possible, of course, counsel should
already have taken the first steps toward securing the client's
release on bail (see paragraph [25](1), (5) *supra*) except in
cases in which bail is legally unavailable or obviously ill-advised
(see paragraph [75-A] *infra*). A second question that the client
will almost invariably ask counsel at the initial interview is what
are the penalties for the offense[s] with which the client is
charged. If counsel knows the charges, s/he should research
the potential penalties in preparation for the interview. If
s/he does not know the charges before leaving for the station
house, it is a good idea to take copies of the criminal code and
the drug code along so that s/he can look up the penalties
when s/he learns the charges from the investigating officer or
the desk officer. Recidivist sentencing provisions and enhance-
ment provisions (for "armed" offenses and the like) are complex in many jurisdictions; they are applicable to a wide range
of offenses. It is useful for counsel to have a photocopy of
these provisions available that s/he can carry around more

handily than a bound volume. Finally, counsel should prepare for the initial interview by obtaining at least a preliminary notion of the elements of the offense with which the client is charged, so as to be able to take the client's story from the outset with an eye to the relevant issues. And if—without wasting time en route to the station house—counsel can pick up a pack of cigarettes, matches, and gum to leave with the client, that is the kind of thoughtfulness that may pave the way toward a good attorney-client relationship.

(B) Counsel will have a lot of questions to ask the client in their first interview. Particularly important are matters that, if not identified and pursued by defense investigation within a few hours after arrest, may later be undiscoverable or discoverable only at inordinate cost. Seeing a client in custody provides a unique opportunity to explore the circumstances surrounding the client's arrest, any attendant search, and the postarrest handling of the client by the police, including interrogation, lineups or other identification confrontations, and tests or examinations conducted in the station house. The police personnel involved may still be on the scene where the client can identify them for counsel, or at least the client's memory of their appearance will be fairly fresh. Another high priority, of course, is the identification of possible witnesses to the charged offense who can still be located at this time but may be difficult or impossible to track down later. Inquiry into these and similar urgent matters obviously must be made of the client immediately. Nevertheless, the interview at this stage had best be kept relatively abbreviated for many reasons, including the client's impatience, counsel's lack of opportunity to prepare, and the absence of guaranteed privacy. An abbreviated initial interview would be directed at the following goals: (a) some examination of the facts of the offense with which the defendant is charged, and particularly its location and any physical characteristics of the place or of objects that should be seen or preserved quickly; (b) discussion of the circumstances surrounding the arrest—whether it was made pursuant to a warrant, whether a search was made, and the results of any search (see paragraphs [234]-[251] *infra*); (c) some discussion of defenses that may be available to the client, particularly factual ones, and an identification of possible witnesses, with attention to factors that may require immediate steps to locate them while the trail is relatively fresh; (d) examination of police activities since the client's arrest, including any abuse of the client, interrogation, viewing by eyewitnesses, physical examinations and tests, and attempts to discuss or implicate the defendant in other crimes (see paragraphs [27]-[30], [36]-[37-A] *supra*; paragraphs [228], [232]-[233], [237]-[238], [363] - [367-A], [374] *infra*); and (e) thorough exploration of facts to be used for bail-setting (see paragraphs [59]-[60], [69] *infra*). Before counsel leaves a client in custody, s/he should give the client (or repeat, if s/he has previously given by telephone) all the instructions described in paragraphs [25] (3), [35]-[37] *supra* for dealing with the police (see paragraph [87] *infra*). S/he should have the client inform the police, in counsel's presence, that the client wishes thereafter to communicate with the police and prosecuting authorities only through the medium of counsel. See paragraphs [35] (D), [37-A] (H) *supra*. Counsel should then give (or repeat) instructions to the investigating officer not to interrogate the client, seek consents or waivers from the client, conduct any tests or examinations on the client, or exhibit the client for identification in counsel's absence. See paragraphs [25] (4), [35]-[37] *supra*. The name, rank, and number of the officer to whom counsel gives these instructions should be noted. Counsel should also inquire of the client whether s/he has any complaints about his or her present treatment in custody. Major abuses should be investigated immediately (see paragraph [84] *infra*); minor grievances can often be resolved quickly through counsel's mediation with the desk officer, the investigating officer, or the commanding officer at the station. The importance of apparently small matters (for example, securing the return of the client's eyeglasses or medications that were taken away at the time of arrest; arranging the release of cash from the client's property envelope) cannot be overstated: These provide opportunities for counsel to do something for the client and thereby win the client's confidence. See paragraphs [79]-[80] *infra*.

(C) It is a wise practice for counsel to make and carry a supply of cards or forms that s/he can give to clients in custody for their use in preserving their rights during police investigation. Such a card may read, for example:

> My lawyer has instructed me not to talk to anyone about my case or anything else and not to answer questions or reply to accusations. On advice of counsel and on the grounds of my rights under the Fifth and Sixth Amendments, I shall talk to no one in the absence of counsel. I shall not give any consents or make any waivers of my legal rights. Any requests for information or for consent to conduct searches or seizures or investigations affecting my person, papers, property, or effects should be addressed to my lawyer, whose name, address, and phone number are _____. I want all communications with the authorities henceforth to be made only through my lawyer. I request that my lawyer be notified and allowed to be present if any identification confrontations, tests, examinations, or investigations of any sort are conducted in my case, and I do not consent to any such confrontations, tests, examinations, or investigations.

The client should be instructed to show this card to any officer or other person who asks the client questions, accuses the client of anything, talks to the client in any way about the case, or starts to examine or exhibit the client while in custody. Cards of this sort serve four important purposes. First, they allow the client to assert his or her rights even if s/he is unable to remember what they are or what to say in order to claim them. Many clients who are simply given the oral advice suggested in paragraph [87] *infra* will forget most of it. Second, they allow the client to make an *express* claim of his or her rights. In some situations, the mere silence of the client may not be sufficient to protect the client's interests fully. See paragraphs [363] (E), [367-A], [390] (I) *infra*. Also, as a practical matter, it may be difficult for the client psychologically to maintain silence in situations that seem to call for some response; the response of flashing the card gives the client something to *do* to relieve this tension. Third, the card makes it easier for the defense to prove in court that the client claimed his or her rights and waived none of them. Any lawyer who has seen a police witness flash a "*Miranda* card" in the courtroom appreciates the probative force of a written record in the inevitable disputes about what was said between officers and arrestees behind the closed doors of a station house. Defense counsel should attempt to give the client something of an even break in this swearing contest. Fourth, the card gives the client a sense of reassurance in his or her capacity to handle the often frightening experience of confronting police investigators in confinement, and it also gives the client an added ground for confidence in counsel's professional ability and concern.

[52] **Wanted client.** The interview with the wanted but unapprehended client has a different focus. Here, unless the client's arrest appears imminent, a thorough initial interview covering all of the matters mentioned in paragraphs [76]-[80], [83], [85-A]-[87] and the relevant portions of the interview checklist in paragraph [90] *infra* should be conducted. If the apparent imminence of arrest makes this impractical, counsel should concentrate upon (1) the facts surrounding the offense for which the client is wanted, including both the facts that would support a charge against the client and the facts relevant to possible defenses against that charge; (2) the client's attitude toward surrendering voluntarily (see paragraphs [42]-[44] *supra*); (3) the specific arrangements that can be made for a voluntary surrender and for the client's prompt release on bail or recognizance thereafter or for the client's protection while in custody if prompt release appears unlikely (see paragraphs [42] - [43] *supra*); (4) advice to the client regarding his or her rights in custody following either a voluntary surrender or arrest and how the client should behave in custody in order to assert and preserve those rights (see paragraph [87] *infra*); and (5) the client's attitude toward contesting guilt, on the one hand, or acknowledging guilt and either beginning plea negotiations or attempting to obtain the dropping or reduction of charges by an appeal to police or prosecutorial discretion, on the other hand (see paragraphs [206]-[219] and [91]-[105] *infra*, respectively). Whether the interview is

thorough or has to be abbreviated, a primary emphasis should be placed upon the facts and considerations relevant to those decisions immediately facing counsel and the client, identified in paragraph [44] *supra*. Before the interview counsel should have obtained from the police as much information as possible about the nature of the charges and the police version of the facts underlying them. These should be discussed with the client for the purpose of determining whether there are any factual defenses or equitable considerations that might persuade the police or a prosecutor not to proceed with the client's arrest but to drop charges. If that outcome appears unlikely, the next questions on the agenda are whether, when, and under what conditions to arrange a voluntary surrender. Next come the questions whether, following surrender, the client ought to make a statement to the police or otherwise cooperate with their investigation and whether, before or immediately after the client's surrender (or arrest), counsel should commence plea bargaining with the prosecutor. Obviously, in an interview that explores these subjects, counsel will need to know and to tell the client the specific penalties for the offense[s] with which the client is, or is likely to be, charged. Even more in the case of the wanted client than in the case of the just-arrested client (see paragraph [51] (A) *supra*), counsel should come into the interview with this information in hand. Counsel will also need to be conversant with the legal elements of the offense[s]. S/he will need to know the procedures for setting and posting bail, the amounts of bail customarily required, and the availability of R.O.R. and other forms of conditional release, for the offense[s] in question. See paragraphs [54]-[75-A] *infra*. Finally, counsel should be prepared to advise the client what to expect concerning police procedures following surrender or arrest and how to respond to those procedures. Under no circumstances should a client be permitted to surrender without first being given detailed advice with regard to how s/he should act in custody. See paragraphs [25](3), [27]-[30], [35]-[37-A] *supra*; paragraph [87] *infra*.

[53] Client at preliminary arraignment. (A) Counsel entering the case at the time of the defendant's first appearance in court (usually at the preliminary arraignment) is particularly likely to be confronted with a drastic curtailment of the opportunity for an initial client interview. Counsel's first task will often be to impress upon the court the necessity for allowing him or her sufficient time to discuss essential matters with the new client. In addition to whatever rights to a continuance and to legal representation at preliminary arraignment may be provided by state law, counsel should invoke the client's federal Sixth and Fourteenth Amendment rights to counsel (see subparagraph (B) *infra*), which guarantee the opportunity for lawyer-client consultation in the course of judicial proceedings when there are "tactical decisions to be made and strategies to be reviewed." *Geders v. United States*, 425 U.S. 80, 88 (1976). If counsel is denied ample time for an adequate interview and investigation, s/he should object and should resist as strongly as possible being pressed to proceed with the preliminary arraignment.

(B) Some information relating to the nature of the charge and to the date of the offense will be available from court records (principally the complaint) at the arraignment. Armed with this information, counsel should interview the client to determine what the client knows about the facts of the case; whether s/he thinks that s/he has any available defense and what that might be; whether the client has a history of mental illness or shows any signs of mental unbalance or incomprehension of the court proceedings; and whether the client has a prior criminal record or has other charges presently pending or outstanding. Counsel should also determine from the court record, from the prosecuting officer, or from the client whether bail has been set and in what amount; s/he should ascertain from the client how much bail the client can make; and if bail has not been set or if it is unreasonably or unmanageably high, s/he should obtain from the client all the facts relevant to the setting or reduction of bail. See paragraphs [59]-[60], [69] *infra*. These facets of the case are generally most critical to the decisions confronting counsel at the preliminary arraignment. See paragraphs [45]-[49] *supra*; and paragraphs [62], [120]-

[122], [125]-[126], [135]-[137] *infra*. Their importance varies, however, depending upon the jurisdiction in which counsel is practicing. In many jurisdictions rights not exercised and motions not made prior to or at the preliminary arraignment may be irrevocably lost. In the absence of firm knowledge about matters that must be handled prior to this arraignment, counsel should seek a continuance pending further research. Requests for a continuance for time to interview, investigate, and research should be predicated upon the defendant's Sixth and Fourteenth Amendment rights to adequate representation by counsel and should be supported by (a) an explicit statement of the circumstances of counsel's belated entrance into the case and (b) an explicit representation that counsel is unprepared to protect the client's interests at arraignment at this time. It is fairly clear that the Sixth and Fourteenth Amendments do guarantee the right to counsel at preliminary arraignment, *White v. Maryland*, 373 U.S. 59 (1963) (per curiam); *Arsenault v. Massachusetts*, 393 U.S. 5 (1968) (per curiam); *Coleman v. Alabama*, 399 U.S. 1 (1970); *Gerstein v. Pugh*, 420 U.S. 103, 122-23 (1975) (dictum); see paragraph [130] *infra*; and the right to counsel in any judicial proceeding ordinarily comports the right to have adequate time to enable counsel to prepare to conduct the proceeding, *e.g.*, *Powell v. Alabama*, 287 U.S. 45 (1932); *Hawk v. Olson*, 326 U.S. 271 (1945); *Megantz v. Ash*, 412 F.2d 804 (1st Cir. 1969); *Rastrom v. Robbins*, 440 F.2d 1251 (1st Cir. 1971); *Moore v. United States*, 432 F.2d 730, 735 (3d Cir. 1970) (en banc); *Twiford v. Peyton*, 372 F.2d 670 (4th Cir. 1967); *Garland v. Cox*, 472 F.2d 875 (4th Cir. 1973); *MacKenna v. Ellis*, 263 F.2d 35, 41-44 (5th Cir. 1959); *Davis v. Johnson*, 354 F.2d 689 (6th Cir. 1966), *aff'd after remand*, 376 F.2d 840 (6th Cir. 1967); *Wolfs v. Britton*, 509 F.2d 304 (8th Cir. 1975); *United States v. King*, 664 F.2d 1171 (10th Cir. 1981). "[T]he denial of opportunity for appointed counsel to confer, to consult with the accused and to prepare his defense, could convert the appointment of counsel into a sham and nothing more than a formal compliance with the Constitution's requirement that an accused be given the assistance of counsel. The Constitution's guarantee of assistance of counsel cannot

be satisfied by mere formal appointment." *Avery v. Alabama*, 308 U.S. 444, 446 (1940) (dictum).

(C) Despite the useful rhetoric of *Avery* and the authorities just cited, which may be invoked in support of a motion for a continuance, counsel should be warned that appellate courts review denials of continuances only under an "abuse of discretion" standard and are slow to find abuse. "Not every restriction on counsel's time or opportunity to investigate or to consult with his client or otherwise to prepare for trial violates a defendant's Sixth Amendment right to counsel. . . . [B]road discretion [is] . . . granted trial courts on matters of continuances; only an unreasoning and arbitrary 'insistence upon expeditiousness in the face of a justifiable request for delay' violates the right to the assistance of counsel." *Morris v. Slappy*, 461 U.S. 1, 11-12 (1983). *See also United States v. Cronic*, 466 U.S. 648, 659-662 (1984); *but see Winston v. Lee*, 470 U.S. 753, 758 n.3 (1985). It is, therefore, imperative to make a detailed factual record both of counsel's unpreparedness and of the justifications for it when requesting a continuance.

IV. BAIL

[54] **Introduction.** As indicated in paragraphs [36], [38] - [41] *supra*, one of defense counsel's first jobs is to arrange for the client's release from custody as quickly as possible. Immediate steps to free the client on bail or another form of conditional release are outlined in those paragraphs. The following paragraphs [55]-[75-A] examine forms of conditional release and their problems in greater detail.

[55] **Arrest and conditional release.** Anglo-American criminal procedure typically calls for an arrest at the outset of prosecution. The purpose of the arrest is to secure the defendant's presence for trial and for punishment in the event of conviction. The assumption underlying arrest is that pretrial detention may be necessary to secure a defendant's presence and that, if necessary, it is authorized. A qualifying assumption, which evolved early in the history of English criminal procedure and became one of the great rallying points in the long English struggle for individual liberty, is that a defendant *should not* be detained prior to trial if some other less oppressive means of securing the defendant's presence is practicable. *See* I STEPHEN, A HISTORY OF THE CRIMINAL LAW OF ENGLAND 233-43 (1883); II POLLOCK & MAITLAND, THE HISTORY OF ENGLISH LAW 582-87 (2d ed. 1952); IX HOLDSWORTH, A HISTORY OF ENGLISH LAW 115-19 (1st ed. 1926); CHAFEE, HOW HUMAN RIGHTS GOT INTO THE CONSTITUTION 51-64 (1952). In early English practice an accused was released in the custody of kinsmen, who obliged themselves to assure the accused's presence for trial. As bailees of the accused's body, they were called bails, and when the custom grew of requiring them to post some valuable security for their obligation, the security posted—and the general practice of releasing a defendant on security or bond conditioned upon appearance at trial—came to be called bail. The right of a criminal accused to pretrial release on bail was protected by the celebrated English Habeas Corpus Act of 1679, whose legacy is the Habeas Corpus Clause

of the federal Constitution and of many state constitutions, and by the Bill of Rights of 1689, whose prohibition of excessive bail survives in the Eighth Amendment and similar state constitutional provisions. Today the bail right is, to some degree, guaranteed by the constitutions and statutes of every American jurisdiction. See paragraphs [57], [57-A] (B) *infra*.

[56] **Forms of conditional release.** Although the constitutions speak only of "bail," their purpose is to approve, if not to require, the defendant's release pending trial on the least onerous conditions likely to assure appearance for trial. Several different forms of conditional release are currently in use. *Bail* involves the defendant's secured promise to appear. S/he signs a bail bond, in which s/he undertakes to be present for trial (or for some other stage in the criminal proceeding), and s/he posts cash or negotiable securities, or pledges personal or real property, to guarantee the performance of that undertaking. It may be required that another person (a "surety") execute the bond, as a joint obligor, and post or pledge negotiables or personal or real property for the defendant's appearance. Surety companies or bonding companies today perform this service in consideration of a premium (usually about 10 per cent of the face of the bond) regulated by law (and often on condition of the defendant's pledging additional collateral to protect the surety). A defendant may also be released on an unsecured promise to pay a designated sum in default of appearance. This is frequently called *release on his or her own bond*. Or s/he may be released on a simple promise to appear, a practice ordinarily called *release on his or her own recognizance*, or *R.O.R.* Occasionally defendants today are still *released into the custody of some other person*, on the informal assurance of that person (sometimes an attorney) that they will appear. This latter practice is used principally in petty cases and cases involving defendants who are minors. Other forms of conditional release, the products of relatively recent legislation, are noted in paragraphs [57] (B) and [63] *infra*.

[57] **General right to bail.** Most jurisdictions give arrested persons an absolute right to have bail set for their release on any noncapital charge. This right may be conferred by constitution, by statute, or by both.

(A) Numerous state constitutions guarantee the right to bail expressly, by providing that all offenses (except certain capital offenses, see paragraph [58] *infra*) shall be bailable. For the most part those constitutions also prohibit "excessive bail." Other constitutions contain only the prohibition of "excessive bail," without explicit recognition of the underlying right to have bail set. The Eighth Amendment to the Constitution of the United States contains a provision of this latter sort. It may be strongly argued that these "excessive bail" clauses assume and thus compel an underlying right to bail. The historical evidence supports this view, *see* Foote, *The Coming Constitutional Crisis in Bail*, 113 U. PA. L. REV. 959, 965-89, 1125 (1965), as does the logic classically expressed by Mr. Justice Butler in *United States v. Motlow*, 10 F.2d 657, 659 (Butler, Circuit Justice, 1926): "The provision forbidding excessive bail would be futile if magistrates were left free to deny bail." *See also Hunt v. Roth*, 648 F.2d 1148, 1156-62 (8th Cir. 1981), *vacated as moot sub nom. Murphy v. Hunt*, 455 U.S. 478 (1982) (per curiam); *United States ex rel. Goodman v. Kehl*, 456 F.2d 863, 868 (2d Cir. 1972) (dictum); *Trimble v. Stone*, 187 F. Supp. 483, 484-85 (D.D.C. 1960). Nevertheless, the Supreme Court of the United States has hinted at a contrary conclusion, *United States v. Salerno*, 107 S. Ct. 2095, 2104, 2105 (1987), citing *Carlson v. Landon*, 342 U.S. 524, 544-46 (1952), and has pointedly reserved the question "whether the Excessive Bail Clause speaks at all to Congress' power to define [that is, to limit] the classes of criminal arrestees who shall be admitted to bail." *United States v. Salerno, supra*, 107 S. Ct. at 2105. The *Salerno* case upheld the facial constitutionality of federal preventive detention legislation enacted in 1984, providing that "[i]f, after a hearing. . . ., [a] . . . judicial officer finds that no condition or combination of conditions [of pretrial release] will reasonably assure . . . the safety of any other person and the community, he shall order the detention of [an arrested] . . . person [charged with a crime of violence, an offense punishable by life imprisonment or death, or an enumerated major drug offense or recidivist felony offense] prior to trial," 18 U.S.C. §3142(e). The legislation also allows detention without bail upon a finding, under similar procedures, that no condition or combination of conditions of pretrial release "will reasonably assure the appearance of the person" for trial, but this latter provision was not at issue in *Salerno*, which raised only the question whether the Eighth Amendment or the Due Process Clause of the Fifth Amendment "limits permissible government considerations [in the regulation of pretrial release] solely to [preventing the accused's possible] . . . flight." 107 S. Ct. at 2105. The Court held that neither constitutional provision had this effect: that although "[i]n our society liberty is the norm, and detention prior to trial or without trial is the carefully limited exception," *ibid.*, the exception includes the power to deny pretrial release "when the government musters convincing proof that the arrestee, already indicted or held to answer for a serious crime, presents a demonstrable danger to the community," *id.* at 2103. In reaching this result, the Court emphasized that the statute (1) "operates only on individuals who have been arrested for a specific category of extremely serious offenses," *ibid.*; (2) permits pretrial detention only when a judicial officer has found both (a) "probable cause to believe that the charged crime has been committed by the arrestee," *ibid.*, and (b) "that no conditions of release can reasonably assure the safety of the community or any person," *ibid.*; (3) requires the latter finding to be made (a) "by clear and convincing evidence," *ibid.*, and (b) after "a full-blown adversary hearing," *ibid.*, which (c) must be "prompt," *id.* at 2101, and (d) is attended by "numerous procedural safeguards," *id.* at 2105 (that is, the arrestee "may request the presence of counsel . . ., may testify and present witnesses in his behalf, as well as proffer evidence, and . . . may cross-examine other witnesses," *id.* at 2099); (4) denies the presiding judge "unbridled discretion in making the detention determination," but rather specifies "the considerations relevant to that decision," which "include the nature and seriousness of the charges, the substantiality of the government's evidence against the arrestee, the arrestee's background and characteristics, and the nature and seriousness of the danger posed by the suspect's release," *ibid.*; (5) provides that a decision to detain (a) must be supported by "written findings of fact and a written statement of reasons for [the] . . . decision," *id.* at 2104, and (b) is subject to "expedited appellate review," *id.* at 2099; (6) restricts "the maximum length of pretrial detention . . . by . . . stringent time limitations," *id.* at 2101; and (7) meanwhile "requires that detainees be housed in a 'facility separate, to the extent practicable, from persons awaiting or serving sentences or being held in custody pending appeal," *id.* at 2102. Even at this, the Court appeared to concede the possibility that the statute "might operate unconstitutionally under some conceivable set of circumstances," *id.* at 2100, and upheld it only against a "facial challenge," *ibid.* (*Compare Schall v. Martin*, 467 U.S. 253 (1984), rejecting a Due Process challenge to a somewhat less protective New York statute authorizing "brief pretrial detention" of juveniles charged with delinquency, *id.* at 263, upon "a finding of a 'serious risk' that [the] . . . juvenile may commit a crime before [the trial] . . . date," *ibid.*; *and see Hilton v. Braunskill*, 107 S. Ct. 2113 (1987).) *Salerno* is a poorly reasoned decision of the Rehnquist Court that deserves little respect from state courts called upon to construe state constitutional "excessive bail" and "due process" clauses; and its reasoning in support of preventive detention has no application at all, of course, to state constitutions that also contain the common form of clause making all noncapital offenses bailable. *See, e.g., In re Underwood*, 9 Cal. 3d 345, 508 P.2d 721, 107 Cal. Rptr. 401 (1973).

(B) State statutes also generally allow a right to bail in all noncapital cases. Most of these statutes give discretion to magistrates and courts of record to set the amount of bail in individual cases, but some contain schedules listing the amounts of bail for specified offenses or authorize courts to promulgate such schedules. A number of jurisdictions have statutes that permit the police to release arrested persons on bail (called station house bail) in specified classes of cases, usually summary offenses and misdemeanors. These statutes also may leave the amount of bail to be determined by police discretion or may contain—or authorize the judicial promulgation of—

bail schedules. (Even in the absence of express statutory authorization, some courts formally or informally promulgate bail schedules to which they conform as a matter of routine in fixing bail, although they will make exceptions in unusual circumstances. Police also frequently operate pursuant to administratively promulgated schedules, and they are less willing than courts to vary the bail-setting in individual cases.) Statutes ordinarily regulate procedures relating to bail in more detail than do constitutional provisions: They identify the authorities who are empowered to set and to receive bail; prescribe proceedings for the setting and posting of bail; describe the allowable forms of bonds; limit charges for commercial bonds and otherwise regulate commercial bail bondsmen; and define the conditions and procedures for forfeiture. Some relatively recent statutes authorize or require forms of conditional release that are more favorable to the defendant than traditional money bail, such as release on the defendant's own recognizance (see paragraph [56] *supra*) or upon the defendant's deposit of the bail-premium amount with the clerk of court (see paragraph [63] *infra*). For example, the Federal Bail Reform Act, 18 U.S.C. §§3146-3152, governing federal criminal cases outside the District of Columbia, provides for a scheme of pretrial release in which money bail is not to be demanded unless other forms of conditional release (*R.O.R.*, release in the custody of a responsible person, travel or residence restrictions, a bail-premium deposit) are not reasonably likely to secure the defendant's appearance at trial, *see Bell v. Wolfish*, 441 U.S. 520, 536 n.18 (1979) (dictum). *Cf.* D.C. CODE, §23-1321, as enacted by the District of Columbia Court Reform and Criminal Procedure Act of 1970, Pub. L. No. 91-358, §210(a), 84 Stat. 642.

(C) Even in jurisdictions where statutes provide a broad right to bail (and where legislatures do not follow the lead of Congress by enacting "preventive detention" legislation, see subparagraph (A) *supra*), the fact that the state constitution also guarantees the bail right may be significant for several reasons. First, it is invariably in the constitutions, not the statutes, that the prohibition of "excessive bail" is found. These constitutional "excessive bail" clauses are the defendant's essential protection both against exorbitant judicial bail-setting in individual cases and against exorbitant amounts prescribed by legislative bail schedules. Second, the statutes regulating bail may be unconstitutional in other respects than exorbitance. For example, the Supreme Court of the United States has construed the Eighth Amendment's Excessive Bail Clause to require that the amount of bail be set in each individual case, in view of the circumstances of each individual defendant, in an amount no greater than is necessary to assure the defendant's appearance for trial. *Stack v. Boyle*, 342 U.S. 1 (1951). (This aspect of *Stack* was reaffirmed in *United States v. Salerno*, subparagraph (A) *supra*, 107 S. Ct. at 2105 (dictum) ("when the government has admitted that its only interest is in preventing flight, bail must be set by a court at a sum designed to ensure that goal, and no more").) Under this construction, uniform bail schedules for offenses, although widely used, appear to be *per se* unconstitutional. *See Ackies v. Purdy*, 322 F. Supp. 38 (S.D. Fla. 1970). Third, where state laws define the jurisdiction of some appellate courts in terms of the presence of a constitutional question, the constitutional status of the bail right permits a resort to those courts that would be unavailable if the right were merely statutory.

[57-A] Federal constitutional rights to bail in state criminal cases. (A) For several additional reasons it would be significant if the federal Constitution guaranteed a right to bail (or a right against excessive bail, see paragraph [57] (A) *supra*) in state criminal cases. First, the substance of such a right would be determined by federal case law, including decisions such as *Stack v. Boyle*, paragraph [57] (C) *supra*, which may be more liberal than state-law bail decisions. Second, a defendant's federal constitutional rights to bail could be enforced not merely in the state courts but (after exhaustion of state-court remedies) by *habeas corpus* in the federal courts. See paragraph [71] *infra*.

(B) It has not yet been authoritatively decided whether a state criminal defendant does have any federal constitutional rights in connection with bail. *See Simon v. Woodson*, 454 F.2d

161, 164-65 (5th Cir. 1972). But strong arguments are available to support these rights:

(1) Beginning with *Mapp v. Ohio*, 367 U.S. 643 (1961), paragraph [227] *infra*, the Supreme Court has followed a course of decisions that has "incorporated" into the Due Process Clause of the Fourteenth Amendment, and thus made binding upon the state courts, all of the other major criminal procedure guarantees of the Bill of Rights. *See Gideon v. Wainwright*, 372 U.S. 335 (1963) (Sixth Amendment right to counsel): *Ker v. California*, 374 U.S. 23 (1963) (Fourth Amendment right against unreasonable search and seizure); *Malloy v. Hogan*, 378 U.S. 1 (1964) (Fifth Amendment privilege against self-incrimination); *Pointer v. Texas*, 380 U.S. 400 (1965) (Sixth Amendment right of confrontation): *Klopfer v. North Carolina*, 386 U.S. 213 (1967) (Sixth Amendment right to speedy trial); *Washington v. Texas*, 388 U.S. 14 (1967) (Sixth Amendment right to compulsory process); *Duncan v. Louisiana*, 391 U.S. 145 (1968) (Sixth Amendment right to jury trial); *Benton v. Maryland*, 395 U.S. 784 (1969) (Fifth Amendment right against double jeopardy); *see generally Faretta v. California*, 422 U.S. 806, 818 (1975); *Herring v. New York*, 422 U.S. 853, 856-57 (1975). The guarantee of the Eighth Amendment against excessive bail eminently qualifies for similar incorporation for several reasons: (a) Historically, the struggle to establish the right to bail was central in the evolution of the English conception of the liberty of the citizen. See paragraph [55] *supra*, and the Foote article cited in paragraph [57] (A) *supra*, at 965-68. Thus the right fairly falls within even the most conservative test for incorporation: It is a "'principle of justice so rooted in the traditions and conscience of our people as to be ranked as fundamental,'" *Palko v. Connecticut*, 302 U.S. 319, 325 (1937). (b) The bail right is universally recognized in American state constitutions. *See Comment*, 70 YALE L.J. 966, 977 (1961); *Comment*, 7 VILL. L. REV. 438, 450 (1962). This, too, is evidence of its fundamental quality. *Cf. Ferguson v. Georgia*, 365 U.S. 570 (1961); *Baldwin v. New York*, 399 U.S. 66, 72-73 (1970). (c) The Supreme Court has recognized that "[u]nless this right to bail before trial is preserved, the presumption of innocence, secured only after centuries of struggle, would lose its mean-

ing." *Stack v. Boyle*, 342 U.S. 1, 4 (1951). And the Court has already held that the other principal reflection of the presumption of innocence—the right against conviction except on proof beyond a reasonable doubt, *see Taylor v. Kentucky*, 436 U.S. 478, 483-86 (1978)—is embodied in the Fourteenth Amendment. *E.g.*, *In re Winship*, 397 U.S. 358 (1970); *Ivan V. v. City of New York*, 407 U.S. 203 (1972); *Mullaney v. Wilbur*, 421 U.S. 684 (1975); *Sandstrom v. Montana*, 442 U.S. 510 (1979); *Francis v. Franklin*, 471 U.S. 307 (1985); *Jackson v. Virginia*, 443 U.S. 307 (1979) (dictum); *cf. Cool v. United States*, 409 U.S. 100, 104 (1972); *County Court of Ulster County v. Allen*, 442 U.S. 140, 156 (1979) (dictum); *and see Estelle v. Williams*, 425 U.S. 501, 503 (1976) (dictum). (*But see Bell v. Wolfish*, 441 U.S. 520, 532-33 (1979).) (d) The Supreme Court has incorporated the Eighth Amendment's prohibition of cruel and unusual punishments, *Robinson v. California*, 370 U.S. 660 (1962); *Furman v. Georgia*, 408 U.S. 238 (1972); *Woodson v. North Carolina*, 428 U.S. 280 (1976); and the reasoning of *Washington v. Texas*, 388 U.S. 14, 17-18 (1967), suggests that this circumstance favors the incorporation of the balance of the amendment as well. (e) Several federal decisions have concluded, albeit usually in dictum, that the Fourteenth Amendment does incorporate the Excessive Bail Clause of the Eighth. *Hunt v. Roth*, 648 F.2d 1148, 1155-56 (8th Cir. 1981), *vacated as moot sub nom. Murphy v. Hunt*, 455 U.S. 478 (1982) (per curiam); *Meechaicum v. Fountain*, 696 F.2d 790 (10th Cir. 1983); *United States ex rel. Keating v. Bensinger*, 322 F. Supp. 784, 786 (N.D. Ill. 1971); *Sistrunk v. Lyons*, 646 F.2d 64, 66-71 (3d Cir. 1981) (dictum); *Henderson v. Dutton*, 397 F.2d 375, 377 n.3 (5th Cir. 1968) (dictum); *Pilkinton v. Circuit Court*, 324 F.2d 45, 46 (8th Cir. 1963) (dictum); *Goodine v. Griffin*, 309 F. Supp. 590, 591 (S.D. Ga. 1970) (dictum); *Hernandez v. Heyd*, 307 F. Supp. 826, 828 (E.D. La. 1970) (dictum), and cases cited. And the Supreme Court has cited the *Pilkinton* case, with apparent approval, for the proposition that "the Eighth Amendment's proscription of excessive bail has been assumed to have application to the States through the Fourteenth Amendment." *Schilb v. Kuebel*, 404 U.S. 357, 365 (1971) (dictum); *see also Baker v. McCollan*, 443 U.S. 137, 144 n.3 (1979) (dictum).

(2) Even if the Eighth Amendment bail right were not incorporated, the Due Process Clause of the Fourteenth Amendment would require the allowance of some form of conditional release in cases in which pretrial incarceration adversely affected the defendant's right to a fair trial; for example, when it impeded his or her ability to locate witnesses important to the defense. *See Kinney v. Lenon*, 425 F.2d 209 (9th Cir. 1970). Pretrial incarceration can be shown to prejudice a defendant's defense in a broad range of ways and situations covering many criminal cases. See the Foote article, cited in paragraph [57] (A) *supra*, at 1137-51.

(3) Whether or not any underlying substantive federal constitutional right to bail exists, it seems plain that "[a]s to . . . offenses . . . for which a state has provided a right of bail it may not, any more than as to other substantive or procedural benefits under its criminal law system, engage in such administration as arbitrarily or discriminatorily to effect denial or deprivation of the right to a particular accused." *Mastrian v. Hedman*, 326 F.2d 708, 711 (8th Cir. 1964) (dictum). *Accord, Atkins v. Michigan*, 644 F.2d 543, 549-50 (6th Cir. 1981); *cf. Connecticut Board of Pardons v. Dumschat*, 452 U.S. 458, 463 (1981) (dictum) ("[a] state-created right can, in some circumstances, beget yet other rights to procedures essential to the realization of the parent right"); *Board of Pardons v. Allen*, 107 S. Ct. 2415 (1987). This is so because the Due Process and Equal Protection Clauses of the Fourteenth Amendment require that all state-law rules be fairly and even-handedly applied, *e.g., Schware v. Board of Bar Examiners*, 353 U.S. 232 (1957), particularly when liberty is at stake in their application, *e.g., Thompson v. City of Louisville*, 362 U.S. 199 (1960); *Shuttlesworth v. City of Birmingham*, 382 U.S. 87, 93-95 (1965); *Papachristou v. City of Jacksonville*, 405 U.S. 156, 170-71 (1972); *Humphrey v. Cady*, 405 U.S. 504, 512 (1972). "Even in applying permissible standards, officers of a State cannot [adversely affect a citizen's interests] . . . when there is no basis for their finding that he fails to meet these standards, or when their action is invidiously discriminatory." *Schware v. Board of Bar Examiners, supra*, 353 U.S. at 239. These concepts forbid the deprivation of liberty by factually baseless or legally arbitrary

applications of *any* legal rules. *Vitek v. Jones*, 445 U.S. 480, 488-89 (1980); *Hicks v. Oklahoma*, 447 U.S. 343, 346-47 (1980); *Evitts v. Lucey*, 469 U.S. 387, 400-1, 403-4 (1985); *Whalen v. United States*, 445 U.S. 684, 690 n.4 (1980) (dictum); *Superintendent v. Hill*, 472 U.S. 445, 454-55 (1985) (dictum); *cf. Logan v. Zimmerman Brush Co.*, 455 U.S. 422, 428-36 (1982); *Goss v. Lopez*, 419 U.S. 565, 572-76 (1975). As applied to the question of bail, they entitle a state criminal defendant to have his or her "motion for bail . . . handled without 'arbitrariness' and 'discriminatoriness,'" *United States ex rel. Keating v. Bensinger*, *supra*, 322 F. Supp. at 787, and require federal constitutional relief if "[w]hat the state court did [in administering its local bail rules can be shown to] . . . be beyond the range within which judgments could rationally differ in relation to the apparent elements of the situation," *Mastrian v. Hedman, supra*, 326 F.2d at 711 (dictum).

(4) The implication of the Equal Protection Clause of the Fourteenth Amendment for pretrial incarceration of indigents in default of bail is considered in paragraph [61] *infra*.

[58] **Capital cases.** (A) In many jurisdictions some or all capital cases are excepted from the right to bail. A common constitutional and statutory formulation provides that all offenses are bailable except capital offenses in which the proof is evident or the presumption great. Some courts read this archaic language to mean capital cases in which the death penalty is likely to be imposed. Others read it more literally to mean capital cases in which the prosecution has strong evidence. Still others construe it to mean cases in which the prosecution has sufficient evidence to get to a jury (that is, to survive a motion for a directed verdict of acquittal) on the capital offense (or the capital degree of an offense divided into capital and noncapital degrees). Under any of these constructions, defense counsel should be alert to the potential of an application for bail as a discovery device for learning what the prosecution's evidence is.

(B) The invalidation of some forms of the death penalty as cruel and unusual punishments in *Furman v. Georgia*, 408 U.S. 238 (1972), spawned considerable litigation over the meaning of the term *capital* in state laws making "capital" offenses nonbailable. Several courts held that offenses punishable by a constitutionally unenforceable death penalty are no longer "capital"; hence they are bailable. Other courts held that offenses remain "capital" and nonbailable if they are statutorily punishable by death, even though the death penalty may no longer be constitutionally imposed. The confusion is compounded by the fact that most of the states have reenacted the death penalty since *Furman* in various forms thought to escape the prohibition of that decision. Some of these states have added laws providing death penalties for restricted classes of offenses without repealing the old, broader death penalty statutes struck down by *Furman*. Decisions of the Supreme Court of the United States in 1976 sustained various forms of the new statutes, invalidated others, and left open the constitutionality of the remainder. See paragraph [468-A] *infra*. These decisions have engendered still a third wave of death penalty laws in many states. What offenses are now "capital" in states with second- or third-generation death penalty statutes is questionable (particularly when the older statutes were not technically repealed by the newer ones or when the newer statutes authorize capital punishment only upon a finding of enumerated "aggravating circumstances" in addition to the elements of the offense)—as is the constitutionality of some of the newer death penalty statutes themselves. *Ibid.*

(C) It is important to note that constitutional and statutory provisions excepting designated capital offenses from the general right to bail are often construed as merely denying an absolute right to bail, not as disallowing release on bail. In the designated cases magistrates and judges may still admit a defendant to bail in their discretion. *E.g., In re Losasso*, 15 Colo. 163, 24 P. 1080 (1890); *State v. Arthur*, 390 So. 2d 717 (Fla. 1980); *State v. Pichon*, 148 La. 348, 86 So. 893 (1921); *Ex parte Bridewell*, 42 Miss. 39 (1879); *In re Corbo*, 54 N.J. Super. 575, 149 A.2d 828 (1959) (dictum), *cert. denied*, 29 N.J. 465, 149 A.2d 859 (1959); *In re West*, 10 N.D. 464, 88 N.W. 88 (1901); *Ex parte Dexter*, 93 Vt. 304, 107 A. 134 (1919).

[59] Amount of bail. If not set by a master bail schedule, the amount of bail is determined by the bail-setting authority (police officer, magistrate, judge, or court clerk by designation of the judge) in light of a number of factors. Most important are (1) the nature of the offense (seriousness of possible penalty, aggravating circumstances that indicate the defendant's dangerousness if released, and so forth), (2) defendant's character and reputation (and particularly criminal record), (3) defendant's financial assets (how much money has to be tied up in bail to keep the defendant in place), (4) defendant's employment status and record (as an indication of reliability and of the defendant's dependence on staying where s/he is; it is also significant that the defendant may lose his or her job if jailed for a period), (5) defendant's family status and roots in the community (length of time the defendant has resided in the location, presence of family there, other factors indicating inconvenience of flight, such as residence in public housing, receipt of social security or welfare payments, and so forth). The Supreme Court of the United States has said, construing the Eighth Amendment, that "when the government['s] . . . only [asserted] interest is in preventing flight, bail must be set by a court at a sum designed to ensure that goal, and no more," *United States v. Salerno*, 107 S. Ct. 2095, 2105 (1987) (dictum), and that individual inquiry into the circumstances of each defendant is required in setting the amount. *Stack v. Boyle*, 342 U.S. 1 (1951). Bail set according to substantive standards (for example—as is common—by reference to the heinousness of the offense) or by procedures (such as use of a bail schedule or refusal of a hearing to consider the defendant's background) that are inconsistent with these canons is unconstitutional (*see Ackies v. Purdy*, 322 F. Supp. 38 (S.D. Fla. 1970)) and can be challenged by *habeas corpus* or any other method of review prescribed by local law. As a general matter, the police, magistrates, and many trial court judges entirely ignore the constitutional conception of bail expressed in *Stack v. Boyle*: Instead of determining the amount of bail in the light of particularized factors relevant to the likelihood of flight and the "function of bail" as an "assurance of the presence of an accused" at trial, 342 U.S. at 5, they set bail exclusively in view of the seriousness of the offense charged and the defendant's prior criminal record. Appellate courts are far more likely to make bail determinations under the proper *Stack v. Boyle* standards. See paragraph [41] *supra*. This means that defense counsel must obtain at the outset factual information pertinent both to the standards that will likely be used at the lower levels (circumstances of the charged offense; defendant's criminal history) and to the standards that will likely be used on any appeals (defendant's stability in the community, general reliability, and financial situation). Counsel should be prepared to vary the emphasis on these several factors as s/he moves from court to court. The following paragraph consists of a form for use in obtaining a sworn statement from a defendant detailing the factors pertinent to setting the amount of bail. It may be used in affidavit form to support a motion for bail, for reduction of bail, or for release on recognizance. Counsel should also attempt to support its assertions by proof from sources other than the defendant, since many judges distrust the interested statements of an accused in these matters. Compare paragraph [466] *infra*.

[60] **Questionnaire for obtaining information pertinent to bail from criminal defendants.** Designed principally for counsel's use in obtaining from a client information pertinent to the amount of bail that should be set, this form may be notarized and submitted to a magistrate or judge in support of an application for bail in a manageable amount or for reduction of bail or for release on nominal bail or on recognizance, as is appropriate. Of course, caution must be observed not to use the form if a client's answers may supply incriminating information or investigative leads that are not already known to the police and the prosecution. The same caution suggests that ordinarily the details of the charged offense should be obtained from the arresting or prosecuting officer, not from the defendant. See paragraph [95] *infra*.

Questionnaire for Bail Information

Name: _____ Age: _____

Address: _____
　　　　　Number　　　　Street　　　　City　　　　State

How long have you lived at this address? _____

Is this public housing (a project)? ☐ Yes　☐ No

Address immediately before present address:

_____
Number　　　　　　Street　　　　　City　　　　　State

How long did you live at that address? _____

Job: _____
　　　　Kind of work　　　　　Employer's name

_____
Employer's address:　Number　　　Street　　　City　　　State

How long have you been employed by this employer?

_____

Amount now earned per week: _____

Is your job waiting for you if you are released at this
time? ☐ Yes　☐ No

Job immediately before present job:

_____
　　Kind of work　　　　　　Employer's name

_____
Employer's address:　Number　　　Street　　　City　　　State

Between what dates were you employed by this employer?

_____ to _____
   Month   Year   Month   Year

Are you enrolled as a student in any school? ☐ Yes   ☐ No

If student: _____
          Name of school   City   State   Your grade

[If you are a student but have a full-time or part-time job, please supply all job information requested previously.]

If unemployed: Since when unemployed? _____

Receiving unemployment compensation? ☐ Yes   ☐ No

Amount per week: _____

Assets: Do you own

     —your own home?   ☐ Yes ☐ No Value: _____
     —an automobile?   ☐ Yes ☐ No Value: _____
     —a bank account? ☐ Yes ☐ No Value: _____
     —other property?   ☐ Yes ☐ No Value: _____

Do you have any other source of income than your job (include social security, if any)?   ☐ Yes   ☐ No

_____
    Nature of source   Amount per week

_____
    Nature of source   Amount per week

Liabilities: Do you have

     —home mortgage(s)?   ☐ Yes   ☐ No

       Creditor: _____ Amount: _____

—debt(s) on installment
　　purchase of a vehicle?　☐ Yes　☐ No

　　Creditor: _____　Amount: _____

—debt(s) on installment
　　purchase of other property?　☐ Yes　☐ No

Item: _____ Creditor: _____ Amount: _____

Item: _____ Creditor: _____ Amount: _____

—other debt(s)?　☐ Yes　☐ No

　　Creditor: _____　Amount: _____

　　Creditor: _____　Amount: _____

—unpaid account(s)?

　　Creditor: _____　Amount: _____

　　Creditor: _____　Amount: _____

Do you have court-ordered obligations to support any person?　☐ Yes　☐ No

| Name of person | Relationship | Amount ordered per month |

| Name of person | Relationship | Amount ordered per month |

Do you have any other dependents?　☐ Yes　☐ No

| Name of dependent | Relationship | Amount contributed per month |

| Name of dependent | Relationship | Amount contributed per month |

Does your family receive public assistance or welfare payments? ☐ Yes ☐ No

    Agency from which payments received: _____

    Amount per month: _____

Present criminal charge(s): _____

_____

Criminal record (include all pending cases other than present charges):

Arrest Date	Place	Charge(s) (Write: convicted, charge(s) dismissed, acquitted, pending, or whatever)	Result
Arrest Date	Place	Charge(s)	Result

With what members of your family, if any, do you now live?

Name	Age	Relationship
Name	Age	Relationship

Do you have any other family in this city/town? ☐ Yes ☐ No
                               county? ☐ Yes ☐ No
                               state? ☐ Yes ☐ No

Name	Age	Relationship
Address: Number	Street	City	State

Name	Age	Relationship
Address: Number	Street	City	State

Do you have any illness or physical disability that makes it difficult to get around?   ☐ Yes   ☐ No

If yes, describe it:

_____

_____

_____

Does anyone in your immediate family have any such illness or disability?   ☐ Yes   ☐ No

If yes, describe it:

_____

_____

_____

_____
Signature

[61] Bail and the indigent. (A) The anomaly and injustice of jailing people simply because they are too poor to make bail have been abundantly argued in the literature since the mid-1960's. *See, e.g.*, FREED & WALD, BAIL IN THE UNITED STATES: 1964 (A Report to the National Conference on Bail and Criminal Justice, Washington, D.C., May 27-29, 1964) (1964); GOLDKAMP, TWO CLASSES OF ACCUSED—A STUDY OF BAIL AND DETENTION IN AMERICAN JUSTICE (1979); WICE, FREEDOM FOR SALE—A NATIONAL STUDY OF PRETRIAL RELEASE (1974); Cohen, *Wealth, Bail, and the Equal Protection of the Laws*, 23 VILL. L. REV. 977 (1977-1978); Foote, *The Coming Constitutional Crisis in Bail*, 113 U. PA. L. REV. 959, 1125 (1965), reprinted in FOOTE, ed., STUDIES ON BAIL 181-283 (1966); Silverstein, *Bail in the State Courts—A Field Study and Report*, 50 MINN. L. REV. 621 (1966). Cognizant of the economic discrimination worked by the requirement of money bail as a condition of pretrial release, courts are increasingly tending to relax the necessity for posting "good" bail if an accused has a stable background in the community. In major metropolitan areas there are agencies (generally called R.O.R. Projects or Bail Projects) that interview defendants shortly after arrest and investigate their backgrounds to determine whether they are eligible under the agency's standards of stability for a recommendation to the court that they be released on recognizance. The courts generally follow these recommendations. Counsel representing an indigent defendant should contact such an agency, if one exists, for help in getting the client released.

(B) On the level of legal right, an argument for the proposition that detention of an indigent in default of bail which s/he cannot make violates the Habeas Corpus Clause, the Eighth Amendment, the Due Process and Equal Protection Clauses of the Fourteenth Amendment, and cognate state constitutional guarantees is fully developed in the Foote article cited in subparagraph (A) *supra*, and may be pressed on *habeas corpus* in state and federal courts. Professor Foote's Equal Protection arguments, in particular, draw strong support from subsequent decisions condemning the incarceration of indigents in default of payment of fines imposed upon conviction.

Williams v. Illinois, 399 U.S. 235 (1970); *Tate v. Short*, 401 U.S. 395 (1971); *In re Antazo*, 3 Cal. 3d 100, 473 P.2d 999, 89 Cal. Rptr. 255 (1970). *Cf. Bearden v. Georgia*, 461 U.S. 660 (1983); *Estelle v. Williams*, 425 U.S. 501, 505-6 (1976) (dictum). In 1977, those arguments prevailed in a path-breaking decision, *Pugh v. Rainwater*, 557 F.2d 1189 (5th Cir. 1977), *rev'd en banc*, 572 F.2d 1053 (5th Cir. 1978). Although the Former Fifth Circuit *en banc* disapproved on narrow grounds the original panel decision in *Pugh* holding Florida's pretrial release system facially unconstitutional, a majority of the court endorsed the panel's essential conclusion that "[t]he incarceration of those who cannot [afford to post money bail], without meaningful consideration of other possible alternatives [that is, other forms of pretrial release], infringes on both due process and equal protection requirements." 572 F.2d at 1057. "We have no doubt that in the case of an indigent, whose appearance at trial could reasonably be assured by one of the alternate forms of release, pretrial confinement for inability to post money bail would constitute imposition of an excessive restraint" and hence violate the Constitution. *Id.* at 1058. A new Florida pretrial release rule, promulgated while the *Pugh* case was pending on appeal, was adjudged "subject to constitutional interpretation and application," *ibid.*, because it did not appear to the *en banc* majority that "the automatic setting of money bails [which had been Florida's prior practice] will continue [under the new rule] and that the unnecessary and therefore constitutionally interdicted pretrial detention of indigents will be the inevitable result," *ibid.* The majority pointed to a drafting committee note on the new Florida rule which said that the rule "'leaves it to the sound discretion of the judge to determine *the least onerous form of release* which will still insure the defendant's appearance,'" *id.* at 1058 n.8 (emphasis added by the court), and expressed confidence that the Florida courts would follow this interpretation of the rule in view of "the absence of a constitutional alternative," *ibid.*

[62] **Procedures for setting bail.** When an arrest warrant is issued for a person, the issuing authority normally sets the amount of bail under which the arrestee is to be held. This

amount is endorsed on the arrest warrant. If there is no such endorsement or if an arrest is made without a warrant, the police, a magistrate, a judge of the criminal court of record, the court clerk, or more than one of them (depending upon the nature of the offense) normally may set bail following the arrest, on request of the arrestee or counsel. If an arrest is made in a county other than that in which the offense is charged, the police officer, magistrate, or court at the place of arrest usually has authority to set bail. In any case in which bail has not been set prior to the preliminary arraignment, it is ordinarily set by the magistrate at that arraignment (except for serious offenses that, in some jurisdictions, are not bailable by magistrates but only by courts of record in *habeas corpus* proceedings). See paragraphs [13], [14], [18], [49] *supra*. Procedures for getting bail set before and after the preliminary arraignment are governed by statute, court rule, and local custom, and they vary widely. See paragraph [57] (B) *supra*. Sometimes counsel is required to obtain a "copy of the charge" from the arresting officers and to present it to a magistrate or judge *ex parte*. Sometimes *habeas corpus* is employed; sometimes, a simple motion for bail with supporting affidavits. Statutory regulation (including applicable bail schedules) should be checked in counsel's jurisdiction to determine the persons who have the authority to set bail and the limitations of authority of each.

[63] **Types of bail allowable.** Three types of bail are normally acceptable: cash or negotiable securities, a surety bond posted by a licensed bonding company, and a real property bond (usually in the form of a deed to property). Whereas cash, securities, and a property deed are returned when the defendant has fulfilled the bail obligation by appearing, the premium paid to a bonding company for the posting of a surety bond is not recoverable. This premium is the surety company's compensation for the risk it incurs in posting its security. Premiums that companies may charge for bail bonds are normally regulated by statute (about 10 per cent of the face of the bond, or a little more or less depending on the face amount), but the companies are free to agree or refuse to serve any indi-

vidual and are usually free to impose conditions when they insure a client, such as a pledge of collateral security to hold the company harmless in the event of default. By statute, in some jurisdictions, a defendant may make bond by depositing the premium amount directly with the clerk of court, recoverable upon appearance. This enlightened reform is spreading but is not yet widespread. Some premium-deposit statutes authorize or require the clerk to retain a small portion of the deposit as an "administration fee"; the Supreme Court of the United States has found such a practice constitutionally unobjectionable. *Schilb v. Kuebel*, 404 U.S. 357 (1971).

[64] **Choice among the types of bail.** If cash, securities, or a property bond can be posted by the client without hardship, these will be the least costly forms of bail in the long run. However, counsel will want to consider the impact on the disposition of the case which might result from the disclosure that the defendant has the means to make bond in these forms. Particularly in gambling, alcohol, drug, prostitution, counterfeiting, and automobile theft cases—and in others involving the lurking suspicion of organized crime—a defendant who posts a sizable cash bond may find that that fact has leaked to the trial judge or jury, with expectable prejudice. Still worse, the fact will likely be considered by the judge at sentencing. In any event, if there is any chance that the defendant will want to dispose of his or her real property in the near future, a property bond should not be used; and if the defendant is one who cannot be easily contacted about appearing or if the chance of the defendant's failure to appear is more than slight, a bonding company is probably the best choice. Bail bondsmen are located near most police stations and are usually available around the clock. Before undertaking to secure the appearance of a client, they will want to know about the client's employment, permanence of residence, criminal record, family status, and the nature of the charge. Of course, they want some immediate cash, but they frequently accept part payment of their premium at the outset. Because of their continuous contact with the police and their familiarity with the neighborhood surrounding the precinct, bondsmen are normally a good

source of information, especially on procedures relating to the quick release of an accused. They differ widely in their helpfulness and in such crucial matters as demands for collateral security (see the preceding paragraph); and, when practicable, counsel not familiar with the local bondsmen should inquire of some reputable attorney who knows them.

[65] Same—deposit of premium; release on personal bond or on recognizance. Counsel should consult local practice concerning the availability of procedures for court deposit of a "premium" amount or fractional portion of the bond, as described in paragraph [63] *supra*. If the client is indigent, counsel should inquire whether there is a local R.O.R. Project of the sort described in paragraph [61](A) *supra*. In any event, the release of arrested persons without security, either on their own bond or on their own recognizance (see paragraph [56] *supra*), is a growing practice (see paragraphs [57](B), [61](A) *supra*), and these forms of release should always be urged on the bail-setting authority. One or the other form is most likely obtainable by a person with strong roots in the community and a stable employment and family situation. The defendant's bail questionnaire set out in paragraph [60] *supra* is useful to document the justifications for a client's release without security; but counsel should support the facts asserted in the statement with proof from sources other than the client if this is practicable.

[66] Procedures for posting bail. After the amount of bail has been set and the means to make up that amount are in hand, the bail is "posted" with the appropriate authority, who orders the defendant's release or issues a receipt or form authorizing the defendant's release. Posting bail involves depositing with the authority the defendant's signed bond (ordinarily a form document), the surety's bond, if any (also a form), and whatever cash, securities, or deeds are put up for bail, and obtaining a receipt and any additional form required to authorize release. If the authority with whom bail is posted is not the same authority that set the bail, the order or endorsement setting the amount of bail must, of course, also be presented. Who is the appropriate authority to receive the bail depends generally on the identity and procedure of the bail-setting official. When set by the police, bail is usually posted with the police; inquiry of the desk officer will locate the proper recipient. Bail set by a magistrate on a copy of the charge or similar procedure (see paragraph [62] *supra*) is ordinarily also posted with the police, whereas bail set by a magistrate at a hearing may have to be posted with the magistrate's clerk. Bail set by a court of record is ordinarily posted with the clerk of the court. In any case in which bail is not posted with the police, counsel or someone acting for the client must deliver the receipt or release order or both to the police. It is usually wise for counsel or a trusted paralegal to do this and to wait until the defendant is physically ushered out of custody, since the investigating officers may delay release to complete their job. When a professional surety is used, the surety usually takes care of these matters, but it should not be forgotten that a professional surety is less likely than counsel to be alert to the defendant's interests and to move quickly.

[67] Problems in getting bail set or in posting bond— locating the defendant and identifying the charges. Counsel will often encounter considerable difficulty in locating an arrested client for the purpose of getting information needed to arrange the setting of bail or of having the client sign an affidavit or other document for use in arranging bail or of having the client sign a bond or of having the client released promptly once the bond is posted. Especially in urban areas arrestees may be shuttled through several police quarters before they come to rest in one or another jail or detention facility to await a judicial hearing. A related problem is the difficulty of identifying the exact charges, and all the charges, against the defendant, since often these are not determined by the police until after their investigation of their prisoner is well advanced. Counsel can obviate some of the frustration in these areas by getting as much information as possible about the client's status from the police when s/he first talks to them about the case. See paragraph [25](4) *supra*. S/he should ask the desk officer and the investigating officer (a) exactly where the client is now; (b) whether the client is going to be taken anywhere else; (c) if so, where; (d) what are the present charges (repeating them to the officer and asking, "Have I got them *all*, now?"); (e) whether other charges are being considered or investigated; and (f) what the other charges are. It is also useful to ask each officer tactfully where *s/he* will be during the next several hours and how *s/he* can be reached so that counsel can locate the officer and ask for an accounting if the officer's information proves wrong (for example, if the client is removed from the station where the officer said that s/he would be held). Frequently it makes sense to leave a client in custody for several hours or even overnight until the specific charges are firmed up. Otherwise, counsel may have bail set and a bond posted only to find that the defendant has been held on additional charges or to learn that a released defendant has been rearrested on additional charges. See paragraph [73] *infra*. Of course, on the other side, the desirability of getting the client out of the hands of the police quickly must be considered. If the police appear uninformative or hostile; if a client cannot be located after reasonable inquiry of them; if the police fail to lodge charges against a client who is detained; if station house bail authorized by law is not quickly set or if it is set in an excessive amount; if the client is being moved around rapidly; if interrogation or improper investigation of a client in custody appears to be going on; or if any other obstruction or problem arises in securing the client's release or admission to bail, a call should be made to the prosecutor's office. Usually in urban areas a deputy prosecutor is assigned to be on call for after-hours emergencies and can be reached through the prosecutor's office switchboard; but if there is no such arrangement, a prosecutor should be telephoned at home. If insufficient assistance is obtained from the prosecutor, an application to a court of record is next in order. Traditionally, *habeas corpus* is available to secure relief in these situations. (See paragraphs [68], [70] *infra*.) If counsel is dissatisfied with the relief s/he gets, s/he may appeal the adverse disposition of the *habeas* petition to an appellate court and seek an expedited hearing, or in most jurisdictions s/he may apply for an original writ of *habeas corpus* from the appellate court or one of its judges.

[68] Same—locating officials to set or receive bond. Counsel will also frequently have trouble identifying or locating the person authorized to set bail or to approve a bond and order the prisoner's release. Police can be very helpful in these regards when they want to cooperate, and inquiry of the desk officer or of the arresting or investigating officers is generally fruitful. If they appear to be acting obstructively, a call on the commanding officer may be advised. Bondsmen in the area are also likely to have helpful tips. If all else fails, an application to a judge for a writ of *habeas corpus* may be required. This should invoke the judge's jurisdiction to entertain *habeas corpus* for the purpose of admitting a detained accused to bail. (See paragraph [70] *infra*.) It should assert that other attempts to secure the prisoner's admission to bail have failed, and it should be supported by an affidavit of counsel reciting counsel's futile efforts and any obstruction of them by the authorities. In a serious case arising after court hours, the judge may be telephoned at home with an inquiry whether s/he will receive a petition there. This frequently results in the judge's telephoning the police and informally arranging to clear up the problem. Obviously, a lawyer who telephones a judge at home should be prepared to show that s/he has made every practicable effort to get relief elsewhere first.

[69] Same—"hold" orders. (A) Even though an arrested person is charged with a bailable offense, s/he may be refused release on bail if a "hold" or "detainer" is lodged against him or her by authorities from other localities where s/he is wanted on outstanding arrest warrants for additional offenses or by local, out-of-county, or out-of-state probation or parole authorities under whose supervision s/he was on probation or parole at the time of the present arrest. (From the standpoint of the latter authorities, the new charges constitute potential probation or parole violations, which may justify the initiation of revocation proceedings.) These detainer practices require close attention and often quick footwork by counsel. In counsel's first discussion with an arrested client, s/he must ask (a) whether the client is on probation or parole; (b) whether there are any warrants out for the client or whether the client is wanted anywhere on any other charges; and (c) whether there is anything the client might be wanted for in any other county or state. Once counsel is aware that s/he is representing a probationer, parolee, or fugitive, s/he may decide to defer attempts to secure bail until the various "detainers" have been lodged and s/he has had a chance to telephone the issuing authorities to try to clear them up. In any event, s/he will avoid paying a bond premium for a defendant who cannot be released by reason of the detainers. On the other hand, some probation or parole authorities may not have a defendant arrested if/she has posted bail on a new offense, whereas they automatically place a "hold" on a probationer or parolee in custody. In this situation counsel may want to hustle to post bail before the "hold" order is lodged with the defendant's custodian.

(B) Probation and parole officers can frequently be persuaded informally to lift detainers (or not to lodge them) by (a) describing the new offense to them in terms which persuade them that the defendant's guilt is dubious or that the offense is trifling even if the defendant is guilty; (b) pointing out, if this is true, that the judge who set bail on the new offense set relatively low bail, thus expressing the belief that the defendant was not likely to flee; (c) pointing out that the new offense is much less serious than the old one, if this is so, and that it would, therefore, be inappropriate to institute heavy back-time revocation proceedings on the basis of a criminal charge for which the defendant will be amply punished (assuming his or her guilt) by the far lighter penalties applicable to the new offense; or (d) persuading them that the new offense is a minor lapse from grace on the part of a probationer or parolee who is otherwise making a good adjustment and that if s/he is jailed for even a short period of time because of the detainer, s/he will lose his or her job, will be dropped from a rehabilitation program in which s/he is enrolled, or will otherwise suffer consequences harmful to the prospect of successfully "making it" on probation or parole. If, notwithstanding these points, the probation or parole officer is adamant on a detainer, counsel may want to insist that an immediate preliminary revocation hearing conformable to the requirements of *Morrissey v. Brewer*, 408 U.S. 471 (1972), and *Gagnon v. Scarpelli*, 411 U.S. 778 (1973), be held or, if it is not held, that the detainer be lifted. (In federal cases, *see also* FED. R. CRIM. P. 32.1, 40(d).) Unless this constitutionally required preliminary hearing is held, the lodging of a detainer resulting in the defendant's nonbailability on a new charge ought to be as assailable as is detention upon a violator's warrant for the old charge alone, *compare Moody v. Daggett*, 429 U.S. 78, 88 (1976); therefore, the detainer may be challenged in *habeas corpus* proceedings (see paragraphs [70]-[71] *infra*) if the probation or parole authorities decline either to lift it or to provide a prompt *Morrissey-Scarpelli* hearing. *Cf. Braden v. 30th Judicial Circuit Court*, 410 U.S. 484 (1973). Counsel should also be aware of the cases suggesting that revocation decisions by probation and parole officials are no longer as immune from substantive judicial review as they were once thought to be. *See Arciniega v. Freeman*, 404 U.S. 4 (1971); *Douglas v. Buder*, 412 U.S. 430 (1973); *Bearden v. Georgia*, 461 U.S. 660, 666 n. 7 (1983); *cf. Superintendent v. Hill*, 472 U.S. 445, 455 (1985) (dictum); *but see Black v. Romano*, 471 U.S. 606 (1985).

(C) If the detainer is based upon an out-of-state warrant, little can be done about it locally (*see Michigan v. Doran*, 439 U.S. 282 (1978); *California v. Superior Court (Smolin)*, 107 S. Ct. 2433 (1987)); efforts will have to be focused upon getting the underlying charges dismissed or upon posting bail for appearance on those charges in the courts of the jurisdiction that issued the warrant. The same may be true in the case of out-of-county but in-state arrest warrants, or it may be possible to post bail locally on both the local and out-of-county charges. Formal procedures permit this in some states; elsewhere, it can be arranged informally through the judges of both courts involved. In federal practice, bail can be set and posted in the district of arrest for appearance in another district, under FED. R. CRIM. P. 40.

[70] Review and renewal of efforts to have bail set. Statutory provisions authorizing station house bail, bail-setting by a magistrate, and bail-setting by a court of record are usually cumulative: that is, they confer concurrent jurisdiction to set bail upon the police, the magistrate, and the judge. In the absence of, or in addition to, any statutory procedures for bail-setting by the court of record, that court almost invariably has jurisdiction to issue writs of *habeas corpus*. By immemorial tradition, *habeas corpus* lies for the admission to bail of persons detained under criminal process, *e.g.*, II HALE, PLEAS OF THE CROWN 143 (1st Amer. ed. 1847); hence the grant of *habeas corpus* power without more ordinarily carries with it the power to set bail for a criminal accused, *e.g.*, *Ex parte Bollman*, 8 U.S. (4 Cranch) 75, 99-100 (1807). As a result of the cumulative or concurrent character of the bail-setting authorizations, counsel for a client who is denied bail or whose bail is set in an excessive or unobtainable amount may proceed to apply *seriatim* for relief to each authorized official. Dissatisfied with the setting of station house bail, s/he may apply first to a magistrate, then to a court of record pursuant to a statutory bail-setting procedure, then to the same court or to a judge of that court by *habeas corpus*, then to other judges of the same court or other courts of record having *habeas corpus* jurisdiction. Denial of relief under the statutory bail-setting procedures may or may not be reviewable by appeal or mandamus; denial of *habeas corpus* relief generally is appealable; and, in addition, in most states appellate courts and their judges also have original *habeas* jurisdiction. Furthermore, the denial of relief, whether under the statutory procedures or by *habeas corpus*, generally presents no technical bar to second or subsequent applications to the same official, court, or judge; renewed motions for the reduction of bail and successive petitions for a writ are frequently entertained. The restrictions upon how repeatedly and how far up the chain of authority counsel may press attempts to get the client admitted to bail are, therefore, practical rather than doctrinal. As a matter of common sense and courtesy to the courts, counsel is advised (a) to go first to the lowest official authorized to set bail and then to proceed up the chain of dignity, passing to a higher court only when a lower one has denied relief or is demonstrably unavailable to receive an application for relief; (b) to avoid repeater applications to the same authority unless a convincing showing of some new and significant fact, not previously discoverable, or some changed circumstance can be made; and (c) to quit wasting time and credit with the courts when s/he thinks s/he has obtained as good a deal as s/he is realistically likely to get in a case. (Judges, too, can count, and they recognize that a $100 difference in the bond set is a $10 difference in the premium.)

[71] **Same—federal habeas corpus.** Paragraphs [57A] and [61] *supra* summarize the arguments that a state criminal defendant has federal constitutional rights to bail. To the extent that the arguments prevail, those rights are not left for their vindication exclusively to the state courts. The federal district courts, in the exercise of the *habeas corpus* jurisdiction given by 28 U.S.C. §2241(c)(3), are authorized to discharge from custody persons confined in violation of the Constitution, hence to release on bail state criminal defendants whom the Constitution requires to be bailed. *See Rivera v. Concepcion*, 469 F.2d 17 (1st Cir. 1972); *Dawkins v. Crevasse*, 391 F.2d 921 (5th Cir. 1968); *Sheldon v. Nebraska*, 401 F.2d 343, 346 (8th Cir. 1968) (dictum); *United States ex rel. Keating v. Bensinger*, 322 F. Supp. 784 (N.D. Ill. 1971); *cf. Schall v. Martin*, 467 U.S. 253 (1984) (by implication); *Kinney v. Lenon*, 425 F.2d 209 (9th Cir. 1970). Federal courts will not grant relief to a state prisoner who has not exhausted available remedies in the state courts. But exhaustion is made out whenever either (a) the state courts have denied relief on the merits, *Braden v. 30th Judicial Circuit Court*, 410 U.S. 484, 489-92 (1973) (speedy trial); *Rivera v. Concepcion*, *supra* (bail); or (b) state court relief is delayed to such an extent that it becomes ineffective in light of the grievance sought to be remedied, *Dixon v. Florida*, 388 F.2d 424 (5th Cir. 1968) (postconviction relief); *St. Jules v. Beto*, 462 F.2d 1365 (5th Cir. 1972) (same); *Dozie v. Cady*, 430 F.2d 637 (7th Cir. 1970) (same); *United States ex rel. Goodman v. Kehl*, 456 F.2d 863, 869 (2d Cir. 1972) (dictum) (bail). Under the latter theory even relatively short delays by the state courts in acting upon bail matters may constitute exhaustion, since "[r]elief

in this type of case must be speedy if it is to be effective." *Stack v. Boyle*, 342 U.S. 1, 4 (1951). Counsel may, therefore, be advised to file a federal petition for *habeas corpus* simultaneously with, or shortly after, an application for bail to the state courts; to bring the federal proceeding to a hearing within not more than eight days in strict conformity to 28 U.S.C. §2243; to file at the hearing a supplemental petition or affidavits reciting that the state courts have denied or delayed release on bail during the preceding eight days or more; and to argue that on this showing the federal court is authorized to entertain on the merits the petitioner's federal claims to pretrial release. *Cf. In re Shuttlesworth*, 369 U.S. 35 (1962). The simultaneous-filing procedure is technically permissible because satisfaction of the exhaustion doctrine is not a prerequisite of federal *habeas corpus* jurisdiction but merely a condition precedent to the federal court's ordering relief on the merits. Exhaustion of state remedies after the filing of the federal *habeas* petition, but before the time when the federal court is asked to act upon it, is quite sufficient. *Sharpe v. Buchanan*, 317 U.S. 238 (1942); *Davis v. Jackson*, 246 F.2d 268 (2d Cir. 1957).

[72] Judicial reduction and increase of the amount of bail; revocation of bail. (A) Apart from the procedures discussed in the preceding paragraphs, a court of record in which a criminal case is pending ordinarily has inherent authority at any time to entertain an application for reduction of the defendant's bail or for the defendant's release on his or her own bond or recognizance. Such a motion would ordinarily be filed on behalf of a defendant who is jailed in default of posting the amount of bail previously set and who seeks reduction as a means of obtaining release on some lesser amount that s/he can make. But a defendant who has posted bond and obtained release may also ask the court to reduce that bond, upon a showing that bail in the amount posted is unnecessary to assure his or her presence for trial. Such a motion will be useless to the defendant who has posted bond with a professional bonding company, since s/he has paid his or her premium already and cannot recover it. But the motion should be considered when cash, securities, or property has been put up as security and the client is in need of funds.

(B) Most jurisdictions also authorize a judge who has set bail or a judge of the criminal court to increase the amount of the bond upon a showing that the bond previously set is insufficient to assure the defendant's presence at trial. In the rare case in which this is done, the defendant who has been released on the old bond is rearrested on a bench warrant and held until s/he posts the new bond. Occasionally trial judges will assert or assume a power to revoke a defendant's bond entirely when s/he has skipped bail or misbehaved (as by threatening witnesses or engaging in courtroom disruption). Such a power is difficult to justify in the absence of explicit statutory authority; and, even under this authority, it may be unconstitutional. To the extent that the defendant's past flight, in violation of a bail obligation, evidences a greater likelihood of future flight, that likelihood should justify only an increase in the amount of bail, not the outright denial of bail, under the ordinary constitutional provisions that confer an absolute right to bail, see paragraph [57] *supra*. Consistent with those provisions, a defendant's bad history of bail-jumping on previous charges could not support denial of bail on a new charge, and the result should be the same if the defendant is recaptured and held on the identical charge from which s/he jumped bail. (Note, however, that under the crabbed construction given to the Excessive Bail Clause of the federal Constitution in *United States v. Salerno*, 107 S. Ct. 2095 (1987), paragraph [57] *supra*, the Court assumed that "a court may refuse bail when the defendant presents a threat to the judicial process by intimidating witnesses," *id.* at 2104.) Certainly, revocation of bail as a *punitive* measure, without regard to the likelihood of future flight, is unconstitutional. It not only denies the bail right upon considerations unrelated to that right but also constitutes punishment without trial. *See Bitter v. United States*, 389 U.S. 15 (1967); *cf. United States v. Salerno, supra*, 107 S. Ct. at 2101 (dictum); *Bell v. Wolfish*, 441 U.S. 520, 535-37 (1979) (dictum).

[73] Duration of bail; effect of additional or superseding charges. Apparently, in many jurisdictions new bail could be demanded for a defendant's appearance at each of the several stages of a criminal prosecution. In a felony case, for example, bond is technically reset at every stage: by a magistrate initially, for appearance at preliminary hearing; by the magistrate again, following bind-over, for the grand jury; by the grand jury, in its indictment, for appearance at the trial. As a practical matter, most bond is set, and bail bonds are written, at whatever pretrial stage, to assure the defendant's appearance at the trial. Interim resettings simply copy or "continue" the amount previously set. (In summary proceedings, however, as noted in paragraph [10] *supra*, new bail is set and actually demanded, sometimes in an increased amount, for appeal from a magistrate's conviction for trial *de novo* in a court of record.) Bail set and a bond written for appearance on one charge may not, however, carry over to other charges growing out of the same incident: A defendant who is bound over and bonded out for assault with a deadly weapon may be rearrested and required to post new bail if the grand jury indicts him or her for assault with intent to kill. Local law and the terms of any bonding contract should be carefully studied in consideration of this problem, which could prove costly for a defendant or even land the defendant in jail despite payment of an irrecoverable bond premium on a superseded charge. Frequently, practical resolutions of the problem can be arranged, by persuading the police, prosecutor, magistrate, or judge to (a) keep the original charge pending in lieu of dismissing it and (b) release the defendant on nominal bail on the second charge, in view of his or her secured obligation to appear on the first.

[74] Legal obligations and consequences of the bond contract and bail status. Complex contractual and noncontractual rights and obligations are created by the transactions involved in a defendant's release on an appearance bond, particularly a bond in which a third party joins as surety. The defendant promises, and the surety guarantees the court, that the defendant will appear; in the event of nonappearance, the posted security is forfeit. Common law, and sometimes statute, gives the surety the right to arrest the defendant at any time without process or cause (and to return the defendant to the state without extradition if s/he is arrested abroad), whether or not the defendant is in default on his or her obligation to appear. By thus seizing and producing the defendant in court, the surety is discharged of its obligation on the bond. (It should be noted that there is a practice in some localities invariably to insist upon the posting of at least a nominal surety bond, even in cases in which release on recognizance is plainly warranted. The purpose of the practice is to create a surety having broad common-law powers to pursue the defendant out of the state and to return him or her without extradition. Its consistency with the constitutional Extradition Clause and with the protective procedural provisions of the widely adopted Uniform Criminal Extradition Act [see *Cuyler v. Adams*, 449 U.S. 433 (1981)] is dubious at best.) However, in a case in which a commercial bond is used, the surety agrees by contract with the defendant to post a bond for the defendant's appearance in consideration of the statutorily regulated premium, and this contractual obligation may explicitly or implicitly qualify the surety's arbitrary common-law power to surrender the non-defaulting defendant. In any event, so long as defendants are not in default, the courts are ordinarily willing to protect them against any attempt by a bonding company to get out of its bail obligation by returning them to custody without some extremely cogent reason. These attempts—or any abuse or overreaching of a defendant by a bondsman—should be promptly reported by counsel to the presiding judge of the criminal court, who will ordinarily deal with it informally but effectively by sending a clear signal to the bondsman to stop. On the other hand, a defendant who *is* in default of his or her obligation to appear for scheduled proceedings thereby is exposed to substantial liabilities in addition to the prospect of arrest on a bench warrant (see paragraph [75] *infra*). The defendant's promise to appear runs in favor of the surety as well as the court; and if, having posted collateral with the surety to secure that promise (see paragraph [63] *supra*), the defendant defaults, the surety contract ordinarily allows the bonding company to forfeit this collateral, to withdraw its own security (to the extent that this is not forfeited by the court), and—as at common law—to arrest the defendant anywhere at any time and return him or her to the jurisdiction without process or extradition. The defaulting defendant also becomes liable to the court for the amount of the bond; in addition, s/he may incur criminal liability in some jurisdictions under statutes that make bail-jumping an offense.

[75] **Forfeiture.** If a defendant defaults on the obligation to appear, the presiding judge normally issues a bench warrant for the defendant's arrest. When the defendant is brought before the court on this warrant, s/he is given the opportunity to explain his or her nonappearance in a summary (and ordinarily feisty) proceeding. Depending upon the merit of the defendant's excuse, the judge may "sue out" (that is, forfeit) the defendant's bail bond or may allow the defendant to be re-released on the bond, usually with a strict admonition to keep his or her judicial appointments in the future. (The court also has power to forfeit bail when the defendant first fails to appear. In such a case it would have to reinstate the bail if it later chose to re-release the defendant on the same bail.) In some jurisdictions if the defendant voluntarily appears within a statutorily specified period of time and before being arrested for failure to appear, s/he will also have the opportunity to plead his or her excuse to the court and thus to avert forfeiture in the court's discretion.

[75-A] **To bail or not to bail.** (A) In most cases clients want to be enlarged on bail or recognizance before trial, and this enlargement is in their best interests. Apart from the obvious point that life is sweeter on the streets than in jail, pretrial detention may be seriously harmful to a defendant in many ways. It may disrupt the defendant's family relations and cause the defendant to lose his or her job. It will certainly interfere, to some extent, with the defendant's ability to assist counsel in preparing his or her defense, particularly in cases in which factual investigation is required among persons or in neighborhoods with which counsel is unfamiliar or where counsel will be seen as an unwelcome stranger (see paragraph [110] *infra*) and in cases in which a site visit is critical to preparation of the defendant's testimony or to counsel's understanding of the facts (see paragraph [111] *infra*). Interviewing clients in jail usually is more troublesome, time-consuming, and unsatisfactory from the point of view of good lawyer-client rapport than interviewing them in counsel's office. While in jail, the client is accessible to such police investigative techniques as renewed interrogation and lineups; s/he is prey to snitches (fellow inmates who will subsequently testify, truly or falsely, that the defendant made incriminatory statements to them in jail); and s/he is exposed to the influence of jail-house lawyers, whose advice can make counsel's job very difficult. Jail conditions are, of course, frequently deplorable; medical care is seldom adequate; and the jailed client is in jeopardy of homosexual attacks and other forms of abuse from fellow inmates. The client who spends the pretrial period in jail often comes to trial looking and feeling like a loser, with the result that s/he is likely to be treated as one by the jury and the judge. Finally, the jailed client cannot—as the bailed client can—be placed in a community situation (a job, job-training program, counseling program, and so forth) in which a good adjustment record can be made that will reap dividends at the time of sentencing. See paragraph [167-A] *infra*. For all these reasons, it is generally advisable for counsel to secure the client's release before trial, if at all possible. Moreover, the best way for a lawyer to gain a client's confidence usually is by *doing* something for the client; and one of the earliest and most appreciated things that the lawyer can do for a criminal defendant is to get the defendant out of jail.

(B) There are, however, some instances in which it is better for the client to remain in jail prior to trial. This may be so when (a) it is clear from the outset that the client is going to plead guilty and will almost certainly receive a sentence including some jail time; (b) it is preferable for the client to do the jail time sooner rather than later; *and* (c) state law or local practice requires that the full period of pretrial incarceration be credited against sentence under computation procedures that compare favorably with the procedures for computing postsentencing time. (Before reaching the conclusion that these latter conditions are met, counsel must usually conduct a thorough study of the intricacies of the sentencing and correctional laws of the jurisdiction. *Cf. McGinnis v. Royster*, 410 U.S. 263 (1973).) A still stronger argument for leaving the defendant in jail before trial appears when the defendant is charged with an offense for which it is the local practice to give a "time served" sentence (that is, a sentence equivalent to the period of pretrial incarceration, with full credit for the pretrial incarceration) when the defendant has served any considerable period of time in jail before trial, whereas a bailed defendant is likely to draw a *longer* sentence. It is common, for example, for judges to want to give defendants convicted of certain offenses some significant "taste of jail" without caring exactly how much. As a rule of thumb, therefore, they may habitually give a time-served sentence to any defendant who has spent, say, a month or more in jail before trial. When the same judge comes to sentence a bailed defendant for the same offense, the judge's habitual practice—or the structure of the state's sentencing law or the processing procedures of the local correctional facility—may require that the shortest jail-time sentence imposed be, say, three months. In this situation a defendant obviously stands to shorten his or her sentence by forgoing bail. Once again, in order to make advised decisions in these matters, counsel must be thoroughly familiar with the details of the jurisdiction's sentencing and corrections law; and also s/he must usually inquire among knowledgeable local criminal lawyers concerning the local judges' sentencing habits.

V. INTERVIEWING THE CLIENT: THE INITIAL INTERVIEW

[76] Establishing the lawyer-client relationship. The initial interview in a criminal case is probably the most important single exchange that counsel will have with the client. It largely shapes the client's judgment of the lawyer. This first judgment may be indelible. At the least, it gravely influences all future dealings of the two. The lawyer's primary objective in the initial interview, therefore, is the establishment of an attorney-client relationship grounded on mutual confidence, trust, and respect.

[77] Same. To gain the client's confidence, counsel must convey a sincere interest in helping the client as well as project the image of a competent, knowledgeable lawyer. The client must be given an adequate opportunity to explain his or her problems, and counsel must be able to respond to them with reasonable assurances and to answer any questions needing immediate attention or preoccupying the client.

[78] Preparing for the interview. Proper preparation for an interview is required if counsel hopes to achieve the objective of inspiring confidence and trust in the client. In the course of locating a client in custody or of checking out the status of a "wanted" client, counsel will ordinarily have spoken to the desk officer in the arrest precinct or in the defendant's home precinct and to the investigating officer. In these conversations counsel should be sure to learn the specific charge against the defendant as well as any other charges being considered. If counsel has the statute books at hand or can get them quickly, s/he should take the time, before the initial interview, to look up the elements of the offense *and particularly the penalty*, including any applicable recidivist sentencing provisions and parole provisions. It is important that counsel be acquainted with the elements of the offense in order to avoid floundering when taking the client's story. Knowledge of the applicable penalty provisions is indispensable in order to answer the question—which the client will almost certainly ask—what kind of a sentence the client is facing. Counsel should also undertake to be as well informed as time permits about the prospects and procedures for getting the client conditionally released from custody. See paragraph [51](A) *supra*. Finally, if counsel has the chance, without significantly delaying the initial interview, s/he should also try to learn from the investigating officer the sort of factual case the police have against the defendant. With a defendant in custody, however, it is usually better to get in to see the defendant quickly than to tarry very long in talking to the police about the case.

[79] **Putting the client at ease.** (A) An understanding of the client's mindset is essential in striking up an attorney-client relationship. Remember that the criminal client is a person in trouble and that the last thing s/he needs is more trouble from counsel. For most people, making a new acquaintance is itself trouble; it places demands upon their personality both by requiring the effort to create a good impression and by exposing them to the fear or sense of failure in that effort—of being judged inadequate or "put down." Counsel should, therefore, make the beginning of the initial interview with the client as undemanding as possible. Questions should be kept very simple until the client's abilities to understand questions, to think, and to articulate answers have been evaluated and should then be kept well within the limits of those abilities. Counsel should avoid displaying any indication that the client is making a bad impression or is failing to provide what counsel wants. To the contrary, counsel should convey the sense that the client is doing well and is giving counsel helpful information.

(B) The client usually enters upon this meeting with certain preconceptions about lawyers that are far from favorable. These include the notions that lawyers are self-interested, uncaring, grasping, and untrustworthy. If the client is rapwise, s/he is also likely to hold the more specific belief that criminal defense lawyers only want to talk their clients into pleading guilty to save themselves the trouble of trying cases. Counsel

should attempt to rectify, or at least alleviate, these preconceptions by showing genuine concern for the client as an individual human being—not just another faceless defendant in
a parade of stereotyped defendants—and by showing a willingness to *work* on the client's behalf. Personalizing touches
help: asking the client's name and then using that name in
addressing the client; offering the client a cigarette (which
counsel should carry whether or not s/he smokes); asking the
client whether smoking bothers him or her before counsel
lights up. Telling the client that counsel has already begun to
exert himself or herself (for example, "On the way in, I
stopped at the desk and copied down the specific charges that
the police have placed against you") and offering to do concrete things for the client (for example, offering to contact the
client's family, see paragraph [88] *infra*) are better and more
credible demonstrations of counsel's willingness to work for
the client than are general self-touting professions of indus-
triousness in the future.

(C) The essential impression to convey is that counsel views
his or her own job as being exclusively to serve and help the
client to the best of counsel's abilities. S/he should avoid
giving the client any grounds for suspicion or confusion about
the lawyer's role or loyalties or motives, which may arise if the
lawyer begins to ask for information without saying why s/he
wants it. The client should be told that the lawyer's only purpose and only interest are to represent the client (see paragraph [80] *infra*) and that, in order to make sure that nothing
is overlooked which could help the client, counsel needs certain
information. If the relevance of counsel's questioning to the
client's needs and interests is not perfectly obvious—obvious,
that is, to a layman, not a lawyer—counsel should explain why
s/he is asking this or that. S/he should ascertain and respond
specifically to anything in the immediate situation that is both-
ering the client or making the client apprehensive and should
promise concrete assistance if s/he can deliver it.

(D) The client should be made to feel comfortable and
secure in the presence of counsel. When explaining something
to the client, it is usually better to ask, "Okay?" than, "Do
you understand that?" Whatever the client tells counsel should

be received with interest and an attempt to understand, even if it does not appear relevant to the immediate tasks at hand as counsel conceives them. Patience in hearing the client out is crucial, since under stress s/he will frequently be rambling and inarticulate. S/he should not be shut off without explanation—or at all unless time is pressing; and, when s/he must be turned from one subject to another, counsel should explain the need to change the subject in a way that does not make the client feel like a fool.

[80] Same—explaining the attorney-client privilege. (A) It is not easy for a lawyer to convince a client to trust him or her when the client has never seen the lawyer before and particularly when the lawyer is of a different race or social background from the client's. As far as the client is concerned, the lawyer is "the law," along with the police and the judge; the client has no reason to believe that the lawyer is on *the client's* side. S/he will likely distrust the lawyer even more if the client is indigent and the lawyer is court-appointed, since, in common experience, things one gets for nothing are ordinarily worth nothing; and the only way to obtain services one can count on is to buy them. Counsel will seldom find that it is possible to overcome these assumptions merely by promising the client that counsel intends to work assiduously in the client's behalf; rather, counsel must actually *do* something for the client. This is why it is so important in building the attorney-client relationship that, when possible, counsel take early action which visibly benefits the client, such as stopping police mistreatment (see paragraph [84] *infra*), getting the client released from jail (see paragraph [75-A] (A) *supra*), or standing up firmly for the client in front of an impatient or overbearing magistrate at preliminary arraignment (see paragraph [46] *supra*). But at the initial interview there is often little of immediate practical consequence that counsel can do for the client in order to earn the client's confidence. Counsel must usually rely on words and intangible expressions of attitude to convey his or her loyalty to the client. S/he can and should state clearly and forcefully, "I am *your* lawyer; my job is to represent *you*, to go to bat for *you*; and I intend to do everything that can possibly be done to help you from now on in this case." However, abstract protestations of this sort cannot be developed or repeated too much without their beginning to sound hollow. A useful way to emphasize that counsel's sole interest lies in serving the client, without sounding like this is a sales pitch learned on a used car lot, is to find some obviously relevant, operational reason for describing counsel's role. Often the best occasion comes in connection with an explanation of the attorney-client privilege—an explanation that is independently desirable, in any event, in order to assure the client that s/he can tell his or her story to counsel in complete confidence.

(B) Counsel may say some of the following, for example: "Now, I am going to ask you to tell me some things about yourself and also about this charge they have against you. Before I do, I want you to know that everything you tell me is strictly private, just between you and me. Nothing you tell me goes to the police or to the District Attorney or to the judge or to anybody else. Nobody can make me tell them what you said to me, and I won't. Maybe you've heard about this thing that they call the attorney-client privilege. The law says that when a person is talking to [his] [her] lawyer, whatever [he] [she] tells the lawyer is confidential and secret between the two of them. This is because the law recognizes that the lawyer's obligation is to [his] [her] client and to nobody else; that the lawyer is supposed to be 100 per cent on the client's side; that the lawyer is only supposed to help [his] [her] client and never do anything—or tell anybody anything—that might hurt the client in any way. The District Attorney is the one who is supposed to represent the government in prosecuting cases; and the judge's job is to judge the cases. But the law wants to make sure that—even if everybody else is lined up against a defendant—there is one person who is not supposed to look out for the government but to be completely for the defendant. That is the defendant's lawyer. As your lawyer, I am completely for you. And I couldn't be completely for you if I were required to tell anybody else the things that you say to me in private. So you can trust me and tell me anything you want without worrying that I will ever pass it along to anyone else because I won't. I can't be questioned or forced to talk about what you tell me, even by a court, and I am not allowed to tell it to anyone else without your permission because I am 100 per cent on your side, and my job is to work for you and only for you; so everything we talk about stays just between us. Okay?"

[81] **Note-taking.** (A) At the outset it is usually good to talk to the client without taking notes, at least for a little while. This establishes a human rapport and does not communicate machinelike dispassion. When counsel is ready to begin taking notes, s/he should ask the client, "Would you mind if I take some notes?" and explain that these are only for counsel's own use, to help counsel to remember details of what the client says. A good way to begin note-taking and to demonstrate counsel's interest and competence is for counsel to summarize aloud the essential material that the client has already given counsel, while counsel writes it down. (This material should not be described to the client as "what is important," since that description implies that everything else the client has said so far is *un*important. Throughout interviews with a client, counsel should be careful to avoid such inadvertently judgmental pronouncements [for example, "I want to go back over the parts of your story that are relevant for our purposes and ask some more about those"].) As counsel summarizes and writes, s/he can ask clarifying or amplifying questions. Long periods of writing in silence should be avoided: If an extended note has to be written, counsel should vocalize it as s/he writes and then ask the client, "Is that correct?" (At later stages of the relationship with a client, writing or reading notes silently for a protracted period may occasionally be useful for particular purposes—for example, to give the client a chance to absorb or think over a point without feeling pressured to respond quickly; to unnerve a client whom counsel believes is lying—but these are exceptions to the general rule that the client should not ordinarily be left hanging while counsel concentrates on counsel's notes.)

(B) Once the client gets into the swing of his or her story (see paragraph [83] *infra*), it is usually wise for counsel to take notes of every significant point while the client is talking. Excessive writing is ill-advised, however, because it impedes counsel's ability to observe the client's nonverbal expressions and also suggests that counsel is more interested in the facts than in the client as a person. Perhaps the best way to take sufficiently detailed notes without excessive writing is to develop the knack of writing down key words and key phrases—using the client's own language rather than translating it or summarizing it in counsel's terminology—and then, *after the interview*, when counsel is back in his or her office, going over the notes while memory is still fresh and writing out or dictating a lengthier and more coherent version of what the client said, together with counsel's observations, interpretations, and impressions. Using the client's exact words in the original notes will stimulate counsel's recall of the things that were said before and after the noted words, particularly if counsel reviews the notes and prepares the refined interview report shortly after the end of the interview. (When counsel has enough control over his or her schedule, s/he will find it useful to leave a half-hour or so free immediately following interviews for the latter purpose. This may appear profligate, but experience shows that it is more efficient than either trying to write out copious notes during an interview or trying to reconstruct the details of information obtained in an interview by going over terse notes half a day or more after they were taken.)

(C) Detailed records of client interviews, particularly of interviews conducted shortly after the time of the offense with which the client is charged, are invaluable tools in criminal defense work. They serve subsequently to refresh both counsel's and the client's memories; they can be used for a variety of practical purposes (for example, to support counsel's representations of fact during efforts to convince the prosecutor to drop or reduce the charges or during plea bargaining [with the caution advised in paragraph [213](B), (C) *infra*]; to support counsel's representation to the court in support of requests for continuances, state-paid investigative or consultative assistance, or *forma pauperis* subpoenas to gather defensive evidence [see paragraphs [304], [301] and [132], [286] respectively]; to support counsel's representations to the court in support of motions for a severance of charges or defendants [particularly when joinder is asserted to be prejudicial because the defendant's testimony at a joint trial would raise problems that could be avoided by separate trials, see paragraphs [260], [263], [264] *infra*], or in support of applications for a pretrial mental examination of the defendant [see paragraphs [120]-[122], [180]-[181]*infra*]; to assist in preparing the defendant to testify); and they may also be admissible at trial in the client's behalf if the prosecution seeks to create the impression that the client's trial testimony is a recent fabrication. In addition, notes will shield counsel from unwarranted attacks (such as inadequate representation and suppression of facts favorable to the defense) should the defendant ultimately be convicted. In some jurisdictions, however, interview notes or reports may be discoverable by the prosecution (see paragraphs [110], [119], [274], [408-A] *infra*) and usable to impeach the client if s/he testifies at trial (see paragraphs [379], [382], [390](G), [394] *infra*). When this is the case, counsel may be able to insulate these materials against disclosure by (1) including within counsel's written notes of the client's oral statements sufficient analytic and evaluative commentary to imbue the whole writing with "work product" protection (*see Upjohn Co. v. United States*, 449 U.S. 383, 397-402 (1981); paragraphs [110], [273-A], [274] (C) *infra*) and (2) *not* reading or submitting the notes to the client for approval after counsel has put them into final form (*cf. Goldberg v. United States*, 425 U.S. 94, 105-7 (1976)). But even with these precautions, "work product" protection is not completely guaranteed, particularly if the client testifies at trial (*cf. United States v. Nobles*, 422 U.S. 225, 236-40 (1975), paragraph [408-A] *infra*; *but see* FED. R. CRIM. P. 26.2), and if disclosure to the prosecution is a possibility under local practice, counsel must weigh its risks against the advantages of note- or record-keeping.

[82] Language problems; the mentally weak or ill defendant. Foreign-language defendants whose English is poor obviously pose a problem. In urban areas an interpreter can usually be found. If there is none in the courthouse complex, other than persons allied in interest with the prosecution, non-governmental social work agencies should be tried. A relatively disinterested interpreter is usually to be preferred to one of the defendant's family who may intrude his or her own personality and biases into the interview and before whom the defendant may be ashamed to tell the truth. But, as a last resort, a family member may have to do. English-speaking defendants with low verbal ability, deficient intelligence, or mental illness have to be handled on an individual basis as counsel's good sense dictates. If counsel is having trouble understanding or being understood by the client, it may aid communication to bring in a relative or a friend who has had longtime dealings with the client, although that procedure raises the dangers just described. Counsel who is dealing with an impaired defendant should be attentive at the outset to determine as well as s/he can the areas and dimensions of the impairment. Careful observation may lay the foundation for a later decision to have the client mentally examined (see paragraphs [120]-[122] *infra*) and may provide facts to support an application to a court, if that proves advisable, for court-ordered and state-paid examination (see paragraphs [180]-[181] *infra*). In addition, the degree of the client's disability may prove significant in later attacks on a confession to police, on purported consent to police searches and seizures, and on other purported waivers of rights by the client in the early stages of the criminal process.

[83] **Getting the client's story.** (A) Obtaining information from the client is ordinarily best done in stages. At the first stage it is wise to encourage the client to tell everything s/he knows about the situation, in his or her own way, without interruptions. This puts the client at ease and informs counsel what the client thinks is important. It gives counsel a collection of unsolicited details on which to cross-examine the client later if counsel suspects untruth. It also shows counsel something about how the client's mind works and his or her intelligence and verbal ability. Counsel can then fashion questions that are within the client's comprehension skills.

(B) After the client has recited his or her story fully, counsel should go back over it at least once—twice is usually better—

to fill in details. In the first re-run the journalistic questions "who, what, why, when, where, and how," combined with requests to "tell me anything else you remember about that," usually work well to elicit the necessary specifics. With some clients a request to "walk me through the events as though they were going on now," coupled with present-tense questioning ("Is anybody saying anything at this point?" "Is it quiet, noisy?" "Okay, so you're hearing trucks go by on the highway; and what else is happening?") is effective as a means of getting the client to relive events and will stimulate maximum recall. Questions should, in any case, be sense-based and use verbs of action (asking what people *did* or what *happened*) and verbs of experience (asking what the client *saw, heard,* and *felt*) rather than asking for interpretations, explanations, or logical connections of occurrences, since these levels of discourse will distract the client from recounting perceptual observations and will cause the loss of concrete details. Then, in the *second* re-run counsel can ask about the *reasons why* things happened, motivations, analytic relationships, explanations, what the client thinks that other participants (or the police) saw, heard, or believe, and can also focus on the particular facts needed to determine whether each of the legal elements of the charge is likely to be easily proved by the prosecution or is contestable, and how.

(C) Besides a full chronology of the defendant's involvement in the case, including police investigative activity and any judicial proceedings to date, a biographical sketch of the client will be required. A checklist of all the necessary information is found in paragraph [90] *infra*. Throughout the initial interview, counsel's emphasis should be upon identifying needs and leads for a prompt commencement of defense investigation (see paragraphs [107]-[108] *infra*) and obtaining other information that counsel must have as the basis for making immediate decisions or taking immediate actions (see paragraphs [51]-[53], [44], [41] and [59] *supra*). Unless the client is obviously lying and unless discovery of the truth appears immediately necessary for effective defense investigation, the client should probably not be cross-examined much during the initial interview. After some independent investigative efforts by counsel and after the attorney-client relationship has had time to solidify, there will be time for cross-questioning the client.

[84] Complaint of police brutality or mistreatment. If a client is being abused by the police, it is counsel's first job to stop the abuse. This is done by complaining to the commanding officer on duty at the precinct station. Unless the precinct commander delivers immediate relief, counsel should telephone the ranking police officer on duty in the city or law enforcement area and, next, the ranking member of the prosecutor's staff who can be reached by telephone. All else failing, resort should be had to a judge. See paragraphs [38], [67]-[68] *supra*. At a later time counsel or the client may want to employ one or another of the remedial processes available to redress police mistreatment: complaint to a police departmental disciplinary board, to a civilian review board, or to the prosecutor; suit for damages in a state court or in the federal courts under the Civil Rights Act, 42 U.S.C. §1983 (*see Monroe v. Pape*, 365 U.S. 167 (1961); *Pembaur v. City of Cincinnati*, 106 S. Ct. 1292 (1986)); complaint to the federal authorities with a request for prosecution of the offending officers under the criminal provisions of the Civil Rights Act, 18 U.S.C. §§241 - 242 (*see Screws v. United States*, 325 U.S. 91 (1945); *United States v. Price*, 383 U.S. 787 (1966)); or a motion to suppress, in subsequent criminal proceedings against the client, evidence obtained by violations of the client's constitutional rights (see paragraphs [223]-[253-A] *infra*). Apart from the Fourth, Fifth, and Sixth Amendment rights discussed in the latter paragraphs, "a detainee [has a Fourteenth Amendment right] . . . not [to] be punished prior to an adjudication of guilt in accordance with due process of law." *Bell v. Wolfish*, 441 U.S. 520, 535 (1979) (dictum); *see also Schall v. Martin*, 467 U.S. 253, 269 (1984) (dictum); *Block v. Rutherford*, 468 U.S. 576, 583 (1984) (dictum). For both immediate and long-range purposes, a client's complaints to counsel of mistreatment or brutality by the police must be investigated with speed and caution. The client should be questioned in detail respecting time, place, and nature of the police conduct complained of, its back-

ground, and the identity or description of all officers involved
or present at the time. The client should be told to keep his
or her eyes open and, if s/he later sees any of these officers,
to try to observe their nameplates or badge numbers. In addition, if misconduct recurs, the client should try to remember
the officer's name, number, and description. Observable con-
tusions and lacerations on the client should be photographed
in color. If possible, a nonpolice doctor should be summoned
to examine major injuries; the county medical society or a civil
liberties group, like the American Civil Liberties Union, can
help find a physician for this purpose. Witnesses who last saw
the client prior to arrest and who can testify concerning his
or her physical condition at that time should be interviewed.
Finally, any observable injuries sustained by any officer handling the client should be noted. Since the defense to most
mistreatment allegations is that the police were required to
use force to effectuate the arrest or subdue an unruly prisoner,
counsel must determine as best s/he can the circumstances of
the arrest or custodial situation when the alleged mistreatment
occurred. S/he should consider what happened to the police
and to the client and then decide whether a claim of mistreatment is justified. The suggestion of caution previously offered
should be heeded because the police are very sensitive to
brutality complaints and may go out of their way to make
certain that a client is convicted if such a complaint is made.
This does not necessarily imply that police will perjure themselves to justify their treatment of an accused, although they
may. It does mean that they will almost certainly prepare their
case more efficiently and also try to cast the client as a police-
hater, a type that is uniquely vilified by judges and punished
accordingly.

[85] **Other custodial complaints.** In addition to physical
abuse a client in custody may complain about lack of medical
treatment, exercise, food, and numerous other things. Most of
these problems can be corrected administratively by informing
the authorities in charge about them. Counsel should see the
commanding officer on duty if the client is in a police station
or the ranking jail official if s/he is in a jail. State court relief

may be available if the conditions of the client's confinement are substantially out of line with civilized standards; federal court relief is available only if they are really egregious (*see Bell v. Wolfish*, 441 U.S. 520 (1979)). Recourse to the courts is appropriate if the client is ill or injured and counsel's requests to the police for necessary medical attention are not promptly honored. In addition to state statutes and regulations that impose responsibility on custodial officers for the well-being of prisoners, the Due Process Clause of the Fourteenth Amendment to the federal Constitution requires that a prisoner's serious medical needs be met by his or her custodians, at least in some presently ill-defined circumstances. *See City of Revere v. Massachusetts General Hospital*, 463 U.S. 239, 244 (1983) (dictum).

[85-A] Settling the roles of lawyer and client. (A) To avoid later misunderstandings, counsel should work out with the client, during the initial interview, the respective roles that the two of them will play in the defense. Counsel should advise the client of the client's major rights—to be released on bail before trial if bail can be made; to have a trial at which the client contests guilt and insists that the prosecution prove its case; to have a jury trial (when applicable); to testify at trial; to attend and to have counsel attend every judicial proceeding in the case. Counsel should inform the client that counsel will present every defense that the law permits and will take every action necessary to protect the client's rights, and that none of the rights just mentioned will be waived without the client's express consent. Also counsel will keep the client advised of all developments in the case; and when decisions of any consequence have to be made, counsel will tell the client about them, describe the possible choices to the client, discuss those choices with the client and—unless time does not permit—make no decision until the client has had full opportunity to consider the choices and to give counsel his or her thoughts about them.

(B) But since counsel is representing the client as an attorney, counsel is ultimately going to have to be responsible for all tactical decisions: Counsel must control the strategy of the defense and have the final say about what points will be raised, what witnesses will be called, what discussions will be had with the prosecutor and the judge, and all the when's and where's of the investigation and the trial. The client must be made to comprehend that counsel is not a "mouthpiece" whose only job is to appear in court and say what the client wants. Rather, counsel's job is to plan, design, and carry out the best defensive strategy possible in the client's interest. That kind of planning requires decisions based upon thorough technical knowledge of the law as well as experience in working with the law, the court system, prosecutors, judges, and juries in a wide range of situations. Counsel is simply not giving the client the kind of representation that the client deserves unless decisions in the conduct of the defense are made on the basis of counsel's best professional judgment, taking into account everything that counsel knows about the legal system. Therefore, counsel ought to tell the client that the client should inform counsel about anything that the client wants or needs or thinks should be done, during their relationship; that counsel wants the client to give counsel any ideas and thoughts the client has about the conduct of the case; that counsel always works with his or her clients in thinking the case through, but that *counsel* has to make the final decisions after considering the client's preferences and all of the tactical needs of the defense.

(C) Counsel should explain the attorney-client privilege (see paragraph [80] *supra*) and then emphasize how important it is for the client to tell counsel the whole truth and the exact truth; that the client should not hold anything back or be embarrassed or afraid to tell counsel anything, even if it makes the client look bad. If the client has done whatever s/he is being charged with, or any part of it, counsel has to know; and the failure of the client to tell counsel every detail about it will badly hurt the presentation of the defense. Counsel's job is not to judge the client; it is to represent the client whether the client is guilty or innocent; and that is exactly what counsel intends to do. But to do it well, counsel has to know the truth. It may be helpful to state that counsel is eventually going to hear the prosecution's version of the facts anyway and that counsel cannot be prepared to handle this version if s/he hears it for the first time in court, in front of the judge and jury. The client should be told, "The question is what a judge or a jury is going to believe, so I want you to tell me the worst possible things that the prosecution's witnesses might say or that the prosecution may be able to prove as well as your own recollection of everything that actually happened." S/he may be told, "I have seen defendants get crucified in court, even when they were innocent, because they didn't tell their lawyer all of the damaging circumstances—all of the evidence that might point to guilt—that the prosecution might come up with." But the most important thing for counsel to remember is that s/he must scrupulously avoid showing any sign of reprobation or moral condemnation of the client's conduct, or the client will take the clue and begin to hide the worst.

[86] **Fee-setting.** Misunderstandings about fees are a vexatious and unnecessary irritant in a lawyer-client relationship. If a case is not a *pro bono* matter, it behooves counsel to come to an early and very clear fee agreement. After determining the nature of the case and the evidentiary and investigatory problems likely to be involved, counsel should calculate a fair fee and agree upon it with the client. Fee-setting in a criminal case is normally based on an advance estimate of the amount of time that will be necessary to handle the case and not on a post-audit hourly basis. What expenses are paid by whom and what exact stages of the criminal process (that is, through to, but not including, trial; through trial; through a first appeal, and so forth) are to be covered by the fee should be explicitly stated and the agreement reduced to writing and signed. Counsel is cautioned to advise the client that failure to pay the full fee before trial will result in counsel's withdrawal from the case: Experience indicates that criminal fees are hard to collect after trial, no matter what its outcome.

[87] **Advising the client.** (A) At the conclusion of the initial interview, whether or not the client is in custody and whether or not s/he has previously been given these warnings, counsel should advise the client as follows. (Most of these admonitions

are described in greater detail in paragraphs [25] (3) and [35]-[37-A] *supra*.) The client should:

(1) Say nothing at all to the police, tell them nothing under any circumstances, and reply to all police questions or approaches by saying that the client's lawyer has told the client not to answer questions or to talk with anyone unless the lawyer is present;

(2) Take the same position with the prosecuting attorneys and under no circumstances discuss any offer or deal with the police or the prosecuting attorneys in counsel's absence;

(3) Discuss the case with no one and particularly not talk to cellmates, codefendants, codefendants' lawyers, or reporters about it but tell anyone who wants to discuss the case or who has information about it to contact counsel;

(4) Neither write nor sign any papers or forms requested by the police or prosecuting attorneys or relating to the case in any way;

(5) Refuse (if the client is at liberty) to go anywhere with the police or with prosecuting attorneys, who may ask the client to accompany them, unless they have an arrest warrant; and tell them that if they want the client to go anywhere or to do anything, they should contact counsel first;

(6) Refuse (if the client is in custody) to participate in any lineup or to appear before any person for possible identification in counsel's absence; refuse to accompany the police or prosecuting attorneys to any place outside of the regular cell and recreation areas of the jail, except to court, in counsel's absence; object to any inspection of the client's body, physical examination, or test of any sort in counsel's absence; request permission to telephone counsel immediately in the event that the police begin any lineup or identification procedure, inspection, examination, or test; and if put in a lineup or exhibited for identification over his or her objection, observe and remember all the circumstances described in paragraph [36] (A) *supra*;

(7) Refuse consent to anyone who may ask the client's permission to search the client's home or automobile or any place or thing belonging to the client unless that person has a search warrant;

(8) Respond to all accusations and to anyone who gives any evidence against the client or says anything against the client by stating that the client's lawyer has told the client not to talk to anybody unless the lawyer is present;

(9) Not make faces, attempt to cover his or her face, or dodge if news photographers try to photograph the client (see paragraph [37] *supra*);

(10) Telephone counsel as soon as possible if anything at all comes up relating to the case—if anyone whom the client does not know tries to talk to him or her about it, if codefendants tell the client that they have made some sort of a deal, if the police tell the client that the codefendants have squealed on the client, or if the client gets any new information or receives any communication from the court about the case; and

(11) If the client goes or is taken to court and counsel is not present when the client's case is called, tell the judge that counsel is supposed to be present and ask the judge to wait for counsel to arrive (if the client knows that counsel is aware of this court date) or ask the judge to phone counsel or permit the client to phone counsel (if the client suspects that counsel does not know about the proceedings).

The client should be given counsel's telephone number and office address, of course. It is extremely useful to give the client the sort of card or form suggested in paragraph [51](C) *supra*. And if the client is in custody, the routine described in paragraph [37] (H) *supra* is imperative.

(B) In some situations counsel may decide that it is in the client's interest to make a statement to the police or to the prosecutor or otherwise to cooperate in their investigations. The usual instance is a case in which counsel believes that the authorities can be persuaded to drop charges (see paragraphs [98]-[103] *infra*) or a case in which a favorable plea bargain appears to be negotiable (see paragraphs [206]-[219] *infra*, with special attention to paragraph [213] (B), (C)), particularly when the authorities and the client are considering the client's turning state's evidence and testifying against accomplices. Even if the client is contesting guilt and a trial appears likely, there are situations (rare, to be sure) in which the defense stands to gain by cooperating with the prosecution's evidence-gathering efforts. For example, defense counsel who has interviewed an eyewitness to the offense and is confident that the witness will not identify the defendant in a lineup may want to have a lineup held. Or if the defendant's story includes an admission of some incriminating facts (for example, presence at the scene of the offense or commission of the *actus reus*) but denies others (for example, participating in the *actus* or having the requisite *mens rea*) or asserts facts supporting some affirmative defense (for example, self-defense; mistake of fact), a written or oral statement to the police may be advised as the best means of putting the defendant's version of the facts before a judge or jury without the defendant's being subject to impeachment. (Prosecutors tend to present these incriminating admissions in their case in chief, even when they have ample independent proof of the facts admitted; and if the prosecution offers only a portion of the defendant's statement, the defense is entitled to put the whole of it into evidence. Thus adduced at trial—whether by the prosecution or the defense—the statement does not open the defendant up to either cross-examination or the sorts of impeaching evidence [for example, prior convictions, see paragraph [390](F) *infra*] to which the defendant would be exposed if s/he told the same story on the stand in court.) Counsel's decisions to cooperate in the staging of a lineup, to permit the client to make a statement, or to provide other evidence to the prosecution in these situations will, of course, qualify the general advice to the client described in subparagraph (A) *supra*. In all these cases, however, counsel should be present during any face-to-face dealings between the client and the police or prosecutors, and counsel should examine any writing or physical evidence before it is turned over to them. The client should never be allowed to communicate with the authorities in counsel's absence. Hence it is best always to give the client the full roster of advice in subparagraph (A) without modification; then, if circumstances justify exceptions to the general rules stated there, counsel can subsequently work with the client to decide upon these exceptions and to implement them.

[88] Offering to contact family. Counsel will ordinarily want to be in touch with the client's family very early in the investigation of a case. See paragraph [118] *infra*. Obviously, the family will often be worrying about the client if s/he has been arrested and retained in custody, and the client will likely be worrying about the family's worrying. It is, therefore, a good idea, if it is at all possible, for counsel to telephone or visit—or at least to send a message to—the client's family, shortly following the initial interview with a client in custody, (a) reassuring them that the client is all right, (b) informing them when and how counsel will subsequently contact them and how they can contact counsel, and (c) informing them when, where, and how they can visit the client. At the close of the initial interview with the client, counsel should offer to get in touch with the family in this way and should ask the client whom to call. Remember that the client is undergoing a frightening experience; any help that counsel can give him or her on a human level is well worth the effort.

[89] Subsequent interviews with the client. (A) Normally the client must be interviewed on more than one occasion. In counsel's preparation for trial, facts will be discovered that were untouched in earlier interviews, and these must be reviewed and analyzed with the client. Increasingly, the client should be cross-examined in a fashion that may range from counsel's mild expression of surprise at a contradiction to open incredulity and grilling, depending upon counsel's best judgment of what is necessary to get at the truth while preserving the lawyer-client relationship. Clients often do lie to their lawyers. If a client is to be saved from himself or herself, s/he must be made to tell counsel the truth. And whether or not s/he is lying, s/he must be confronted with any inconsistencies among the pieces of the story s/he is telling or between the client's story and other information obtained by counsel, since these may be exposed at trial.

(B) One way to cross-question the client vigorously without creating the impression that counsel disbelieves or distrusts the client is to engage in an explicit exercise of role-playing, in which counsel first prepares and rehearses the testimony that the client might give in his or her own defense at trial and then plays prosecutor for purposes of cross-examining the client. This kind of dry run of cross-examination, as well as direct examination, will be necessary anyway in any case in which the client is actually going to take the stand at trial (see paragraphs [279]-[280] *infra*); it can simultaneously be used to confront the client with any embarrassing holes or contradictions in the client's story while maintaining an attitude of complete confidence in the client's truthfulness. At some point during these interviews with the client, preferably near the time of trial when counsel has all the information that s/he will have at trial, the client should be given an objective appraisal of the case, with counsel avoiding unfounded optimism or pessimism.

[90] **Interview checklist.** What follows is the substance of a "model" or "ideal" interview, covering most of what the lawyer will have to learn from the client in order to defend the client adequately throughout the several stages of an ordinary criminal case. Circumstances often will not permit coverage in the initial interview of everything that is included here. When this is so, inquiry concerning less immediate background matters (educational history, military service history, employment history, family history, medical history) and the details of the police investigation may be deferred until subsequent interviews.

(to be completed by attorney
following interview)

Attorney's file no.: _____

Criminal case no.: _____

Client's name: _____

Charges: _____

_____

Date and hour of interview: _____

Place of interview: _____

_____

Name of interviewer: _____

INTERVIEW SHEET

Name (have the client spell even common names):

All aliases:

Address (if apartment or room, include number):

Phone (or phone at which client can be reached and name of person there):

Date of birth:

Place of birth:

Place of residence at time of arrest:

Prior places of residence (from latest to earliest):

Residence	From (date)	To (date)

Education:

	Name of school and location	Highest grade completed	Date last attended
Elementary:			
High School:			
Trade School:			
College:			
Other:			

Armed Forces:

Branch of service:

Date of beginning of active duty:

Date of discharge:

Type of discharge:

Rank at time of discharge:

Any honors or medals:

Combat service:

Time overseas:

place	from (date)	to (date)
place	from (date)	to (date)

Court martial charges:

Charge:

Finding:

Date of finding:

Sentence, if any:

Portion of sentence remitted:

Portion of sentence served:

   Where:

   From (date):

   To (date):

Charge:

Finding:

Date of finding:

Sentence, if any:

Portion of sentence remitted:

Portion of sentence served:

Where:

From (date):

To (date):

Present employment (separate notation of each employer if more than one):

Name of employer:

Address:

Phone:

Type of business:

Client's immediate supervisor:

Client's job designation:

Client's type of work:

Pay (starting):   (present):

Employed since (date):

Indicate season if seasonal:

If presently unemployed, check   ☐

   Since (date):

   Receiving unemployment compensation?   ☐ Yes   ☐ No

      Amount:

Other means of support:

Prior employment (all employers, from latest to earliest):

Name of employer:

Address:

Phone:

Type of business:

Client's immediate supervisor:

Client's job designation:

Client's type of work:

Pay (starting):   (at termination):

Employed from (date):   to (date):

Indicate season if seasonal:

Reason for leaving:

Name of employer:

Address:

Phone:

Type of business:

Client's immediate supervisor:

Client's job designation:

Client's type of work:

Pay (starting):   (at termination):

Employed from (date):   to (date):

Indicate season if seasonal:

Reason for leaving:

Social security number:

Marital status:
- ☐ Single
- ☐ Divorced
- ☐ Married: ceremonial ☐   common-law ☐

Spouse:

Name:

Address:

Phone:

Employed: ☐ Yes ☐ No

Type of work:

Employer's name:

Employer's address:

Employer's phone:

Children:

Name: Age:

Name: Age:

Client's father:

    Name: Type of work:

    Living ☐   Deceased ☐

    If living:

      Address:

      Phone:

Client's mother:

    Name: Type of work:

    Living ☐   Deceased ☐

    If living:

      Address:

      Phone:

Client's brother(s):

    Name: Type of work:

    Living ☐   Deceased ☐

    If living:

      Address:

      Phone:

Client's sister(s):

    Name: Type of work:

    Living ☐   Deceased ☐

    If living:

        Address:

        Phone:

By whom was client raised? Indicate if parents were separated during childhood. If client was raised by persons other than a parent, get data from those persons as for parents, *supra*.

Does (or did) client use drugs?   ☐ Yes ☐ No

    Type(s):

    Beginning (date):

    Ending (date) [write "present" if client is still on drugs]:

    Greatest dosage:

    Present dosage, if applicable:

    Greatest frequency of use:

    Present frequency of use, if applicable:

Has client received treatment for drug problem or participated in any form of detoxification program?   ☐ Yes ☐ No

    Agency:

    Address:

    Phone:

Names of personnel who worked with client:

Describe program:

Beginning (date):

Ending (date):

Does (or did) client use alcohol?   ☐ Yes   ☐ No

Type(s):

Beginning (date):

Ending (date) [write "present" if client still uses alcohol]:

Greatest amount:

Present amount, if applicable:

Greatest freqency of use:

Present frequency of use, if applicable:

Has client received treatment for alcohol problem or participated in any form of detoxification program?   ☐ Yes   ☐ No

Agency:

Address:

Phone:

Names of personnel who worked with client:

Describe program:

Beginning (date):

Ending (date):

Physical and mental condition:

Present physical disabilities:

Present physical illnesses:

Is client presently under medical care?   ☐ Yes   ☐ No

Doctor's name:

Address:

Phone:

Serious physical injuries (and all head injuries):

Type:

Cause:

Date:

If hospitalized, name, address, and phone of hospital and dates of hospitalization:

If treated by physician, name, address, and phone of physician and dates when client was under physician's care:

Has client ever been in a mental hospital or institution?
☐ Yes   ☐ No

Name, address, and phone of hospital:

Name[s] of physician[s]:

Admission date: Discharge date:

Event[s] leading to hospitalization:

Diagnosis:

Has client ever been found mentally incompetent by a court?   ☐ Yes   ☐ No

Name and location of court:

Name of judge:

Name[s] of attorney[s]:

Date of adjudication:

Nature of proceeding:

Event[s] leading to proceeding:

Has client ever been treated by a psychiatrist or psychologist?   ☐ Yes   ☐ No

Name, address, and phone of psychotherapist:

Date treatment began: Date treatment ended:

Event[s] leading to treatment:

Diagnosis:

Nature of treatment:

Has client ever undergone psychiatric or psychological evaluation?   ☐ Yes   ☐ No

Name, address, and phone of evaluator[s]:

Date of evaluation:

Event[s] leading to evaluation:

Diagnosis:

Prior criminal record (all *arrests,* from latest to earliest, *including pending charges, including juvenile arrests,* and in all jurisdictions):

Incident #1.

Date of arrest:

Jurisdiction (city and state):

Street location of arrest:

Charge[s]:

Disposition if not by court:

Plea: ☐ not guilty   ☐ insanity   ☐ guilty   ☐ *nolo*

If guilty or *nolo*, to what charges:

Trial by judge or jury:

Name of judge:

Court disposition: ☐ acquittal   ☐ conviction   ☐ other

If conviction, of what charges:

If "other," describe disposition:

Sentence:

Date sentence imposed:

Name, address, and phone of defense attorney:

Length of sentence served:

From (date):   To (date):

Institution:

Location:

Client's prison number:

Length of time on probation or parole:

From (date):   To (date):

Name of probation or parole officer:

Was client ever charged with violation of probation or parole conditions?   ☐ Yes   ☐ No

Date of charge:

Nature of violation charged:

Disposition:

Incident #2.

Date of arrest:

Jurisdiction (city and state):

Street location of arrest:

Charge[s]:

Disposition if not by court:

Plea: ☐ not guilty ☐ insanity ☐ guilty ☐ *nolo*

If guilty or *nolo,* to what charges:

Trial by judge or jury:

Name of judge:

Court disposition: ☐ acquittal ☐ conviction ☐ other

    If conviction, of what charges:

    If "other," describe disposition:

Sentence:

Date sentence imposed:

Name, address, and phone of defense attorney:

Length of sentence served:

    From (date):   To (date):

    Institution:

    Location:

    Client's prison number:

Length of time on probation or parole:

From (date):   To (date):

Name of probation or parole officer:

Was client ever charged with violation of probation or parole conditions?   ☐ Yes   ☐ No

Date of charge:

Nature of violation charged:

Disposition:

WAS CLIENT ON PROBATION OR PAROLE AT THE TIME OF THIS ARREST?   ☐ Yes   ☐ No

On which of the above prior charges?	check whether probation or parole	amount of back time owed
Incident #_____	☐	☐	_____
Incident #_____	☐	☐	_____

WAS CLIENT UNDER ANY PENDING CHARGES AT THE TIME OF THIS ARREST?   ☐ Yes   ☐ No

On which of the above prior charges?	Form of conditional release:	Amount of bond or recognizance:	Name, address & phone of bondsman & attorney:
Incident #__ _____	_____	_____
Incident #__ _____	_____	_____

WAS CLIENT WANTED FOR ARREST ON OTHER CHARGES IN
ANY JURISDICTION AT THE TIME OF THIS ARREST?
    ☐ Yes   ☐ No

    Jurisdiction:

    City, town, or county:

    Charge(s):

    Nature of incident:

    How client knows s/he is wanted:

    Name of law enforcement agency involved, if known:

    Name of officers involved, if known:

    Has client consulted an attorney
    about these charges?   ☐ Yes ☐ No

        Name, address, and   _____
        phone of attorney:

                                            _____

Present custodial status:

    Jail (name and address):

    Prison (name and address):

    Prison number:

    Bail:

        Where posted:

        When posted:

Amount:

Form (cash, property, professional surety):

   If professional surety:

Name, address, and   _____

phone of bondsman: _____

Who paid for the bail: _____

                     _____

Has collateral security been put up? ☐ Yes ☐ No

   If so:

Nature of collateral: _____

Amount secured: _____

Who put up the collateral: _____

                     _____

   Other form of conditional release:

   Describe:

THE CLIENT SHOULD BE ASKED TO TELL EVERYTHING S/HE KNOWS ABOUT THE PRESENT CHARGE, IN CHRONOLOGICAL ORDER: WHAT S/HE DID, WHAT HAPPENED TO HIM OR HER, WHO WAS INVOLVED, WHEN AND HOW THE CLIENT WAS ARRESTED, AND EVERYTHING THAT THE POLICE HAVE DONE WITH THE CLIENT SINCE ARREST. AT THE CONCLUSION OF THE CLIENT'S STORY, COUNSEL SHOULD ASK QUESTIONS—WHO, WHAT, WHY, WHEN, WHERE, AND HOW—FOR CLARIFICATION. BEFORE TER-

MINATING THE INTERVIEW, COUNSEL SHOULD BE SURE S/HE
KNOWS AT LEAST THE FOLLOWING:

Client's version of the events on which the charge is based or,
if the client denies involvement, where the client was and what
s/he was doing at the time of the events on which the charge
is based:

Witnesses (indicate if immediate contact is advised for any
reason):

> Witnesses to the events on which the charge is based
> (including the complainant and persons who may be pros-
> ecution witnesses):
>
> Alibi witnesses:
>
> Background and character witnesses:

For each witness:

> Name (get spelling and all aliases and nicknames)
>
> _____
>
> _____
>
> Address: _____
>
> _____
>
> Phone: _____
>
> Other information helpful in locating the witness (where
> does s/he work, where does s/he hang out, union affili-

ation, friends, probation/parole officer, kind of car s/he drives, public assistance contacts, and so forth):

Arrest:

Who, what, why, when, where, and how?

Who was with the client when s/he was arrested? Were they also arrested? Get information as for witnesses, *supra*.

Was client drunk when arrested, or had s/he taken alcohol recently?

Was s/he under the influence of drugs, or had s/he taken drugs recently?

Was client ill when arrested? Describe illness:

Was client struck or roughly handled in arrest or thereafter? Describe any injuries:

Date and time of arrest:

Exact location of arrest:

Names of arresting officers:

Did they have a warrant? ☐ Yes ☐ No

What did they say the charge was:

What questions did they ask the client:

What did the client tell them:

Did police at the time of arrest or any other time take property from the client's person, home, place of work, automobile, place where the client was, home or workplace of any other person: ☐ Yes ☐ No

Kind of property:

Did police have a search warrant: ☐ Yes ☐ No

Describe circumstances under which property was taken:

For all persons present during search or seizure, get information as for witnesses, *supra*:

After arrest:

List every location to which client was taken by police:	Exact times of confinement in each place:	Number of officers present
_____	From: _____	
_____	To: _____	_____
_____	From: _____	
_____	To: _____	_____

For all officers present in each place:

Name, squad, rank, description, and other identifying information:

Was the client interrogated? ☐ Yes ☐ No

For each interrogation session:

Where did the interrogation take
place?

What time did it begin?

What time did it end?

Was questioning continuous or
on and off between these times?

Number of officers present? [Key the names
or identifying in-
formation for

Number of officers involved in each officer to
questioning? the list of offi-
cers above.]

Other persons present: [For each person, get name,
description, and

Other persons involved in ques- description, and
tioning: other identifying
information.]

Was a lie detector test given? ☐ Yes ☐ No

Describe machine:

Name, description, and
other identifying infor-
mation for operator:

What specific questions did the interrogators ask? [This is
often a good means of learning something about the prosecution's case.]

Did the interrogators confront the client
with any evidence against the client? ☐ Yes ☐ No

    Describe the evidence:

    Name, description, and other identi-
fying information for each person
who was, or was said by the interrogators to be, a source of the information:

    Name, description, and other identi-
fying information for each person
who was said to be involved in the
incriminating events:

Did the police tell the client that any
person had incriminated the client? ☐ Yes ☐ No

    Name, description, and other identi-
fying information for each person
who was said to have provided incriminating information:

    Content of the information:

    Name, description, and other identi-
fying information for each person
who was said to be involved in the
incriminating events:

Did the police tell the client that any
codefendant had confessed? ☐ Yes ☐ No

Name, description, and other identifying information for each codefendant who was said to have confessed: [For each, indicate whether s/he was said to have incriminated the client.]

Content of the information said to have been given by the codefendant:

Name, description, and other identifying information for each person who was said to be involved in the incriminating events:

Did any codefendant confess or incriminate the defendant in his or her presence?   ☐ Yes   ☐ No

Name, description, and other identifying information for each such codefendant: [For each, indicate whether s/he incriminated the client.]

Content of the information given by the codefendant:

Name, description, and other identifying information for each person who was said to be involved in the incriminating events:

Did the client tell the police anything?   ☐ Yes   ☐ No

What, in detail:

Did the client make a written statement: ☐ Yes   ☐ No

How many written statements:

For each written statement:

  Length of statement:

  Other identifying characteristics:

  Did the client sign the statement?   ☐ Yes   ☐ No

Did the client fill out or sign any
forms?   ☐ Yes   ☐ No

  Describe the forms:

Did the client make an oral statement?   ☐ Yes   ☐ No

  Was it videotaped?   ☐ Yes   ☐ No

  Was it audiotaped?   ☐ Yes   ☐ No

  Was it stenographically transcribed?   ☐ Yes   ☐ No

  Did anybody write it out or take
  notes on it?   ☐ Yes   ☐ No

Name, description, and other
identifying information for each
person who transcribed, wrote
out, or took notes on the
client's oral statments:

Other circumstances at the time of the client's statement, in
detail:

What officers were present at the
time when the client made each
statement?

What other persons were present at
the time when the client made each
statement?

[Key the names
or identifying in-
formation for
each officer and
person to the
lists of officers
and persons
present during
interrogation.]

Before making each statement, was
the client told by the police:

That s/he had a right to remain
silent?   ☐ Yes   ☐ No

That anything s/he said could be
used against him or her?   ☐ Yes   ☐ No

That s/he had a right to a lawyer
before making a statement?   ☐ Yes   ☐ No

That if s/he could not afford a
lawyer, one would be appointed
before any questioning?   ☐ Yes   ☐ No

What did the client say in response to these warnings:

Was the client asked whether s/he
understood each warning?   ☐ Yes   ☐ No

How did s/he respond:

Was s/he asked whether s/he was willing to make a statement after having
been given the warnings?   ☐ Yes   ☐ No

How did s/he respond:

Was s/he asked to sign a form with
these warnings written on it?   ☐ Yes   ☐ No

How did s/he respond:

When were the warnings given, in relation to the client's making of each statement:

Was the client given any physical exami-
nation?   ☐ Yes   ☐ No

Was a blood sample taken from the
client?   ☐ Yes   ☐ No

Was a breath sample taken from the
client?   ☐ Yes   ☐ No

Was a urine sample taken from the
client?   ☐ Yes   ☐ No

Was a hair sample taken from the client?   ☐ Yes   ☐ No

Were fingernail parings taken from the
client?   ☐ Yes   ☐ No

Was any part of the client's body
swabbed, vacuumed, or brushed?   ☐ Yes   ☐ No

Was the client's clothing swabbed, vacuumed, or brushed?   ☐ Yes ☐ No

Was the client given any alcohol test? ☐ Yes ☐ No

Was the client given any drug test?   ☐ Yes ☐ No

Was the client examined by a psychiatrist
or psychologist?   ☐ Yes ☐ No

    For each such examination, test, or
inspection:

      Where did it occur?

      At what time did it begin?

      At what time did it end?

      Describe the examination, test, or inspection:

      Who conducted it?   [Key the names
                                       or identifying in-
      What officers were present?   formation for
                                       each officer to
                                       the list of offi-
                                       cers above.]

      What other persons were present? [Name, descrip-
                                       tion, and other
                                       identifying infor-
                                       mation for each
                                       person who con-
                                       ducted or was
                                       present during
                                       any examination,
                                       test, or inspec-
                                       tion:]

Did anyone say anything about what the
examination, test, or inspection showed: ☐ Yes ☐ No

    Who:

    What was said:

Was the client asked for permission to
make any examination, test, or inspection (whether or not the examination,
test, or inspection was actually conducted)? ☐ Yes ☐ No

    Was s/he told that s/he had a right
    to refuse the examination, test, or
    inspection? ☐ Yes ☐ No

    Was s/he told that s/he had a right
    to talk to an attorney or to have an
    attorney present before or during
    the examination, test, or inspection? ☐ Yes ☐ No

    How did the client respond:

    Was the client told that a warrant or
    court order allowing the examina-
    tion, test, or inspection had been is-
    sued? ☐ Yes ☐ No

    What was the client told about the
    warrant or order:

    How did the client respond:

Who spoke to the client on these subjects?

What officers were present?

[Key the names or identifying information for each officer to the list of officers above.]

What other persons were present?

[Name, description, and other identifying information for each person who spoke to the client or was present during discussions of these subjects:]

Was the client exhibited in a lineup or brought, under any circumstances, before any person for identification?

☐ Yes   ☐ No

Where:

At what time did the exhibition begin:

At what time did it end:

Describe the circumstances (see paragraphs [36](A), [37-A](F) *supra*):

List all persons present:

    police officers

[Key the names or identifying information for each officer to the list of officers above.]

    subjects in the lineup or presented for possible identification

    identifying witnesses and persons asked to try to make an identification

[Name, description, and other identifying information for each person:]

    codefendants present

    other persons present

What did the police say to each identifying witness:

What did each identifying witness say:

Was the client asked to say anything during the lineup or identification exhibition?   ☐ Yes ☐ No

    How did s/he respond:

Was s/he told that s/he had a right not to say these things?   ☐ Yes ☐ No

    How did s/he respond to this advice:

Was the client asked to do anything during the lineup or identification exhibition (walk around, gesture, step forward)?   ☐ Yes ☐ No

What did s/he do or say:

Was s/he told that s/he had a right not to do these things?   ☐ Yes ☐ No

How did s/he respond to this advice:

Was the client asked for permission to put him or her in the lineup or to exhibit him or her for identification?   ☐ Yes ☐ No

Was s/he told that s/he had a right to refuse to be exhibited for identification?   ☐ Yes ☐ No

Was s/he told that s/he had a right to talk to an attorney or to have an attorney present before or during the identification exhibition?   ☐ Yes ☐ No

How did the client respond:

Was the client told that a warrant or court order allowing the identification exhibition had been issued?   ☐ Yes ☐ No

What was the client told about the warrant or order:

How did the client respond:

Who spoke to the client on these   [Key the names
subjects?   or identifying in-
                                           formation for
What officers were present?   each officer to
                                           the list of offi-
                                           cers above.]

What other persons were present?   [Name, descrip-
                                           tion, and other
                                           identifying infor-
                                           mation for each
                                           person who
                                           spoke to the
                                           client or was
                                           present during
                                           discussions of
                                           these subjects:]

Did the client reenact any events?   ☐ Yes   ☐ No

   Where:

   At what time did the reenactment
   begin:

   At what time did it end:

   What did the client do:

   Describe the surrounding circumstances:

List all persons present:

police officers

[Key the names or identifying information for each officer to the list of officers above.]

other actors in the reenactment

codefendants present

other persons present

[Name, description, and other identifying information for each person:]

Did the police give any instructions to the client about what to do?   ☐ Yes ☐ No

What were those instructions:

How did the client respond:

Did the police give any instructions to any other actor in the reenactment, about what to do?   ☐ Yes ☐ No

What were those instructions:

How did the actor respond:

Did the police say anything else during or about the reenactment?   ☐ Yes ☐ No

What:

Did anyone else say anything else during or about the reenactment?   ☐ Yes ☐ No

What:

Prior to the reenactment, was the client asked whether s/he would participate in it?   ☐ Yes   ☐ No

    Was s/he told that s/he had a right to refuse to participate?   ☐ Yes   ☐ No

    Was s/he told that s/he had a right to talk to an attorney or to have an attorney present before or during the reenactment?   ☐ Yes   ☐ No

    How did the client respond:

    Was the client told that a warrant or court order allowing the reenactment had been issued?   ☐ Yes   ☐ No

    What was the client told about the warrant or order:

    How did the client respond:

    Who spoke to the client on these subjects?

    What officers were present?

[Key the names or identifying information for each officer to the list of officers above.]

    What other persons were present?

[Name, description, and other identifying information for each person who spoke to the client or was present during discussions of these subjects:]

Was the client asked to give permission
for the search of any place or thing: ☐ Yes   ☐ No

    Where was the request made:

    When was the request made:

    What was the client told was the
    place or thing for which permission
    to search was being requested:

    What was said about what the search
    was supposed to be looking for:

    What else was said to the client by
    the person requesting permission:

    What did the client say:

    Was the client told that s/he had a
    right to refuse permission?   ☐ Yes   ☐ No

    Was the client told that s/he had a
    right not to have the place or thing
    searched without a search warrant?   ☐ Yes   ☐ No

    Was s/he told that s/he had a right
    to talk to an attorney or to have an
    attorney present before consenting
    to the search or during the search? ☐ Yes   ☐ No

    How did the client respond:

    Was the client told that a search
    warrant allowing the search had
    been issued?   ☐ Yes   ☐ No

    What was the client told about the
    warrant:

How did the client respond:

Who spoke to the client on these
subjects?

What officers were present?

[Key the names
or identifying in-
formation for
each officer to
the list of offi-
cers above.]

What other persons were present?

[Name, descrip-
tion, and other
identifying infor-
mation for each
person who
spoke to the
client or was
present during
discussions of
these subjects:]

Was the client present when the police
searched any place or thing?

☐ Yes   ☐ No

What place or thing:

Where:

At what time did the search begin:

At what time did it end:

What was said about what the search
was supposed to be looking for:

What else did the client hear said
about the search:

Who spoke to the client on this subject?

What officers were present?

[Key the names or identifying information for each officer to the list of officers above.]

What other persons were present?

[Name, description, and other identifying information for each person who spoke to the client or was present during discussions of this subject:]

Describe the search:

Describe the surrounding circumstances:

Who conducted the search?

What officers were present?

[Key the names or identifying information for each officer to the list of officers above.]

What other persons were present?

[Name, description, and other identifying information for each person:]

Was anything found during the
search? ☐ Yes ☐ No

What:

Where was it found:

When was it found:

By whom was it found:

Describe the thing(s) found:

What did the client hear said
about the things found:

Who spoke to the client on this sub-   [Key the names
ject?   or identifying in-
    formation for
    each officer to
What officers were present?   the list of offi-
    cers above.]

What other persons were present?   [Name, descrip-
    tion, and other
    identifying infor-
    mation for each
    person who
    spoke to the
    client or was
    present during
    discussions of
    this subject:]

Has the client appeared in court on the
present charges? ☐ Yes ☐ No

For each prior court appearance:

What court:

Address or location of court:

Nature of proceedings:

Who was the judge?

Who was the prosecutor?

Were charges read or shown to the
client?   ☐ Yes   ☐ No

What were they:

Was the client asked to plead?   ☐ Yes   ☐ No

What did s/he plead:

Did the client testify?   ☐ Yes   ☐ No

What did s/he testify:

Did any other witnesses testify?   ☐ Yes   ☐ No

What did they testify   [Name, descrip-
                                           tion, and other
What codefendants were present?   identifying infor-
                                           mation for each
What other persons were present?   witness and
                                           other person:]

What police officers were present?   [Key the names
                                           or identifying in-
                                           formation for
                                           each officer to
                                           the list of offi-
                                           cers above.]

Was the client represented by a lawyer?   ☐ Yes   ☐ No

    Name, description, and other identi-
    fying information for the lawyer:

    [Did the lawyer give the client a
    business card, and does the client
    still have it?]

    How did this lawyer come to repre-
    sent the client:

    If the client was not represented by
    a lawyer:

        Was the client told that s/he had
        a right to have a lawyer represent
        him or her in court?   ☐ Yes   ☐ No

        That if s/he could not afford a
        lawyer, one would be appointed to
        represent him or her without cost?   ☐ Yes   ☐ No

        How did the client respond?

    Who spoke to the client on these   [Key the names
    subjects?   or identifying in-
                                              formation for
                                              each officer to
    What officers were present?   the list of offi-
                                              cers above.]

What other persons were present?

[Name, description, and other identifying information for each person who spoke to the client or was present during discussions of these subjects:]

What else happened in court:

[Was the client given a slip of paper or a form of any sort, and does the client still have it? If the slip or form is retrievable, counsel wants to get it as soon as s/he can obtain it from the client or the client's family, since it will state the charges and the next court appearance date more accurately than the client is likely to remember them and will contain the court's case number.]

Were any other person(s) arrested along with the client?   ☐ Yes   ☐ No

Has the client been informed that any other person(s) have been charged along with the client?   ☐ Yes   ☐ No

    For each person arrested or charged along with the client:

    Name, description, and other identifying information:

    With what offenses is s/he charged:

Is s/he in custody?   ☐ Yes   ☐ No

If so, name, location, or description of facility:

If not, get information as for
witnesses, *supra.*

Is s/he represented by a lawyer?   ☐ Yes   ☐ No

Name, description, and other
identifying information for the
lawyer:

WHEN APPROPRIATE, COUNSEL SHOULD OBTAIN:
    (1) Information relating to bail, paragraph [60] *supra;*
    (2) The client's signed release giving counsel the right to
        inspect all hospital, prison, court, and juvenile court
        records relating to the client (releases for each on
        separate sheets);
    (3) A signed retainer and fee agreement, paragraph [86]
        supra.

VI. DEALINGS WITH THE POLICE AND PROSECUTOR

[91] Summary. Counsel should usually establish contact with the investigating officers as early as possible in the course of a case. Thereafter, s/he should feel free to speak to them whenever the needs of the client dictate. Similarly, counsel should establish contact with the prosecuting attorney as soon as one is assigned to the case and should communicate with him or her periodically thereafter. The purposes of these contacts with the police and the prosecutor are (a) to learn as much as possible about the prosecution's evidence, the temperament and attitudes of any officer who may testify, the prosecutor's goals, objectives, and plans in the case, and the prosecutor's attitude toward the defendant; (b) to protect the defendant during police and prosecutorial investigative activity; (c) to persuade the police or the prosecutor to drop or reduce charges; and (d), if appropriate, to negotiate a mutually agreeable disposition or settlement of the case.

[92] Discussions with the police generally. Except in cases in which there are particular reasons to keep a low profile (for example, when counsel's independent researches disclose that the police conducted a slipshod initial investigation and are doing no further investigating, so that counsel prefers to let sleeping hounds lie), the more frequently counsel speaks with the police, the better. Every conversation with an officer gives counsel a little additional information about how the officer views the case, what the officer will testify, what the officer knows concerning other prosecution evidence, and how eager the officer is to see the client convicted. Details that the officer tells counsel may be useful in impeaching the officer if the case goes to trial. (These statements may be used in questioning the officer on cross, see paragraph [379] *infra*; and if s/he denies making them or professes not to remember making them, they may be proved extrinsically to the extent that they are "noncollateral," see paragraphs [382], [394] *infra*.)

167

Equally important, the more frequent the conversations between an officer and counsel, the more difficult it is for the officer to recall what s/he has said to counsel, and the more cautious s/he will be not to embroider the facts when testifying. Discussions with the police are usually most fruitful before a prosecuting attorney is assigned to the matter because until that stage the officers regard it as "their case," are freer to talk about it, and have more influence in relevant decisions (see paragraphs [98]-[105] *infra*).

[93] **Discussions with the prosecutor generally.** Once a prosecutor has been assigned to the case, frequent conversation with him or her is also fruitful as a means both of acquiring factual information and of learning and affecting the prosecutor's attitude. The more the prosecutor sees that counsel is involved with the case, the more s/he is likely to conclude that counsel is working hard at it. The value of this is twofold. First, if the prosecutor thinks that defense counsel is going all out, the prosecutor's estimate of the time and trouble involved in trying the case will increase and so may the prosecutor's willingness to offer concessions in order to settle the case before trial. Second, counsel's visible dedication to a client often tends to make the prosecutor's own attitude toward the client more sympathetic, in the view that the client probably has something on the ball to inspire all that zeal. Both of these impressions can, of course, backfire in some cases, causing the prosecutor to prepare more thoroughly or to develop a more competitive turn of mind. Counsel should seek to learn as much as possible about this particular prosecutor's psychology by asking other informed defense practitioners. Sometimes counsel will decide to keep contact with the prosecutor at a minimum in order to decrease the visibility of the case or avoid arousing the prosecutor's combativeness.

[94] **The importance of amiability and honesty.** In any event, frequent contact is likely to be productive only if it is amiable contact, and counsel should cultivate the art of diplomacy. It is wise to establish two distinct levels of discourse with the police and the prosecuting attorney: (a) things said

that counsel is free to disclose and to use in presenting the case at trial and (b) things said "off the record" or in confidence. Counsel should always make clear the level on which s/he is talking with the police and prosecution. If police officers or the prosecutor get the feeling that they have been "double-crossed"—that counsel has revealed information communicated in confidence—*all* communications to counsel in this and future cases are likely to be terminated abruptly.

[95] Initial discussions with the arresting and investigating officers. Before (or, if that is impracticable, then immediately after) the initial interview with the client, counsel should speak to the investigating officer and ask what are the charges against the defendant and the facts of the case as the officer understands them. Counsel should ask whether any other or additional charges are being considered and, if so, what charges. S/he should ask the names of all witnesses. S/he should ask to see the police report, which the officer may or may not be willing to disclose. Counsel should also speak to the arresting officer to ask what s/he observed, what s/he was told, whether s/he knows of other witnesses, and what their names and addresses are. Counsel should tell both officers that s/he will probably speak to them again and ask what times and places are convenient to see them. Counsel should not attempt to bargain or argue with the officers. Rather, s/he should restrict the conversation to ascertaining what evidence the police have against the client, what they think of the client as a person (or as a problem), and whether they are hostile, sympathetic, or indifferent to the client. If counsel does not know the officers involved, it is useful to check out their reputations with an experienced local criminal lawyer, reliable bondsman, or R.O.R. Project staffer, with special regard to whether information given by these particular officers can be trusted. Even when they are trustworthy, however, it is generally not prudent to tell the police of counsel's plans, the facts counsel knows, or the client's reaction to the charge. The only *quid pro quo* that counsel can offer for their information at this early stage is friendliness, courtesy, and sincere appreciation for their willingness to be helpful.

[96] Later discussions and interviews with police and the prosecutor for the purpose of gathering information about the prosecution's case. See paragraphs [102]-[103], [116] *infra*.

[97] Protecting the client in custody. If the client is in custody, the investigating officer should be told in the most amiable and inoffensive manner possible (1) that the police are not to interrogate or speak to the client or to confront the client with any evidence or witness except in counsel's presence; (2) that they are not to ask the client for any permissions, consents, or waivers but should address these requests to counsel; (3) that the client is not to be taken or removed from the present place of detention for any purpose without notice to counsel; (4) that the client is not to be put in a lineup or exhibited for identification in the absence of counsel; and (5) that the client is not to be subjected to any physical or mental examination, personal inspection, or scientific test in counsel's absence. See paragraphs [25] (4), [35]-[37-A] *supra*. Counsel should offer to be available on reasonable notice to attend any lineups, identification viewings, examinations, or tests or to discuss the case or its investigation with the police. Counsel should ask whether the police intend to conduct any of these proceedings. If they do, s/he should try to arrange with the investigating officer to have them all done at a mutually convenient time. If they do not, or if they have not yet decided, counsel should give the officer his or her phone number and request that the officer phone counsel in the event that they subsequently do decide to conduct any of these sorts of investigations, so that counsel can be present. Counsel should also have the client personally advise the investigating officer or one of the custodial officers, in counsel's presence, that the client henceforth does not want to converse with the police or prosecuting authorities without counsel's assistance but wants to deal with them only through counsel. See paragraphs [35] (D), (F), [37] (H) *supra*. (To guard against the possibility that the police do not notify counsel or will not wait for counsel to appear, the client must also be advised to make appropriate objections and to look for and remember the things which counsel would have wanted to observe. See paragraphs [25] (3), [36], [37-A], [51] (B), (C), [87] and the relevant items in the checklist, paragraph [90] *supra*.) Police may well disregard counsel's requests or harass counsel by scheduling lineups, identification viewings, examinations, or tests at inconvenient hours or scheduling them one a day over a period of time. If counsel concludes that the police are conducting improper investigative proceedings or are scheduling investigative proceedings abusively or without adequate notice to counsel, s/he should call the prosecutor and ask the prosecutor to mediate a reasonable agreement with the police regarding the methods and timing of subsequent investigation. If the prosecutor declines to intervene or cannot solve the problem, counsel should consider whether there are grounds to move the court to enjoin further police investigations, suppress the results of those already conducted, or both. See paragraphs [36] (A), [37-A], [38] *supra*; paragraphs [223], [224] (B), [228], [232], [233], [237] (A), [238], [270] (H), [374] *infra*. In this connection particular attention should be paid to the potential interaction of the constitutional doctrines of *Gerstein v. Pugh*, 420 U.S. 103 (1975), discussed in paragraph [127] *infra*, and of *Kirby v. Illinois*, 406 U.S. 682 (1972), discussed in paragraph [233] (B) (1) *infra*. *Gerstein* requires that any person arrested without a warrant be given a prompt postarrest determination of probable cause by a judicial officer unless perhaps s/he is equally promptly indicted by a grand jury. Failing either a prompt probable cause determination or a prompt indictment, his or her detention becomes unconstitutional, and s/he is entitled to release on *habeas corpus* (see paragraph [38] *supra*). Any evidence obtained as a consequence of the unconstitutional detention should be suppressed on motion (see paragraphs [127] (C), (D) and [236] (A) *infra*). On the other hand, the judicial probable cause determination required by *Gerstein* should mark the initiation of "adversary judicial proceedings"—the "first formal charging proceeding," *Moran v. Burbine*, 106 S. Ct. 1135, 1145 (1986)—that, according to *Kirby*, triggers the defendant's Sixth Amendment right to counsel and thereby invalidates any police investigative procedures involving the defendant that are subsequently conducted in the absence of counsel. (See paragraph [233] (A) *infra*; *e.g.*, *Michigan v. Jackson*, 106 S. Ct. 1404, 1407-9 (1986).) And, of course, an indictment plainly triggers this Sixth Amendment right, with its exclusionary consequences. (*E.g.*, *Estelle v. Smith*, 451 U.S. 454, 469-70 (1981).)

[98] **The exercise of discretion by police and prosecutor: (1) the police.** The criminal process, particularly in its early stages, is honey-combed with police and prosecutorial discretion. Not all persons who are guilty of a crime and who are known by the police to have committed the crime are arrested. Many minor infractions are handled by a warning from the officer. When a person is arrested, the arresting officer initially decides what the charge is, arrests the person on that charge, and takes the person to the precinct. Here again, if the charge is not serious, the desk officer reviews the facts and may send the arrestee home or have the arrestee slated on the same charge as, or a different charge from, that made by the arresting officer. If the charge is serious, the arrestee will be taken (either routinely or after the exercise of similar discretion by the desk officer) to an investigating officer or detective. See paragraph [28] *supra*. Now it is the investigating officer's job to determine whether the arrestee has committed a crime and, if so, what crime. The investigating officer, too, may decide that the arrestee is not guilty or that the case is weak or that for some reason it should not be prosecuted and may send the arrestee home. Or the officer may decide to charge the arrestee with one or more offenses, which may or may not be those for which s/he was arrested. After further investigation the officer may change or add to those charges. The fact that the arrestee has been booked initially on one charge does not guarantee that s/he will not subsequently be charged with other offenses growing out of the same set of facts or with other crimes growing out of other facts that s/he has admitted or to which s/he has been connected.

[99] **Same: (2) the prosecutor.** The prosecutor reviews the charges placed by the police. On the basis of the police report,

discussion with the investigating officers and, sometimes, an independent investigation, the prosecutor may decide to drop the charges or to proceed on the charges made by the police or to charge more serious or less serious or different offenses. S/he thus determines the charges to be presented at the preliminary hearing. Thereafter it is the function of the magistrate or judge at the preliminary hearing to determine the charges on which the defendant is to be held for trial or for the grand jury. The prosecutor in a nonindictable case, however, is often permitted to charge by information offenses shown at the preliminary hearing for which the defendant was not bound over; and in indictable cases, the prosecutor is usually free to present to the grand jury whatever charges s/he pleases. See paragraphs [16], [20]-[21] *supra*. After the bind-over and after the information or indictment, ordinarily the prosecutor is still free to drop the prosecution (a) formally, by entering a *nolle prosequi* (usually called *nol pros*)—for which leave of court is sometimes required but ordinarily given routinely when requested (*cf. Rinaldi v. United States*, 434 U.S. 22, 29-30 n.15 (1977) (per curiam), discussing federal practice)—or (b) informally, by an indefinite continuance (called *stetting*). The prosecutor also retains discretion—again, sometimes subject to leave of court or to the requirement that the prosecutor file a statement of reasons with the court—to accept a plea of guilty to a lesser offense than that charged in the information or the indictment. Whether the defendant pleads guilty or goes to trial, the prosecutor may recommend a sentence to the court or may inform the court that the defendant is cooperating. The court has complete discretion to accept or reject the prosecutor's sentencing recommendation, and practice varies locally in this regard; but it is fair to say that there are few places where the position taken by the prosecutor on sentence is wholly unimportant. Additionally, when the defendant is a recidivist, the prosecutor generally exercises considerable discretion (sometimes lawfully, sometimes in the teeth of mandatory recidivist-sentencing statutes) to "charge the priors": that is, to invoke the stiffer penalties allowed by law for second or successive convictions.

[100] **Factors influencing discretion.** The factors that influence the police and prosecutor not to press charges or to press less serious charges or otherwise to exercise discretion in favor of the accused are innumerable. A few important ones, however, deserve mention. No matter how strong the evidence, many prosecutors will not charge an individual who they personally believe is innocent. This matter of personal belief is far less important to the police, but not unimportant. The likelihood of conviction—the strength of the prosecution's case—is also more important to the prosecutor than to the police. (It is the prosecutor who stands to look like a fool in court; police efficiency is judged in terms of clearance by arrest.) In assessing the strength of the prosecution's case, the prosecutor must consider the weight of the evidence, the likely availability of the evidence at the time of trial, and the habits, attitudes, and sympathies of judges and juries in the locality. Docket congestion and his or her own workload tell with the prosecutor. Particularly if a case is relatively unimportant (in terms of the egregiousness of the crime and the probable future dangerousness of the accused) and if preparing and presenting it in court are going to involve much time and work, the prosecutor will tend to favor a noncourt disposition. This is particularly so if s/he is confident that the disposition will leave pertinent parties—principally the police, the complainant, and the news media—satisfied. Both the police and the prosecutor are concerned with the accused's past record, which they view as indicative of whether the defendant is a likely source of future trouble to them or of danger to the community. A defendant with a good record is likely to get a break, especially if the offense charged is one that carries a penalty that seems unduly harsh. Both police and prosecutor are also concerned with the question whether, if a case goes to trial, the evidence will disclose serious police misconduct or ineptitude. Finally, both police and prosecutor are likely to view favorably the accused's willingness to cooperate in apprehending or in convicting other offenders or in solving other crimes.

[101] **The role of defense counsel.** The implications of the large discretion exercised by police and prosecutors, of its exercise at numerous points in the criminal proceeding, and of the variety of factors that affect it should be obvious. Counsel must begin early and work continuously to project the best possible image of the client and of the facts surrounding the charge in the minds of these officials. At the same time, hard practicality, as well as the compulsions of professional and personal integrity, precludes the projection of an image that subsequently is likely to be found inaccurate. Counsel also has to worry about his or her own image. If s/he is not trusted, s/he either will not be dealt with or s/he will not be dealt with fairly. If s/he appears lazy, careless, or weak, s/he is likely to be taken advantage of, and the police or the prosecutor may bear down heavily in the hope that s/he will capitulate. The stronger counsel appears to be, the more trouble the case will appear to be to prosecute. On the other hand, if s/he is too combative, s/he may raise the spirit of combat in the police or the prosecutor. Usually, counsel's most effective posture is one of complete sincerity, of unquestioning commitment to protect every right that the law gives the client, of unflagging willingness to work as hard as necessary in the client's behalf, yet of infinite reasonableness in seeking some fair accommodation that will dispose of the case in the most efficient and just manner. When counsel takes a hard line on a point, it must appear to be because the facts of the case are strong, not because s/he is an inventive, tricky, or obstructive lawyer. Counsel is merely doing the right thing and knows how to do it well. If the alternative to a reduced charge is a long trial, this is not because counsel wants to make trouble for the prosecutor but because the greater charge requires the finding of a certain state of mind; counsel's client certainly did not have the state of mind; the stories of a dozen witnesses make this clear; counsel has statements from them all; and s/he is going to have to call them all. If the complainant is unconvincing, the police and the prosecutor should not believe the complainant's version of the story; and it is a matter of some, but secondary, importance that a jury also is not likely to believe the complainant or to convict the defendant. At all

events, the important thing is that the criminal process not bear so harshly on the defendant that it will defeat its own aims and leave everybody concerned with a mess of troubles.

[102] **Dealings with the police.** Counsel should ordinarily not bargain or negotiate with the police. The costs in disclosure are too great, the dispositive power of the police is too limited, and counsel's later opportunities to negotiate with the prosecutor are ample. But in cases in which the facts already known to the police will support an argument that no charges are warranted or that the charges should be less severe than those the police have made or contemplate, counsel should urge the police to drop or reduce the charges. For this purpose counsel may want to discuss the legal elements of a particular charge and demonstrate that some required element is missing. When it is clear that the client is going to be charged with something, a suggestion of an appropriate lesser charge is advised. Discussion of legal and factual weaknesses in the evidence against the client is recommended, however, *only if* those weaknesses are not likely to teach the police something and to encourage police fabrication or further investigation that could be damning. References to the client's good record and to the harm a serious and dubious charge will do to that record may help. Portraying the client sympathetically or explaining apparent unfavorable traits ("That kid is not being tough, officer; he's scared stiff in this police station") may also be helpful. Generally counsel does better to try to persuade the investigating officer that facts discovered since the arrest or ambiguities in the facts cleared up since the arrest exonerate the client than to argue that there was no basis for the arrest itself. Police feel called upon to defend their arrests and may reject any notion that the arrest was unfounded.

[103] **Early dealings with the prosecutor.** Counsel's early dealings with the prosecutor are principally aimed at learning the prosecutor's evidence and the prosecutor's attitude toward the seriousness of the offense and the character of the defendant. Counsel should ask the prosecutor what the prosecution's proof consists of and what the prosecutor thinks is an

appropriate and reasonable disposition of the case. Counsel should ask to see specific items in the file, such as the police report or a confession. If counsel can honestly and convincingly urge the client's innocence or the unfounded nature of a given charge, s/he may attempt to convince the prosecutor at this stage to drop charges or to present lesser ones. Counsel should remember that the prosecutor's personal view of guilt or innocence is important and that it is based on information—both favorable and unfavorable to the defendant—that may not be admissible as evidence in court. A complainant's shabby character or prior unfounded complaints may do counsel no good when the case goes to trial; it is with the prosecutor that they can be put to good effect. In rare cases, when counsel is very sure of the client, s/he may consider suggesting a lie detector test. This should never be suggested without the client's prior consent and only in a case in which counsel, after a thorough factual investigation and a skeptical cross-examination of the client in the light of that investigation, is completely persuaded of the client's innocence. Almost never should the suggestion of a lie detector test include a stipulation of its admissibility in evidence. Polygraphs are fairly reliable, but when they err, it is on the side of false positives (incorrect indications that a truthful answer is a lie). In the more usual case counsel's greatest effectiveness will be in urging reduced charges based on factual weaknesses in the prosecution's evidence, the defendant's good record or sympathetic character, the harshness of the penalty for the greater charge, and the availability of a lesser charge with a more fitting penalty. Occasionally, a prosecutor who is indisposed to exercise discretion favorably will profess to have none. Defense counsel faced with an unbudging protestation that the prosecutor's "hands are tied" may find it useful to write a short letter or memorandum to the prosecutor demonstrating that they are not (*see, e.g., United States v. Lovasco,* 431 U.S. 783, 794-95 & n.15 (1977); *Bordenkircher v. Hayes,* 434 U.S. 357, 364-65 (1978); *United States v. Batchelder,* 442 U.S. 114, 123-25 (1979); *Rummel v. Estelle,* 445 U.S. 263, 281 (1980); *United States v. Goodwin,* 457 U.S 368, 380 & n.11 (1982); *Wayte v. United States,* 470 U.S. 598, 607-8 (1985); *Ball v. United States,* 470 U.S. 856, 859 (1985);

McCleskey v. Kemp, 107 S. Ct. 1756, 1768, 1777 (1987); *Young v. United States ex rel. Vuitton et Fils*, 107 S. Ct. 2124, 2137 (1987); *Town of Newton v. Rumery*, 107 S. Ct. 1187, 1194 (1987) (plurality opinion); *cf. Marshall v. Jerrico, Inc.*, 446 U.S. 238, 248 (1980); *Heckler v. Chaney*, 470 U.S. 821, 831-32 (1985)), before calling the prosecutor to resume discussions. (This tells the prosecutor nothing that s/he does not already know, but it is a nicer way of pointing out that you also know it than by calling the prosecutor a liar.) In dealing with the prosecutor, counsel should always have a thorough grip of all the possible lesser charges on the books. Counsel will often find that it is most effective to urge the prosecutor to drop or reduce charges prior to preliminary hearing, since, once the magistrate has bound a defendant over on a charge, there is considerable inertial pressure on the prosecutor to take it to trial. This is especially so when the prosecutor and magistrate are of different political parties and the prosecutor is required to project a public image of being no less rough on crime than is the magistrate. Plea negotiation, which may follow unsuccessful attempts to persuade the prosecutor to drop or reduce charges without a guilty plea or other *quid pro quo*, is discussed in paragraphs [206]-[219] *infra*.

[104] **Complainants.** By law, by police or prosecutorial routine, or by judicial practice, some minor charges are pressed only on private complaint. In these cases particularly, efforts to persuade the complainant to drop charges are important. But they may also be important in cases in which the offense is prosecuted or the prosecution is continued past the stage of the complaint without formal concern for the complainant's wishes. As a practical matter the complainant's attitude, even in the latter cases, is likely to affect the exercise of the prosecutorial discretion. There is nothing wrong with defense counsel's talking to a complainant so long as counsel is honest and not overbearing. It is usually a good idea, however, to have a reliable witness present during the discussion, or unfounded charges against counsel may later be made. In cases in which the complainant appears sympathetic, the damaging effect of the prosecution on the defendant's record or the

harshness of the possible penalty may be mentioned. When guilt is clear, offers of restitution will frequently satisfy complainants who have suffered property loss as a result of minor offenses. With the client's consent these offers may properly be made.

[105] Offers to cooperate with the police or prosecution. The police or the prosecution will sometimes offer a client the opportunity to "cooperate" by testifying against accomplices in exchange for dismissal or reduction of charges or in exchange for a recommendation of leniency to the trial judge. Such an arrangement should rarely be made with the police. Unless the prosecutor is brought in, counsel should decline to discuss it. In evaluating an offer to which the prosecutor is a party, counsel must be sure to learn the nature of the evidence that the prosecution has against the client or else s/hc may buy a bad bargain. Some prosecutors use cooperation offers to "break" multidefendant cases that they cannot prove against *any* of the defendants; therefore, counsel should ask to see the police reports or the witnesses' statements establishing the client's guilt before counsel discusses "cooperation." There are basically three kinds of promises that the prosecution can make. (a) An immunity grant under an applicable immunity statute or "state's evidence" statute is legally binding and can be relied upon to protect the client. (b) An informal promise by the prosecutor not to prosecute or not to press certain charges is only as good as the prosecutor's word. (c) A sentencing recommendation by the prosecutor is not even that good, since judges may ignore the recommendation. This third kind of promise should never be accepted without inquiry of experienced criminal lawyers in the area who know the judge or judges (and often then, only if the prosecutor can assure counsel that the case will be brought on for sentencing before a particular judge). Neither the second nor the third kind of promise should be accepted without a basis for trust in the prosecutor. Local statutes should be studied to see whether the bargain can be cast in a mold that brings it within the scope of a legally enforceable immunity provision. The prosecutor should also be asked what s/he can do to assure the client against retaliation by codefendants: for example, an arrangement that they be committed to an institution other than the client's. Then after counsel has learned exactly what is expected of the client and what the client will receive, and after counsel has decided how good the bargain is, s/he should explain it to the client. The contingencies in the promised benefits (particularly those relating to sentencing recommendations) should be very carefully pointed out. Counsel should also warn the client of the possibility of recrimination by other prisoners if the client testifies against a codefendant, even though the client and codefendant are sent to different institutions. Ultimately, the decision must be the client's. Advising the client in the matter involves many of the same considerations involved in advising a client whether to accept a negotiated plea. See paragraphs [201]-[219] *infra*. The final agreement with the prosecutor should specify precisely the proceedings in which the client is required to testify and should not leave unclear the scope of the client's obligations in the event that proceedings against the codefendant later take varying twists (for example, prosecution of the codefendant on multiple charges involving separate trials; reprosecution of the codefendant following reversal of an initial conviction). *See Ricketts v. Adamson*, 107 S. Ct. 2680 (1987).

VII. DEFENSE INVESTIGATION

[106] Importance of the facts. The story of the indigent defendant who, upon being offered counsel by the court, replied, "If it's all the same to you, Judge, I'd rather have a couple of good witnesses," summarizes what defense counsel will quickly learn: Most cases turn on the presentation of evidence and not on legal argument. This is true whether or not a case goes to trial on the issue of guilt. The *facts* are counsel's most important asset not only in arguing before a jury but also in every other function counsel performs: seeking advantageous terms of bail, urging the prosecutor to drop or reduce charges, negotiating a plea bargain with the prosecutor, urging a favorable sentencing recommendation on a probation officer or sentencing disposition on a judge. Investigation is counsel's instrument for getting the facts. One key aspect of defense investigation, the interview with the client, is discussed in paragraphs [76]-[90] *supra*. Several other important aspects are discussed here. The discussion is brief, since it is required to be general and there are few helpful generalities in the highly particularistic business of gathering facts. Related matters will be discussed later: discovery procedures and devices in paragraphs [265] - [275] *infra*; defense trial preparation in paragraphs [277] - [297] *infra*.

[107] Directing investigation toward a theory of the defense. If counsel's time and resources were unlimited, counsel's investigation could be unlimited. Since they are not, the investigation must be selective—often painfully so. Conscious selectivity and a thoughtful assignment of priorities must direct the defense investigative effort at all times. This means, for the most part, having a theory of the defense and going after the facts that the theory makes material. At the same time, counsel must avoid becoming a prisoner of his or her theory. In the search for facts that support it, s/he must be alert to those that do not and to facts that suggest a preferable theory. In short, counsel must go to the sources that are most likely to contain information relevant to his or her theory, but while s/he is at those sources, s/he must gather all other information potentially germane to the case that can be gathered with little additional time and effort. Counsel must constantly reevaluate what s/he has thus gathered and determine whether to keep on the same track or switch to a new one. Almost always, one issue, or a very few issues, should stand out as having paramount importance. Although the prosecution must prove all the elements of its case, the defense needs to destroy only one. It is seldom profitable to take on more than one or, at most, a couple. Hence the defense should aim at the few weakest points in the prosecution's case or at the few strongest points in the defendant's case, as these points appear to counsel's best judgment at any moment. But counsel should be sure to reconsider that judgment from time to time as investigation progresses. By keeping his or her eyes open and plans flexible as s/he pursues the places of most likely paydirt, s/he may find unexpected nuggets that call for digging in new directions. S/he must always have priorities but be willing to change them.

[108] **Starting promptly.** The first priority is establishing a rational order of priorities. To do this, counsel must know something about the case in broad outline. The two most likely sources of general information are obvious—the investigating officers and the defendant. Counsel has to go to these two sources at the outset of the case, in any event, for other purposes. S/he must do so, as indicated in paragraphs [23]-[53] *supra*, to protect the client against police investigation and to get or keep the client out of custody. S/he should have an initial discussion with the officers, see paragraph [95] *supra*, and an initial interview with the client, see paragraphs [76]-[90] *supra*, as early as possible, both because the client most needs protection immediately after arrest and because defense investigation should begin promptly. Speed may not be essential in a particular case, but counsel cannot know this until s/he learns something about the case. Generally speed *is* essential. Physical facts change. An object of importance may be discarded. Witnesses may disappear or forget. Particularly in urban areas, individuals are highly mobile. They may suddenly

go away and leave no trace. Or if they remain in the area, they may quickly blend into the neighborhood, becoming impossible to locate, as their principal indentifying characteristic—proximity to the offense or arrest—dissolves. If and when they are ever found again, they may be useless as witnesses. Most people (except lawyers) keep no diaries or deskbooks. Their lives are not punctuated by unforgettable adventures. One day is like another. Whether they were with the defendant on a Wednesday or a Thursday a week ago makes little difference to them, although it may mean conviction or acquittal to the defendant. So it is that, with awareness of these realities, counsel is in a position to make his or her initial decisions concerning the priorities of defense investigation immediately after talking to the police and client. The first things to go after are those that are perishable: physical items that are mobile or changeable; witnesses who are mobile or indefinitely identified but related to some specific location at a recent point of time; witnesses whose involvement is such that they may forget if not questioned quickly. Counsel should move on these items as rapidly as s/he can. This is so not only because of the risk of irreparable losses but also because early investigation makes the most efficient use of counsel's limited resources: An hour's search while the track is warm may be worth days later. Once a reasonable effort has been made to find the known perishable items, counsel should evaluate everything s/he has, estimate the points of strength, and proceed with further investigation to consolidate them.

[109] Witnesses the defendant wants called. There is one major exception to counsel's order of priorities. When the defendant tells counsel that the defendant wants certain named, or reasonably identifiable, witnesses called or that certain witnesses will "clear" the defendant (this usually involves alibi witnesses), counsel should ordinarily seek them out and interview them. S/he should keep file notes of the interviews or, if the witnesses cannot be located, of the efforts to find them. Counsel may decide not to use the witnesses (when, for example, they are entirely unconvincing), but if s/he so decides, s/he should discuss the reasons with the defendant and make a file note both of the reasons and of the discussion of them with the defendant.Looking for these witnesses and interviewing them are important, even if counsel believes in advance that they are not going to be worthwhile. In the first place, counsel may be wrong. Second, every client is entitled to the small comfort, at least, that his or her lawyer does not disbelieve the client without fair inquiry. Third, failure to look for witnesses named by a defendant is, perhaps, the most frequent ground of postconviction attacks upon the competence of trial counsel.

[110] **Use of an investigator.** Whether counsel should hire an investigator or conduct the investigation personally will depend in part, of course, upon the financial resources available to the defense. An investigator is recommended when practicable for several reasons. Money spent to hire an investigator is usually economically spent, since an investigator's time is less costly than counsel's. Counsel does or will have other things to do in the case that can be done only by a lawyer, which may occupy counsel at times when investigative needs are critical. An investigator is apt to make headway more freely and efficiently, particularly in neighborhoods where counsel may be perceived as a detective, truant officer, finance company agent, welfare department inspector, or the like and may encounter only closed doors. A good investigator also has sources of information unavailable to all but the most experienced criminal lawyers in a locality—community contacts, official contacts (acquaintances in the police department, prison records department, juvenile court, probation department, and so forth), and contacts with other professional fact-gatherers (news reporters, social workers, local politicians and their staffers). Furthermore, the investigator can readily be called upon to testify if any conflicts arise between the stories given by witnesses at trial and the stories they previously gave to the defense. And if counsel decides that photographs are necessary for the defense, a person other than counsel will have taken them and will be available to testify to lay a foundation for their admission into evidence, should the prosecutor not stipulate to their accuracy. (This is important, whether or

not an investigator is being used generally.) Intelligent use of an investigator, however, requires thoughtful attention by counsel. Counsel must explain the case and the initial theories of the defense fully to the investigator at the outset and must inform the investigator periodically of counsel's current thinking, in order to avoid squandering defense resources in the collection of useless information. Frequent, regularly scheduled check-ins by phone ordinarily serve this purpose best; most of the time, they can be kept brief. Defense investigators should be cautioned that their notes, reports, and memoranda may become discoverable by the prosecution in some situations (see paragraphs [274], [408-A] *infra*) and must, therefore, be drafted prudently. When practicable, it is generally wise to have an investigator first report orally to counsel and then reduce his or her report to writing with counsel's approval. Counsel may prefer to make all of the written notes, based upon the investigator's oral report, since counsel's notes will very probably enjoy greater "work product" protection (see paragraphs [273-A], [274] (C) *infra*) than an investigator's written report. See paragraph [81] *supra*; *Upjohn Co. v. United States*, 449 U.S. 383, 397-402 (1981); *United States v. Nobles*, 422 U.S. 225, 252-54 (1975) (concurring opinion of Justice White); *cf. Goldberg v. United States*, 425 U.S. 94, 105-7 (1976).

[111] **Site visits.** Whether or not counsel uses an investigator, it is usually wise for counsel personally to inspect the site of any important event in the case: the offense, the arrest, a search and seizure. Although counsel will be principally looking for specific items, s/he will often perceive others that put a whole new complexion on the case—items having a significance that would escape anyone but counsel. Frequently, for example, at the time of trial, when a prosecution witness is testifying about events in detail not previously known to the defense, it becomes apparent to counsel who has been at the scene, and only because s/he has been at the scene, that the witness is mistaken or confused on matters of spatial relations. (A witness who, on direct examination, has carefully drawn a diagram of an unobstructed street corner can be quite visibly flustered by the question on cross-examination whether there

is not, in fact, a telephone booth on that corner.) It is also helpful in many cases for counsel to participate in a reenactment of pertinent events, such as a search-and-seizure episode in which the client claims the police pushed their way through an apartment door, whereas the police will expectably claim that they knocked and saw illicit activities inside when the door was opened. By playing the role of the police officer in this situation, counsel can become dramatically aware of physical restrictions on the witness's field of vision that may break the officer's testimony wide open on a motion to suppress. Of course, counsel should be sure that the scene has not undergone changes between the time of the critical events and that of counsel's visit. And reenactments should not be undertaken, if avoidable, in places where the public or the police can watch the replay.

[112] **Miscellaneous sources of information.** There are as many sources of information as there are different factual situations. Among the most useful to keep in mind are police reports, logs, and dockets; in a death case, the medical examiner's files or the coroner's transcript and report; newspaper files and photographs; United States Weather Bureau records; relevant records maintained by business concerns (such as time clock cards and invoices); and hospital, prison, and court records. In investigating a client's history, counsel should consider school records, juvenile court records, military service records, records of the client's employers, union records, social security and welfare department records, records of a personal or family physician, and records of hospital admissions. Counsel should also talk to clergy, schoolteachers, and social workers who have come in contact with the client's family and to the neighborhood political ward leader.

[113] **Locating witnesses.** Primary sources for names, addresses, and locations of witnesses include the prosecution, police, news media and their reporters, and the defendant. If these provide inadequate leads, counsel must resort to visiting the scene as quickly as possible and to contacting any person that might be remotely connected with the incident to inquire

who knows or saw anything relevant to the defense. This aspect of defense investigation is time-consuming and often frustrating. Its importance, however, cannot be overemphasized. Counsel should always ask any person interviewed whether other witnesses were present and then get the fullest possible description of them. When identification is by name, the spelling of the name *and* its phonetic spelling should be taken, if possible. Counsel should always ask whether the witness has any aliases or nicknames; where the witnesses lives or lived; where s/he works or worked; whether s/he was on relief and where s/he collected his or her welfare check, foodstamps, or any other regular source of income; whether s/he belonged to a union or frequented a hiring hall and, if so, which one; where s/he "hangs out" and with whom; whether s/he has a girlfriend or boyfriend, and where the friend lives; whether the witness plays the numbers and where; whether s/he has ever been in prison, been arrested, or been in the service. In trying to locate a witness when only the witness's name is known, checks should be made of the telephone directory, telephone company, electric and gas companies, voting registrars, tax assessors, traffic court, department of motor vehicles, credit card companies, credit-rating bureaus, hospital and department store billing records, probation and parole departments, Veteran's Administration, and the department of public welfare. If the neighborhood is known as well, counsel should also check the social work agencies, settlement houses, churches, finance companies, debt-collection agencies, employment agencies, labor union offices and hiring halls, political ward leaders, liquor stores, bars, and the precinct station. When counsel for a ghetto-resident defendant goes out on the street in the ghetto looking for witnesses, s/he should take a member of the defendant's family or a friend of the defendant along to introduce counsel as the defendant's lawyer. Otherwise, s/he will be thought to be "the law" and will find nothing and nobody.

[114] **Keeping track of witnesses.** Having located and interviewed the witnesses, counsel must make an initial determination of their usefulness. Information needed to retrieve

potentially important defense witnesses—their addresses, telephone numbers, places of employment, union memberships, and so forth—should be verified *independently* by counsel. Frequently, although witnesses may possess information helpful to the defendant, their appearance, background, or uncertainty of recollection militates against their being called to testify. Seldom, however, is it possible for counsel to know with certainty that in *no* future contingency will s/he need such a witness. Therefore, it is wise to keep tabs on every witness interviewed who knows anything about the case. Counsel should ask not only (a) the witness's current address and telephone number but also (b) any plans to move, and when and where and (c), in any event, the names, addresses, and telephone numbers of other persons through whom the witness can be contacted. If counsel's style and witness's mood lend themselves to this, it is often a wise idea to chat a little with the witness, so as to pick up unobtrusively some of the facts about his or her interests and activities listed in the preceding paragraph as potential leads in locating witnesses. People do move around; if and when a trial eventually is held, a witness may be needed on short notice; and the ability to reach the witness through various sources can alleviate some of the worst headaches of last-minute trial preparation.

[115] **Interviewing witnesses.** (A) Counsel must develop his or her own interviewing techniques to obtain cooperation and information. Witnesses frequently "don't want to get involved" because of the uncertainty of what they must do and the inconvenience to them. Counsel must overcome this reticence by an effective pitch of some sort. One argument that sometimes works is to stress the importance of the witness's giving information, since s/he is the only one who has it and the client's life or liberty is at stake. Counsel can also state that as a citizen the witness has a duty to tell what s/he knows and that if s/he were, unfortunately, placed in the predicament of counsel's client, s/he would expect others to come forward. If all else fails and counsel believes the witness has important information, counsel must subpoena the witness and hope that the witness will talk to counsel prior to trial. Of course, except

in an otherwise hopeless case, this should not be done if the prosecutor is unaware of the witness and if there is a substantial chance that the witness's story will be damning.

(B) The basic technique described in paragraph [83] *supra* is usually effective in taking a witness's story. Counsel should always ask every witness whether the witness has discussed the case with anyone else, with whom, and what was said. Particular care should be taken to have the witness describe in detail what s/he has told the police or any prosecution investigator to whom s/he has spoken. S/he should also be asked what the investigators said, including their specific questions. These may give counsel investigative leads and insight into the other side's theory of the case. Just as counsel must cross-examine his or her client when interviewing the client, so s/he must cross-examine other witnesses. This has several purposes: to find out the truth; to elicit details as an aid to counsel's further investigation; to evaluate the witness for the purpose of deciding whether to use the witness at trial; and to educate and prepare the witness for cross-examination by the prosecutor. The latter two purposes can generally be served at a subsequent interview (see paragraph [279] *infra*); therefore, unless the first purpose is compelling, counsel may be advised to forgo too vigorous cross-examination in an initial witness interview. Counsel stands to gain considerably by being in the witness's good graces, and it makes no sense to anger the witness unnecessarily by pressing the witness hard before favorable relations are established. If a witness finds it an uncomfortable or unpleasant experience to be interviewed by counsel, the witness will not be readily available for subsequent interviewing and may even shade his or her story so as to discourage counsel from calling him or her at trial. The approach to cross-examining one's client suggested in paragraph [89] *supra*—describing the questioning as a role play or dry run of the cross-examination that the prosecutor might conduct at a trial—is also a useful device for asking other potential defense witnesses the probing questions that are necessary to test the durability of their stories without implying that counsel personally has any doubts about their truthfulness. If cross-questioning shakes a witness (or may leave the witness feeling shaken) but counsel concludes that the witness's story is nevertheless sufficiently solid to be potentially usefully to the defense, counsel should follow up with some supportive questioning that will assist the witness to regain a warranted measure of confidence and should end by reassuring the witness that the witness is doing just fine. Never should counsel let a witness leave an interview feeling that his or her story has been demolished or disbelieved unless, in fact, counsel is convinced that the story is a fabrication. Minor inconsistencies and errors that counsel realizes are unimportant because they are perfectly natural and will not seriously impair the witness's credibility may nevertheless cause a legally unsophisticated witness to experience painful self-doubts. Unless those doubts are assuaged by some comfort from counsel at the end of the interview, the witness is likely to dwell on them following the interview and the witness's story is likely to become weaker, more hesitant, and more heavily qualified than it needs to be or should be.

[116] Special problems—prosecution witnesses; complainants; police. (A) Witnesses do not belong to one party to a litigation. Counsel has a right to interview any witness or prospective witness who may have information pertinent to the client's case. Canon 39 of the American Bar Association's Canons of Professional Ethics (which remains authoritative because of the omission of the subject from the Code of Professional Responsibility) makes the point entirely clear: "A lawyer may properly interview any witness or prospective witness for the opposing side in any civil or criminal action without the consent of opposing counsel or party." Many laypersons do not understand this, however, and witnesses (particularly complainants) who have given incriminating information to the police or prosecutor may *think* that they belong to the prosecution. Counsel should explain that this is not so; that the witness has as much obligation as a citizen to talk to defense counsel as to the prosecution; and that if the witness does not do so, the trial will be unfair. Of course, a witness has no *legal* obligation to talk to either the prosecution or the defense (*e.g.*, *United States v. White*, 454 F.2d 435, 438-39 (7th Cir. 1971)), and counsel must not suggest that s/he has. But the witness's *moral* obligations to tell what s/he knows to the defense, as well as to the police or prosecutor, should be stressed.

(B) If a prospective prosecution witness, the complainant, or a police officer continues to refuse to talk to counsel, counsel should ask whether the prosecutor (or a police officer) has told the witness not to talk to the defense. If the answer is yes or if counsel is not satisfied with the truth of a no answer, counsel should call the prosecutor and ask whether any instructions of this sort have been given to any witness. If they have, counsel should point out the caselaw and ethical proscriptions cited below and should ask that the prosecutor phone the witnesses immediately and tell them that they are free to talk to the defense. This should be done with defense counsel also on the phone, so that s/he can monitor what the prosecutor says and follow up immediately by arranging an appointment for an interview. Instructions by a prosecutor or by the police that witnesses should not talk to the defense (or that they should talk to the defense only with the prosecutor's consent or in the prosecutor's presence) are both unprofessional and unconstitutional. *See United States v. Carrigan*, 804 F.2d 599, 603 (10th Cir. 1986); *Gregory v. United States*, 369 F.2d 185 (D.C. Cir. 1966); *United States v. Enloe*, 15 U.S.C.M.A. 256, 35 C.M.R. 228 (1965); *United States v. Munsey*, 457 F. Supp. 1, 4-5 (E.D. Tenn. 1978); *Kines v. Butterworth*, 669 F.2d 6, 8-9 (1st Cir. 1981) (dictum), and cases cited; *State v. Simmons*, 57 Wis. 2d 285, 203 N.W.2d 887, 892-93 (1973) (dictum), and cases cited; AMERICAN BAR ASSOCIATION PROJECT ON STANDARDS FOR CRIMINAL JUSTICE, STANDARDS RELATING TO THE PROSECUTION FUNCTION 3.1(c) (1971); AMERICAN BAR ASSOCIATION, MODEL RULES OF PROFESSIONAL CONDUCT, Rule 3.4(f) (1983). Unless the prosecutor gives complete satisfaction, counsel should move the court of record having jurisdiction of the case for a rule on the prosecutor to show cause (a) why the charges against the client should not be dismissed with prejudice, on the ground that the prosecutor has unconstitutionally interfered with the preparation of the defense and that there is no way either of knowing how much harm has been done or of setting it right at this stage, or (b) why the court should not order a deposition of each witness with whom the prosecutor or any police officer has discussed the case, at which counsel can ask the witness the questions that s/he would have asked in an investigative interview if it had not been for the prosecutor's or officers' interference, *see United States v. Carrigan, supra,* or, at least (c) why all witnesses with whom the prosecutor or any police officer has discussed the case should not be brought before the court and instructed by the court that they are free to speak to the defense, *cf.* the procedure approved in *United States v. Mirenda,* 443 F.2d 1351, 1355 n.3, 1356 (9th Cir. 1971); *and see United States v. Vole,* 435 F.2d 774, 778 (7th Cir. 1970): "[W]itnesses are the special property of neither party and in the absence of compelling reasons, the . . . court should facilitate access to them before trial whenever it is requested."

(C) Arguing by analogy from *Curran v. Delaware,* 259 F.2d 707 (3d Cir. 1958), counsel may also want to try to get a judicial order compelling uncooperative police witnesses to tell counsel what they know (even when their unwillingness to talk to counsel is not the result of instructions from the prosecutor or a superior officer or of departmental policy forbidden by *Gregory, Enloe,* and *Munsey,* respectively), on the ground that police officers are not mere private witnesses but are state officials with criminal law enforcement duties and hence may no more instruct themselves than they may instruct one another to refuse information to the defense. *Cf. Coppolino v. Helpern,* 266 F.Supp. 930 (S.D.N.Y. 1967). Of course, counsel may decide that the trouble and friction involved in this procedure are not justified by its likely yield or that at least this course of action should be delayed until counsel sees whether the preliminary hearing (see paragraphs [124]-[147] *infra*) or more ordinary discovery procedures (see paragraphs [265]-[275] *infra*) reveal what counsel wants.

[117] Same—codefendants. Before questioning codefendants, counsel should ascertain whether they are represented by an attorney. If they are, courtesy dictates that each codefendant's lawyer be contacted for permission to interview the lawyer's client. An interview with a codefendant should explore thoroughly what information s/he has given to the authorities. If a codefendant admits guilt, counsel should determine whether the codefendant intends to testify for the prosecution and implicate the defendant. Whether or not the codefendant admits an intention to testify, counsel should take the codefendant's story in detail. A codefendant may turn state's evidence at any time; and his or her testimony is likely to be decisive at trial. If s/he denies guilt, counsel should ascertain what s/he knows about the crime and what his or her defense is. Counsel should ask the codefendant's lawyer the same questions. Trial tactics relating to severance and jury trial or waiver may hinge on answers to these inquiries. See paragraphs [260], [262], [264], [282], [317], [362] *infra*.

[118] **Same—defendant's family.** A client's family should be interviewed to enlist investigative support. Stress should be placed on the importance and difficulty of thorough investigation and the help that the client's family can render in this regard. Additionally, if a client is in custody, the family should be encouraged to visit the client in order to keep up his or her morale as s/he awaits trial. Counsel may also want to have the family make efforts to persuade the client's employer not to fire the client or, if the client has already lost that job as a result of arrest, to find the client a new job in anticipation of the time of sentencing when the defendant's prospective employment status will be a vital factor.

[119] **Taking statements from witnesses; arranging to be accompanied to interviews with adverse witnesses.** (A) Counsel should ordinarily reduce interviews to writing and have them dated and signed by the person interviewed. If the person is reluctant to sign, counsel should ask whether s/he would nevertheless be willing to look over counsel's notes and to correct any inaccuracies in counsel's recording of the witness's story. An unsigned record of an interview that the interviewee has corrected with his or her own hand is every bit as useful as a signed statement for most purposes; and even an unsigned and uncorrected written record that the interviewee has approved orally may be invaluable in assisting coun-

sel to collate information when preparing for trial (see paragraph [297] *infra*), in refreshing the witness's recollection during pretrial preparation (see paragraph [279] *infra*), and in impeaching the witness in court if that turns out to be necessary (see paragraphs [379], [382], [394], [409] *infra*). *Cf. Goldberg v. United States*, 425 U.S. 94, 105, 107-8 n.12, 110-11 & n.19 (1976). Since witnesses' statements may be discoverable by the prosecution under some circumstances (see paragraphs [274], [408-A] *infra*), they should be prepared with considerable care. If at the conclusion of an initial interview, counsel thinks that the witness's memory or phraseology might be improved by subsequent interviewing, it may be wise to defer taking a written statement until counsel has seen the witness a second or third time. But in this situation the follow-up interviews should be scheduled as soon as possible after the first because the persuasive value of a witness's statement decreases sharply with the passage of time following the events s/he is recalling and describing. Particularly in the case of a witness who has not yet been interviewed by the police or the prosecution but who may be so interviewed at any time, defense counsel is usually advised to take a written statement without delay. One important *caveat* should be considered, however, before reducing any witness's statement to writing. If local law or practice permits prosecutorial discovery of defense witnesses' written statements but protects counsel's own written notes of witnesses' oral statements from discovery under the "work product" doctrine or some similar principle (see paragraph [81] *supra*; paragraphs [273-A], [274] (C), [408-A] *infra*), counsel may prefer to take only the protected form of notes. See paragraphs [81], [110] *supra*; paragraph [274] (C) *infra*. Or when all defense witnesses' statements are theoretically unprotected against discovery by the prosecution but the only forms of discovery devices available reach written and not oral statements (for example, when motions for the production of documents are recognized but not depositions or interrogatories, see paragraphs [265], [274] *infra*), counsel who is sufficiently confident of a witness's faithfulness, capacity to remember, longevity, and persuasiveness—*and* who does not anticipate any undue trial delay—may decide that it is best to leave the witness's statement completely unrecorded.

(B) Whenever practical, counsel should arrange to conduct interviews with potentially adverse witnesses in the presence of another person who would make a good and convincing witness. This "shot-gun rider" serves two principal functions. First, s/he will be available to testify concerning what the adverse witness said out of court, should occasion arise for the defense to impeach that witness with a prior inconsistent statement. Second, the "shot-gun rider" can protect counsel against possible charges of berating, overbearing, or attempting to corrupt the witness.

[120] Giving consideration to psychiatric evaluation of the client. Fairly early in the course of defense investigation, counsel should give some thought to the possibility of having the client undergo a psychiatric evaluation. Such an evaluation should obviously be considered if the client is demonstrating symptoms of mental disorder so severe as to impede counsel's ability to communicate with the client or to relate to the client or if a history of mental illness suggests the availability of the defenses of lack of criminal responsibility or (when recognized) diminished capacity. But it is also a good idea to seek psychiatric aid in any serious case when the circumstances of the crime or the history, behavior, or appearance of the defendant suggests that s/he is having significant trouble in getting along in society in his or her present mental or emotional condition. Certainly, it does not follow from the fact that all criminal conduct is, in a sense, aberrant that this client, assuming s/he committed the criminal acts charged, is mentally unsound. But the client's history or the unusual circumstances of the crime (particularly in sex cases) may suggest that the client does have a psychiatric problem. If s/he does, counsel wants to know about it early, for several reasons. Although the problem may not be obvious, it may be serious enough to affect the client's capacity to stand trial. It may affect the reliance that counsel is willing to place on the client's judgment or on the truth of what the client says. It may support an early recommendation to the prosecutor that the case be treated medically rather than criminally: for example, by a voluntary civil commitment followed by a *nol pros*. It may suggest the possibility of a psychiatric defense on the issues of guilt or degree of the offense charged or the possibility of developing psychiatric material useful to the client at the sentencing stage. In any event, counsel will want to assist the client to get the medical help s/he needs, both for medical reasons and for the potential effect the help may have in the litigation. A client who begins some form of therapy program early in the case has the advantage of appearing before the sentencing judge— if the case goes to conviction—in the posture of a person on the road to voluntary reform and rehabilitation. An opinion from the psychiatrist working with the client that the client is not dangerous in society or that imprisonment would interrupt a productive course of outpatient therapy will be very important to the judge and may alone make the difference between a prison sentence and probation. Even if incarceration is indicated, the judge may be persuaded that a short county jail sentence, which will allow early resumption of the client's therapy program, is to be preferred over a term in the penitentiary.

[121] **Same.** There are generally two kinds of ways to have the client examined. One is to invoke the provisions of law authorizing a defendant's pretrial commitment to a state mental facility for evaluation or the appointment of psychiatric experts to examine the defendant on behalf of the court. See paragraph [180] *infra*. The other is for counsel to arrange a private examination. Since the cost of a private examination is prohibitive for most clients, this alternative, in turn, presents a choice whether to request the court to appoint a state-paid psychiatrist for the defense (see paragraphs [180]-[181], [298]-[301] *infra*) or to attempt to find a psychiatrist who will do the job free of cost on an informal basis. One problem with both a motion for pretrial commitment or examination and a request for state-paid psychiatric aid is that these actions alert the court and the prosecution to the psychiatric dimension of the case. This can be seriously harmful to the defense for a number of reasons that are described in paragraph [180] *infra*. In addition, under some circumstances at least, the motion for

commitment or examination will constitute a waiver of objections to admission into evidence of the results of the examination—a very risky business. *Compare Buchanan v. Kentucky*, 107 S. Ct. 2906 (1987), *with Estelle v. Smith*, 451 U.S. 454 (1981). Accordingly, at least in the case of a client who is not jailed pending trial and whose examination can therefore be arranged without alerting the prosecution, it is generally wise for counsel to investigate the resources available in the community for nonofficial examination. These include hospital clinics (which often offer individual or group therapy as well as evaluation at nominal or no cost), hospitals with psychiatric residencies, the county medical society, and social welfare agencies. Of course, counsel should not begin to make arrangements to have the client examined without the client's agreement. Unless the client is obviously incompetent, s/he should have the final say on whether s/he will be subjected to a psychiatric evaluation. Counsel can attempt to be persuasive, however, and may be most effective if s/he can get the client to understand that psychiatrists work with "sane" people as well as with "nuts," that they are very useful in helping "well" people with adjustment problems, and that many people who are not at all "sick" see psychiatrists.

[122] Choosing the psychiatrist. To oversimplify a complex subject, there are basically three kinds of psychiatrists: the so-called A-P (analytic-psychological) type, the so-called D-O (directive-organic) type, and the eclectic type. A-P's tend to predominate in private practice, D-O's in state and county institutions, and eclectics in teaching hospitals, research facilities, and private patient-care services. Younger doctors will probably be A-P's or eclectics, particularly if they are American-trained. A-P psychiatrists are generally flexible and relativistic; they do not conceive or describe mental and emotional conditions in clear-cut, either/or, sane/insane terms; they are less concerned with diagnostic labels than with explaining how a particular individual functions and why. They view the individual within the context of his or her overall life situation and complex of relationships with other people. They are attentive to degrees of "stress" and "anxiety," and—since most people are subject to a certain amount of stress and anxiety—A-P psychiatrists tend to talk about the behavior of most criminal clients in terms that suggest, if not pathology, at least the influence of factors other than calculated rationality and deliberate choice. A-P psychiatrists speak a language that counsel can grasp fairly readily and will be of considerable help in understanding the client—what the client's needs, vulnerabilities, problems, weaknesses, and strengths were at the time of the offense charged and are now. D-O psychiatrists are more categorical and dogmatic. They tend to treat mental disease like a classical physical illness: Either the client has the bug or s/he does not; and it is either this specific bug or that specific bug. D-O psychiatrists are apt not to want to describe an individual as "mentally ill" or "insane" unless s/he is psychotic (that is, grossly out of touch with reality); but if the symptoms of some classified psychosis are present, the D-O psychiatrist can sound very sure and be very convincing that the individual is "insane." In short, defense counsel asserting a psychiatric defense of nonresponsibility or other psychiatric position that depends on convincing a prosecutor, judge, or jury that the client has a "mental disease" will do better with an A-P expert witness if the client is unstable and disturbed and is generally having a rocky time adjusting to life; but, on the other hand, counsel will often do better with a D-O expert if the client has some sort of condition that is described among the "psychoses" in the American Psychiatric Association's DIAGNOSTIC AND STATISTICAL MANUAL OF MENTAL DISORDERS (3d ed. 1980) [DSM-III]. Eclectic psychiatrists are familiar with both the A-P and the D-O approaches and generally stand midway between them. These considerations would indicate that if an examination of the client is to be made during the early stages, generally an A-P or eclectic psychiatrist should be consulted first. These doctors will be more useful in giving counsel an idea of what the client is all about, whether the client has serious mental or emotional problems, and of what kinds. If, on this basis, it appears that the client is quite sick and that the client's form of sickness is one of the classically recognized ones (A-P or eclectic psychiatrists can tell counsel this, although they may debunk the classification scheme), then counsel can bring in a D-O psychiatrist. Apart from this distinction between types of psychiatrists, counsel would do well to check, if possible, (1) the area of specialization (that is, work with particular kinds of illnesses or patients), (2) the impressiveness of credentials (that is, Board certification, senior staff position, recognition as a researcher), (3) the degree of forensic experience, and (4) the reputation, if any, among local criminal lawyers and judges of the particular psychiatrist that counsel is thinking of consulting. The psychiatrist's past demonstrated attitude in dealing with criminal defendants is particularly important to ascertain. Many psychiatrists are sympathetic to criminal defendants (or to some sorts of criminal defendants), whereas others can be quite hostile. Some psychiatrists are indeed notorious for writing flamboyant reports on defendants of the "here-is-our-next-mass-killer" kind. The effect of such a report, should it be read by a sentencing judge, is evident.

VIII. SUMMARY OF THINGS TO DO BEFORE FIRST COURT APPEARANCE

[123] Checklist of things to do for an arrested client between the times of arrest and the client's first court appearance.

I.   *Locate client.* [Paragraphs [31]-[34] *supra*]

II.   *Telephone precinct or place of detention.*[Paragraphs [25], [35]-[37] *supra*]

A. Ask charges and amount of bail from desk officer and investigating officer.

B. Tell investigating officer not to question client until counsel arrives, not to request consents or waivers from client, and not to exhibit client for identification or to make any examinations or tests on client in counsel's absence.

C. Speak to client, tell client that counsel is coming to see client immediately, and advise client:

1. To speak to no one about the case;

2. To decline to answer any questions by police or to give consents or waivers to police, on advice of counsel;

3. Not to write or sign any papers or forms;

4. To decline to consent to any lineups, identifications, examinations, or tests in counsel's absence;

5. Not to offer physical resistance if placed in a lineup or subjected to any examinations or tests, but to remember the circumstances of all lineups, identifications, examinations, and tests in counsel's absence, and to write out a description of them for counsel as soon as they are over;

6. Not to dodge news photographers or cover face.

D. Have client inform a police officer, with counsel listening on the phone, that client wishes all future dealings and communications with the authorities to be conducted solely through counsel.

III. *Telephone family or bondsman or both and arrange to have bail money or bond or both brought to place of detention.* [Paragraphs [25], [38]-[40], [62]-[64] *supra*]

IV.   *Review elements of charge and penalty.* [Paragraphs [51], [78] *supra*]

V.   *With proper identification, immediately go to place of detention.*
   A. Interview client. [Paragraphs [37-A], [50]-[51],[76]-[90] *supra*]
      1. Establish rapport [Paragraphs [76]-[77],[79]-[80] *supra*]
      2. Obtain biographical sketch. [Paragraph [90] *supra*]
      3. Obtain defendant's version of events leading to and following arrest. [Paragraphs [51], [83]-[84], [90] *supra*]
      4. Obtain names of all witnesses. [Paragraphs [108], [113] *supra*]
      5. Obtain statement or affidavit relating to bail factors if needed. [Paragraph [60] *supra*]
      6. Establish roles of lawyer and client. [Paragraph [85-A] *supra*]
      7. Set fee and state clearly what it covers. [Paragraph [86] *supra*]
      8. Repeat warnings and advice relating to conduct in custody and in response to police investigative procedures, and have client tell a police officer, in counsel's presence, that all subsequent communications between the client and the authorities are to be conducted through counsel [Paragraphs [37-A], [51], [87] *supra*]
      9. Offer to talk to family. [Paragraph [88] *supra*]
   B. Speak to investigating officer.
      1. Verify charges. [Paragraphs [67], [95] *supra*]
      2. Ask police version of the offense and arrest. [Paragraphs [60], [91]-[92], [95], [108] *supra*]
      3. Obtain names of all witnesses. [Paragraphs [108], [113] *supra*]
      4. Repeat requests not to question client, exhibit or examine client in counsel's absence, and so forth. [Paragraphs [25], [35]-[37-A], [97] *supra*]
      5. Ask whether there are any plans to move client elsewhere, exhibit client, and so forth. [Paragraphs [67], [97] *supra*]
      6. Ask how counsel can contact officer again. [Paragraphs [67], [95] *supra*]

C. Accompany and represent client at any identification confrontations or testing procedures. [Paragraph [37-A] *supra*]

VI.   *Complete any arrangements necessary to secure client's release on bail or recognizance, including resort to court, if necessary.* [Paragraphs [38]-[41], [54]-[72] *supra*]

VII.   *Begin field investigation.*

A. Locate objects and witnesses that may be lost if search is delayed. [Paragraphs [108], [113] *supra*]

B. Retain investigator or photographer, if desired. [Paragraph [110] *supra*]

C. Interview:

1. Police. [Paragraphs [91]-[92], [95], [102], [116] *supra*]
2. Prosecutor. [Paragraphs [93]-[94], [103] *supra*]
3. Complainant. [Paragraphs [104], [116], [119] *supra*]
4. Witnesses. [Paragraphs [113]-[115], [119] *supra*]
5. Codefendants. [Paragraph [117] *supra*]
6. Client's family. [Paragraph [118] *supra*]

D. Visit site. [Paragraph [111] *supra*]

E. Consider sources of information, such as newspapers and records. [Paragraph [112] *supra*]

F. Consider psychiatric examination of client. [Paragraphs [120]-[122] *supra*]

VIII.   *Maintain contacts with police and prosecutor, looking to dropping or reducing of charges.* [Paragraphs [98]-[105] *supra*]

[123-A] A note on the coroner's inquest and similar institutions. In many jurisdictions a coroner or a coroner's jury or a medical examiner or an examining magistrate is required to investigate all cases of possible homicidal death to determine whether a criminal homicide has been committed. The statutes governing these investigations vary widely. They may or may not require a formal hearing as a part of the investigation, and they may or may not require a finding of homicidal death as the precondition of filing of a complaint (or an indictment or information) charging a particular person with the offense of homicide. Whether or not it is a statutory prerequisite to a homicide prosecution, this sort of investigation will have important implications for the course of an ensuing prosecution because (a) it memorializes, often in the form of sworn testimony, both medical and nonmedical evidence bearing on the cause and circumstances of death that may be favorable to the defense; (b) it constitutes a source of discovery by defense counsel of similar evidence that may be favorable to the prosecution (see paragraphs [266], [299] *infra*); (c) it commits witnesses to their stories in a fashion that may shape or explain their later trial testimony and in a form that can be used for impeachment at trial (see paragraphs [379], [382], [394] *infra*); and (d) it frequently generates pretrial publicity that may be helpful or harmful to the defense. The same consequences may attach to fire marshal's investigations in arson cases, when these are authorized by statute in a particular jurisdiction. They may also attach to legislative committee hearings or administrative "crime commission" investigations, as these are conducted in a number of states for the purpose of uncovering criminal activity and referring it to the prosecuting authorities. Since, theoretically, none of these proceedings is directed against specific individuals, the statutes and resolutions authorizing them ordinarily make no allowance for any sort of participation by defense attorneys. However, when the proceedings are, in fact, aimed at particular persons or when they necessarily implicate identifiable persons (as in a homicide case in which the identity of the killer is clear and undisputed and the only question is whether the killing was justifiable), the federal Constitution may give these persons a right to appear by counsel, to cross-examine witnesses, and to present defensive evidence. The Supreme Court held in *Jenkins v. McKeithen*, 395 U.S. 411 (1969), that persons under investigation by one form of "crime commission" were entitled to these rights; and the logic of the *Jenkins* opinion appears to extend not only to most of the other common forms of "crime commissions" and legislative crime-investigating committees but also to the older and more pervasive institutions of the coroner (or equivalent) and the fire marshal. *But see Securities and Exchange Commission v. Jerry T. O'Brien, Inc.*, 467 U.S. 735 (1984).

IX. PRELIMINARY HEARING

[124] **The preliminary hearing.** The first judicial appearance of the defendant is called the preliminary hearing (or, in some states, the commitment hearing or the examining trial). This is the proceeding described in paragraphs [13] - [15], [19] *supra*. A magistrate (or a justice of the peace, municipal court judge, or other member of the minor judiciary) usually presides, although in most jurisdictions judges of courts of record also have statutory authority to sit as committing magistrates (see paragraph [134] *infra*). Arrested defendants are brought before the magistrate for a preliminary hearing shortly after arrest. See paragraphs [125] (C), [126] (B), [127] *infra*. Summoned defendants are required by the summons to appear before the magistrate.

[125] **Formal functions of the preliminary hearing.** (A) The traditional function of the preliminary hearing is to provide an early postarrest safeguard against improvident detention. The magistrate hears the prosecution's evidence against an arrested person (or as much of it as the prosecution chooses to present at this stage) for the purpose of determining whether that person should be released from custody or whether s/he should be "bound over" or "held over" or "committed"—that is to say, incarcerated or required to post bail for his or her appearance—pending subsequent stages of a criminal prosecution. The standard used for this determination is "probable cause" (see paragraph [241] *infra*) or, in some states, a *prima facie* case (see paragraph [154] *infra*). If the prosecution's evidence establishes probable cause to believe that an offense was committed and that the arrested person committed it, the arrestee is bound over to await the filing of an information in the criminal court of record (see paragraph [16] *supra*) or to await the action of the grand jury upon a bill or bills of indictment (see paragraphs [20]-[21] *supra*; paragraphs [153]-[155] *infra*). If the magistrate fails to find probable cause, the arrestee is discharged from custody.

S/he may nevertheless be indicted (or, in some jurisdictions, prosecuted by information) and required to stand trial; but if s/he has been discharged by the magistrate at the preliminary hearing, s/he remains at liberty throughout the trial (unless either (1) s/he is rearrested, given a second preliminary hearing, and bound over (see paragraph [147] *infra*) or (2) s/he is indicted and thereafter arrested and committed on a bench warrant supported by the indictment (see paragraph [21] *supra*; paragraph [167] *infra*)).

(B) In many jurisdictions the preliminary hearing today has a second function: to weed out and foreclose prosecutions on groundless charges, so as to spare the accused the expense and degradation of a full-scale criminal trial. In these jurisdictions the prosecutor may not file an information (or may file an information only with leave of court) against a defendant who has not been bound over at a preliminary hearing. Some of the jurisdictions, in addition, limit the offenses that may be charged in an information to those specific charges upon which the magistrate bound the defendant over. Other jurisdictions permit an information to charge any offense (or at least any offense "related" to the charges upon which the defendant was bound over) that is supported by probable cause appearing in the transcript of the evidence presented at the preliminary hearing, whether or not the magistrate bound the defendant over upon those specific charges. See paragraph [16] *supra*. These various restrictions upon prosecutions by information assign to the preliminary hearing a pretrial screening function that is complementary to the grand jury's (see paragraph [154] *infra*): A defendant may be charged in a criminal court only after the prosecutor has first made a showing of probable cause (or a *prima facie* case) either at preliminary hearing or before the grand jury.

(C) In addition to the two functions just described, the preliminary hearing has gradually accreted others that have received formal or theoretical recognition in varying degrees. Obviously, any procedure requiring the production of arrested individuals before a magistrate or judge shortly following arrest potentially protects citizens against police mistreatment and assures the early implementation of several procedural rights given to accused persons by the federal and state constitutions and laws. A postarrest judicial proceeding will realize this potential insofar as (1) a notation is made in court records that an arrested person is in custody and where s/he is in custody, thereby preventing secret imprisonments and enabling the arrestee's friends or attorney to locate the arrestee and to secure his or her release by *habeas corpus* if the confinement is unlawful (see paragraphs [38], [67], [71], [97] *supra*); (2) the police are required to justify the arrest by showing probable cause (see paragraphs [236] (C), [241] *infra*); (3) the arrested person is informed of his or her rights, principally the privilege against self-incrimination (see paragraphs [161] (C), (E), [232], [363] (E), [367-A] *infra*), the right to bail (see paragraphs [54]-[75-A] *supra*), the right to an attorney (see paragraphs [130], [233], [270] (A) *infra*), and the right to a preliminary examination (see subparagraphs (A), (B) *supra*; paragraphs [127]-[128] *infra*); (4) some of those rights are immediately implemented, for example, through the setting of bail and the appointment of counsel by the magistrate; and (5) custody of the accused is transferred from the arresting and investigating officers to other authorities—jailers responsible to the court for the arrested person's safekeeping and not charged with prosecutive duties. Increasingly, these various protective steps have been recognized as components of the preliminary hearing and as rights of the accused. Most of them, though not all, are now given by statute, judicial decision, or practice in the large majority of jurisdictions. To assure their timely effectuation, almost every jurisdiction now requires by statute or court rule that an arrested person be brought before a judicial officer "promptly" or "forthwith" or "without unnecessary delay" following arrest.

[126] The trend toward bifurcation of the preliminary hearing. (A) With the emergence of these additional functions, the preliminary hearing has tended to evolve from a single proceeding into two distinct procedural stages: the preliminary arraignment (sometimes called the preliminary appearance) and the preliminary examination (often nicknamed the PX or the "prelim"). As long as the hearing was concerned almost exclusively with the justifiability of pretrial detention, the important thing was the examination by the magistrate of the evidence against the arrestee. To the extent that a preliminary arraignment of any sort was held, it was either (as at common law) an inquisition of the prisoner (that is, a part of the taking of the evidence) or else a mere reading of the charges against the prisoner as a prelude to taking evidence. But as various procedural rights came to be afforded to an accused, the preliminary arraignment began to assume an independent significance: It became the stage of the proceedings at which the accused was informed of those rights and afforded an opportunity to exercise them. And once the right to counsel at the preliminary examination was given (see paragraph [130] *infra*), a strong pressure was generated to split the originally unitary preliminary hearing into two separate court appearances. The defendant seldom had a lawyer when s/he first appeared in court; it was necessary either to adjourn the hearing for appointment or retainer of counsel or else to appoint counsel at the preliminary arraignment itself. Particularly when the preliminary examination had become increasingly important by reason of the addition of the screening function described in paragraph [125] (B) *supra*, lawyers appointed at the preliminary arraignment began more frequently to seek continuances of the examination in order to obtain time to prepare for it.

(B) This development has proceeded at differing speeds and produced different practices in various localities. In some courts it is still customary to hold a single preliminary hearing shortly following arrest, at which (1) a complaint is filed against the defendant and is given or read to the defendant; (2) s/he is advised of his or her rights (the privilege against self-incrimination, the right to counsel, the right to bail, if any, and the right to have a preliminary examination at which the prosecution will have to show probable cause or a *prima facie* case to justify the defendant's detention); (3) counsel is appointed to represent the defendant (or if s/he has sufficient funds to retain counsel, s/he is given a brief recess for that purpose); (4) s/he is asked either to plead to the complaint or to elect or waive preliminary examination; and (5) unless s/he pleads guilty or waives examination or asks for a continuance of the examination, the court proceeds immediately to hear the prosecution's evidence. When the defense does seek a continuance of the preliminary examination, some of these courts may set it for a date several days or weeks later; others may adjourn for only an hour or two, with the admonition to counsel to "take a couple of hours to talk to your client and get prepared, if you want, but the prosecution has its witnesses here and we are going to proceed with the preliminary hearing today." At the other end of the spectrum, there are now many localities that maintain entirely separate preliminary-arraignment and preliminary-hearing calendars. The arraignment, comprising steps (1) through (4) *supra* and the setting of bail (see paragraph [62] *supra*), is held soon after arrest, but the prosecution is not then expected to have its witnesses in court. The examination (unless the defendant waives examination) is set (either by the magistrate at the preliminary arraignment or routinely by an administrative judge or calendar clerk) for a date a week or two following the preliminary arraignment.

[127] **The federal constitutional rights to a prompt post-arrest determination of probable cause and to a prompt preliminary appearance.** (A) In *Gerstein v. Pugh*, 420 U.S. 103 (1975), the Supreme Court of the United States held that the Fourth Amendment to the federal Constitution (see paragraphs [229]-[231] *infra*), which has long been construed as forbidding arrests without probable cause (see paragraph [236] (C) *infra*), entitles every arrested person to "a judicial determination of probable cause as a prerequisite to extended restraint of liberty following arrest." 420 U.S. at 114. Consequently, persons arrested without an arrest warrant (and hence without a prearrest judicial finding of probable cause) may not be confined pending trial unless they are given the opportunity for a probable cause determination "by a judicial officer . . . promptly after arrest." *Id.* at 125. *Accord, Baker v. McCollan*, 443 U.S. 137, 142-43 (1979) (dictum). *Gerstein* is a very narrow decision in several regards. First, it fails, by its terms, to protect persons arrested under arrest warrants (*see Michigan v. Doran*, 439 U.S. 282, 285 n.3 (1978)) and may also be inapplicable to persons indicted by a grand jury (see par-

agraphs [20]-[21] *supra*; paragraphs [129]-[131] *infra*). *Gerstein v. Pugh*, *supra*, 420 U.S. at 117 n.19. (*But see In re Walters*, 15 Cal. 3d 738, 543 P.2d 607, 126 Cal. Rptr. 239 (1975), extending *Gerstein* to require a postarrest probable cause determination in cases of arrests made under a warrant.) Second, *Gerstein* does not say *how* "promptly" after arrest the constitutional probable cause determination must be afforded. There is language in the opinion (clearly echoing that in *Mallory v. United States*, subparagraph (C) *infra*) which can be construed to mean that only "a brief period of detention to take the administrative steps incident to arrest" will be tolerated before the probable cause determination must be made, 420 U.S. at 114, but the Court does not appear to be taking this language very seriously, *see Schall v. Martin*, 467 U.S. 253, 274-77 & n.28 (1984). Third, *Gerstein* does not speak to the question whether the timetable can be enlarged for various reasons of prosecutorial convenience or necessity—for example, the unavailability of witnesses—although it does contain a footnote that may be cited in opposition to any such enlargements on the ground that the police are required to have probable cause *before* they make an arrest and can, therefore, properly be obliged to demonstrate probable cause without any delay following the arrest. *Id.* at 120 n.21. Fourth, *Gerstein* does not require that the probable cause determination be "accompanied by the full panoply of adversary safeguards—counsel, confrontation, cross-examination, and compulsory process for witnesses." *Id.* at 119. To the contrary, it sanctions "[t]he use of an informal procedure," *id.* at 121, in which there is no constitutional right to the appointment of counsel, *id.* at 122-23, no "confrontation and cross-examination" need be allowed, *id.* at 121-22, and the determination of probable cause may presumably be made "on hearsay and written testimony," *id.* at 120. All that is constitutionally required is "a fair and reliable determination of probable cause." *Id.* at 125; *see also Baker v. McCollan*, *supra*, 443 U.S. at 143 & n.2; *Hewitt v. Helms*, 459 U.S. 460, 475 (1983). Finally, failure to give an accused a prompt probable cause determination does not foreclose subsequent prosecution or provide grounds for its dismissal; it merely renders the accused's pretrial confinement unconstitutional. *Gerstein v. Pugh, supra*, 420 U.S. at 119; *see Bell v. Wolfish*, 441 U.S. 520, 534 n.15 (1979).

(B) Notwithstanding all of these limitations—which cumulatively render *Gerstein's* "probable cause determination" a pale shadow of the preliminary examination already allowed by state law in most jurisdictions—*Gerstein* does have significant implications for state preliminary examination practice. Most states had traditionally provided no other forum than preliminary examination for the making of a postarrest probable cause determination, and they responded to *Gerstein* by relying on their traditional preliminary examination procedures to satisfy the requirements of that decision. In the absence of alternative procedures for a prompt probable cause determination, an "acceleration of existing preliminary hearings [that is, examinations]" may be required, 420 U.S. at 124; and undue delay of the preliminary examination in any particular case is subject to federal constitutional challenge. The filing or the threat of a federal *habeas corpus* petition (see paragraph [71] *supra*] seeking an accused's release on the ground that s/he has not been given a timely probable cause determination under *Gerstein* will therefore probably stir the prosecutor into listing the matter for preliminary examination without further delay.

(C) Violations of the *Gerstein* requirement may also entail evidentiary consequences. Explaining them requires a description of the history and the current somewhat muddy status of the so-called *McNabb-Mallory* rule. In *McNabb v. United States*, 318 U.S. 332 (1943), the Supreme Court enforced a federal prompt-appearance statute (of the sort mentioned in paragraph [125] (C) *supra*) by an exclusionary rule forbidding the admission into evidence, in federal criminal trials, of confessions obtained from arrested persons during a period of unlawful delay in bringing them before a judicial officer. By the time of *Mallory v. United States*, 354 U.S. 449 (1957), the statute had been superseded by FED. R. CRIM. P. 5(a), requiring arrestees to be produced before a magistrate "without unnecessary delay"; and the lower federal courts had largely eviscerated *McNabb* by holding (1) that postarrest delays to permit the completion of police investigation (including interrogation of the arrestee) were not "unnecessary" and (2) that even unnecessary delay did not require the exclusion of an arrestee's confession unless the delay *caused* the confession—a principle effectively limiting *McNabb*'s exclusionary rule to confessions which would have been inadmissible as involuntary regardless of *McNabb* (see paragraph [363] (C) *infra*). *Mallory* firmly rejected both of these doctrines. It held that postarrest delay for investigative purposes was *per se* unnecessary under Rule 5(a) because "[p]resumably, whomever the police arrest they must arrest on 'probable cause.' It is not the function of the police to arrest . . . at large and to use an interrogating process at police headquarters in order to determine whom they should charge before a committing magistrate on 'probable cause.'" 354 U.S. at 456 (quoted with approval in *Gerstein v. Pugh*, subparagraph (A) *supra*, 420 U.S. at 120 n.21). And confessions obtained following unnecessary delay in the production of an arrestee before a magistrate were also excludable *per se*, not because (or only when) they were involuntary but because their exclusion was required in order to compel obedience to the command of Rule 5(a). This prophylactic character of the *McNabb-Mallory* exclusionary sanction was both its greatest strength and its greatest possible weakness. For, as an exercise of the Supreme Court's supervisory authority over the lower federal courts, it had (as yet) no constitutional stature; and Congress undertook to abrogate it by enacting section 701 of the Omnibus Crime Control and Safe Streets Act of 1968, Pub. L. No. 90-351, 82 Stat. 210, codified at 18 U.S.C. §3501. Subsection (a) of this poorly drafted statute provides that confessions shall be admissible in federal criminal cases if they are "voluntarily given." Subsection (b) provides that, in determining the voluntariness of a confession, the trial judge shall consider, *inter alia*, certain enumerated circumstances, including "the time elapsing between arrest and [preliminary] arraignment of the defendant making the confession, if it was made after arrest and before arraignment," but that "[t]he presence or absence of any of the above-mentioned factors to be taken into consideration by the judge need not be conclusive on the issue of voluntariness. . . ." Subsection (c) provides that a confession made by a person while s/he is

> under arrest or other detention in the custody of any law-enforcement officer . . . shall not be inadmissible solely because of delay in bringing such person before a commissioner [for preliminary arraignment] . . . if such confession is found by the trial judge to have been made voluntarily . . . and if such confession was made or given by such person within six hours immediately following his arrest or other detention: *Provided,* That the time limitation contained in this subsection shall not apply in any case in which the delay in bringing such person before such commissioner . . . beyond such six-hour period is found by the trial judge to be reasonable considering the means of transportation and the distance to be traveled to the nearest available such commissioner. . . .

Thus, although subsections (a) and (b) appear to overrule *McNabb-Mallory* altogether, subsection (c) appears to preserve the exclusionary rule of those cases in instances of prearraignment delays exceeding six hours and not justified by transportation problems. From the defensive viewpoint the argument that *McNabb-Mallory* continues to require the exclusion of confessions obtained during unwarranted delays of more than six hours in arraignment seems solidly based upon the proposition that subsection (c) is immediately and solely directed at the *McNabb-Mallory* rule and hence prevails over the more general provisions of subsections (a) and (b). In any event, even under subsections (a) and (b), unnecessary prearraignment delay is a factor to be taken into account as affecting the voluntariness of a confession; and the trial judge apparently *may* give that factor conclusive effect, although s/he "need not." This is consistent with the Supreme Court's decisions applying the constitutional requirement of voluntariness to exclude confessions in state criminal cases (see paragraphs [228], [363] (C) *infra*): Those cases, although declining to impose the *McNabb-Mallory* rule as a Due Process command upon the states, have consistently considered prearraignment delay as *a* factor tending to show involuntariness. *See Culombe v. Connecticut,* 367 U.S. 568, 601-2 (1961) (plurality opinion of Justice Frankfurter); *Haynes v. Washington,* 373 U.S. 503,

513-15 (1963); *Davis v. North Carolina*, 384 U.S. 737, 742-53 (1966); *Clewis v. Texas*, 386 U.S. 707, 711 (1967).

(D) Arguably, *Gerstein* now provides a constitutional basis for the *McNabb-Mallory* rule or something very close to it. As noted in subparagraph (B) *supra*, most jurisdictions (including the federal courts) rely exclusively upon preliminary examinations to provide the postarrest probable cause determination that *Gerstein* demands; the failure to give an accused a preliminary examination "promptly after arrest" therefore renders his or her continued detention federally unconstitutional, 420 U.S. at 125; *see also id.* at 114, 119, 126; and any evidence that is "'come at by exploitation'" of a federally unconstitutional detention is required constitutionally to be excluded, *Wong Sun v. United States*, 371 U.S. 471, 488 (1963); *Brown v. Illinois*, 422 U.S. 590, 597-605 (1975); *Dunaway v. New York*, 442 U.S. 200, 216-19 (1979); *Taylor v. Alabama*, 457 U.S. 687, 689-90 (1982); *Lanier v. South Carolina*, 106 S. Ct. 297 (1985) (per curiam); *cf. Rawlings v. Kentucky*, 448 U.S. 98, 106-10 (1980) (dictum), just as other unconstitutionally obtained evidence must be excluded (see paragraphs [223]-[233], [236] (A), [237] (B), [251] *infra*). The conclusions follow that, in the preponderantly common situation of the defendant who is arrested without a warrant, (1) the 1968 congressional attempt to overrule *McNabb-Mallory* is unconstitutional, *cf. United States v. Brignoni-Ponce*, 422 U.S. 873, 878 (1975); (2) the *McNabb-Mallory* rule continues to govern federal criminal trials, *cf. Gerstein v. Pugh*, subparagraph (A) *supra*, 420 U.S. at 123 n.24; and (3) a similar constitutional rule governs state criminal trials, *cf. id.* at 120 n.21.

(E) However, as subparagraph (A) *supra* also indicates, *Gerstein* does not reach persons who are arrested on a warrant; it may not reach persons who have been indicted, *cf.* paragraph [130] *infra*); and in states that so provide, its requirements could conceivably be satisfied by the postarrest determination of probable cause in an *ex parte* proceeding that does not even involve the defendant's appearance in court. (*But see In re Walters*, subparagraph (A) *supra*.) These loopholes in *Gerstein* necessitate consideration of the question whether, apart from that decision, the Supreme Court's refusal to constitutionalize the *McNabb-Mallory* rule (*see, e.g., Stein v. New York*, 346 U.S. 156, 187-88 (1953)) is still good law. Strong grounds exist to contend that it is not and that the federal Constitution does now require every defendant's personal appearance in court, promptly after arrest with or without a warrant, for the purpose of preliminary arraignment proceedings which afford the defendant the protections described in paragraph [125](C) *supra*. A detailed argument to this effect is presented in Broeder, *Wong Sun v. United States: A Study in Faith and Hope*, 42 NEB. L. REV. 483, 564-94 (1963). Another route to the same conclusion proceeds as follows: (1) The Supreme Court last considered the question of the constitutional status of the *McNabb-Mallory* rule in 1961. A dictum in a plurality opinion of that year reaffirmed several earlier decisions that had declined to adopt a *per se* rule requiring the exclusion from evidence, in state criminal cases, of confessions obtained during periods of protracted delay between arrest and preliminary arraignment. *Culombe v. Connecticut*, subparagraph (C) *supra*, 367 U.S. at 598-601. (2) These decisions, however, did not imply that there was no federal constitutional right to a prompt postarrest judicial appearance. That issue could hardly have been considered prior to 1961 because, at that time, the Supreme Court was committed to the view that evidence was not required to be excluded from state criminal trials even if it *was* obtained in violation of the federal Constitution. *See, e.g., Wolf v. Colorado*, 338 U.S. 25 (1949); *Lisenba v. California*, 314 U.S. 219 (1941). It was only in *Mapp v. Ohio*, 367 U.S. 643 (1961), that the Court first adopted the principle, which has since become pervasive, of enforcing federal law by exclusionary rules that are binding upon the state courts. *See, e.g., Escobedo v. Illinois*, 378 U.S. 478 (1964); *Miranda v. Arizona*, 384 U.S. 436 (1966); *Gilbert v. California*, 388 U.S. 263 (1967); *Lee v. Florida*, 392 U.S. 378 (1968); *Brown v. Illinois*, subparagraph (D) *supra*; *Smith v. Illinois*, 469 U.S. 91 (1984) (per curiam). (3) It was also in 1961 that the Supreme Court began the process of "incorporating" the criminal-procedure guarantees of the Bill of Rights into the Due Process Clause of the Fourteenth Amendment. See paragraphs [57-A] (B) *supra*; paragraph [227] *infra*. That process now secures to state criminal defendants the Fifth

Amendment privilege against self-incrimination, *Malloy v. Hogan*, 378 U.S. 1 (1964); *Miranda v. Arizona, supra,* the Sixth Amendment right to counsel, *Gideon v. Wainwright,* 372 U.S. 335 (1963); *Michigan v. Jackson,* 106 S. Ct. 1404, 1407-8 (1986), and the Eighth Amendment right to bail, see paragraphs [57-A], [61] *supra.* As paragraph [125] (C) *supra* indicates, all of these rights—together with the privilege of the writ of *habeas corpus* (U.S. CONST. art. I, §9, cl. 2; *see Smith v. Bennett,* 365 U.S. 708, 712-13 (1961); *Jones v. Cunningham,* 371 U.S. 236, 238 (1963); *Fay v. Noia,* 372 U.S. 391, 405-6 (1963))—depend upon a timely preliminary arraignment for their implementation. Put another way, federal constitutional rights are so deeply implicated in the protective functions which the preliminary arraignment has come to serve in contemporary criminal procecure that the prompt conduct of the arraignment itself is now a constitutional necessity. *Cf. Michigan v. Jackson, supra.* In "the context of the criminal processes maintained by the American States" (*Duncan v. Louisiana,* 391 U.S. 145, 150 n.14 (1968))—the "actual systems" of state criminal procedure (*id.* at 149 n.14) that require reliance upon the preliminary arraignment to safeguard federal constitutional rights (*cf. Miranda v. Arizona, supra,* 384 U.S. at 467-79)—a prompt postarrest judicial appearance for preliminary arraignment is a "protective device" (*id.* at 465) that is constitutionally needed and, therefore, demanded. *Cf. North Carolina v. Pearce,* 395 U.S. 711, 725-26 (1969). It "provides 'practical reinforcement' for the . . . [underlying constitutional] right[s]," *New York v. Quarles,* 467 U.S. 649, 654 (1984).

[128] **The state law right to a full preliminary examination.** Neither *Gerstein v. Pugh,* 420 U.S. 103 (1975), nor the argument made in paragraph [127](E) *supra* supports a federal constitutional right to a full-scale adversary preliminary examination. (*Compare* Amsterdam, *Perspectives on the Fourth Amendment,* 58 MINN. L. REV. 349, 390-92 (1974).) Rather, by a 5-4 vote, *Gerstein* holds that there is no such constitutional right. 420 U.S. at 119-25. *See also Baker v. McCollan,* 443 U.S. 137, 143 & n.2 (1979); *Schall v. Martin,* 467 U.S. 253, 274-77 (1984). Most states do secure the right by statute, however, and some

state court decisions enforce it by the strong remedy of reversing an otherwise valid conviction for no reason except that an adequate preliminary examination was denied. *E.g.*, *Manor v. State*, 221 Ga. 866, 148 S.E.2d 305 (1966); *Mascarenas v. State*, 80 N.M. 537, 458 P.2d 789 (1969).

[129] **Devices by which the right is defeated.** There are two classic devices by which magistrates and prosecutors have long defeated the state law right to preliminary examination. One is for the magistrate to accept a waiver of the examination from an uncounseled defendant. The other is for the prosecutor to request, and the magistrate to grant, a continuance of the examination, and then for the prosecutor to obtain a supervening indictment the effect of which is to deprive the defendant of any right to a further hearing. As noted in paragraph [21] *supra*, since the return of the indictment is alone sufficient to sustain the defendant's detention, it has traditionally been thought that indictment renders the preliminary examination unnecessary. Indeed, in federal criminal cases, a statute enacted in 1968 (now 18 U.S.C. §3060(e)) explicitly provides that "[n]o preliminary examination . . . shall be required to be accorded an arrested person . . . if at any time subsequent to the initial appearance of such person [at preliminary arrignment] . . . and prior to the date fixed for the preliminary examination . . ., an indictment is returned or . . . an information is filed. . . ." (*See also* FED. R. CRIM. P. 5(c).) *Gerstein v. Pugh*, 420 U.S. 103, 116-19 (1975), plainly renders the "information" provision of this statute invalid insofar as preliminary examination remains the exclusive method for providing a postarrest probable cause determination in federal prosecutions of defendants arrested without warrants; but, as noted in paragraph [127](A) *supra*, the *Gerstein* decision leaves the question of the effect of a supervening indictment unsettled.

[130] **Attacks on the devices.** The first device—securing waiver from an uncounseled defendant—is assailable if the defendant has a right to counsel at preliminary arraignment. S/he is given that right by statute in some jurisdictions (and

by FED. R. CRIM. P. 5(c) in federal prosecutions). In theory, the question whether s/he also has a federal constitutional right to counsel depends upon whether, in the light of local law and practice, the preliminary arraignment is a "critical stage" in the proceeding—one at which a defendant may be prejudiced by the absence of counsel. *Hamilton v. Alabama*, 368 U.S. 52 (1961); *White v. Maryland*, 373 U.S. 59 (1963) (per curiam); *Arsenault v. Massachusetts*, 393 U.S. 5 (1968) (per curiam); *Sigler v. Bird*, 354 F.2d 694 (8th Cir. 1966); *and see Michigan v. Jackson*, 106 S. Ct. 1404, 1407-8 n.3 (1986). But the opinions in *Coleman v. Alabama*, 399 U.S. 1 (1970), and *Gerstein v. Pugh*, 420 U.S. 103, 122-23 (1975), leave little doubt that the common form of preliminary examination known in most American jurisdictions involves "critical" litigation opportunities that require the appointment of counsel; and it follows from *Estelle v. Smith*, 451 U.S. 454, 470-71 (1981), that counsel is similarly required at preliminary arraignment, when the decision whether to take or waive those opportunities must be made. After *Adams v. Illinois*, 405 U.S. 278 (1972)—which held the *Coleman* decision nonretroactive but apparently saw no other question raised by its extension from Alabama to Illinois practice—it is probably safe to assert categorically that there *is* a federal constitutional right to counsel at preliminary arraignment in virtually every state. See paragraph [53] *supra*; *cf. Moore v. Illinois*, 434 U.S. 220 (1977). The second device— the supervening indictment—is more difficult to attack. The device may be fought at the time of the first appearance for hearing, by defense counsel's objecting to any prosecution request for a continuance (see paragraph [145] *infra*); but frequently defense counsel is in no position to oppose a continuance because s/he is not prepared to go forward with the hearing at this time, particularly if s/he has just been appointed. Thereafter, when an indictment is returned, it is technically true that the two formal functions of the preliminary examination (see paragraph [125](A), (B) *supra*) are mooted. Successful challenge of the second device consequently depends upon defense counsel's ability to persuade the courts either (1) that this is a case in which *Gerstein v. Pugh, supra*, requires a constitutional probable cause determination for which no other procedure is provided by state law than the preliminary examination (see paragraph [127](A), (B) *supra*) and that the question unresolved by *Gerstein* whether an indictment by a grand jury satisfies the requirement of a probable cause determination by a "judicial officer" (420 U.S at 125; compare *id.* at 117 n.19) must be answered in the negative in light of the grand jury's practical domination by the prosecutor (*see, e.g., Hawkins v. Superior Court*, 22 Cal.3d 584, 589-92, 586 P.2d 916, 919-21, 150 Cal. Rptr. 435, 438-40 (1978), and authorities cited; Goldstein, *The State and the Accused: Balance of Advantage in Criminal Procedure*, 69 YALE L.J. 1149, 1171 (1960), and authorities cited); or (2) that the defendant has a state law right to a preliminary examination under the applicable statute, that the statute makes no express provision for the termination of this right by indictment (compare 18 U.S.C. §3060(c), paragraph [129] *supra*), and that the statute should not be construed as implying such a termination because defendants would be legally prejudiced by the denial of a preliminary examination even when their detention is supported by an indictment and need not depend upon a bind-over (see paragraph [131] *infra*).

[131] Informal functions of the preliminary examination. Denial of the preliminary examination may result in prejudice in fact, arising from two informal, or extralegal, functions of the examination. First, although in most jurisdictions the magistrate's legal role at the preliminary hearing is limited to determining whether there is probable cause, or a *prima facie* case against the accused, some magistrates are willing to decline a bind-over in a sympathetic case if they are convinced that the defendant is innocent, notwithstanding the prosecution's technical showing of probable cause. This is a significant fact, and counsel appearing before such a magistrate (they are usually known by reputation) will certainly want to take it into account in deciding how to handle the case at the preliminary examination if there is one. But the magisterial practice of "acquitting" is so plainly inconsistent with the legislated function of the examination in most jurisdictions that it is difficult to imagine that a court could be persuaded to accord it weight in holding the denial of a hearing *legally* prejudicial. Particularly is this so in indictable cases, since the grand jury may lawfully indict notwithstanding a magistrate's discharge; the advantages of the discharge to the defendant are merely to require his or her release from custody and (it is hoped) to persuade the prosecutor not to go to the grand jury. The second extralegal function of the examination is defense discovery. By hearing the prosecution's witnesses and cross-examining them, defense counsel can learn a good deal about what s/he is going to have to meet at trial. The discovery function of the preliminary examination is all the more important because in most jurisdictions other opportunities and procedures for criminal discovery are rather limited. (See paragraphs [265]-[273-B] *infra*.) And the discovery function has more claim to judicial recognition than the "acquittal" function because, although not required by the legislated purposes of the examination, it is also not inconsistent with those purposes. A plurality of the Supreme Court of the United States adverted to the discovery function of the preliminary examination as a legitimate defense interest in *Coleman v. Alabama*, 399 U.S. 1, 9 (1970), in reasoning that the examination was a "critical stage" requiring the appointment of counsel. See paragraph [130] *supra*. Another plurality of the Court recognized that interest in *Adams v. Illinois*, 405 U.S. 278, 282 (1972), although holding it insufficient to warrant the retroactive application of *Coleman* in the absence of a showing of "actual prejudice," 405 U.S. at 285, at least in a jurisdiction that provided "alternative [discovery] procedures," *id.* at 282. See paragraph [140] *infra*. The Georgia Supreme Court in the *Manor* case, paragraph [128] *supra*, mentioned the denial of discovery opportunities in holding that a defendant whose waiver of preliminary examination was coerced is entitled to a reversal of the ensuing conviction, notwithstanding the supervention of an otherwise valid indictment. 221 Ga. at 868-69, 148 S.E.2d at 307. Recognition of the defendant's discovery interest also appears in a significant line of District of Columbia cases, which, prior to the 1968 statute described in paragraph [129] *supra*, held that denial of certain preliminary hearing rights are not cured by a supervening indictment. *Blue v. United States*, 342 F.2d 894

(D.C. Cir. 1964); *Dancy v. United States*, 361 F.2d 75 (D.C. Cir. 1966); *Ross v. Sirica*, 380 F.2d 557 (D.C. Cir. 1967). (In the federal courts themselves these cases have been overturned by the subsequent statute, *see Coleman v. Burnett*, 477 F.2d 1187, 1198-1200 (D.C. Cir. 1973); *United States v. Anderson*, 481 F.2d 685, 691-92 (4th Cir. 1973), *aff'd*, 417 U.S. 211 (1974), and cases cited; but the reasoning of the *Blue-Dancy-Ross* line should remain persuasive in state jurisdictions where no statute expressly dictates a contrary result.) The same recognition of "the important discovery function served by an adversarial preliminary hearing" figures prominently in the decision of the California Supreme Court in *Hawkins v. Superior Court*, 22 Cal.3d 584, 588, 586 P.2d 916, 918-19, 150 Cal. Rptr. 435, 437-38 (1978), holding that a defendant who is denied a preliminary examination by the prosecutor's discretionary decision to proceed by indictment instead of by information is thereby denied the equal protection of the laws under the California Constitution. As the New York Court of Appeals has put it:

> [S]ince the prosecutor must present proof of every element of the crime claimed to have been committed, no matter how skeletally, the preliminary hearing conceptually and pragmatically may serve as a virtual minitrial of the prima facie case. . . . In its presentation, the identity of witnesses, to greater or lesser degree, testimonial details and exhibits, perforce will be disclosed. Especially because discovery and deposition, by and large, are not available in criminal cases, this may not only be an unexampled, but a vital opportunity to obtain the equivalent. It has even been suggested that "in practice [it] may provide the defense with the most valuable discovery technique available to him." . . .
>
> . . . Most important, early resort to that time-tested tool for testing truth, cross-examination, in the end may make the difference between conviction and exoneration.

People v. Hodge, 53 N.Y.2d 313, 318-319, 423 N.E.2d 1060, 1063, 441 N.Y.S.2d 231, 234 (1981). These cases lay the foundation for an argument that would invalidate the use of the grand jury by the prosecutor to end-run preliminary examinations. The argument is that the supervening return of an indictment does not avoid the defendant's right to a preliminary examination, which accrues as an incident of his or her arrest prior to indictment, because the indictment—even if it justifies the defendant's detention for trial—leaves the defendant prejudiced by denial of a major benefit of the examination: discovery adequate to "provide the defense with valuable information about the case against the accused, enhancing its ability to evaluate the desirability of entering a plea or to prepare for trial," *Hawkins v. Superior Court, supra,* 22 Cal.3d at 588, 586 P.2d at 919, 150 Cal. Rptr. at 438, together with the opportunity for "skilled interrogation of witnesses by [the defense] . . . lawyer [that] can fashion a vital impeachment tool for use in cross-examination of the State's witnesses at the trial, or preserve testimony favorable to the accused of a witness who does not appear at the trial," *Coleman v. Alabama, supra,* 399 U.S. at 9. The prosecution cannot fairly be permitted to proceed in a fashion that gives it the advantages of two differing procedures—arrest without prescreening of the grand jury; indictment without discovery at the preliminary examination—and the disadvantages of neither. *Cf. People v. Hodge, supra,* 53 N.Y.2d at 318-20, 423 N.E.2d at 1063-64, 441 N.Y.S.2d at 234-35; *Coleman v. Burnett, supra,* 477 F.2d at 1207-12; *and see United States v. Milano,* 443 F.2d 1022, 1025 (10th Cir. 1971) (holding that under 18 U.S.C. §3060(e) a preliminary examination is not required after indictment but reserving the question whether the same result would obtain in a case of "deliberate prosecutorial connivance to deprive a person of a preliminary hearing by delay until after indictment"). The recognition of the legitimacy of defense use of the preliminary examination for discovery purposes also has implications for some of the procedures at that hearing itself: broader rights of cross-examination than some magistrates now allow, more liberal allowance of defense subpoenas of adverse witnesses, and so forth. See paragraphs [140]-[141] *infra.*

[132] **Rights at preliminary hearing; transcription of proceedings.** The defendant's right to counsel at the preliminary hearing—and, if s/he is indigent, the right to appointed counsel under *Gideon v. Wainwright,* 372 U.S. 335 (1963)—is dis-

cussed in paragraph [130] *supra*. An indigent defendant should have a federal constitutional right to the transcription of the proceedings at state expense, since (a) the transcript would be an important aid to defense trial preparation as well as to impeachment of prosecution witnesses at trial, *cf. Coleman v. Alabama*, paragraph [131] *supra*, 399 U.S. at 9 (plurality opinion); *Britt v. North Carolina*, 404 U.S. 226, 228 (1971); (b) a solvent defendant could employ a stenographer to make a transcript; and (c) the Equal Protection Clause of the Fourteenth Amendment, as construed in *Griffin v. Illinois*, 351 U.S. 12 (1956), forbids the states to deny an indigent, for the sole reason of indigency, an important litigation tool that a solvent defendant could buy. *See Roberts v. LaVallee*, 389 U.S. 40 (1967); *Britt v. North Carolina, supra* (dictum); *Bounds v. Smith*, 430 U.S. 817, 822 & n.8 (1977) (dictum); *United States ex rel. Wilson v. McMann*, 408 F.2d 896 (2d Cir. 1969); *Peterson v. United States*, 351 F.2d 606 (9th Cir. 1965); *cf. Washington v. Clemmer*, 339 F.2d 715, 717-18 (D.C. Cir. 1964); *compare United States v. MacCollom*, 426 U.S. 317 (1976). In localities where it is not routine practice to have preliminary examinations attended by a court reporter or stenographer, counsel should be sure to have a stenographer or recording device present (see paragraph [144] *infra*) and should move for payment of the cost by the state if the client is indigent. In addition, the defendant is ordinarily given by state law the rights at preliminary examination (a) to cross-examine the prosecution's witnesses (this may now be protected by the federal guarantee of confrontation incorporated in the Fourteenth Amendment, *Pointer v. Texas*, 380 U.S. 400 (1965); *Barber v. Page*, 390 U.S. 719 (1968); *Delaware v. Van Arsdall*, 106 S. Ct. 1431, 1435-36 (1986)(dictum); *compare California v. Green*, 399 U.S. 149, 165-66 (1970); *and see Mascarenas v. State*, 80 N.M. 537, 458 P.2d 789 (1969), or by the Due Process Clause, see paragraph [140](B) *infra*); (b) to present evidence, *see, e.g., United States v. King*, 482 F.2d 768, 773-75 (D.C. Cir. 1973) (a right also arguably guaranteed by the federal Constitution, *cf. Jenkins v. McKeithen*, 395 U.S. 411 (1969), paragraph [123-A] *supra*); and (c) to subpoena witnesses, *see, e.g., Coleman v. Burnett*, 477 F.2d 1187, 1202-7 (D.C. Cir. 1973), *in forma pauperis* under the Equal

Protection principle of *Griffin v. Illinois, supra,* if the defendant is indigent and makes an adequate showing that the witness's testimony will be material and helpful to the defense on the issue of probable cause, *see Washington v. Clemmer, supra,* 339 F.2d at 718-19, 725-28; *cf. United States v. Valenzuela-Bernal,* 458 U.S. 858, 867-72 & n.7 (1982). (Although *Gerstein v. Pugh,* 420 U.S. 103 (1975), holds that these rights are not necessary incidents of the probable cause hearing required by the Fourth Amendment, *Gerstein* does not deny that they may be constitutionally obligatory in the "full preliminary hearing . . . procedure used in many States to determine whether the evidence justifies going to trial under an information or presenting the case to a grand jury." *Id.* at 119. Rather, *Gerstein* says that "[w]hen the hearing takes this form, adversary procedures are customarily employed" and "[t]he importance of the issue to both the State and the accused justifies the presentation of witnesses and full exploration of their testimony on cross-examination." *Id.* at 120. Analogously, *Gerstein* recognizes no constitutional right to counsel at a Fourth Amendment probable cause hearing, *id.* at 122-23, but asserts that if the state chooses to conduct a full preliminary examination in lieu of a minimal probable cause hearing, then "appointment of counsel for indigent defendants" is required. *Id.* at 120.) The judge or magistrate presiding at the preliminary hearing has bail-setting authority (see paragraphs [49], [62], [70], [73] *supra*); and defense counsel should move for the release of the client on reasonable bail or on recognizance or for the reduction of bail previously set, both (1) pending the preliminary examination if that is continued or protracted and (2) following the bind-over if the client is held. See paragraph [72] *supra;* and see paragraphs [54]-[75] generally in regard to bail.

[133] Procedure to challenge denial of rights to or at preliminary hearing—before hearing. Counsel who, prior to the stage of bind-over, is dissatisfied with the preliminary arraignment or preliminary examination procedures should apply to the court in which the case will ultimately be tried for an order to rectify the deficiencies. In most jurisdictions the appropriate form of action will be a prerogative writ proceeding—prohibition or mandamus—directed to the magistrate or to the prosecutor. For example, if a magistrate refuses to subpoena defense witnesses or refuses a defense request for free transcription of the testimony in the case of an indigent, counsel should seek mandamus to compel the magistrate to provide these services or prohibition to restrain the examination without them. If the prosecutor obtains a continuance and if defense counsel suspects that the prosecutor is going to the grand jury, counsel may seek mandamus to compel the magistrate to proceed forthwith with the preliminary examination or prohibition to restrain the prosecutor from presenting the case to the grand jury before the examination has been had. In some jurisdictions a bill in equity is used in lieu of the prerogative writs; in others, a simple motion in the court of record is entertained. If a preliminary arraignment or a preliminary examination is being unduly delayed by the real or supposed unavailability of a magistrate to conduct it, counsel should also consider applying to one of the judges of the court of record to conduct the proceedings in the judge's capacity as a committing magistrate. See paragraph [134] *infra*.

[134] **Same—after hearing or bind-over.** If counsel is retained or appointed following the preliminary hearing stage, s/he should immediately ascertain from the client, the prosecutor, or court records whether both a preliminary arraignment and a preliminary examination have been held. (Since the client is unlikely to know what a "preliminary examination" is or to distinguish it from a preliminary arraignment, the best question to ask the client is whether there was a hearing at which people took the witness stand and testified.) If any part of a preliminary hearing has been held, ordinarily counsel should have the stenographic notes transcribed or, if the client is an indigent, move for their transcription at state expense. See paragraphs [144], [299] *infra*. If the transcript shows defects in the hearing that counsel wishes to challenge or if there has been no hearing and no valid waiver or if there is no transcript of the hearing and no valid waiver of a transcript, counsel should decide whether s/he wants a preliminary hearing at this time. (See paragraph [137] *infra*.) If s/he decides

that s/he does want a preliminary hearing, one or more of several procedural devices may be available. First, in many jurisdictions courts of record are given statutory authority to conduct a "court of inquest" or their judges are empowered to sit as committing magistrates. Where this authority exists, a motion to the trial court to have one of its judges conduct a preliminary hearing that will afford the defendant the rights that s/he has heretofore been denied seems appropriate. Second, in jurisdictions where *habeas corpus* is traditionally available to review the magistrate's decision to bind a defendant over, the writ would seem equally appropriate to challenge denial of, or procedural defects in, the preliminary hearing. Third, motions to quash the bind-over or the magistrate's transcript, to dismiss any outstanding charging paper, and to remand the case to the magistrate for preliminary hearing would generally seem proper. (*Gerstein v. Pugh*, 420 U.S. 103 (1975), described in paragraph [127](A) *supra*, does not appear to permit an attack on a charging paper upon the sole ground that *Gerstein's* requirement of a Fourth Amendment probable cause determination has not been satisfied. For that particular defect, standing alone, *habeas corpus* is the exclusive remedy. *See* 420 U.S. at 119. If, however, any *other* federal constitutional rights have been infringed by proceedings at the preliminary arraignment or the preliminary examination (see paragraphs [130], [132] *supra*), a motion to dismiss or quash the charging papers is in order. *See Hamilton v. Alabama*, 368 U.S. 52 (1961); *Coleman v. Alabama*, 399 U.S. 1, 10-11 (1970) (plurality opinion).)

[135] Defensive conduct of the preliminary arraignment—pleading. The general nature of the proceedings at preliminary arraignment is described in paragraphs [13]-[14], [126] (B) *supra*. Three points deserve further mention here:

(A) In some jurisdictions the defendant is asked to plead to the complaint at the preliminary arraignment. In other jurisdictions s/he does not plead but simply elects to have or waive preliminary examination. Where pleading is required, local practice differs regarding the significance of a plea of guilty. It is sometimes treated merely as a waiver of preliminary examination, authorizing the defendant's bind-over without the presentation of evidence by the prosecution. Sometimes it is treated as a waiver of both preliminary examination and indictment in indictable cases (see paragraph [20] *supra*; paragraphs [153]-[157] *infra*). Sometimes it is additionally treated as an indication by the defendant that s/he intends to plead guilty in the trial court to which s/he is bound over. The defendant may subsequently switch signals and plead not guilty in the court of record; but if s/he does so without good reason, the prosecutor and the trial judge will be displeased and will remember their displeasure at the time of sentencing in the event of a conviction. (These effects of a guilty plea to a complaint charging a felony or a misdemeanor must, of course, be distinguished from the effect of the defendant's plea of guilty to a summary offense that is a lesser included offense of the one charged in the complaint. Since a summary offense is within the dispositive jurisdiction of the magistrate (see paragraphs [9]-[10] *supra*), the defendant is convicted and sentenced by the magistrate upon this latter plea, and the greater charges are then dismissed. Some jurisdictions do, and others do not, recognize special pleas (see paragraph [193] *infra*) at preliminary arraignment. Where they are recognized, they are ordinarily required to be entered prior to a general plea of not guilty, or they are waived (*cf.* paragraphs [192]-[194] *infra*), with the consequence either (1) that they may not later be made in the trial court or (2) that they may later be made only upon leave granted within the trial court's discretion. Motions to dismiss the complaint for failure to state an offense within the jurisdiction of the court (*cf.* paragraph [173] *infra*) or for technical deficiencies (see paragraph [136] *infra*) usually must also be made before a plea of not guilty is entered. Obviously, careful consideration of local practice is required prior to pleading.

(B) Counsel who is first appointed at preliminary arraignment should therefore request adequate time to interview the defendant and to do whatever investigation and research appear to be necessary before pleading. See paragraphs [45]-[49], [53] *supra*. In particular, counsel should not succumb to browbeating by a hurried magistrate who urges counsel to "go ahead and enter a safe plea of not guilty," since such a plea may, in fact, be far from safe. The decision whether to demand or to waive preliminary examination also requires thoughtful consideration. See paragraph [137] *infra*.

(C) Some courts appoint counsel for indigent defendants at preliminary arraignment only *after* the defendant (1) has pleaded, (2) has demanded or waived a preliminary examination, or (3) has done both. Counsel appointed at this juncture should immediately inform the court that s/he wants to consult with the client and will also need time to do additional research and investigation in order to advise the client whether to stand upon or to change the pleas and elections already made. If counsel then concludes that the defendant's pleas or elections were improvident, counsel should move to vacate them on the ground that the defendant's Sixth Amendment right to counsel at preliminary arraignment (see paragraphs [53], [130] *supra*) would be violated by holding the defendant to any decisions which s/he made prior to the appointment of an attorney. *See Hamilton v. Alabama*, 368 U.S. 52, 53-54 (1961).

[136] **Same—technical objections.** Objections to the form of a complaint may be made at preliminary arraignment by a motion to dismiss the complaint as insufficient or defective on its face. Also in some states the magistrate's jurisdiction depends on the validity of the arrest, with the result that a successful attack on the arrest (see paragraph [236] *infra*) requires dismissal of the complaint. These technical defenses should be raised very sparingly. In most instances the defects can be cured by the filing of a new complaint or by a rearrest, and the defendant gains nothing of substance. In fact, s/he may have to post new and higher bail for being vexatious. On the other hand, local rules may sometimes require that certain objections be taken or that certain motions be made at the preliminary arraignment in order to preserve the right to make the contentions involved subsequently at trial or on appeal.

[137] **Same—the decision whether to demand or waive preliminary examination.** Defense counsel should not ordinarily waive preliminary examination; it provides unique opportunities for discovery of the prosecution's case. See para-

graphs [265] - [266] *infra*. Waiver of the examination is usually appropriate only in one of the following situations:

(1) A witness essential to the prosecution is able to testify at the preliminary hearing, but there is a strong likelihood that s/he will not be able to appear at trial because of declining health, plans to leave the jurisdiction, or other considerations. If s/he testifies at the preliminary hearing and is later unavailable, the recorded testimony may be used against the defendant at trial. *See Ohio v. Roberts*, 448 U.S. 56 (1980).

(2) The prosecution has a solid case, and the chances are less than slight that a preliminary examination will produce anything but high bail and intensification of the hostility of prosecution witnesses. Frequently, with the passage of time a complainant will mellow, but once s/he has testified under oath, s/he is unlikely to change the story and is impeachable if s/he does. Moreover, once s/he has testified for the prosecution, s/he may refuse to be interviewed by anyone representing the defendant's interests. See paragraph [116] *supra*.

(3) The likely adverse publicity outweighs any possible gain from the examination.

(4) Counsel learns of a defect in the prosecution's case that, in all probability, would not be corrected before the case went to trial if not brought to the prosecutor's attention at the preliminary examination. This may happen especially in metropolitan areas where the prosecutor's office is handling an enormous caseload and relies primarily upon the police to make sure that all needed witnesses and essential elements of a case are produced at trial.

(5) The defendant is undercharged. If facts known to counsel suggest that the defendant is guilty of more, or more serious, offenses than those charged in the complaint, counsel may want to avoid a preliminary examination that could alert the prosecutor to the additional or more serious offenses.

Other exceptional reasons to waive may occasionally appear. When in doubt whether to waive or demand the examination, counsel should demand it.

[138] **Proceedings at preliminary examination.** The preliminary examination is in most respects conducted like a trial. The rules of evidence are ordinarily enforced (although counsel handling a federal matter should note FED. R. EVIDENCE 1101(d)(3)), often with some relaxation of the hearsay rule. (Indeed, in some jurisdictions magistrates may bind a defendant over on nothing but hearsay evidence.) The prosecution must make a showing of probable cause of every element of the offense and of the defendant's identity as its perpetrator. The *corpus delicti* must ordinarily be proved before any admissions of the defendant may be received in evidence, but the magistrate has some discretion to allow variance from this order of proof. Compare paragraph [363] (A) *infra*. Witnesses are questioned in the ordinary fashion, and real evidence is admitted as exhibits. Cross-examination of witnesses is permitted, although some magistrates tend to limit its scope to a narrower compass than would be allowed at trial. See paragraph [140] *infra*. Sequestration of witnesses is allowed within the sound discretion of the magistrate. There is modification of these rules in varying degrees in some jurisdictions, and local practice must be checked. In a number of localities preliminary examination in misdemeanor cases is conducted for the prosecution by a police officer rather than a law-trained prosecutor; here, the proceedings are somewhat more informal, and the magistrate plays a greater role in questioning witnesses.

[139] **Defensive conduct of the examination—cross-examining for discovery and impeachment.** (A) Defense counsel has three principal goals at the preliminary examination: (1) to secure the dismissal or reduction of the charges against the defendant if the prosecution does not meet its burden of proof; (2) to put the testimony of the prosecution witnesses on record in a way that makes them most impeachable at trial; and (3) to discover as much of the prosecutor's case as pos-

sible. Once the prosecution has made out its *prima facie* case, there is no great likelihood that cross-examination will destroy it so completely as to warrant a dismissal, and therefore, counsel must proceed with the objectives of discovery and of nailing down impeachable prosecution testimony. As a practical matter these are the major objectives of the defense from the outset of most preliminary hearings, since most magistrates will predictably find probable cause to bind most defendants over most of the time.

(B) Frequently, counsel may find that s/he is working at cross-purposes in seeking to discover and to lay a foundation for impeachment simultaneously. S/he will obviously have to accommodate these objectives in particular situations with an eye to which objective is more important in dealing with an individual prosecution witness. If counsel vigorously cross-examines the witness, in an effort to get a contradiction or concession on record, the witness will normally dig in and give a minimum of information in an effort to save his or her testimonial position; and, more than likely, s/he will be uncooperative if counsel thereafter attempts to interview the witness prior to trial. On the other hand, if counsel engages the witness in routine examination, amiable and ranging, counsel may be able to pick up many clues for investigation and for planning of the defense. Of course, some witnesses resent any kind of cross-examination. If counsel thinks that this type of witness is lying or confused, counsel may wish to pin the witness down. Under no circumstances, however, should counsel educate the witness about the weaknesses of his or her testimony. To avoid mutual education by prosecution witnesses, counsel should ordinarily ask that all witnesses be excluded from the courtroom during one another's testimony. See paragraph [348] *infra*.

(C) The probable utility of cross-examining for impeachment depends almost as much on the prosecutor as on the witness. If the prosecutor is one who prepares witnesses as carefully for preliminary examination as for trial, the likelihood of getting anything out of the witness on the examination that will be useful to impeach him or her at trial is small. Most prosecutors, however, do not have the time to prepare witnesses thoroughly for the preliminary hearing, with the result that the examination provides a unique opportunity to catch the prosecution witnesses, on record, with their guards down. On the other hand, the importance of using the preliminary hearing for discovery depends largely upon the amount of funds available to conduct an independent investigation and the liberality of practice with respect to other criminal pretrial discovery devices in the locality. Investigation can be very expensive, and counsel must recognize that most clients simply cannot afford it. The investigative services made available to appointed counsel in indigent cases are generally woefully inadequate. As for other discovery procedures, it is fair to say that although there is a trend toward more liberal discovery, the trend has not yet gone very far—and *least* far in the area of defense access to the statements of prosecution witnesses. For a fuller discussion of pretrial discovery, see paragraphs [265]-[275] *infra*. Counsel, at the preliminary examination stage, should therefore be careful to avoid undue optimism about what s/he will learn later if s/he lets this opportunity for some discovery go by.

[140] Resisting limitations on cross-examination. (A) Many magistrates allow defense counsel very grudging room for cross-examination at preliminary hearing on the reasoning that guilt is not at issue, that the prosecution need only show a case the jury could believe, and that, therefore, nothing which cross-examination might disclose is relevant. The theoretical answers to this reasoning are (a) that it would be plainly relevant if cross-examination forced the witness to withdraw his or her testimony on direct examination and (b) that the statute expressly permitting the defendant to cross-examine prosecution witnesses, call defense witnesses, or both at preliminary hearing (as most statutes do) assumes that the magistrate is not to restrict the inquiry to a bare-bones hearing of the prosecution's evidence, untested for credibility. (Most of the cases cited in paragraph [131] *supra* contain quotable language endorsing the right of the defense to conduct a probing cross-examination at the preliminary hearing. See particularly the two *Coleman* opinions, *Hawkins*, and *Hodge*.) Magistrates, however, like to push the hearing along and will often not be persuaded by these theories. Counsel should continue to attempt to cross-examine, as long as s/he can decently do so, in order to make clear for the record the extent of the limitations imposed on cross-examination. S/he should then respectfully ask the magistrate whether all cross-examination is going to be disallowed and, if not, what areas the magistrate is not going to let counsel go into. If the magistrate says that s/he cannot tell until counsel asks the questions, counsel should resume attempts to cross-examine. Eventually the magistrate will shut counsel off altogether. Counsel should then object to the denial of cross-examination on the grounds of the client's statutory right to a preliminary examination (paragraph [128] *supra*) and the statutory and constitutional rights to confrontation (paragraph [132] *supra*; see paragraph [270] (C) *infra*), effective representation by counsel (paragraph [130] *supra*; see paragraph [270](A) *infra*), and a fair hearing (see paragraph [270] (C) *infra*), as well as on the ground that the statute giving defendants a right to present testimony evisions that the magistrate will hear both sides of the case. The record should be clear that this objection has been overruled if it has. Counsel is now in a position to challenge the propriety of the bind-over by the procedures enumerated in paragraph [134] *supra* if s/he can convince a higher court that upon one or another of these legal grounds, s/he had a right to cross-examine which was unduly restricted.

(B) An unfortunate *dictum* in a plurality opinion of the Supreme Court appears to accept, without federal constitutional quarrel, a state-law practice permitting the magistrate "to terminate the preliminary hearing once probable cause is established," *Adams v. Illinois*, 405 U.S. 278, 282 (1972). This language, predictably, will be seized upon by lower courts as giving an examining magistrate virtually unlimited power to curtail defensive cross-examination. But the Supreme Court did not, in fact, have before it in the *Adams* case any instance of curtailment of the defensive conduct of a preliminary hearing. The plurality opinion was merely noting, as relevant to the question of the retroactivity of the constitutional requirement of appointed counsel at preliminary examination (see paragraphs [130]-[131] *supra*, that "because of limitations upon the use of the preliminary hearing for discovery and impeachment purposes, counsel cannot be as effectual as at trial." 404 U.S. at 282. So it is fair to urge that the *Adams* *dictum* must be read narrowly: as allowing magisterial discretion to curb cross-examination pursued "for discovery and impeachment purposes" only, "once probable cause is established," *ibid.*, but not as authorizing the restriction of cross-examination designed to test the foundation of the probable cause showing itself, even if the cross-examination does also provide some discovery. For it seems plain that if, with one exception not presently relevant, a *parolee* has a right "to confrontation and cross-examination" at a preliminary parole-revocation hearing, *Morrissey v. Brewer*, 408 U.S. 471, 487 (1972), a criminal defendant has rights that are at least as ample at a preliminary examination, which is "part of a criminal prosecution," *id.* at 480. *See also Gagnon v. Scarpelli*, 411 U.S. 778, 781-82, 788-90 (1973); and see paragraph [270](C) *infra*. (*Gerstein v. Pugh*, 420 U.S. 103 (1975), does not hold to the contrary. See paragraph [132] *supra*.) Certainly, counsel is on far firmer ground when s/he can justify his or her questions on cross-examination as going to probe the prosecution's showing of probable cause than when they have no other justification but discovery. Only when there is no possibility of successfully urging that a line of questioning goes to probable cause and, therefore, that it is within the purview of the classic functions of preliminary examination (see paragraph [125](A), (B) *supra*) should counsel attempt to justify it on the basis of a right to discovery as such (see paragraphs [265]-[271] *infra*; *cf.* paragraph [131] *supra*), pointing out, if possible, why in the case at bar, unlike *Adams*, there are no effective "alternative procedures" for discovery. 404 U.S. at 282.

[141] **Calling adverse witnesses.** One rather venturesome method of discovery at preliminary examination is to call adverse witnesses whom the prosecution fails to call. Since the prosecution normally wants to present just enough evidence to satisfy its burden of making a *prima facie* case and does not want to show more than it has to, it will frequently not call all

the witnesses it plans to use at trial. The defense can call these witnesses as its own, but if it does so, it is ordinarily limited to nonleading questions (see generally paragraph [383] *infra*), since the witness is on direct examination. The prosecutor may then lead the witness on cross-examination. Although the story that is thus unfolded may be enlightening, it may also be calamitous for the defendant. At best, defense counsel may get some favorable testimony at the cost of giving the prosecutor the opportunity to hammer it into the worst possible shape. At worst, counsel may perpetuate damning evidence. Ordinarily, then, counsel should not use this tactic in the case of any witness who is not already known to the prosecutor; nor, even then, unless the witness has refused to be interviewed by the defense notwithstanding strenuous efforts by counsel to get him or her to talk out of court (see paragraph [116] *supra*). The presiding magistrate or judge may also permit defense counsel, on request, to call a person as a hostile witness for purposes of cross-examination. This will work only very infrequently, partly because hostility is difficult for the defense to show without confessing guilt (except when the witness has a demonstrable animosity to the defendant apart from the events giving rise to the charge or when other prosecution witnesses have related incriminating hearsay declarations of the witness) and partly because most magistrates apparently feel that the calling of adverse witnesses by the defense has no place in a proceeding in which the only purpose is to require that the prosecution show probable cause. Certainly, the best case for a defensive claim of the right to call a witness as hostile is the case in which that witness's hearsay declarations have been put in by the prosecution; here defense counsel can legitimately purport to be challenging the prosecutor's *prima facie* showing and can also make some mileage out of the constitutional rights of confrontation and due process, see paragraph [132] *supra*; paragraph [270] (C), (D) *infra*.

[142] Calling defense witnesses. Counsel should never present defense testimony at a preliminary examination unless there is the strongest likelihood that the defendant will be discharged after it is presented. See paragraph [131] *supra*.

This is a very rare case. See paragraph [139] (A) *supra*. Before presenting testimony, counsel should always ask for the dismissal of the charge based upon the inadequacy of the prosecution's evidence. Argument on the question of dismissal at this point, even if dismissal is refused, will often reveal whether the judge would be inclined to dismiss the case on the basis of the defense that counsel is considering putting on.

[143] Objecting to inadmissible evidence. To the extent that under local practice the rules of evidence are applied in preliminary examinations (see paragraph [138] *supra*), counsel will sometimes have the opportunity to object to prosecution evidence as inadmissible. Generally s/he should object only if (a) there is a good chance that the prosecution will fail to make a *prima facie* case; (b) counsel is sure s/he already knows everything s/he could learn from the evidence; or (c) the evidence is likely to be seriously damaging, and either (i) an objection is required under local rules in order to preserve a claim of its inadmissibility at trial (see paragraph [136] *supra*), or (ii) there is substantial reason to believe that the witness may become unavailable to the prosecution by the time of trial (see paragraph [137] (1) *supra*). If the prosecution has a good case on its face, counsel will need investigative leads to defend against it. Much discovery can be obtained by permitting prosecution witnesses at preliminary hearing to make all the hearsay and other inadmissible statements that they want. More can often be obtained by cross-examining them on these statements. By allowing the testimony to come in, counsel can also lay a foundation for earlier objection at trial when the direct examination of a witness starts down an impermissible track: referring to the transcript of the witness' testimony at preliminary hearing, s/he can show the trial judge exactly where this line of examination leads. See paragraph [359] *infra*. Of course, the tactic of nonobjection is a two-edged sword, for the prosecution may also discover facts, previously unnoticed, that might be helpful to its case. Here again, it matters how careful or careless the prosecutor is known to be in his or her out-of-court investigation.

[144] Obtaining a transcript. Many of the tactical suggestions just made have assumed that there will be a reporter or stenographer transcribing the testimony. Whether a court reporter routinely attends preliminary examinations depends on local practice. Counsel should not assume that a reporter will be in attendance but should inquire. If local practice does not provide for a court reporter, the expense of a stenographer should be considered by the defense. Alternatively, a tape recorder might be used. The obvious advantage of a transcript is its utility at trial to impeach a witness who alters his or her testimony. Additionally, it is an invaluable aid in preparing for cross-examination at the trial. In some jurisdictions where preliminary hearing testimony is routinely recorded, it is nevertheless not transcribed unless specially ordered by a party. Again, counsel should inquire whether this is the situation and should order a transcript if necessary. Where both recording and transcription are routine, the transcripts are normally forwarded several days or weeks after the hearing to the office of the clerk of court. Counsel may wish to examine the hearing transcript in the clerk's office before deciding whether to order a defense copy. (For the procedure in federal prosecutions, see FED. R. CRIM. P. 5.1(c).) If the client is unable to afford a transcript (or a stenographer, when testimony is not reported), counsel should request transcription (or reporting and transcription, as the case may be) at state expense. In the event that local law does not give counsel a right to what s/he wants, s/he should invoke the federal Equal Protection doctrine adverted to in paragraph [132] *supra*; paragraphs [266], [299] *infra*. Procedures for enforcing the demand are considered in paragraphs [133]-[134] *supra*.

[145] Continuances. In a few jurisdictions a continuance of the preliminary hearing of a defendant in custody may be made only with his or her personal assent. The more ordinary practice permits continuances in the discretion of the magistrate upon the application of either prosecution or defense. That discretion is limited by *Gerstein v. Pugh*, 420 U.S. 103 (1975), paragraph [127] (A) *supra*; and the citation of *Gerstein* in opposition to a prosecution-sought continuance is appropriate *unless* local law can be construed to permit the magistrate to make a probable cause determination upon affidavits without a full preliminary examination. The prosecutorial tactic of using a continuance to permit presentation of the case to the grand jury is discussed in paragraph [129] *supra*, and objections to the tactic are described in paragraphs [130]-[131] *supra*. If defense counsel is ready for the hearing and if the prosecutor seeks a continuance during a period when the grand jury is in session, counsel should oppose the continuance except on a representation by the prosecutor in open court that s/he will not present the matter to the grand jury. If the prosecutor refuses to make such a representation and the continuance is, nonetheless, granted, counsel has made a record on which s/he can seek either mandamus against the magistrate to proceed forthwith or prohibition or an injunction against the prosecutor to forbid the prosecutor's presenting bills to the grand jury. See paragraph [133] *supra*. In other situations in which the magistrate grants the prosecution a continuance that defense counsel believes is excessive, counsel may challenge it for abuse of discretion by mandamus or bring *habeas corpus* if the client is in custody. Counsel should consider, alternatively, asking a judge of the court of record to assume jurisdiction as a committing magistrate and to conduct the examination. See paragraph [134] *supra*. Or counsel might be willing to agree to a relatively long continuance desired by the prosecution in exchange for the prosecutor's recommendation of favorable terms of bail and a promise not to go to the grand jury during the continuance. The defense itself may want a continuance for various reasons—to investigate and prepare the case; to let a complainant's temper cool off; to demonstrate to the prosecutor that a defendant released on bail is behaving as a law-abiding citizen or has gotten a job or is starting to make restitution or that some other change of circumstances warrants the favorable exercise of the prosecutor's discretion to drop or to reduce the contemplated charges (see paragraphs [99]-[101], [103] *supra*). When counsel is unprepared to conduct the preliminary examination and can show adequate justification for being unprepared, a defense request for a continuance may invoke the defendant's federal Sixth and

Fourteenth Amendment rights to counsel (see paragraphs [53], [130] *supra*) as well as the magistrate's state-law discretion. During the period of any continuance, the magistrate should be asked to release the defendant on bail or on some form of conditional release. See paragraphs [14], [54]-[73] *supra*. If a defendant cannot make bail, the magistrate may be asked to hold the defendant in the courthouse cellblock or to commit the defendant to jail rather than leave the defendant in the police lockup where s/he will remain in the hands of the investigating officers.

[146] **Bind-over; review.** The defendant may ordinarily be bound over to the grand jury or for trial for any offense shown by the evidence, even though not charged in the complaint. (This practice, although traditionally accepted in many jurisdictions, should be subject to challenge on due process grounds, as depriving the defendant of fair notice and an opportunity to defend at the preliminary examination. See paragraph [270](B) *infra*. "Few constitutional principles are more firmly established than a defendant's right to be heard on the specific charges of which he is accused," *Dunn v. United States*, 442 U.S. 100, 106 (1979); *see also Cole v. Arkansas*, 333 U.S. 196 (1948); *Presnell v. Georgia*, 439 U.S. 14 (1978) (per curiam); and the principle is not restricted to the trial stage of a criminal case, *see Jenkins v. McKeithen*, 395 U.S. 411, 429 (1969) (plurality opinion), paragraph [123-A] *supra*; *Morrissey v. Brewer*, 408 U.S. 471, 486-87 (1972) (preliminary hearing in parole revocation proceedings).) In some jurisdictions the bind-over is essentially unreviewable. In others a motion to dismiss the consequent information may lie in a nonindictable case on the ground that the preliminary examination transcript fails to show probable cause to hold the defendant to answer or probable cause to charge a particular offense. In still others *habeas corpus* or a motion to quash the bind-over or the magistrate's transcript is available to review the magistrate's finding of probable cause. Ordinarily the issue on the writ or motion is decided on the basis of the preliminary examination transcript, since the magistrate's order to commit the defendant for court was based on that record. In some states, however, the *habeas*

corpus court will hold its own hearing on the question of probable cause. The simple admission of inadmissible evidence at a preliminary examination is not usually sufficient to sustain the vacating of the bind-over on motion or *habeas corpus* unless the remaining admissible evidence fails to support a finding of probable cause; but the admission of unconstitutionally obtained evidence at the hearing may require that the bind-over be vacated. See paragraph [172] *infra*. Defense counsel's decision to proceed with a motion to dismiss or with *habeas* involves some of the same considerations as the decision to move to dismiss a complaint before the magistrate for technical reasons (see paragraph [136] *supra*), since the prosecution can rearrest and present evidence that it neglected or did not deem necessary at the first hearing. Thus the defendant has gained only a Pyrrhic victory, the results of which are (A) that s/he must go through the arrest process again and post new bail and (B) that the prosecution is alerted to defects in its case while there is still time for it to cure them before jeopardy attaches (see paragraphs [177], [222] (D), [422] *infra*). As a matter of probabilities, though, the likelihood of rearrest is usually considerably less in overturning a bind-over than in sucessfully urging a technical objection before the magistrate. (Counsel should be alert to the consideration that in some jurisdictions the scope of review of the magistrate's bind-over is broader on *habeas corpus* than on a motion to quash. When this is the case and when *habeas corpus* is available only to applicants in actual custody—that is, when state practice does not follow the recent liberal evolution of federal case law recognizing bail status as "custody" for *habeas corpus* purposes (see paragraph [311](B) *infra*)—counsel may well be advised not to post bail at the preliminary hearing but to apply for bail in the *habeas* case after filing the petition for the writ.)

[147] **Discharge; rearrest.** If it appears at preliminary examination that there is no probable cause to believe that an offense was committed or no probable cause to believe that the defendant committed it, the magistrate "discharges" the defendant from custody. Following such a discharge, counsel should ask the magistrate to order the defendant's arrest rec-

ord expunged or, alternatively, marked to reflect that the defendant was discharged for want of probable cause upon preliminary examination. See paragraph [459-A] *infra*. When the prosecutor disagrees with a magistrate's discharge (or if new evidence is discovered subsequent to the discharge), the prosecutor may order the defendant rearrested and presented for a second hearing, usually before a different magistrate. In some localities, by rule or practice, this second hearing is held before a higher ranking member of the judiciary—the chief magistrate or a judge of the court of record sitting as a committing magistrate. Although the rearrest practice is lawful, it is disfavored by many judges, and defense counsel may properly wear an air of abused innocence to the second hearing. Obtaining a transcript of the first hearing is especially useful in these cases, since the prosecution can be made to look bad, whether its evidence is the same or different.

X. DEFENSIVE PROCEDURES BETWEEN BIND-OVER AND THE FILING OF THE CHARGING PAPER

[148] **Checklist.** The routine prosecutive steps that immediately follow bind-over are the drafting and filing of an information or informations in a misdemeanor (nonindictable) case (see paragraph [16] *supra*) or, in a felony (indictable) case, the presentation of a bill or bills to the grand jury and the jury's return of the bills as "true bills" or indictments (see paragraph [20] *supra*). Between the time of the bind-over and the filing of the charging paper—information or indictment—in the court of record having jurisdiction to try the defendant, there are a number of moves that defense counsel should consider making. These are as follows:

A. *Matters looking backward to the preliminary hearing.* [Paragraph [149] *infra*]

1. Arranging transcription of the notes of testimony of the preliminary hearing.

2. Obtaining review of the bind-over by *habeas corpus*, motion to quash the transcript, or other appropriate procedure.

3. Securing reopening of the preliminary hearing or a new preliminary hearing or attacking waiver of the preliminary hearing.

4. Obtaining review by *habeas corpus*, motion for reduction of bail, or other statutory bail-setting procedure, of the magistrate's setting or denial of bail at the preliminary hearing.

B. *Matters looking forward to the information.*

1. Discussing charges with the prosecutor. [Paragraph [150] *infra*]

C. *Matters looking forward to the grand jury.*

1. Challenging the array of grand jurors, or individual grand jurors, on grounds of improper selection, disqualification, and so forth. [Paragraph [158] *infra*]

2. Moving to suppress illegally obtained evidence before its presentation to the grand jury. [Paragraph [159] *infra*]

3. Requesting recording of the grand jury testimony. [Paragraph [160] *infra*]

4. Considering waiver of indictment. [Paragraphs [156]-[157] *infra*]

5. Discussing bills with the prosecutor. [Paragraph [150] *infra*]

D. *Matters immediately relating to the grand jury.*

1. Advising the defendant and defense witnesses with respect to testifying before the grand jury. [Paragraphs [161]-[162] *infra*]

2. Presenting matters to the grand jury. [Paragraph [164] *infra*]

3. Resisting grand jury process. [Paragraph [163] *infra*]

4. Investigating grand jury witnesses. [Paragraph [165] *infra*]

E. *Matters looking forward to trial.*

1. Conducting defense investigation in light of new matter disclosed at the preliminary examination. [Paragraph [151] *infra*]

2. Discussing with the client the prosecution's case presented at the examination. [Paragraph [151] *infra*]

3. Having the defendant committed for pretrial mental examination. [Paragraph [152] *infra*]

4. Negotiating a plea with the prosecutor. [Paragraph [150] *infra*]

F. *The matter of delay.* [Paragraph [166] *infra*]

G. *Anticipation of a bench warrant.* [Paragraph [167] *infra*]

H. *Matters looking forward to sentencing.* [Paragraph [167-A] *infra*]

1. Placing the defendant in a job, rehabilitation program, or other situation in which s/he can make a good adjustment record.

2. Advising the defendant in regard to other changes of life style that may increase his or her attractiveness to a sentencing judge.

[149] Matters looking backward to the preliminary hearing. These have already been discussed. Concerning review of the magistrate's bail decision, see paragraphs [70]-[72] *supra*. Concerning transcription of the notes of testimony of the preliminary hearing, see paragraphs [132], [134], [144] *supra*. Concerning review of the bind-over, see paragraph [146] *supra*. Concerning procedures for reopening the preliminary hearing or challenging a waiver of that hearing, see paragraph [134] *supra*. Procedures seeking review of the bind-over or reopening of the preliminary hearing or challenging waiver of the hearing had best be taken as early as possible and, in any event, before the presentation of the case to the grand jury, since the doctrine that a supervening indictment moots all attacks on the preliminary hearing or bind-over, although assailable (see paragraphs [130]-[131] *supra*), remains strong in most jurisdictions. Under the practice prevailing in some localities, the filing of a petition for *habeas corpus* or other application for review may work an automatic supersedeas of all proceedings in the criminal case. When it does not, counsel should be careful to move in the review proceeding for an order restraining the prosecutor from presenting the case to the grand jury during the pendency of that proceeding.

[150] Discussions with the prosecutor. As indicated in paragraph [99] *supra*, the prosecutor retains considerable discretion concerning the charges s/he will press or drop (or, in some jurisdictions, add) by information following the bind-over, and s/he has still greater discretion regarding the charges s/he presents to the grand jury. Accordingly, counsel will find it useful to discuss the case with the prosecutor at this stage and, in light of the evidence presented at the preliminary examination, urge the dropping or reducing of charges. The events surrounding the commission of the offense and apprehension of the defendant will often have cooled somewhat by this time; the complainant may have calmed down or been impressed at the preliminary hearing with the gravity of the defendant's situation; hence the time may be ripe for urging a favorable exercise of the prosecutorial discretion. See paragraphs [100], [103] *supra*. If the prosecutor is indisposed to drop or reduce charges without a *quid pro quo*, plea negotiation is sometimes best begun at this time. See paragraphs [206]-[218] *infra*. The further along the process goes, the more work the prosecutor will have already done and the less s/he will save by dealing with the defense. Once the prosecutor has calendared the case for trial, s/he has made something of a psychological commitment to try it and has arranged his or her other affairs so as to leave the trial date free. Before this happens, s/he is likely to be more negotiable.

[151] **Defense investigation.** Matters learned at the preliminary examination may cast a new light on the nature of the prosecution's case and may open up new leads or establish new priorities for defense investigation. See paragraph [107] *supra*. Shortly after the examination counsel should review the case and consider whether redirection or intensification of defense investigation is advised. This may also be a good time to pursue cross-examination of the client, confronting the client with items of prosecution evidence presented at the examination and pointing out that the magistrate apparently credited them. See paragraph [89] *supra*.

[152] **Commitment for mental examination.** In some jurisdictions a defendant may be committed for pretrial mental examination to determine competence to stand trial at any time following bind-over. Counsel dealing with a client who may be mentally ill should consider moving for such a commitment. See paragraphs [120]-[122] *supra*; paragraphs [180]-[181] *infra*.

[153] **Matters looking forward to, and immediately relating to, the grand jury—in general.** As a prelude to discussion of several points of defensive procedure and strategy, a few words should be said about the institution of the grand jury. The majority of the states, by constitution or statute, require the prosecution of some or all serious crimes by indictment. (The Fifth Amendment to the federal Constitution similarly requires that prosecutions for any "capital, or otherwise infamous crime [in the federal courts be by] . . . indictment.")

The requirement is conceived principally as a protection to the defendant, and s/he may waive it. Indictments are the product of a grand jury. See paragraph [20] *supra*. Grand juries are convened, ordinarily at the outset of, or shortly preceding, each criminal term of court and are composed of a number of citizens (usually 15 to 23) selected by statutorily prescribed methods (see paragraphs [320]-[324] *infra*) and possessing statutorily prescribed qualifications (usually age, residence, "good moral character"). There are also a few nonstatutory restrictions on juror selection practices and nonstatutory grounds of disqualification:

(A) The Equal Protection Clause of the Fourteenth Amendment to the federal Constitution forbids the systematic exclusion of racial, ethnic, religious, or economic groups from jury service, *Coleman v. Alabama*, 389 U.S. 22 (1967), and cases cited (blacks); *Turner v. Fouche*, 396 U.S. 346, 356-61 (1970) (same); *Hernandez v. Texas*, 347 U.S. 475 (1954) (Mexican-Americans); *Castaneda v. Partida*, 430 U.S. 482 (1977) (same); *Schowgurow v. State*, 240 Md. 121, 213 A.2d 475 (1965) (atheists); *Labat v. Bennett*, 365 F.2d 698 (5th Cir. 1966) (wage earners). This principle applies to grand juries as well as to petit juries, *e.g.*, *Turner v. Fouche, supra*; *Alexander v. Louisiana*, 405 U.S. 625, 626 n.3 (1972); *Castaneda v. Partida, supra*; *Rose v. Mitchell*, 443 U.S. 545, 551-59 (1979); *Vasquez v. Hillery*, 106 S. Ct. 617 (1986); *Batson v. Kentucky*, 106 S. Ct. 1712, 1716 n.3 (1986) (dictum), and condemns the systematic exclusion of any "distinct class" of citizens shown to be viewed or treated differently from other classes in the local community, *Hernandez v. Texas, supra*, 347 U.S. at 478; *Castaneda v. Partida, supra*, 430 U.S. at 494-95; *compare Lockhart v. McCree*, 106 S. Ct. 1758, 1765-66 (1986). In *White v. Crook*, 251 F. Supp. 401 (M.D. Ala. 1966) (three-judge court), women were recognized as a distinct class for this purpose; but the Supreme Court's subsequent decision in *Taylor v. Louisiana*, 419 U.S. 522 (1975), holding unconstitutional the systematic exclusion of women from *petit* juries, emphasizes the right implicit in the Sixth Amendment to a "petit jury [drawn] from a representative cross section of the community," *id.* at 528; and its ambiguous treatment of the derivation of the "representative cross section" requirement from

Equal Protection and from Sixth Amendment cases (*see also Daniel v. Louisiana*, 420 U.S. 31, 32 (1975); *Duren v. Missouri*, 439 U.S. 357, 368 n.26 (1979)) leaves somewhat unclear whether the systematic exclusion of women from grand juries would be constitutionally condemned. Probably it would, as the Eleventh Circuit has held. *Machetti v. Linahan*, 679 F.2d 236 (11th Cir. 1982). Gender discrimination violates the Equal Protection Clause unless " 'an "exceedingly persuasive justification" ' " for it is established by demonstrating that it " 'serves "important governmental objectives and [is] . . . substantially related to the achievement of those objectives," ' " which cannot include an " 'objective . . . to exclude or "protect" members of one gender because they are presumed to suffer from an inherent handicap or to be innately inferior.' " *Heckler v. Mathews*, 465 U.S. 728, 744 (1984) (dictum); *see Reed v. Reed*, 404 U.S. 71 (1971); *Craig v. Boren*, 429 U.S. 190, 197-99 (1976); *Califano v. Goldfarb*, 430 U.S. 199, 206-7, 210-11 (1977); *Mississippi University for Women v. Hogan*, 458 U.S. 718, 723-28 (1982). Whether the systematic exclusion of particular age groups—for example, young people—would also be condemned is a more difficult question, which the Court has reserved. *Hamling v. United States*, 418 U.S. 87, 137 (1974). *See* Zeigler, *Young Adults as a Cognizable Group in Jury Selection*, 76 MICH. L. REV. 1045 (1978); *cf. Lockhart v. McCree, supra*, 106 S. Ct. at 1765 ("[w]e have never attempted to precisely define the term 'distinctive group,' and we do not undertake to do so today"). A grand jury whose composition is affected by systematic racial exclusion may be challenged even by a defendant who is not a member of the excluded class. *Peters v. Kiff*, 407 U.S. 493 (1972). This same broad "standing" rule was applied in *Taylor v. Louisiana, supra*, to other sorts of unconstitutional exclusions in the selection of petit juries, *see Duren v. Missouri, supra*, 439 U.S. at 359 n.1; but its applicability to unconstitutional nonracial exclusions in grand jury selection remains unsettled. In *Hobby v. United States*, 468 U.S. 339 (1984), the Court held that a white federal criminal defendant was not entitled to reversal of his conviction on the ground that discrimination had been practiced against blacks and women in the selection of grand jury foremen, "as distinguished from discrimination in the selection of the grand jury itself," *id.* at 344. A muddy opinion briefly questions and then elaborately distinguishes the assumption made in *Rose v. Mitchell, supra,* that a black defendant's state criminal conviction would have to be reversed upon a showing that blacks had been systematically excluded from selection as grand jury foremen under Tennessee practice. *Hobby* both emphasizes differences between federal and Tennessee law in regard to the powers of grand jury foremen and the effects of discrimination in selecting them upon the composition of the grand jury as a whole (468 U.S. at 347-49) and also notes that "*Rose* involved a claim brought by two Negro defendants under the Equal Protection Clause," whereas Hobby "has alleged only that the exclusion of women and Negroes from the position of grand jury foreman violates his right to fundamental fairness under the Due Process Clause" (*id.* at 347). Whether the Court is saying that Hobby lacked standing to assert an Equal Protection claim or merely that he did not assert one is unclear; its suggestion that the black defendants in *Rose* were given such standing not because of any harm to their legitimate interests in the criminal proceeding but rather because "[a]s members of the class allegedly excluded . . ., the[y] . . . had suffered the injuries of stigmatization and prejudice associated with racial discrimination" (468 U.S. at 347) is thoroughly inconsistent with the Court's rejection in a later case of a state prosecutor's submission that "discrimination in the grand jury has no effect on the fairness of the criminal trials that result from that grand jury's actions," *Vasquez v. Hillery, supra,* 106 S. Ct. at 623; *Vasquez* finds explicitly that improper grand jury selection does adversely affect legitimate interests of a criminal defendant because

> [t]he grand jury does not determine only that probable cause exists to believe that a defendant committed a crime, or that it does not. In the hands of the grand jury lies the power to charge a greater offense or a lesser offense; numerous counts or a single count; and perhaps most significant of all, a capital offense or a noncapital offense—all on the basis of the same facts. Moreover, "[t]he grand jury is not bound to indict in every case where a conviction can be obtained." . . . When consti-

tutional error calls into question the objectivity of those charged with bringing a defendant to judgment, a reviewing court can neither indulge a presumption of regularity nor evaluate the resulting harm.

Ibid. Consequently, *Hobby* seems to stand for little beyond its immediate holding; and even that is obscure. Technically, the case decides only that appellate reversal of a white defendant's conviction on the ground of discrimination against blacks and women in the selection of grand jury foremen is unwarranted (*see* 468 U.S. at 350) because "vacating criminal convictions" is inappropriate when "[l]ess Draconian measures will suffice to rectify the problem" (*id.* at 349). This narrow reading would leave it open for a federal district court to entertain a pretrial motion to dismiss the indictment in a case identical to Hobby's: *Hobby* would mean only that the denial of such a motion was not cognizable on appeal following conviction. *Cf. United States v. Mechanik*, 106 S. Ct. 938 (1986), declining to reverse a conviction because of the presence of an unauthorized person during the taking of grand jury testimony, although "[w]e assume for the sake of argument that . . . the District Court would have been justified in dismissing portions of the indictment on that basis had there been actual prejudice and had the matter been called to its attention before the commencement of the trial," *id.* at 941; *see also id.* at 943.

(B) Common-law doctrine in some (but not all) jurisdictions requires that grand jurors be unbiased.

(C) Finally, the Fourteenth Amendment's Due Process Clause may impose some, albeit not stringent, restrictions on service by grand jurors who have been prejudiced against a defendant through adverse newspaper publicity and the like. *See Beck v. Washington*, 369 U.S. 541, 546 (1962) (dictum). *Cf.* paragraph [315] (C) *infra*.

[154] **Same.** Once the jurors for a term have been selected, their names are published or made available through the office of the jury commissioners or the clerk of court. They meet in closed session, with no judicial officer in attendance. By statute or common law doctrine, no one except the prosecutor, a

stenographer, and the single witness testifying is permitted to be present during testimony to the grand jury; and the prosecutor and witnesses are also barred from the jury's deliberations. The jury is theoretically free, on its own initiative, to consider any matters of felony (and sometimes other matters) within its jurisdiction and to call any witnesses it pleases; but as a matter of actual practice, grand juries generally limit their consideration to cases presented by the prosecutor and to the witnesses whom the prosecutor suggests they call. The prosecutor drafts "bills" charging defendants with offenses, presents witnesses to the grand jury in support of the bills, and, at the conclusion of the testimony, asks the jury to return bills as "true bills," or indictments. The grand jury is supposed to indict a defendant if, upon the evidence presented to it, it finds that there are sufficient grounds to believe the defendant guilty of an offense. In some jurisdictions the test of sufficiency of the grounds is described as "probable cause" or "reasonable cause"; in others it is described as a *prima facie* case—that is, evidence which, if believed, unexplained and uncontradicted, would warrant the defendant's conviction by a trial jury.

[155] **Same.** The grand jury ordinarily takes its legal advice from the prosecutor, although it may also request instructions from the presiding judge of the felony court. (The judge's general "charge" to the jury at the beginning of a session usually consists of administrative instructions and civic exhortations, conveying no principles of substantive law.) The jury has the subpoena power; witnesses who refuse to testify before it are taken into court, ordered to testify by the judge, and, upon further refusal, punished by the judge for contempt. Practice varies regarding the applicability of rules of evidence to the grand jury; in some jurisdictions the jurors are adjured by statute to receive only legally admissible evidence; in others they are left relatively unrestricted with regard to what they may hear. (For example, except with respect to privileges the Federal Rules of Evidence are explicitly made inapplicable to federal grand jury proceedings by Rule 1101(d)(2).) In practice, with no judge and no defense counsel present, grand juries hear just about whatever the prosecutor wants them to

hear. (Concerning the possibility of judicial review of the sufficiency, admissibility, and legality of evidence received by the grand jury, see paragraph [172] (B) - (D) *infra*; *cf.* paragraphs [161], [163] *infra*.) Following their deliberations on the evidence, the jurors by majority vote return bills of indictment into the felony court, signed as "true bills" by their foreman. These are the indictments required by constitution and statute and constitute the charging papers on which felony defendants are subsequently put to trial. Although grand juries differ in their tempers, for the most part they simply rubber-stamp the prosecutor's work product and obligingly return as "true" all the bills which the prosecutor presents, excepting those which s/he quietly lets it be known that s/he does not want returned. In "no-billing" the latter cases, the grand jury serves the function of taking the heat off the prosecutor for not going forward with prosecutions that s/he prefers not to undertake but cannot overtly decline without arousing the ire of some political or personal constituency.

[156] **The defensive decision to waive indictment—advantages of the indictment.** The various legal rules governing grand jury proceedings present a number of grounds of potential challenge to the composition and conduct of any particular jury. These, obviously, are lost if a defendant waives indictment and consents to be prosecuted by information. The defendant who waives also loses the slight chance that the grand jury may rebuff the prosecutor and no-bill the indictment. Finally, s/he loses one rather significant trial advantage. Informations may be amended substantially by the prosecutor prior to or during trial. Indictments may not be amended so as to charge "an offense that is different from that alleged in the grand jury's indictment," without resubmission to the grand jury. *United States v. Miller*, 471 U.S. 130, 142 (1985) (dictum). *See id.* at 142-45; *Ex parte Bain*, 121 U.S. 1 (1887); *Russell v. United States*, 369 U.S. 749, 770-71 (1962) (dictum). And, by reason of the prohibition against double jeopardy (see paragraphs [177], [422] *infra*), a prosecutor who finds at trial that the evidence is varying from the allegations of the indictment cannot stop the trial in order to resubmit the case

to the grand jury. The consequence is that an indictment imposes a much tighter check on the prosecution's proof at trial than does an information. Significant variance of the proof from the facts alleged in an indictment requires an acquittal (*see Sanabria v. United States*, 437 U.S. 54, 68-69 (1978), recognizing the principle and holding that double jeopardy bars a prosecutor's appeal from such an acquittal, even when the trial judge has taken an erroneously narrow view of the indictment's allegations), whereas a similar variance in an information case would ordinarily allow the defendant nothing more than a continuance. Similarly, the trial judge may not, in his or her charge, submit to the petit jury theories or grounds for conviction which an indictment does not support, *see Stirone v. United States*, 361 U.S. 212 (1960); *United States v. Miller, supra*, 471 U.S. at 138-40 (dictum); although s/he may submit such theories or grounds in an information case, provided that the defendant has been given sufficient notice and preparatory opportunity to meet those theories or grounds at the trial.

[157] Same—considerations affecting waiver. The advantages just mentioned suggest that generally a defendant should not waive indictment unless there is some affirmative reason for doing so. This is particularly true in the case of a defendant who is a member of a racial minority that has traditionally been underrepresented on juries in this area. Frequently, in these cases, a systematic-exclusion claim is as strong as any defense that the defendant is likely to have. Sound affirmative reasons for waiving indictment are presented in the following circumstances:

(1) *There is a substantial certainty of indictment; the next grand jury term is some time away; and the defendant is in jail or otherwise inconvenienced by the delay.* A proceeding by information, of course, need not await the next term of the grand jury, which may be several weeks (or, in rural counties, months) after bind-over. This delay can be particularly oppressive to a defendant who has not made bail. The period of pretrial incarceration may or may not be credited against a subsequent sentence, depending on local practice. (See paragraph [75-A] (B) *supra*.) In any event, some defendants who are bound over for the

grand jury and detained in default of bail are being held on charges for which they will not be sentenced to imprisonment, with the result that the whole period of pretrial detention is wasted. In such a case, anything that speeds the process up is advantageous. There may be other situations, too, in which a speeding-up is desirable. A defendant on bail may be planning a move and may, therefore, want to conclude the case quickly. In some jurisdictions a pretrial commitment for mental examination to determine competency to stand trial is authorized only after the charging paper is filed. Defense counsel may want to have that commitment as early as possible, since the nearer to the time of the offense a psychiatric evaluation is made, the more persuasive its results may prove in connection with a possible insanity defense. (See paragraphs [180]-[181] *infra*).

(2) *The defendant intends to plead guilty at trial.* There are two considerations here. First, in a plea case, even more than in a case that goes to trial, waiver of the grand jury tends to speed up final disposition. Second, in negotiating with the prosecutor, a defendant's willingness to save the prosecution the trouble of going before the grand jury is worth something.

(3) *The grand jury proceeding or the indictment may occasion substantial adverse publicity.*

(4) *Counsel has reason to believe that testimony before the grand jury may alert the prosecutor to defects in the prosecution's case that have gone unnoticed through the stage of the preliminary hearing and are not otherwise likely to be noticed by the prosecutor prior to trial; or counsel apprehends that testimony before the grand jury may give the prosecutor other investigative leads or alert the prosecutor to additional charges.*

(5) *The prosecutor is known to call prospective defense witnesses before the grand jury to badger them or to get their testimony on record for purposes of impeachment at trial.*

Other affirmative reasons for waiver, of course, may occasionally appear.

[158] **Challenge to the array or to the polls.** Unless compelling considerations call for waiving indictment, counsel should consider whether there is any available ground of attack

on the selection procedure or composition of the grand jury. See paragraph [153] *supra*; paragraphs [320]-[324] *infra*. Objections to the method of selection or to the qualifications of the jurors generally (including claims of systematic exclusion of a racial, ethnic, religious, economic, sexual, or other "distinct class" (paragraph [153] *supra*)) are made by a challenge to the array (that is, to the group of jurors collectively). Objections to a particular juror (on grounds of bias, lack of statutory qualifications, and so forth) are made by a challenge to the polls (that is, to specified individuals). Both sorts of challenges are ordinarily required to be made in writing and prior to the convening of the jury (or, in some jurisdictions, prior to indictment). Counsel should therefore obtain from the clerk of court or the office of the jury commission, as soon after bind-over as it is available, the list of grand jurors or of the grand jury "pool," "box," or "wheel," as the case may be, for the ensuing term. This list is often required by local law to be made accessible for inspection by counsel; if not, counsel should move the court having control over the grand jury to order the list disclosed on the grounds that "without inspection, a party almost invariably would be unable to determine whether he has a potentially meritorious jury challenge," *Test v. United States*, 420 U.S. 28, 30 (1975), and that the federal constitutional right against systematic exclusion of classes of citizens from the grand jury implies an ancillary right to fair opportunities to discover and prove systematic-exclusion claims, *Coleman v. Alabama*, 377 U.S. 129, 133 (1964); *cf. Ham v. South Carolina*, 409 U.S. 524 (1973). The grand jury list usually notes name and address, and sometimes occupation. Thus individual jurors can be checked out if desired. In larger cities there are jury investigating services, but these tend to be costly, and checking out grand jurors is seldom worth the cost. The jurors are probably individually qualified as far as the statutory criteria go; the kind of bias that disqualifies is narrow, and if the juror's name has not come up in counsel's investigation of the case and the complainant, the juror is probably not technically challengeable. The accepted method of proving claims of systematic exclusion has been described as follows:

The first step is to establish that the group [claimed to be excluded] is one that is a recognizable, distinct class, singled out for different treatment under the laws, as written or as applied. . . . [Blacks and women qualify *per se, see Rose v. Mitchell,* 443 U.S. 545, 565 (1979) (blacks); *Duren v. Missouri,* 439 U.S. 357, 364 (1979) (women; but note the *caveat* concerning gender-based exclusion in paragraph [153] *supra*); Mexican-Americans may now also qualify *per se, see Lockhart v. McCree,* 106 S. Ct. 1758, 1765-66 (1986) (dictum); other groups must be shown to qualify under the test of *Hernandez v. Texas,* 347 U.S. 475, 478 (1954), paragraph [153] *supra.*] Next, the degree of underrepresentation must be proved, by comparing the proportion of the group in the total population to the proportion called to serve [as jurors] . . . , over a significant period of time. . . . This method of proof, sometimes called the "rule of exclusion," has been held to be available as a method of proving discrimination in jury selection against a delineated class. . . . Finally . . . a selection procedure that is susceptible of abuse or is not racially neutral supports the presumption of discrimination raised by the statistical showing. [*Duren v. Missouri, supra,* implies that underrepresentation alone is not sufficient; it must also be shown that "this underrepresentation is due to systematic exclusion of the group in the jury-selection process," 349 U.S. at 364, as the result of "discriminatory purpose," *id.* at 368 n.26. However, *Duren* also recognizes that both systematic exclusion and discriminatory purpose may be inferred from a "significant discrepancy shown by the statistics" comparing a group's numbers in the general population with its numbers in jury pools and panels, and on juries, *ibid.*]

Rose v. Mitchell, 443 U.S. 545, 565 (1979), quoting *Castaneda v. Partida, supra,* 430 U.S. at 494. Counsel will therefore want to investigate both grand and petit jury lists, going back ten years or more, in order to demonstrate a pattern of discrimination. These are public records, available from the jury clerk or commissioners. If the clerk's or commissioners' records contain racial designations, the jury is probably challengeable upon the showing of even a relatively small discrepancy between the percentages of the racial minority group in the general population and on jury panels. *Avery v. Georgia,* 345 U.S. 559 (1953); *Whitus v. Georgia,* 385 U.S. 545 (1967); *Alexander v. Louisiana*, 405 U.S. 625 (1972); *cf. Castaneda v. Partida*, 430 U.S. 482, 493-95 (1977). When racial designations or indications of a selection process that "is not racially neutral" (*Rose v. Mitchell, supra*, 443 U.S. at 565) do not appear in the records, it is important to seek out other aspects of the procedure that are "susceptible of abuse" (*ibid.*). Any nonrandom method of culling or cutting prospective jurors would seem to be "susceptible of abuse" in this sense (*see id.* at 548 n.2, 566; *and see Castaneda v. Partida*, 430 U.S. 482, 497 (1977), describing the key-man system as "highly subjective"; *cf. Batson v. Kentucky*, 106 S. Ct. 1712, 1723 (1986)); but in the absence of some form of identification of prospective jurors by nonneutral characteristics in the records available to jury-selection officials, a stronger statistical showing of underrepresentation is apparently required. In any event, counsel should conduct the most thorough statistical study practicable for a period going back at least a decade, comparing the proportion of minority individuals in the general population of the country (as reflected in the latest federal census figures) with the proportions of minority individuals (a) who are on the jury rolls and (b) who have actually served as jurors. *See* the *Alexander* case, *supra*. If the jury records do not contain racial identifications, tax digests may. Sophisticated statistical methods of analyzing the data are available, and it is wise to consult a statistician for possible use as an expert witness. *See, e.g.*, NATIONAL JURY PROJECT (Bonora & Krauss, eds.), JURYWORK—SYSTEMATIC TECHNIQUES 5-1 to 6-15 (2d ed. 1983); NATIONAL JURY PROJECT & NATIONAL LAWYERS GUILD, THE JURY SYSTEM: NEW METHODS FOR REDUCING PREJUDICE (Kairys, ed. 1975); Finkelstein, *The Application of Statistical Decision Theory to the Jury Discrimination Cases*, 80 HARV. L. REV. 338 (1966); Kairys, *Juror Selection: The Law, a Mathematical Method of Analysis, and a Case Study*, 10 AM. CRIM. L. REV. 771 (1972); Sperlich & Jaspovice, *Statistical Decision Theory and the Selection of Grand Jurors: Testing for Discrimination in a Single Panel*, 2 HASTINGS CONST. L. Q. 75 (1975). Judicial receptivity to these statistical modes of proof is reflected in *Castaneda v. Partida, supra*, 430 U.S. at 496-97 n.17; *see also International Brotherhood of Teamsters v. United States*, 431

U.S. 324, 339-40 (1977); *Vasquez v. Hillery*, 106 S. Ct. 617, 621 (1986); *cf. McCleskey v. Kemp*, 107 S. Ct. 1756, 1767 (1987) (dictum).

[159] **Motions to suppress.** Motions to suppress illegally obtained evidence are considered in greater detail in paragraphs [223]-[253] *infra*. Although ordinarily made after indictment, in most jurisdictions they may be made earlier. The advantage of moving to suppress prior to the convening of the grand jury is that evidence suppressed at that time cannot be presented to the grand jurors. *Compare Silverthorne Lumber Co. v. United States*, 251 U.S. 385 (1920), *with United States v. Calandra*, 414 U.S. 338 (1974). The importance of forestalling its presentation is obviously intensified in jurisdictions which follow the rule that an indictment will not be quashed on the grounds of the receipt of illegally obtained evidence by the grand jury. See paragraph [172] *infra*. Counsel should accompany a preindictment motion to suppress with an application for a stay of all other proceedings in the case pending determination of the motion so that the prosecutor cannot go to the grand jury with the evidence while the question of its legality is under consideration by the court.

[160] **Requesting recording of grand jury proceedings.** (A) In a few jurisdictions the grand jury proceedings are routinely recorded, and a transcript of the notes of testimony is delivered to the defendant following indictment. There are slip-ups in the routine, however, and defense counsel may be wise to telephone the prosecutor to obtain an express assurance that a stenographer will be present when the case against the client is presented.

(B) In most jurisdictions the practice relating to disclosure of grand jury records to the defense has traditionally gone to the far extreme of illiberality. Although the prosecutor makes free use of the grand jury transcript (if there is one), defense counsel has very limited access to it. Defense counsel is generally forbidden to inspect it at all before trial except in a case in which the client is charged with perjury committed before the grand jury or in which counsel can show that grounds may exist for a motion to dismiss the indictment on account of matters occurring before the grand jury (see paragraphs [161]-[163], [172] *infra*). Even after a prosecution witness has testified at trial, defense inspection of the witness's transcribed grand jury testimony for purposes of impeachment is said to rest in the discretion of the trial court. This discretion, however, is increasingly being exercised in favor of permitting defense inspection at trial for impeachment purposes; in some jurisdictions (as in the federal courts), such at-trial inspection has become virtually a matter of right (see paragraph [380] *infra*). A few jurisdictions are beginning to move in the direction of more liberal pretrial disclosure of grand jury minutes to the defense as well (see paragraph [271] (A) *infra*), and constitutional arguments supporting the requirement of disclosure are available (see paragraph [270] *infra*). Depending upon the extent to which defense inspection of any notes of testimony taken before the grand jury is likely to become available at a later time, counsel may or may not want to try to make certain that notes are, in fact, taken and transcribed. Frequently, the decision whether or not to have a stenographer record or transcribe particular grand jury proceedings is made by a budget-conscious prosecutor. Prosecutors usually like to have grand jury testimony transcribed, since they get far more use out of it than the defense does (both because of its greater accessibility to them and because, in the *ex parte* grand jury proceedings, the prosecutor can lead and cross-question witnesses without equal privileges for the defense). If the proceedings are not recorded, therefore, it is usually for financial reasons. Defense counsel who concludes that (notwithstanding the prosecutorial advantages just described) it would be in a client's interest to preserve a record of the grand jury proceedings, and whose client can afford it, may want to consider offering to pay for a stenographic transcript, either on condition that counsel receive a copy in the event of indictment or without condition. (The condition would be illegal in a number of jurisdictions whose statutes flatly prohibit disclosure of grand jury proceedings to any person without court order.) Alternatively, counsel may want to move the criminal court for an order requiring the recording and transcription of grand jury proceedings at public expense, under the theory of *McMahon v. Office of the City and County of Honolulu*, 51 Hawaii 589, 590-91, 465 P.2d 549, 550-51 (1970) ("a defendant is under some circumstances constitutionally entitled to some part of the grand jury transcript"; "[w]e have no difficulty in requiring that presentations of evidence to grand juries . . . shall be recorded" because "[o]therwise there would be no remedy to make effective a constitutional right which may clearly exist"). In any event, if the defendant or prospective defense witnesses are subpoenaed to appear before the grand jury, counsel should telephone the prosecutor and insist that a transcript of their testimony be made. The prosecutor will have one made anyway, if s/he wants one for later impeachment, so counsel loses little by the demand. A transcript will be necessary to support the defendant's claim that his or her privilege against self-incrimination was violated before the grand jury if it was. See paragraph [161] *infra*. Counsel may also later wish to contend that the defendant or defense witnesses were called before the grand jury for the purpose of harassing and intimidating them; and either the transcript or the prosecutor's refusal to order a transcript will provide helpful support for that contention.

[161] **Protecting and advising defendants subpoenaed by the grand jury.** (A) In a few jurisdictions a prospective defendant or a person who is a target of a grand jury investigation cannot be compelled to testify before the grand jury. *E.g.*, *People v. Avant*, 33 N.Y.2d 265, 307 N.E.2d 230, 352 N.Y.S.2d 161 (1973). Elsewhere (and so far as the federal Constitution is concerned), prospective defendants and targets of investigation can be subpoenaed to testify (*United States v. Wong*, 431 U.S. 174, 179-80 n.8 (1977)), and they need not be advised of their target status by the prosecutor (*United States v. Washington*, 431 U.S. 181 (1977)), although, like any other witness, they may decline to answer specific questions asked them on examination before the grand jury under a valid claim of the privilege against self-incrimination. *See United States v. Mandujano*, 425 U.S. 564, 571-76 (1976) (plurality opinion). That privilege is given to witnesses, whether or not they are "sus-

pects," *Zurcher v. Stanford Daily*, 436 U.S. 547, 562 n.8 (1978) (dictum), both by state constitutions and laws and by the Fifth Amendment to the Constitution of the United States, which is made applicable to state proceedings by the Fourteenth Amendment, *Malloy v. Hogan*, 378 U.S. 1 (1964); see paragraph [57-A] (B) *supra*; paragraphs [227], [232] *infra*, and has been applied specifically to protect state grand jury witnesses, *Lefkowitz v. Turley*, 414 U.S. 70 (1973); *Lefkowitz v. Cunningham*, 431 U.S. 801 (1977); *Stevens v. Marks*, 383 U.S. 234 (1966). Although a plurality of the Supreme Court of the United States has said that grand jury witnesses need not be given *Miranda* warnings (see paragraph [29] *supra*; paragraph [363] (E) *infra*) such as those which are required prior to police interrogation of persons in custody, *United States v. Mandujano, supra*, 425 U.S. at 578-81; *see Minnesota v. Murphy*, 465 U.S. 420, 431 (1984) (dictum), the question remains open in the light of two concurring opinions in *Mandujano, id.* at 598-602, 609. Even the plurality opinion does not purport to decide whether a grand jury witness must be warned at least (1) that s/he may invoke the Fifth Amendment and refuse to answer any potentially incriminating question and (2) that s/he may have an attorney stand by outside the grand jury room and may interrupt his or her testimony to consult with that attorney whenever s/he wishes advice during the course of the examination, *see id.* at 582 n.7; *United States v. Washington, supra*, 431 U.S. at 186, 190. The contention that these latter warnings must be given to witnesses whom the grand jury has reasonable grounds to suspect of a crime—if not to all grand jury witnesses—is strongly supported by *Estelle v. Smith*, 451 U.S. 454 (1981), paragraph [232] *infra*; *see also Satterwhite v. Texas*, 56 U.S.L.W. 4470 (U.S., May 31, 1988), and by the dictum in *Schneckloth v. Bustamonte*, 412 U.S. 218 (1973), see paragraph [240] (C) *infra*, that in "trial-type situations" like formal grand jury proceedings (412 U.S. at 238), a "waiver of trial rights . . . such as the waiver of the privilege against compulsory self-incrimination" (*ibid.*) and the right to counsel (*id.* at 237) can be effective only upon the basis of an explicit and adequate prior warning of the right. *See, e.g., Carnley v. Cochran*, 369 U.S. 506 (1962). This is particularly true when, as in the case of a witness whom the grand jury has cause to suspect, "the in-

quiring government is acutely aware of the potentially incriminating nature of the disclosures sought," *Garner v. United States*,
424 U.S. 648, 657 (1976); *see also id.* at 660; *cf. Roberts v. United
States*, 445 U.S. 552, 559 (1980); *Minnesota v. Murphy*, *supra*,
465 U.S. at 429-30; *but see id.* at 428-29, with the result that it
is both practicable to require warnings and unfairly heedless
of "the fundamental purpose of the Fifth Amendment—the
preservation of an adversary system of criminal justice," *Garner
v. United States*, *supra*, 424 U.S. at 655—to omit giving them.
Therefore, counsel who enters a case after a client has already
appeared and testified before a grand jury should move the
court, at the earliest opportunity, for an order requiring transcription and disclosure to counsel of the stenographic notes
of the client's grand jury appearance, so that counsel can determine whether there has been any infringment of the client's
Fifth Amendment privilege, and what corrective measures—
such as a motion to quash the grand jury's use of the client's
testimony, *cf. Silverthorne Lumber Co. v. United States*, 251 U.S.
385 (1920), or a motion to quash any indictment based upon
that testimony, *cf.* paragraph [172] (D)(2)(b) and (D)(4)
infra—may be advised. (FED. R. CRIM. P. 6(e)(3)(C) supports
such a motion for transcription and disclosure in federal practice.) If the client is again summoned to testify before that or
another grand jury, counsel should instruct the client to decline
to answer any questions until the transcript of the client's
earlier grand jury appearance has been furnished to counsel,
on the grounds that without it counsel cannot make an intelligent decision regarding the extent to which the client now
can and should claim privilege and that any interrogation of
the client before the grand jury under these circumstances
would violate both the Fifth Amendment and due process. *Cf.
Stevens v. Marks*, *supra*; *Raley v. Ohio*, 360 U.S. 423 (1959).

   (B) When counsel has entered a case before the service of
a grand jury subpoena upon a client, counsel's primary role
at the grand jury stage lies in advising and assisting the client
to claim such protections as the law gives the client against
grand jury process. The available grounds for motions to quash
grand jury subpoenas *duces tecum* or *ad testificandum* are reviewed
in paragraph [163] *infra*. They are lamentably few. The

grounds upon which a duly subpoenaed witness may refuse to answer particular questions before the grand jury are also lamentably few. *See United States v. Calandra,* 414 U.S. 338 (1974). Basically, the latter grounds are:

(1) A claim of the Fifth Amendment privilege against self-incrimination (discussed in the following subparagraphs (C) through (E));

(2) A right not to answer questions based upon illegal electronic surveillance in violation of the Omnibus Crime Control and Safe Streets Act of 1968 (see paragraphs [243] (B), [245] *infra*), *Gelbard v. United States,* 408 U.S. 41 (1972), and, therefore, to have proceedings conducted pursuant to 18 U.S.C. §3504 to determine whether, in fact, some illegal surveillance occurred and underlies the grand jury questioning, *see Gelbard v. United States, supra,* 408 U.S. at 52-58; *cf.* the *Alderman* procedures described in paragraph [251] (A) *infra*;

(3) A right not to answer questions that seek disclosure of associations protected by the First Amendment, *see Branzburg v. Hayes,* 408 U.S. 665, 708 (1972) (dictum); *cf. Gibson v. Florida Legislative Investigation Committee,* 372 U.S. 539 (1963); *DeGregory v. Attorney General,* 383 U.S. 825 (1966); *Liveright v. Joint Committee,* 279 F. Supp. 205 (M.D. Tenn. 1968), or disclosure of information protected by any "valid [evidentiary] privilege . . . established by the Constitution, statutes, or the common law," *United States v. Calandra, supra,* 414 U.S. at 346 (dictum); and

(4) Possibly a right to relief against questioning pursued entirely for purposes of harassment, *United States v. Dionisio,* 410 U.S. 1, 12 (1973), or demonstrably unrelated to any legitimate function of grand jury inquiry, *see In re National Window Glass Workers,* 287 F. 219 (N.D. Ohio 1922), particularly in cases in which the grand jury investigation may trench upon freedom of association or other First Amendment concerns, *see Branzburg v. Hayes, supra,* 408 U.S. at 707-8, 709-10 (concurring opinion of Justice Powell).

Except for the Fifth Amendment, most of these grounds for refusing to answer grand jury questions are not factually presented in the ordinary criminal case; counsel who does have a case presenting them should consult NATIONAL LAWYERS GUILD (GRAND JURY PROJECT), REPRESENTATION OF WITNESSES BEFORE FEDERAL GRAND JURIES (3d ed. 1984).

(C) Advising a client under grand jury subpoena concerning the Fifth Amendment privilege often requires examination of an applicable immunity statute. In most jurisdictions immunity statutes permit the compulsion of testimony notwithstanding the fact that it is self-incriminating; they replace the privilege with a grant of immunity that, depending on the terms of the statute, may protect the witness against any prosecution on account of matters concerning which s/he is questioned or testifies (so-called transactional immunity) or may protect the witness only against the use of the witness's answers to prosecute him or her (so-called use immunity). The latter, more limited, form of immunity was held insufficient to displace the privilege and hence inadequate to support compulsion of a witness's testimony in *Counselman v. Hitchcock*, 142 U.S. 547 (1892); *see Albertson v. Subversive Activities Control Board*, 382 U.S. 70, 79-81 (1965), and it may still be held inadequate under some state constitutional privileges against self-incrimination. In *Kastigar v. United States*, 406 U.S. 441 (1972), however, the Supreme Court overruled *Counselman's* requirement of "transactional immunity" as far as the federal Fifth Amendment is concerned. *See also Lefkowitz v. Cunningham*, subparagraph (A) *supra*, 431 U.S. at 809 (dictum). An immunity statute satisfies the Fifth Amendment, the Court held in *Kastigar*, if it provides "use and derivative-use immunity," 406 U.S. at 457, which the Court defined as immunity "from the use of compelled testimony, as well as evidence derived directly and indirectly therefrom," *id.* at 453. *Kastigar* sustained a federal immunity-grant statute that, as construed, imposed a "total prohibition on use" of compelled self-incriminating testimony, *id.* at 460: "a comprehensive safeguard, barring the use of compelled testimony as an 'investigatory lead,' and also barring the use of any evidence obtained by focusing investigation on a witness as a result of his compelled disclosures," *ibid.* The Court emphasized that a criminal defendant "raising a claim under this statute need only show that he testified under a grant of immunity in order to shift to the government the heavy burden of proving that all of the evidence it proposes to use was derived from legitimate independent sources," *id.* at 461-62. The *Kastigar* opinion implies that not only the statute but also the Constitution "imposes on the prosecution the affirmative duty to prove that [its] . . . evidence [derives] . . . from a legitimate source wholly independent of the compelled testimony." *Id.* at 460. *See also Pillsbury Co. v. Conboy*, 459 U.S. 248, 255, 261 (1983). (A witness's testimony compelled under an immunity statute may be used against the witness in a subsequent prosecution for perjury committed before the grand jury, *United States v. Apfelbaum*, 445 U.S. 115 (1980); but, subject to this single exception, statements made by the witness after s/he has claimed the privilege and been granted immunity "may not be put to any testimonial use whatever against him in a criminal trial," *New Jersey v. Portash*, 440 U.S. 450, 459 (1979) (holding that "a person's testimony before a grand jury under a grant of immunity cannot constitutionally be used to impeach him [as a witness] when he is a defendant in a later criminal trial," *id.* at 459-60).) Counsel should examine closely the terms and the judicial construction of any state immunity statute possibly relevant to the client's situation. Particularly if enacted prior to *Kastigar* or under the requirements of state constitutional holdings following *Counselman*, it may provide the client with full transactional immunity. This immunity would, of course, be binding upon the state that offers it in consideration for a witness's testimony, whether or not the federal Fifth Amendment obliged the state to go so far. *See Piccirillo v. New York*, 400 U.S. 548 (1971). On the other hand, if the statute purports to grant only "use" immunity, counsel should examine the scope of that immunity to assure its conformance to the *Kastigar* requirements. Unless it conforms to those requirements, testimony may not be compelled under it.

(D) In terms of the mechanism by which immunity is conferred, the immunity statutes may again be classified into two categories. One, the automatic or "immunity bath" statute, protects the witness who testifies in certain described proceedings (grand jury proceedings, legislative investigations, and so forth) relating to certain described subjects (gambling, narcotics, and so forth), whether or not the witness claims the privilege and even though the witness may volunteer incriminating information. The other, the "claim" statute, protects the witness only if s/he claims the privilege (again, in certain described proceedings relating to described subjects) and if s/he is then expressly granted immunity under the statute. Defense counsel whose client is subpoenaed to appear before the grand jury in any situation in which the client's testimony may result in his or her indictment or may in any way incriminate the client with regard to any criminal offense (whether s/he has previously been bound over or charged by complaint or is merely under investigation) should ordinarily advise the client not to testify unless an "immunity bath" statute clearly applies and clearly provides full "transactional immunity" precluding future prosecution of the client for any and all matters relating to the testimony s/he may give. Under any other circumstances testimony given before the grand jury in the absence of an explicit claim of the privilege may be used against the client (*see United States v. Washington*, subparagraph (A) *supra*; *United States v. Mandujano*, subparagraph (A) *supra*, 425 U.S. at 572-76 (plurality opinion); *cf. Garner v. United States*, subparagraph (A) *supra*, 424 U.S. at 653-56); *Minnesota v. Murphy*, subparagraph (A) *supra*, 465 U.S. at 427-31; and even apparently innocuous testimony can often turn out subsequently to assist the prosecution in constructing a case along some line or theory that neither the client nor counsel has sufficient information to anticipate at this early stage of the proceeding. Accordingly, the client should almost always claim the Fifth Amendment right to refuse to answer grand jury questioning and should avoid appearing before the grand jury if at all possible. If the jurisdiction is one that forbids the calling of a prospective defendant, the prosecutor should be advised that counsel's client will not appear and should be asked to withdraw the subpoena. If the prosecutor refuses to do so, counsel should then move the court to quash it. In a jurisdiction that allows the defendant to be called, counsel should advise the prosecutor that if the client is compelled to appear before the grand jury, the client intends to claim the

Fifth Amendment in response to all questions except the client's name. Counsel should ask the prosecutor, therefore, to discharge the client from the obligation to appear, since his or her compelled appearance would only harass and prejudice the client before the grand jury, without serving any legitimate purpose in furtherance of the jury's inquiry. If the client is not then excused from appearing, counsel should instruct the client to appear and claim the privilege. (This claim may not, of course, subsequently be used against the client at any criminal trial, *United States v. Washington*, subparagraph (A) *supra*, 431 U.S. at 191 (dictum), nor may the client be made by the state to suffer any "grave [adverse] consequences solely because he refused to waive immunity from prosecution and give self-incriminating testimony," *Lefkowitz v. Cunningham*, subparagraph (A) *supra*, 431 U.S. at 807; see paragraph [232] (B) *infra*.)

(E) Specifically, counsel should give the following instructions to the client (which may be typed on a card for the client to carry into the grand jury room):

In answer to *every* question, say:

I RESPECTFULLY REQUEST PERMISSION TO LEAVE THE GRAND JURY ROOM TO CONSULT WITH MY LAWYER, SO THAT COUNSEL MAY ADVISE ME OF MY CONSTITUTIONAL RIGHTS IN REGARD TO ANSWERING THAT QUESTION.

If permission to leave is granted, come out and tell me what the question was.

If permission to leave is refused and you are directed to answer the question, say:

I RESPECTFULLY DECLINE TO ANSWER ON ADVICE OF COUNSEL, ON THE GROUNDS OF MY STATE AND FEDERAL PRIVILEGES AGAINST SELF-INCRIMINATION.

Never say anything other than these two things in the grand jury room unless I instruct you specifically that you can.

The client should be told to give these answers to all questions except his or her name, even though s/he may believe that the answer to a particular question would not, in fact, be incriminating. The test of a valid claim of privilege is whether any conceivable answer the witness might give *could* furnish a link in a chain of evidence incriminating the witness, not whether a specific answer *would* do so. *Blau v. United States*, 340 U.S. 159 (1950); *Hoffman v. United States*, 341 U.S. 479 (1951); *and see Maness v. Meyers*, 419 U.S. 449, 461 (1975). A witness who claims the privilege is not required to explain how the answer will incriminate him or her—or even to assert that it will (since that assertion is obviously incriminating), *Hoffman v. United States*, *supra*, 341 U.S. at 486-87; s/he need only assert that it *may*. And counsel is not obliged to leave a client to make unassisted determinations of the applicability of the Fifth Amendment to particular questions that the client is asked in closed-door grand jury proceedings; rather, counsel may properly instruct the client to make a routine claim of privilege— if the client's right to consult counsel about each question is refused—as a means of forcing the constitutional issue out of the grand jury room into open court, where an attorney can properly instruct and defend the client. Counsel should emphatically warn the client not to *ad lib* in the grand jury room, to watch out for the trick questions that prosecutors often snap back disarmingly at witnesses who claim the privilege— "Would that really incriminate you?" or "Now how could that possibly incriminate you?"—and to answer these questions, like all others, by saying, "I respectfully decline to answer, on advice of counsel, on the grounds of my state and federal privileges against self-incrimination." The client should be told that if anyone offers the client immunity, s/he should say nothing; but, once again, answer the next question by saying: "I respectfully request permission to leave the grand jury room to consult with my lawyer, so that counsel can advise me of my constitutional rights in regard to answering that question." Counsel should always accompany the client to the grand jury session and remain immediately outside the grand jury room, available for consultation. If immunity is offered, counsel should confer with the prosecutor and ask the statutory basis for the immunity. After inspecting the statute, counsel may conclude that it does not apply to the case or that it is constitutionally insufficient in the scope of immunity it allows and may then advise the client to persist in refusing to testify. If the prosecutor or the grand jury wishes to press the point, the client will then be taken before a judge, in open court, for proceedings to compel the client's testimony. *See United States v. Mandujano*, subparagraph (A) *supra*, 425 U.S. at 575-76 (plurality opinion). The judge will order the client to testify before the grand jury and, upon the client's refusal, will hear counsel's objections to the compulsion of the client. If the objections are overruled, the client will again be ordered to testify prior to being held in contempt. Counsel who continues to think that s/he has valid objections to the client's compelled testimony should request that the final order to testify be stayed pending counsel's proceeding by appeal or prerogative writ (whichever local practice allows) to obtain review of the judge's order. If a stay is refused, the client should be instructed to state politely that s/he refuses to answer questions, on advice of counsel, because of his or her privilege against self-incrimination. As long as the client's manner is inoffensive, counsel is now in a strong position to urge that the question of the validity of the claim of privilege should be tested in civil, rather than criminal, contempt proceedings. *See Shillitani v. United States*, 384 U.S. 364, 371 n.9 (1966); *Young v. United States ex rel. Vuitton et Fils*, 107 S. Ct. 2124, 2134 (1987) (dictum). Either form of contempt commitment may be challenged by appeal or by *habeas corpus* in state and federal courts. See paragraphs [70]-[71] *supra*. The trial judge should be asked to stay the contempt order pending appeal or to release the client on bail or recognizance pending appeal. *Cf. Pillsbury Co. v. Conboy*, subparagraph (C) *supra*, 459 U.S. at 251. If the judge refuses, the same relief may be sought by motion on the appeal or in *habeas*. *In re Grand Jury Proceedings (Lewis, Applicant)*, 418 U.S. 1301 (Douglas, Circuit Justice, 1974); *cf. In re Roche*, 448 U.S. 1312 (Brennan, Circuit Justice, 1980). Many judges are reluctant to release recalcitrant grand jury witnesses from confinement pending appeal of contempt commitments because the purpose of these commitments is coercive and they believe that immediate coercion of the witness is necessary to enable the grand jury to proceed expeditiously with its investigation. Counsel faced with a judge of this mind may find it useful to call the court's attention to a dictum of the Supreme Court of the United States in *United States v. Wilson*, 421 U.S. 309, 318 (1975): "A grand jury ordinarily deals with many inquiries and cases at one time, and it can rather easily suspend action on any one, and turn to another while [contempt] proceedings . . . are completed. . . . 'Delay necessary for a hearing would not imperil the grand jury proceedings.' " Under no circumstances should the client be left to make his or her own unaided decision before the grand jury whether or not to claim the privilege against self-incrimination or whether or not to testify under an immunity grant. S/he is always entitled to have the matter brought out into open court, through the procedures described in this paragraph, so that counsel can address the complex issues involved. *Cf. Maness v. Meyers, supra*, 419 U.S. at 465-70; *Pillsbury Co. v. Conboy*, subparagraph (C) *supra*, 459 U.S. at 261-62.

[162] Advising defense witnesses subpoenaed by the grand jury. Some prosecutors will issue grand jury subpoenas for witnesses whom they expect to testify favorably to the defense, in order to tie the testimony of these witnesses down on record for possible use to impeach them at a subsequent trial. Defense witnesses may, of course, be compelled to testify unless they have a valid ground for invoking the privilege against self-incrimination on their own behalf or unless their testimony is otherwise privileged (under the lawyer-client, doctor-patient, priest-penitent, or other recognized privileges) or unless they are questioned on matters irrelevant to the grand jury's investigations. Counsel should advise a witness with a claim of privilege other than self-incrimination to claim it and should support the witness in that claim through the same procedures that are suggested in paragraph [161] (E) *supra* to present the client's claim of self-incrimination. A witness with a potential self-incrimination claim should be advised to secure a lawyer to represent him or her independently. Other witnesses should be interviewed by counsel prior to their grand jury appearance, and their testimony should be prepared much as it would be prepared for trial. See paragraph [279] *infra*. Counsel should also explain to the witness the nature of grand jury proceedings, in order to make the witness as comfortable as possible while testifying. In the case of a particularly apprehensive witness, it may be advisable for counsel to accompany the witness to the antechamber of the grand jury room and stand by while s/he testifies. The statutes relating to the grand jury in the jurisdiction should be checked. If they do not prohibit a grand jury witness from disclosing to any person matters occurring before the grand jury, counsel should interview the witness after s/he appears before the grand jury, for the purpose of learning both the testimony s/he gave (as an arm against future impeachment) and the questions s/he was asked (as a possibly profitable discovery device). If an applicable statute does purport to forbid grand jury witnesses to reveal what occurred during their grand jury appearances, counsel may want to interview the witness in any event, challenging the statute on the ground that it is unconstitutional as applied to defense counsel's interviewing of a potential defense witness because it precludes fair opportunity to prepare and present a defense. See paragraph [116] *supra*; paragraphs [270], [410-A] *infra*. Of course, counsel undertaking such a challenge must advise the witness about the statute before the interview and should secure legal representation for the witness if the witness is going to talk. In cases in which it is apparent that the prosecutor is subpoenaing defense witnesses simply for harassment—subpoenaing a witness repetitively, for example—counsel may move to quash the subpoenas as abusive, on the ground that the prosecution is using the grand jury to intimidate defense witnesses and deprive the defendant of a fair trial. *Cf. Webb v. Texas*, 409 U.S. 95 (1972), described in paragraph [410-A] *infra*.

[163] **Resisting grand jury process.** (A) Motions to quash grand jury subpoenas *ad testificandum* may be made on the grounds that:

(1) The person subpoenaed is a prospective defendant (in jurisdictions that recognize the "prospective defendant" rule, see paragraph [161] (A) *supra*);

(2) The subpoena has no legitimate purpose in furtherance of an investigation within the jurisdiction of the grand jury but is being used solely for "harassment," *United States v. Dionisio*, 410 U.S. 1, 12 (1973) (dictum); *cf. United*

States v. Mandujano, 425 U.S. 564, 582-83 n.8 (1976) (plurality opinion) (dictum); or

(3) The grand jury is not pursuing a *bona fide* inquiry looking to indictment but is employing its subpoena power for some other purpose—for example, to gather evidence against a defendant who has already been indicted, *In re National Window Glass Workers*, 287 F. 219 (N.D. Ohio 1922); *cf. United States v. Mandujano*, *supra*, 425 U.S. at 594 (concurring opinion of Justice Brennan).

(B) Grand jury subpoenas *duces tecum* seeking the production of documents, records, or writings are susceptible to a motion to quash predicated on the same grounds or on the ground that the materials sought are privileged. A motion to quash may invoke the state and federal privileges against self-incrimination, *see United States v. Dionisio*, *supra*, 410 U.S. at 11 (dictum); *Zurcher v. Stanford Daily*, 436 U.S. 547, 562 n.8 (1978) (dictum); *United States v. Judson*, 322 F.2d 460 (9th Cir. 1963), if:

(1) The production of the documents, records, or writings would constitute an admission of their existence or possession in a context in which such an admission poses a substantial threat of incrimination, *United States v. Doe*, 465 U.S. 605 (1984); *Fisher v. United States*, 425 U.S. 391, 410-12 (1976) (dictum), or would constitute an implicit authentication of them, when the authentication poses such a threat, *id.* at 412-13 & n.12 (dictum); *Andresen v. Maryland*, 427 U.S. 463, 473 & n.7 (1976) (dictum), or

(2) The writings are "private books and papers" of the person who is ordered to produce them and their contents are potentially incriminating, *Boyd v. United States*, 116 U.S. 616, 633, 634-35 (1886).

(Boyd has been substantially undercut by four decisions of the Burger Court holding respectively that the Fifth Amendment privilege is not abridged by compelling the production from an individual of his or her accountant's papers, *Fisher v. United States*, *supra*, 425 U.S. at 405-14, or his or her "business records," *United States v. Doe*, *supra*, 465 U.S. at 606, or by compelling a bank to produce an individual's account records, *United States v. Miller*, 425 U.S. 435, 440-45 (1976) (by implication; the technical question decided was a Fourth Amendment issue with Fifth Amendment overtones), or by seizing an individual's business records under a valid search warrant, *Andresen v. Maryland, supra,* 427 U.S. at 470-77. The opinions in the first three of these cases, however, take pains to distinguish *Boyd* by pointing out that the writings in question were not the personal records or "private papers" of the persons whom they incriminated, *Fisher v. United States, supra,* 425 U.S. at 414; *United States v. Doe, supra,* 465 U.S. at 610 n.7; *United States v. Miller, supra,* 425 U.S. at 440. In addition, *Miller* neither involved a Fifth Amendment contention nor could support one, inasmuch as the compulsion of the subpoena there was not directed to the person incriminated (*Securities and Exchange Commission v. Jerry T. O'Brien, Inc,* 467 U.S. 735, 742-43 (1984); see paragraph [232](B) *infra*). And *Andresen* rests squarely on the cognate ground (*see ibid.*) that a search warrant, unlike a subpoena, authorizes the seizure of documents but does not compel their possessor to take any action to produce them, *Andresen v. Maryland, supra,* 427 U.S. at 473-77. For these reasons *Boyd* may yet survive in drastically narrowed form, to the extent of forbidding subpoenas addressed to an individual for the production of his or her own private papers whose contents potentially incriminate the individual, *cf. G.M. Leasing Corp. v. United States,* 429 U.S. 338, 355-56 (1977) (treating *Boyd* ambiguously); *United States v. Ward,* 448 U.S. 242, 251-54 (1980) (same); *United States v. Doe, supra,* 465 U.S. at 610-11 n.8 (same), or may at least survive to this extent in the case of peculiarly private papers such as nonbusiness letters and diaries, *cf. Hill v. California,* 401 U.S. 797, 805-6 (1971) (reserving the question); *Fisher v. United States, supra,* 425 U.S. at 401 n.7 (same).) Regarding the development of Fifth Amendment law in relation to document subpoenas generally, *see* Mosteller, *Simplifying Subpoena Law: Taking the Fifth Amendment Seriously,* 73 VA. L. REV. 1 (1987).

(C) Subpoenas *duces tecum* seeking records of witnesses that are protected by the lawyer-client, doctor-patient, or other privileges may also be quashed. *Continental Oil Co. v. United States,* 330 F.2d 347 (9th Cir. 1964); *cf. Fisher v. United States, supra,* 425 U.S. at 402-5 (dictum). It is a recognized ground for quashing or limiting a subpoena *duces tecum* that the subpoena is oppressively overbroad or indefinite. *See In re Certain Chinese Family Benevolent and District Ass'ns*, 19 F.R.D. 97 (N.D. Cal. 1956), and cases cited. And "[t]he Fourth Amendment provides protection against a grand jury subpoena *duces tecum* too sweeping in its terms 'to be regarded as reasonable.' *Hale v. Henkel*, 201 U.S. 43, 76 [(1906)]; *cf. Oklahoma Press Publishing Co. v. Walling*, 327 U.S. 186, 208, 217 [(1946)]." *United States v. Dioniso, supra*, 410 U.S. at 11-12 (dictum). *Accord, United States v. Calandra*, 414 U.S. 338, 346 (1974) (dictum); *Fisher v. United States, supra*, 425 U.S. at 401 (dictum); *United States v. Miller, supra*, 425 U.S. at 445-46 (dictum); *Donovan v. Lone Steer, Inc.*, 464 U.S. 408, 415 (1984) (dictum); *cf. United States v. Doe, supra*, 465 U.S. at 607-8 n.3. Local law should be consulted respecting both additional substantive grounds for attacking grand jury process and the exact procedures by which attack can be made.

(D) Recently grand juries (and occasionally prosecutors in support of their own criminal investigations) have begun to seek and obtain court orders requiring that named individuals submit to fingerprinting, photographing, or blood-testing or provide exemplars for handwriting or voice comparison. These kinds of orders, compelling responses beyond the scope of traditional subpoenas *ad testificandum* or *duces tecum*, were virtually unknown until the last few years, probably because of doubts that they were consistent with the state and federal privileges against self-incrimination and also—more basically—because there existed no authority in law for courts to make them. But in the wake of the *Schmerber*, *Wade*, and *Gilbert* decisions by the Supreme Court of the United States, holding the Fifth Amendment inapplicable to non-"testimonial" compulsions (see paragraph [232] (B), (C) *infra*), prosecuting authorities were emboldened to begin to seek these orders; thereafter, orders compelling suspects to speak and write for voice and handwriting comparisons were sustained over constitutional objection in *United States v. Dionisio, supra*, and *United States v. Mara*, 410 U.S. 19 (1973). In both cases, the Supreme Court considered only Fourth and Fifth Amendment contentions made against the orders (see paragraphs [230]-[232]

infra); the parties apparently did not ask, and the Supreme Court certainly did not answer, the question what authority empowered criminal courts to issue these unprecedented orders, whether or not they were consistent with the Constitution. Obviously, a litigant applying to a court for some sort of affirmative judicial order ordinarily has to show something more in support of the application than that the order, if issued, would not violate anybody's constitutional rights. S/he must show that there is some authority in law for the court to enter that kind of an order and that s/he has some legal right to invoke the court's authority. Prosecutors have not generally been thought exempt from these rudimentary requirements. *See, e.g., Lynch v. Overholser*, 369 U.S. 705 (1962); *State v. Olson*, 274 Minn. 225, 143 N.W.2d 69 (1966), paragraph [180] (B) *infra*. Therefore, counsel should oppose prosecutorial requests for the kinds of orders described in this subparagraph on the grounds that, whether or not it would be constitutional for the legislature to authorize them, the legislature has not done so; and in the absence of legislation, courts are not at liberty to entertain applications for orders alien to the common-law tradition. *Cf.* paragraph [274] (B) *infra*. Although this contention now appears to be foreclosed in the federal courts (*see United States v. Euge*, 444 U.S. 707 (1980), construing a general statutory grant of the subpoena power as authorizing the compulsion of handwriting exemplars), it remains open as a matter of state law when state grand juries or prosecutors ask state courts to issue these orders.

[164] **Advocacy to the grand jury.** In some jurisdictions defense counsel is permitted to communicate directly with the grand jury by a letter or other written submission, which may urge the grand jury not to indict (giving supporting reasons), or may request that the jury call the defendant or defense witnesses to testify. Letters urging against indictment may sometimes be quite fruitful, particularly when they offer constructive alternatives to criminal prosecution: for example, the representation that the client is prepared to enlist in the army; that military discipline will do more to shape up the client than a term in prison; and that an indictment would bar the client's

acceptance by the armed services. On the other hand, it is generally very unwise to put defense testimony in before the grand jury because the prosecutor has virtually complete control of witnesses before the jury and may examine them there in the absence of defense counsel. The prosecutor also has an almost unlimited right to use the grand jury transcript for investigation and subsequent impeachment. In any event, before addressing any communication to the grand jury, counsel should consult local statutes, rules, and customs. In many jurisdictions *any* communication by counsel to the grand jurors is improper; indeed, it may be punishable criminally or by contempt.

[165] **Identifying grand jury witnesses.** The secrecy of the grand jury does not extend beyond matters occurring in the grand jury room. There is nothing to preclude counsel or an investigator from going to the place where the grand jury meets in order to observe what witnesses the prosecutor has called. In some jurisdictions grand jury subpoenas, like others, are available for inspection through the office of the clerk or the bailiff of the court; these provide, of course, an easier method of identifying prosecution witnesses than does observation. In situations in which other means of discovery are not productive and the defendant's case is being presented to the jury at a time when few other cases are on, counsel may want to use one or another of these means to learn the identity of prosecution witnesses so that counsel can subsequently interview them. This will be unnecessary in jurisdictions which provide that the defense must be furnished a list of grand jury witnesses at or after the time of indictment (see paragraph [183] *infra*) unless the grand jury's investigation is protracted or counsel suspects that the prosecutor is not complying in good faith with the witness-listing requirement.

[166] **The matter of delay.** Questions relating to a criminal defendant's constitutional, statutory, and common-law rights to a speedy trial, including rights (a) to have the proceedings expedited; (b) to be released on recognizance if the proceedings are inordinarily delayed; and (c) to have the proceedings

dismissed with or without prejudice, by reason of the inordinate delay, are discussed in paragraphs [306]-[311] *infra*. Those sections should be consulted. Suffice it to say here that in some jurisdictions statutes require that an information be filed or an indictment be returned within a specified period of time after a bind-over (or after "commitment," which may be construed to mean either bind-over or arrest). In other jurisdictions, statutes require that a defendant must be tried within a specified time after bind-over or after commitment. Remedies under the statutes range from the release of the defendant from custody on his or her own recognizance to the dismissal of the prosecution with prejudice. Backstopping the statutes are constitutional provisions and the power of the court (sometimes expressly given by statute or rule, sometimes implied as "inherent") to dismiss charges for want of prosecution. Under these various guarantees of the right to speedy trial, counsel may (and sometimes must) make appropriate motions prior to the filing of the charging paper. These may be in the nature of a demand for expedition of the proceedings, or they may be an application for relief by way of discharge from custody or from prosecution. After considering paragraphs [306]-[311] *infra*, counsel should consult local statutes, rules, and practice.

[167] **Anticipation of a bench warrant.** Once an indictment is returned against a defendant who has not been previously arrested, a bench warrant authorizing his or her arrest will ordinarily be issued by the criminal trial court upon the prosecutor's request. A bench warrant may also be issued for a defendant previously released on bail if the grand jury indicts on new or additional charges. See paragraphs [73], [99] *supra*. Therefore, when counsel represents an unarrested or bailed client and knows that the prosecutor is presenting the case to the grand jury, counsel should suggest to the prosecutor prior to indictment an arrangement to surrender the client, without warrant, in the event an indictment is returned or new charges are added. The arrangements for surrender are similar to those at an earlier stage, discussed in paragraphs [42]-[44] *supra*, except that in the bench warrant phase it is easier to arrange for the client's surrender before a judge of the trial court instead of a magistrate if that seems advisable. Should the prosecutor be uncooperative, counsel may be able to block a warrant by appearing before the judge prior to indictment. Counsel should inform the judge about counsel's offers to surrender the client in the event of indictment and about the prosecutor's refusal and should request that the court notify counsel when a warrant is sought so that counsel may surrender the client in court. Alternatively, counsel may request that the judge issue a summons in lieu of a warrant when this is authorized by local law or practice.

[167-A] Anticipation of possible conviction and sentencing; assisting the client to make a favorable appearance at the time of sentence. Even while working to prevent a client's being charged and convicted, counsel cannot afford to forget the possibility that the client *may* be convicted and that some day, sooner or later, s/he will stand before the court for sentencing. To prepare for this contingency, counsel should begin at a very early stage of the case to think about things that can be done to improve the client's image at sentencing—while there is still time to do them. The client who comes before a sentencing judge on a presentence report showing that s/he has successfully completed four months of a six-month job-training program since arrest and release on bail or recognizance, for example, is a far more likely candidate for probation than the client who remains just as unemployed and unemployable during those four months as s/he was at the time of the offense. Counsel should, therefore, advise and assist the client at the earliest possible opportunity to find a situation in the community in which the client can make and document a good, solid record of adjustment prior to trial and sentencing. In particular, counsel should consider the possibilities of getting the client placed in (a) a steady, responsible job (see paragraph [118] *supra*); (b) a job-training program; (c) an out-patient psychiatric or psychological counseling program (see paragraph [120] *supra*); (d) a community-based rehabilitation program for alcoholics or drug addicts, if appropriate (and if (i) the client's enrollment in such a program would not furnish unprivileged evidence against the client or otherwise prejudice the defense on the criminal charge in the event of a not guilty plea and trial, and (ii) counsel has determined by inquiries in the probation department or among local criminal lawyers that the particular program is well regarded by the court); or (e) any other sort of counseling program— family counseling, vocational counseling, speech therapy, remedial reading—that responds to the basic problems that apparently got the client into trouble (see paragraph [463] *infra*). Counsel should also consider whether the client would look better to the probation department or the court if the client altered his or her place of residence, life style, or companions and should advise the client accordingly with all possible tact. The client's family and various social-service agencies may prove helpful in all of these regards; but counsel will find that sometimes there is simply no substitute for counsel's advising the client or for counsel getting on the telephone and running down a job or placement opportunity for the client.

XI. DEFENSIVE PROCEDURES AFTER FILING OF THE CHARGING PAPER AND BEFORE ARRAIGNMENT

[168] Proceedings after filing of the charging paper. The prosecutive stage next following the filing of an information or indictment in the court of record is arraignment.

(A) When a defendant is in custody, ordinarily the defendant, defense counsel who appeared at the preliminary hearing, or both of them will be notified of the arraignment date by the prosecutor, court clerk, or court administrator. (If new counsel has entered a case following bind-over, s/he should immediately advise the prosecutor, jail authorities, and clerk of the criminal court that s/he is now representing the defendant and should ask to be informed as soon as any charging paper is filed. Once advised of the filing, s/he should enter an appearance for the defendant in the criminal number, so as to be sure that s/he will be notified of all subsequent proceedings.) When a defendant is on bond, the arraignment notice may be sent to the defendant, to defense counsel who appeared at the preliminary hearing, to the bonding company or other surety, or to all of them. For obvious reasons, bonding companies are usually pretty faithful about relaying the notice to the defendant and to counsel, but they may slip up; and defendants themselves will sometimes fail to notify their lawyers of the receipt of notices from the court. Therefore, if counsel has received no notice within a short time after the end of a grand jury term when a bill against a client should have been presented—or within a short time after bind-over in a case that can be prosecuted by information—counsel should make inquiries of the client, the bonding company, and the clerk of the court, in that order.

(B) When a defendant who has never been arrested is indicted, the prosecutor will usually obtain a bench warrant from a judge of the court in which the indictment has been filed. The bench warrant is executed by arrest; the defendant is brought immediately before the court; an arraignment date is set; the defendant is committed without preliminary examination; and bail is set by the presiding judge.

[169] Checklist. During the prearraignment stage, there are a number of steps that defense counsel may want to take. Counsel should consider:

A. *Matters relating to arrest.* [Paragraph [170] *infra*]

B. *Matters looking backward to preliminary hearing.* [Paragraph [171] *infra*]

1. *Habeas corpus* or a motion to quash the transcript or the information or for other relief on the ground of denial of a preliminary hearing or on the ground of defects in the procedures at preliminary hearing or on the ground of insufficiency of the evidence to support a bind-over.

2. In a nonindictable case a motion to quash the information as unsupported by the preliminary hearing transcript or bind-over.

C. *Matters looking backward to the grand jury: motions to quash or to dismiss the indictment* [paragraph [172] *infra*] based on:

1. Objections to the procedures used in selecting grand jurors, to the composition of the jury, or to the qualifications of jurors.

2. Objections to procedural irregularities before the grand jury.

3. Objections to the evidence before the grand jury on grounds of:

    a. Insufficiency;

    b. Inadmissibility or illegal procurement.

4. Objections based on compelled self-incrimination of the defendant before the grand jury or on immunity grants.

D. *Matters relating to the face of the charging paper: motions to quash or to dismiss* on grounds of:

1. Failure to charge an offense or lack of jurisdiction. [Paragraph [173] *infra*]

2. Objections to venue. [Paragraph [174] *infra*]

3. Technical defects. [Paragraph [175] *infra*]

4. A statute of limitations. [Paragraph [176] *infra*]

5. Double jeopardy, pardon, and like matters. [Paragraph [177] *infra*]

6. Misjoinder. [Paragraph [178] *infra*]

E. *Matters looking forward to arraignment and trial.*

1. Discussions with the prosecutor. [Paragraph [179] *infra*]

2. Objections to the defendant's mental competency to plead; motions for commitment of the defendant for mental examination. [Paragraphs [180]-[181] *infra*]

3. Defensive investigation. [Paragraph [182] *infra*]

4. Motions for state-paid investigative or consultative assistance or for other support services that the defendant cannot afford. [Paragraphs [299]-[301] *infra*]

5. Defensive discovery, including a motion for a bill of particulars, a demand for a list of witnesses, and the initiation of other pretrial discovery procedures. [Paragraph [183] *infra*]

6. Motions to suppress illegally obtained evidence. [Paragraph [184] *infra*]

7. Motions for change of venue. [Paragraph [185] *infra*]

8. Challenges to the venire of trial jurors. [Paragraph [186] *infra*]

F. The matter of delay. [Paragraph [187] *infra*]

In the drafting and presentation of the prearraignment motions discussed in paragraphs [171]-[178], [180]-[181], [183]-[187], and [301] *infra*, counsel should also consult paragraphs [221]-[222] *infra*, dealing with practice on pretrial motions generally.

[170] Matters relating to arrest. If counsel has not taken steps before indictment to head off the issuance of a bench warrant, s/he should do so immediately after indictment (see paragraph [167] *supra*) or should arrange the surrender of the client (see paragraphs [42]-[44] *supra*). If these efforts fail and the client is arrested, counsel must take the usual steps to protect the client in custody and to obtain the client's release on bail or recognizance as quickly as possible. See paragraph [123] (I)-(VI) *supra* and the references therein. If the case is one in which the defendant has been previously bailed, then surrendered or rearrested after indictment because of the addition of charges by the grand jury, counsel should urge the court to release the defendant on recognizance or nominal bail on the additional charges, in light of the defendant's obligation, secured by the bail previously posted, to appear for trial on the original charges. See paragraph [73] *supra*.

[171] **Matters relating to preliminary hearing.** In nonindictable cases many of the objections to denial or inadequacy of a preliminary hearing that are summarized in paragraph [149] *supra* survive the filing of an information. After the information is filed, they may be raisable—depending upon local practice—by the procedures previously available (see the paragraphs referenced by paragraph [149] *supra*) or by a motion to quash or to dismiss the information or by both. Motions to quash or to dismiss informations on the ground that illegally obtained evidence was presented before the magistrate at preliminary hearing are considered in paragraph [172] (D) (3), (4) *infra*. A motion to quash or to dismiss the information will also lie to raise the objection that the information charges offenses not shown in the transcript of the preliminary examination or offenses for which the defendant was not bound over (in the jurisdictions where bind-over on a specific charge is a prerequisite to an information for that charge). See paragraphs [16], [125] (B) *supra*. If the argument made in paragraphs [130]-[131] *supra*—that indictment does not moot the right to a preliminary examination—prevails, certain attacks on the preliminary examination will also survive indictment in an indictable case and may be raised by the procedures enumerated in paragraph [134] *supra*, including a motion to quash or to dismiss the indictment.

[172] **Motions to quash or to dismiss an indictment on grounds relating to defects in the composition or functioning of the grand jury.** (A) Motions to quash or to dismiss an indictment are available in most jurisdictions on various grounds that challenge the composition or procedures of the grand jury or the sufficiency or legality of the evidence presented to it. Particularly important are:

(1) Challenges to the method of selection of the grand jurors or to their qualifications collectively or individually, including claims of systematic exclusion of a racial, ethnic, religious, economic, sexual, or other distinctive demographic group; claims that the jury panel was prejudiced by inflammatory publicity; and claims of bias of an individual juror (see paragraphs [153], [158] *supra*; paragraph [321] *infra*);

(2) Challenges to the manner of proceeding or to the functioning of the grand jury, for example, claims that unauthorized persons were present during the jury's deliberations or that the prosecutor engaged in prejudicial misconduct before the grand jury (*see State v. Joao*, 53 Hawaii 226, 491 P.2d 1089 (1971); *cf. United States v. Mechanik*, 106 S. Ct. 938, 941, 943 & n.2 (1986)(leaving unresolved the status of such objections in federal practice) or that less than a majority of the grand jurors concurred in returning the indictment (see paragraphs [154]-[155] *supra*);

(3) Claims that the defendant's rights were violated in the course of his or her appearance before the grand jury, for example, by compulsion of the defendant's testimony in violation of the privilege against self-incrimination (see paragraph [161] *supra* and subparagraph (D) (2) (b) *infra*); and

(4) Claims that the indictment was returned in violation of a grant of immunity given the defendant before the grand jury (see paragraph [161] *supra*).

(B) In some jurisdictions a motion to quash or to dismiss will lie upon the ground that there was insufficient evidence before the grand jury to support a finding of probable cause or to meet whatever other burden of proof is required by local law for the return of an indictment. *See, e.g., People v. Nitzberg*, 289 N.Y. 523, 47 N.E.2d 37 (1943); *but see Costello v. United States*, 350 U.S. 359 (1956), subparagraph (C) *infra* (federal practice). In other jurisdictions there are judicial decisions purporting to authorize these motions on the ground that *no* evidence was presented to the grand jury; but attempts to satisfy the no-evidence standard are obviously rarely successful.

(C) Attacks on the admissibility of evidence received by the grand jury will support a motion to quash or to dismiss an indictment only in jurisdictions that both permit review of the grand jury transcript for probable cause (see subparagraph (B) *supra*) and restrict grand juries to legally competent evidence (see paragraph [155] *supra*). In these jurisdictions an indictment will be set aside if exclusion of the inadmissible evidence would leave insufficient remaining evidence to support it.

(D) A more complex question is presented by attacks on an indictment on the ground that illegally or unconstitutionally obtained evidence was presented before the grand jury (for example, coerced confessions, evidence procured by unlawful searches and seizures or electronic surveillance, perjured testimony known by the prosecutor to be perjured).

(1) In *United States v. Calandra*, 414 U.S. 338, 344-45, 346 (1974), the Supreme Court of the United States repeated with approval a collection of *dicta* in earlier cases to the effect that, in the federal courts, indictments need not be dismissed by reason of the grand jury's use of unconstitutional evidence, *see Lawn v. United States*, 355 U.S. 339, 349-50 (1958); *United States v. Blue*, 384 U.S. 251, 255 n.3 (1966); *Gelbard v. United States*, 408 U.S. 41, 60 (1972), because: "[a]n indictment returned by a legally constituted and unbiased grand jury, . . . if valid on its face, is enough to call for trial of the charge on the merits. The Fifth Amendment requires nothing more." *Costello v. United States*, 350 U.S. 359, 363 (1956). But this conclusion manifestly does not follow from its premise. For, *in addition* to the requirements of the Fifth Amendment (or whatever state-law counterpart it may have in any jurisdiction, conferring a right to prosecution by indictment of a grand jury), criminal procedures must satisfy the requirements of other constitutional and statutory safeguards, including those that proscribe impermissible methods of obtaining evidence (see paragraphs [223]-[250] *infra*) and that have been read by implication to exclude the use of evidence obtained by the proscribed methods, *e.g.*, *Mapp v. Ohio*, 367 U.S. 643 (1961). The purposes of the exclusionary rules (see paragraphs [228], [251] *infra*) appear to forbid *any* use of unconstitutionally obtained evidence to aid a prosecution, as Justice Holmes recognized in *Silverthorne Lumber Co. v. United States*, 251 U.S. 385, 392 (1920): "The essence of a provision forbidding the acquisition of evi-

dence in a certain way is that not merely evidence so acquired shall not be used before the Court but that it shall not be used at all." Particularly in light of the doctrine that illegally obtained evidence may not "legally form the basis for an arrest or search warrant," *Alderman v. United States*, 394 U.S. 165, 177 (1969) (dictum); *cf. United States v. Giordano*, 416 U.S. 505, 529-34 (1974); and see paragraph [251] (C) *infra*, it is difficult to comprehend how the same evidence can "legally form the basis for" an indictment or a bind-over. And if the police may not even use the evidence to advance their investigation, *see Wong Sun v. United States*, 371 U.S. 471, 487-88 (1963), surely the prosecutor should not be permitted to use it to advance the prosecution by obtaining an indictment or a commitment. So the argument is logically forceful that the federal Constitution does compel the voiding of an indictment returned by a grand jury, or of a bind-over issued by a magistrate, before whom was presented evidence obtained in violation of federal statutory or constitutional guarantees. *See* Note, *Disclosure of Grand Jury Minutes to Challenge Indictments and Impeach Witnesses in Federal Criminal Cases*, 111 U. PA. L. REV. 1154 (1963); *compare United States v. Tane*, 329 F.2d 848 (2d Cir. 1964). This requirement would apply in both federal and state cases, to the same extent and for the same reasons that the exclusionary rules governing trial evidence do. See paragraph [57-A] (B) *supra*; paragraphs [227], [228], [251] *infra*. It would require the dismissal of indictments and the quashing of bind-overs whenever the unconstitutional evidence cannot be said to have been harmless in its impact on the grand jury or the magistrate, as the case may be, within the rule of *Chapman v. California*, 386 U.S. 18 (1967); *Harrington v. California*, 395 U.S. 250 (1969); *United States v. Hasting*, 461 U.S. 499, 508-12 (1983); and *Satterwhite v. Texas*, 56 U.S.L.W. 4470 (U.S., May 31, 1988)—not merely when the other, constitutionally untainted evidence is sufficient to support a finding of probable cause, *cf. Vasquez v. Hillery*, 106 S. Ct. 617, 623-24 (1986).

(2) The broad language of the *Calandra* opinion, however, expressly refuses "to extend the exclusionary rule to grand jury proceedings . . . , " 414 U.S. at 390. Technically, this language is *dictum* insofar as it implies that indictments are not to be quashed on the ground of the grand jury's receipt of

illegally obtained evidence. *Calandra* did not involve a motion to quash by an indicted defendant but held only that an unindicted grand jury witness was not entitled to a judicial order immunizing the witness from grand jury questioning based upon leads obtained through an unreasonable search and seizure. Counsel may therefore wish to contend:

(a) That *Calandra* does not foreclose a motion to quash by "a criminal defendant" who has been "indicted by the grand jury," 414 U.S. at 352 n.8, because these motions do not entail the sort of "interruption of the grand jury proceedings," *id.* at 353 n.8, with which *Calandra* is primarily concerned, *see id.* at 349-50.

Alternatively, it is arguable at least:

(b) That *Calandra* is limited to cases in which grand jury evidence is challenged on Fourth Amendment grounds, as distinguished from other grounds of illegality (such as coercion, *see, e.g., Mincey v. Arizona*, 437 U.S. 385, 397-98 (1978)) which implicate its "trustworthiness," *cf. Harris v. New York*, 401 U.S. 222, 224 (1971), paragraph [390] (H) *infra*, or involve the grand jury more directly in a constitutional violation, *compare United States v. Calandra*, *supra*, 414 U.S. at 353-54, *with New Jersey v. Portash*, 440 U.S. 450, 458-59 (1979); *cf.* paragraphs [250] (C), [251] (A) (2), [253] (B) *infra*; *but see United States v. Blue*, *supra*, 384 U.S. at 255 n.3 (dictum);

or

(c) That *Calandra* is limited to cases in which no motion to suppress has been filed prior to submission of the case to the grand jury, *see United States v. Calandra*, *supra*, 414 U.S. at 352-53 n.8; *cf.* paragraph [159] *supra*.

(These arguments would not bar the defendant's reindictment following new grand jury proceedings in which his or her constitutional rights were observed; they would merely require the dismissal of indictments obtained "'by exploitation of . . . illegality,'" *Wong Sun v. United States*, 371 U.S. 471, 488 (1963), paragraph [251] (A) *infra*, so as to provide a "remedy . . . denying the prosecution the fruits of its transgression," *United States v. Morrison*, 449 U.S. 361, 366 (1981).)

(3) However, the tone of *Calandra* bodes ill for these several distinctions and plainly implies that—until the present membership of the Supreme Court significantly changes—there is no real hope for the argument of a constitutional right to dismissal of indictments based on illegally obtained evidence. *See also United States v. Washington*, 431 U.S. 181, 185 n. 3 (1977); *United States v. Ceccolini*, 435 U.S. 268, 275 (1978); *Bracy v. United States*, 435 U.S. 1301 (Rehnquist, Circuit Justice, 1978). The hope is stronger that *Calandra* can be distinguished:

(a) In *information* cases, in which *Calandra*'s solicitude for the "special role" of the grand jury, 414 U.S. at 343, is obviously beside the point, upon a motion to quash an information or a magistrate's transcript on the ground of receipt of illegally obtained evidence at the preliminary examination (*but see* FED. R. CRIM. P. 5.1(a)); and

(b) In both information and indictment cases in which the motion to quash is based upon a claim of illegal electronic surveillance in violation of the Omnibus Crime Control and Safe Streets Act of 1968 (see paragraphs [243] (B), [245] *infra*) and can therefore draw support from 18 U.S.C. §2515, which "directs that '. . . no part of the contents of [an illegally intercepted] . . . communication and no evidence derived therefrom may be received in evidence in any [trial, hearing or other] . . . proceeding in or before any [court,] . . . grand jury . . . [or other authority of the United States, a State, or a political subdivision thereof] if the disclosure of that information would be in violation of this chapter,'" *Gelbard v. United States*, 408 U.S. 41, 43 (1972). *Compare id.* at 59-61, *with United States v. Calandra, supra*, 414 U.S. at 355-56 n.11.

(4) In any event, *Calandra* does not affect the right given by state law in some jurisdictions (see subparagraph (C) *supra*) to have informations and indictments set aside on the ground that the magistrate's or grand jury transcript contain insufficient legally competent evidence to support them. For this purpose, illegally obtained evidence is not legally competent evidence, *see, e.g., Priestly v. Superior Court*, 50 Cal. 2d 812, 330 P. 2d 39 (1958)—not because of the federal "exclusionary rule" that *Calandra* declined to apply to grand juries but be-

cause the state law screening function of preliminary examinations and indictments in these jurisdictions forbids
magistrates or grand juries to act upon evidence that will not
be admissible at trial.

(E) The various motions to quash or to dismiss an indictment
on the grounds suggested in this paragraph are ordinarily
required to be made before arraignment, or at least before the
defendant pleads. Local time limitations should be checked
and carefully observed, since untimelinesss can irrevocably forfeit meritorious claims of error in the proceedings leading up
to indictment. *See Davis v. United States*, 411 U.S. 233 (1973);
Francis v. Henderson, 425 U.S. 536 (1976); *cf. Wainwright v. Sykes*,
433 U.S. 72 (1977). But see paragraph [192] *infra*. Success
on any of the motions does not, of course, bar reindictment
following new grand jury proceedings that avoid the defects
of the old. Reindictment is precluded only if the statute of
limitations has run; and in many jurisdictions there are provisions that toll the statute during the pendency of a technically
deficient indictment or that permit reindictment within a specified time after its dismissal, even though the limitations period
has expired. Counsel may sometimes decide that, in light of
the probabilities of reindictment, available motions are not
advised. But knocking out an indictment is often a victory that
demoralizes the prosecution considerably and commensurately
improves the bargaining posture of the defense. See paragraph
[212] *infra*. Fringe benefits of the motions to quash or dismiss
should also not be ignored: (1) If denied, they leave a claim
of error that may be pressed on appeal from conviction; (2)
if granted, they ordinarily delay the trial at least one criminal
term (which may, of course, be a blessing or a bane, depending
on the circumstances of the defense); and (3) whether granted
or denied, they may occasion some inquiry into the proceedings before the grand jury (perhaps even serving as the basis
for a defense request to examine all or portions of the grand
jury transcript), knowledge of which may enable counsel to
gain some measure of informal discovery of the prosecution's
case.

[173] Challenges to the face of a charging paper—failure to charge an offense; lack of jurisdiction. (A) A motion to quash or to dismiss an indictment or information, or a demurrer to it, is used to challenge the legal sufficiency of its allegations. They may be legally insufficient for several different reasons, often confusingly grouped under the single rubric, "failure to charge a public offense."

(1) The allegations may state fully and clearly the specific acts the defendant is charged with doing, but these acts may be no crime. For example, a defendant might be charged under a statute penalizing one who "resists an officer in the execution of his duty" by an information alleging that the defendant did "run away and refuse to stop when called upon to stop by" the officer. A motion to dismiss or demurrer here tests the prosecution's legal theory. Specifically, it raises the issue of law whether one who runs away from a police officer thereby "resists" the officer within the meaning of the statute. There are, of course, no general rules of pleading or procedure that address themselves to this sort of "failure to charge a public offense." The question in each case is one of construction of the statute defining the substantive offense.

(2) Second, a charging paper may quite simply have something missing. The conduct with which it charges the defendant is perfectly consistent with criminality, but some ingredient of the crime or of the charge is omitted. The missing ingredient may be more or less important: Deficiencies in this regard range from those of the infamous burglary indictment that charged the defendant "did enter the dwelling house of A.B. in the nighttime" (the grand jury omitting "with intent to commit a felony therein") to the omission in a perjury indictment of the allegation that the person who administered the oath to the defendant in Courtroom No. 344 was a person "duly authorized by law to administer an oath in the matter." In this second regard, local practice varies enormously respecting the significance that an omission must have in order to be fatal. Most jurisdictions require allegations of (1) the name of the defendant, (2) a description or characterization of the defendant's conduct that asserts (in factual or conclusory terms) every legal element of the offense charged (including

acts done, any circumstances surrounding them that are necessary to make them unlawful, and the requisite mental state—
or *mens rea*), (3) enough about the place of the crime to disclose
that venue lies in the court, and (4) enough about the date of
the crime to disclose that it is within the statute of limitations).
Beyond these rudiments, the jurisdictions differ (and often
differ from offense to offense) regarding what must be
charged. Some jurisdictions require the identification of the
victim and great particularization of the means or instrumen-
talities of the offense. Others disregard these matters. Some
disregard even the rudiments just described. Conspicuous
among the latter are jurisdictions that provide statutory "short
forms," declaring that a charging paper shall be sufficient for
the crime of *x* if it alleges: "On [date], A.B. *x*'d C.D. within
the jurisdiction of this Court."

　　(3) Finally, a charging paper may be wholly unspecific and
conclusory. It may duplicate the language of the criminal statute (A.B. "did commit a lewd act") without giving the slightest
idea what the defendant *did*. Again, the jurisdictions vary considerably in the factual specificity required. Many permit allegations in conclusory statutory language under all but the
vaguest statutes. *Cf. Michigan v. Doran*, 439 U.S. 282, 290
(1978) (dictum). The following formulation of federal pleading rules is also common in state practice: "It is generally
sufficient that an indictment set forth the offense in the words
of the statute itself, as long as 'those words of themselves fully,
directly, and expressly, without any uncertainty or ambiguity,
set forth all the elements necessary to constitute the offence
intended to be punished' ... 'Undoubtedly the language of
the statute may be used in the general description of an offence,
but it must be accompanied with such a statement of the facts
and circumstances as will inform the accused of the specific
offence, coming under the general description, with which he
is charged .' ... " *Hamling v. United States*, 418 U.S. 87, 117-
18 (1974); *see also United States v. Bailey*, 444 U.S. 394, 414
(1980). Conclusory pleading has several recognized vices. It
(1) impairs the defendant's rights to be "'fairly inform[ed]
... of the charge against which he must defend,' " *ibid.*; see
paragraph [270] (B) *infra*], and to have "'the record ...

sho[w] with accuracy to what extent he may plead a former acquittal or conviction,'" *Sanabria v. United States*, 437 U.S. 54, 66 (1978), for purposes of double jeopardy in the event of a subsequent prosecution, see paragraph [177] *infra*; (2) deprives the defendant of any opportunity to test the prosecution's legal theory by demurrer to its facts (subsection (A)(1) *supra*), *see Russell v. United States*, 369 U.S. 749 (1962); and (3) deprives the defendant, in an indictable case, of any opportunity to obtain judicial review of the concurrence of findings of fact by the grand jury and the trial jury or judge that the right to prosecution by indictment supposes, *see Stirone v. United States*, 361 U.S. 212 (1960); *United States v. Miller*, 471 U.S. 130, 138-40, 142-45 (1985). It should be noted that the bill of particulars (see paragraph [183] *infra*), which some courts assert supplies the need for factual allegations in the charging paper, in fact remedies only the first of these three vices. It does not touch the second because of the general rule that a demurrer will not lie to a bill of particulars; and it does not touch the third because the bill is the product of the prosecutor, not the grand jury. Defense counsel whose other interests are not harmed by delay at the pleading stage may do well to attack even venerable and accepted forms of conclusory charging papers, particularly indictments, on the ground that these disempower the court to perform its function of testing the sufficiency of the prosecutor's case in law and that they subvert the defendant's constitutional right of indictment by grand jury.

(B) Demurrers and motions to quash or to dismiss that attack the facial sufficiency of a charging paper are ordinarily required to be filed before the defendant's plea, although the contention that what is charged is not a crime (subsection (A)(1) *supra*) will usually be heard at any time. Similarly, motions to quash or to dismiss for lack of jurisdiction in the court will ordinarily be heard any time.

[174] **Same—venue.** (A) A charging paper is generally held fatally defective if it does not allege facts establishing venue in the court where it is filed. Allegations in terms of "*X* street" or "*Y* township" are ordinarily sufficient; the court will judi-

cially notice that *X* street or *Y* township is within the geographical jurisdiction of the court, if it is.

(B) Criminal venue is governed by statute within constitutional limitations. The prevalent state constitutional provision insuring trial by a jury of the vicinage, for example, embodies a time-honored common-law venue restriction; and even those forms of jury trial guarantees that omit explicit reference to "vicinage" may be read as implying a similar restriction, *see Alvarado v. State*, 486 P.2d 891 (Alaska 1971). The Sixth Amendment to the federal Constitution requires trial "by an impartial jury of the State and district wherein the crime shall have been committed, which district shall have been previously ascertained by law." *See United States v. Johnson*, 323 U.S. 273, 275 (1944); *Platt v. Minnesota Mining & Mfg. Co.*, 376 U.S. 240, 245-46 (1964); *cf.* U.S. CONST. art. III §2, cl. 3. The incorporation of the Sixth Amendment into the Fourteenth by *Duncan v. Louisiana*, 391 U.S. 145 (1968), paragraph [57-A] (B) *supra*; paragraph [315] *infra*, may, therefore, entail some measure of federal constitutional restraint upon state legislative power to manipulate criminal venue. *See Williams v. Florida*, 399 U.S. 78, 92-97 (1970); *cf. People v. Jones*, 9 Cal.3d 546, 510 P.2d 705, 108 Cal. Rptr. 345 (1973).

(C) The general constitutional and statutory rule is that offenses are triable only in the county (or circuit or other judicial unit) comprising the place where the offense was committed. The "crime-committed" formula depends principally on the statutory elements of the offense: If a defendant mails a false application to a state agency in another county, for example, venue may turn on whether the statue punishes "making" a false statement or "filing" one. Crimes, the operative elements of which occur in more than one county, are generally triable in either. Conspiracies are triable wherever the conspiracy was maintained (a mystic notion meaning, in practice, wherever any one of the conspirators spent any considerable amount of time during the conspiracy) or wherever any act in furtherance of the conspiracy was done. When the substantive law of conspiracy requires an overt act, venue demands at least one overt act within the territorial jurisdiction of the court. (At the trial stage, this latter rule may become quite significant. In the course of forum-shopping, prosecutors—particularly federal prosecutors—frequently pick a jurisdiction having only very attenuated contacts with a conspiracy and allege only one or two overt acts within it. If they fail to prove these specific overt acts at trial, an acquittal is compelled, even though the conspiracy is otherwise abundantly proved.) Local practice should be consulted for the intricacies of venue lore.

[175] Same—technical defects. Charging papers may be asailed by motion on a host of technical grounds, some relating to the nature of the charging language ("duplicity," vagueness, noncompliance with prescribed statutory forms), others relating to strictly formal matters (failure of an indictment to carry the signature or endorsement of the grand jury foreman or the prosecutor as required by law, failure of the indictment to carry an endorsement of the names of the witnesses who testified before the grand jury as required by law, and so forth). Some of these defects are remediable and will be ordered remedied without resubmission of the bill. Others are fatal. Again, local practice must be consulted.

[176] Same—statute of limitations. Statutes of limitations of prosecutions, like statutes of limitations governing civil matters, prescribe the permissible period of time within which a charging paper may be filed after an event, asserting liability based on that event. In many jurisdictions a charging paper is subject to demurrer or dismissal if it either (a) does not allege the date of the offense charged with reasonable specificity ("on or about" will do) or (b) alleges a date that is beyond the period of limitations. The demurrer or motion to dismiss is ordinarily required to be made before plea. In other jurisdictions questions of limitations are raised by a special plea at arraignment. In still others the defendant must go to trial and raise the issue by a demurrer to the evidence or a motion for acquittal at the close of the prosecution's case. Local practice should be consulted.

[177] **Same—double jeopardy, pardon, and so forth.** (A) At common law, matters such as double jeopardy, pardon, and abatement of the prosecution were ordinarily raised by special pleas at arraignment. Today, in many jurisdictions they must be raised by prearraignment motion. Most of these motions turn on technical issues of local law. Double jeopardy, however, is a complex and developing constitutional doctrine. (See the general discussions of double jeopardy principles in *United States v. Wilson*, 420 U.S. 332, 339-44 (1975); *United States v. Scott*, 437 U.S. 82, 87-101 (1978); *Swisher v. Brady*, 438 U.S. 204, 214-18 (1978); *United States v. DiFrancesco*, 449 U.S. 117, 126-38 (1980); *Justices of Boston Municipal Court v. Lydon*, 466 U.S. 294, 304-10 (1984).)

(B) Guarantees against being "twice put in jeopardy" may be found in the Fifth Amendment to the federal Constitution and in most state constitutions. In *Benton v. Maryland*, 395 U.S. 784 (1969), the Supreme Court held that the Fifth Amendment guarantee was "incorporated" in the Due Process Clause of the Fourteenth and thereby made binding upon state criminal trials. See paragraph [57-A] (B) *supra*; paragraph [227] *infra*. The Court has since declared its *Benton* decision fully retroactive, *Ashe v. Swenson*, 397 U.S. 436, 437 n.1 (1970); *and see Robinson v. Neil*, 409 U.S. 505 (1973), but it has reserved the question whether "each of the several aspects of the [federal] constitutional guarantee against double jeopardy" developed by its Fifth Amendment cases is now applicable in state prosecutions, *Waller v. Florida*, 397 U.S. 387, 390-91 (1970); *cf. Illinois v. Somerville*, 410 U.S. 458, 468 (1973). Subsequent cases strongly imply an affirmative answer to this question, *see Greene v. Massey*, 437 U.S. 19, 24 (1978); *Crist v. Bretz*, 437 U.S. 28, 32 (1978); *Hudson v. Louisiana*, 450 U.S. 40, 42 n.3 (1981), but they are not categorical on the point, *see Crist v. Bretz, supra*, 437 U.S. at 37-38; *Whalen v. United States*, 445 U.S. 684, 689-90 n.4 (1980). An affirmative answer is supported by numerous decisions holding that the incorporation of other Bill of Rights guarantees into the Fourteenth Amendment requires the application of each in state cases in a fashion identical to its application in federal cases. *Ker v. California*, 374 U.S. 23, 30-34, 46 (1963) (Fourth Amendment guarantee against unreasonable search and seizure); *Malloy v. Hogan*, 378 U.S. 1, 9-11 (1964) (Fifth Amendment privilege against self-incrimination); *Lakeside v. Oregon*, 435 U.S. 333, 336 (1978) (same); *New Jersey v. Portash*, 440 U.S. 450, 456-57 (1979) (same); *Washington v. Texas*, 388 U.S. 14, 22 (1967) (Sixth Amendment right to compulsory process); *Baldwin v. New York*, 399 U.S. 66, 68-69 (1970) (Sixth Amendment right to jury trial); *cf. Ludwig v. Massachusetts*, 427 U.S. 618, 624-30 (1976).

(C) The state and federal constitutional double jeopardy guarantees commonly bar a second prosecution for the same offense if the first trial passed the stage at which "jeopardy attached" (ordinarily, the swearing of the jury in a jury-tried case, *Crist v. Bretz*, subparagraph (B) *supra*, or the commencement of the presentation of evidence in a nonjury case, *id.* at 37 n.15 (dictum); *see also, e.g., Downum v. United States*, 372 U.S. 734 (1963); *Serfass v. United States*, 420 U.S. 377, 388 (1975); *United States v. Sanford*, 429 U.S. 14, 15 (1976) (per curiam) (dictum); *Lee v. United States*, 432 U.S. 23, 27 n.3 (1977) (dictum); *cf. Finch v. United States*, 433 U.S. 676 (1977) (per curiam)), and resulted in

(1) Acquittal, *Fong Foo v. United States*, 369 U.S. 141, 143 (1962) (per curiam); *United States v. Martin Linen Supply Co.*, 430 U.S. 564 (1977); *Sanabria v. United States*, 437 U.S. 54, 64, 68-69, 75 (1978); *Bullington v. Missouri*, 451 U.S. 430, 437-38, 445 (1981); *Arizona v. Rumsey*, 467 U.S. 203 (1984); *Arizona v. Washington*, 434 U.S. 497, 503 (1978) (dictum); *United States v. DiFrancesco*, 449 U.S. 117, 129-30 (1980) (dictum); *Arizona v. Manypenny*, 451 U.S. 232, 246 (1981) (dictum); compare *Abney v. United States*, 431 U.S. 651, 665 (1977)—that is, "a resolution, correct or not, of some or all of the factual elements of the offense charged" by a finding against the prosecution, *United States v. Martin Linen Supply Co., supra*, 430 U.S. at 571; *see also Sanabria v. United States, supra*, 437 U.S. at 71; *Burks v. United States*, 437 U.S. 1, 10-11 (1978); *United States v. Scott*, 437 U.S. 82, 97 (1978); *Smalis v. Pennsylvania*, 106 S. Ct. 1745, 1748 & n.6 (1986) [technically, the double jeopardy plea here is *autrefois acquit*]; or

(2) Conviction, *Brown v. Ohio*, 432 U.S. 161 (1977); *Harris v. Oklahoma*, 433 U.S. 682 (1977) (per curiam), unless the

defendant succeeds in getting the conviction set aside by a posttrial motion, an appeal, or postconviction proceedings, *United States v. Tateo*, 377 U.S. 463, 465-68 (1964); *Tibbs v. Florida*, 457 U.S. 31, 39-40 (1982); *Poland v. Arizona*, 106 S. Ct. 1749, 1753 (1986); *Montana v. Hall*, 107 S. Ct. 1825 (1987) (per curiam); *see also Price v. Georgia*, 398 U.S. 323, 326-30 (1970) (dictum); *Breed v. Jones*, 421 U.S. 519, 533-35 (1975) (dictum); *Jeffers v. United States*, 432 U.S. 137, 152 (1977) (dictum); *Burks v. United States, supra*, 437 U.S. at 13-18 & n.9 (dictum); *United States v. Scott*, subparagraph (A) *supra*, 437 U.S. at 88-92, 99 (dictum); *Oregon v. Kennedy*, 456 U.S. at 667, 676 n.6 (1982) (dictum), on any other ground than that the evidence was insufficient to support the conviction (in which case retrial is barred, whether the evidence is held insufficient by the trial judge on a motion for a new trial or for a judgment of acquittal, *Hudson v. Louisiana*, 450 U.S. 40 (1981), or by an appellate court, *Burks v. United States, supra*; *Greene v. Massey*, subparagraph (B) *supra*; *see Bullington v. Missouri, supra*, 451 U.S. at 442-43 (dictum); *Richardson v. United States*, 468 U.S. 317, 325 & n.5 (1984)(dictum); *Poland v. Arizona, supra*, 106 S. Ct. at 1753-54 (dictum), as long as the conviction is set aside for *insufficiency of the evidence*, and not merely as *against weight of the evidence, see Tibbs v. Florida, supra*) [technically, the double jeopardy plea here is *autrefois convict*]; or

(3) An inconclusive disposition by which the trial is terminated before verdict (*see Sanabria v. United States, supra*, 437 U.S. at 75) without the defendant's assent, *Downum v. United States, supra*; *United States v. Jorn*, 400 U.S. 470 (1971); *Crist v. Bretz*, subparagraph (B) *supra*, 437 U.S. at 33-35; and see paragraph [422] (B) *infra*, unless the failure to conclude the trial is occasioned by circumstances presenting "a manifest necessity" for a mistrial, *United States v. Perez*, 9 Wheat. 579, 580 (1824); *see Arizona v. Washington, supra*, 434 U.S. at 505-16; *United States v. Scott*, subparagraph (A) *supra*, 437 U.S. at 92-93 (dictum)—such as a hung jury, *e.g.*, *United States v. Sanford, supra*; *Richardson v. United States, supra*, 468 U.S. at 323-26—which are not referable to prosecutorial misconduct, see paragraph [422] (C) *infra*. (However, when the defendant moves for a mistrial or for any other disposition that would "terminate

the trial before verdict on grounds unrelated to factual guilt or innocence," a retrial is not barred, *United States v. Scott, supra,* 437 U.S. at 87; *see id.* at 92-101 (dictum); *United States v. Dinitz,* 424 U.S. 600 (1976); *Oregon v. Kennedy, supra,* unless the defendant's motion was occasioned by prosecutorial misconduct "intended to 'goad' the defendant into moving for a mistrial," *id.,* 456 U.S. at 676; *see also United States v. Scott,* subparagraph (A) *supra,* 437 U.S. at 94 (dictum); *United States v. DiFrancesco,* subparagraph (A) *supra,* 449 U.S. at 130 (dictum).)

(D) These rules do not preclude a second prosecution in certain "special circumstances," *Ricketts v. Adamson,* 107 S. Ct. 2680, 2685 (1987). Three such circumstances are:

(1) When "the State is unable to proceed on the [second] . . . charge at the outset because the . . . facts necessary to sustain that charge have not occurred or have not been discovered despite the exercise of due diligence," *Brown v. Ohio,* subparagraph (B) *supra,* 432 U.S. at 169 n.7 (dictum); *see Diaz v. United States,* 223 U.S. 442 (1912); *Garrett v. United States,* 471 U.S. 773, 789-92 (1985);

(2) When the prosecution makes multiple charges in the alternative at the outset and the defendant elects to obtain a disposition of some of them prior to the others, *Jeffers v. United States,* subparagraph (C) *supra,* 432 U.S. at 151-54; *Ohio v. Johnson,* 467 U.S. 493 (1984); and

(3) When the disposition of the earlier charges was effected pursuant to a plea bargain that the defendant later breaches, *Ricketts v. Adamson, supra.*

(E) The criteria for determining whether a prior charge involved the "same offense" differ considerably among the jurisdictions. Some courts apply an "identity of elements" test (are all the elements of one offense also elements of the second?); other courts use an "identity of proof" test (would the proof advanced by the prosecution on one charge support conviction on the second?); still others employ the "same transaction" or compulsory-joinder approach articulated by Justice Brennan, concurring, in *Ashe v. Swenson,* subparagraph (B) *supra,* 397 U.S. at 450-60; see the authorities collected in *Brooks v. Oklahoma,* 456 U.S. 999, 1000 (1982) (opinion of Justice Brennan, dissenting from denial of *certiorari*). The federal Fifth Amendment test is not entirely clear. At the least, the Fifth Amendment forbids successive prosecutions for two offenses if one subsumes all the elements of the other. *Harris v. Oklahoma*, subparagraph (C) *supra*; *Whalen v. United States*, subparagraph (B) *supra*, 445 U.S. at 693-94; *Illinois v. Vitale*, 447 U.S. 410, 417-21 (1980); *Payne v. Virginia*, 468 U.S. 1062 (1984) (per curiam); *Jeffers v. United States*, subparagraph (C) *supra*, 432 U.S. at 147-51 (dictum); *Morris v. Mathews*, 106 S. Ct. 1032, 1037 (1986) (dictum), as in the classic "lesser included offense" relationship, *e.g.*, *Brown v. Ohio*, subparagraph (C) *supra*; *Ricketts v. Adamson*, subparagraph (D) *supra*, 107 S. Ct. at 2685 (dictum); *compare Garrett v. United States*, subparagraph (D) *supra*, 471 U.S. at 787-89. Decisions reaching this result usually support it by reference to the so-called *Blockburger* test (from *Blockburger v. United States*, 284 U.S. 299, 304 (1932)), originally a rule of statutory construction, which is now sometimes said to be the rule of the Fifth Amendment, *see*, *e.g.*, *Albernaz v. United States*, 450 U.S. 333, 344-45 n.3 (1981). Despite its occasional characterization as a "'same evidence' test," *see*, *e.g.*, *Sanabria v. United States*, subparagraph (C) *supra*, 437 U.S. at 70 n.24, the *Blockburger* test "emphasizes the elements of the two crimes [and asks whether] . . . 'each requires proof of a fact that the other does not . . . .' " *Brown v. Ohio*, subparagraph (C) *supra*, 432 U.S. at 166. *See also Whalen v. United States*, subparagraph (B) *supra*, 445 U.S. at 691-93; *Illinois v. Vitale*, *supra*, 447 U.S. at 416-17; *Albernaz v. United States*, *supra*, 450 U.S. at 337-39, 343-45; *Ball v. United States*, 470 U.S. 856, 861 (1985); *United States v. Woodward*, 469 U.S. 105, 108 (1985) (per curiam). There have been hints, however, that this may not mark the outer limits of the Fifth Amendment's prohibition of multiple prosecutions for the "same offense." *See Brown v. Ohio*, subparagraph (C) *supra*, 432 U.S. at 166-67 n.6; *Ashe v. Swenson*, subparagraph (B) *supra*, 397 U.S. at 445-46.

(F) In any event, in addition to the three aspects of double jeopardy previously described (*autrefois acquit*, *autrefois convict*, and former jeopardy for the same offense), the Supreme Court has held that the federal Fifth Amendment embodies a "rule of collateral estoppel in criminal cases," *Ashe v. Swenson*, subparagraph (B) *supra*, 397 U.S. at 444; so that, following acquittal at a first trial, a defendant may not be retried for any offense (whether or not it be the "same offense") which depends upon proof of facts inconsistent with the facts established in the defendant's favor by the prior acquittal. *E.g.*, *Simpson v. Florida*, 403 U.S. 384 (1971) (per curiam); *Harris v. Washington*, 404 U.S. 55 (1971) (per curiam); *Turner v. Arkansas*, 407 U.S. 366 (1972) (per curiam); *and see United States v. Powell*, 469 U.S. 57, 64 (1984) (dictum). Significantly, the Court has also held that conviction of a lesser included offense or degree of offense constitutes an implicit acquittal of the greater offense or degree, *Price v. Georgia*, subparagraph (C) *supra*; *De Mino v. New York*, 404 U.S. 1035 (1972) (per curiam); and although this rule has so far been applied only in *autrefois acquit* situations, there is no reason why it should not obtain in collateral estoppel situations as well.

(G) Double jeopardy does not apply to successive civil and criminal proceedings, *see One Lot Emerald Cut Stones and One Ring v. United States*, 409 U.S. 232 (1972); *United States v. One Assortment of 89 Firearms*, 465 U.S. 354 (1984); *United States v. Ward*, 448 U.S. 242, 248 (1980) (dictum), but does apply to successive proceedings that are both of a criminal nature, such as criminal contempt citations, *see Colombo v. New York*, 405 U.S. 9 (1972), or juvenile delinquency petitions, *see Breed v. Jones*, subparagraph (C) *supra*; *Illinois v. Vitale*, subparagraph (E) *supra*, 447 U.S. at 415. It does not bar successive prosecutions by different sovereigns, *Heath v. Alabama*, 106 S. Ct. 433 (1985) (two states): so, for example, a defendant convicted of bank robbery in a state court may subsequently be prosecuted for federal bank robbery of the same bank. *See, e.g.*, *Abbate v. United States*, 359 U.S. 187 (1959); *United States v. Wheeler*, 435 U.S. 313 (1978). (The harshness of this result is somewhat ameliorated in practice because federal prosecutors tend generally to permit state authorities to proceed first against a defendant who has committed acts that might give rise to both federal and state charges; and the Department of Justice has a formal policy forbidding United States Attorneys to prosecute an individual for conduct that was an ingredient in a previous state prosecution, except when the Department expressly authorizes the federal prosecution in advance, upon a finding that it will serve compelling interests of federal law enforcement. *See, e.g., Watts v. United States*, 422 U.S. 1032 (1975) (per curiam); *Rinaldi v. United States*, 434 U.S. 22 (1977) (per curiam); *Thompson v. United States*, 444 U.S. 248 (1980) (per curiam). This "Petite Policy" is frequently violated in practice through inadvertence, and defense counsel may have to remind the federal prosecutor of it in cases in which it applies.) The "two sovereignties" principle does not permit successive prosecutions by a state and its political subdivisions (for example, municipalities); these are barred by double jeopardy whenever successive prosecutions by the same prosecuting agency would be. *Waller v. Florida*, subparagraph (B) *supra*; *United States v. Wheeler, supra*, 435 U.S. at 318-22 (1978) (dictum).

[178] **Same—misjoinder.** State statutes, rules of court, and common-law doctrines restrict the circumstances under which (a) a single charging paper may charge more than one offense against a single defendant and (b) a single charging paper may charge an offense or offenses against more than one defendant. In some jurisdictions a separate bill of indictment is returned for each offense charged, even though several charges are based on the same event or episode (for example, housebreaking, larceny, receiving, and conspiracy). Other jurisdictions permit the joinder of any number of separate charges in a single charging paper (usually in separate paragraphs, or "counts") if they are based on the same transaction or series of transactions or are part of a "common plan" or "common scheme" by the defendant or if the charges, although based on distinct transactions, are legally the same or similar (for example, housebreaking May 5, housebreaking June 12). More than one defendant may usually be joined if all were involved in the criminal transaction, whether or not conspiracy is alleged. The usual remedy for misjoinder (or for prejudicial joinder) is severance of the charges for trial (see paragraphs [259]-[264] *infra*). In some jurisdictions, however, charging papers that misjoin offenses or defendants are subject to dismissal on that ground. In researching local law on the question, counsel should keep in mind the possible contention that under a statute permitting joinder in specified circumstances (for

example, "common scheme"), a charging paper is defective for misjoinder if it fails to *expressly* allege facts supporting an inference that the specified circumstances ("common scheme") exist. These allegations are frequently omitted, even in traditional forms of charging papers. Another question common under many of the joinder statutes is whether things joinable to joinable things are thereby joinable to each other; that is, whether, under a statute that allows joinder of (a) different offenses arising out of one transaction and (b) the same or similar offenses arising out of different transactions, an indictment may charge: (1) housebreaking and (2) larceny, both on May 5, *plus* (3) housebreaking and (4) arson, both on June 12. The statutes are full of grounds for legal argument, and they should be read with a critical eye.

[179] Discussions with the prosecutor—negotiation and discovery. As the case progresses toward the trial stage, defense counsel will want to continue and intensify discussions with the prosecutor concerning possible dispositions without trial. See paragraphs [103], [150] *supra*. Plea negotiation is discussed in paragraphs [206]-[219] *infra*. In addition to the possibility that negotiation will lead to agreement on a favorable disposition, counsel should keep in mind its discovery potential. Whether s/he offers to negotiate or not, counsel is often advised to discuss the prosecution's evidence with the prosecutor shortly before arraignment and to request inspection of the prosecutor's file or items in it: the police report, laboratory reports, statements of prosecution witnesses, the defendant's prison record and probation or parole records (vital documents that defense counsel often cannot obtain from their sources but that the prosecutor will usually have), the criminal records of the complainant and prosecution witnesses, and so on. At this stage the file is likely to be fuller and the prosecutor more knowledgeable than heretofore.

[180] Raising the question of the defendant's competency to plead or to be tried; pretrial commitment for mental examination. (A) In some jurisdictions objections to the defendant's mental competency to plead or to be tried are raised by special plea at arraignment; in others they may or must be raised by prearraignment motion. Some jurisdictions provide that, upon the filing of these objections, the defendant is automatically committed to a state mental institution or specialized facility for psychiatric evaluation (commitment periods generally ranging from 30 to 90 days, although theoretically required by the federal Constitution to be "strictly limited" to a duration reasonably necessary for evaluation of the defendant's competency, *cf. McNeil v. Director*, 407 U.S. 245, 250 (1972)), or one or more "neutral and impartial" psychiatric experts are appointed by the court to examine the defendant and to make reports to the judge concerning the defendant's present competency.

(B) In other jurisdictions defense counsel or the prosecutor by motion or the court *sua sponte* may initiate a hearing on the advisability of committing the defendant for psychiatric examination or of appointing neutral experts to examine the defendant, and the court may thereafter enter an order for commitment or examination in its discretion. In addition to any neutral experts whose appointment is required or permitted by law, the court may also appoint psychiatric expert consultants to assist defense counsel, at state expense, upon defense motion and upon a satisfactory showing that the defendant cannot afford to hire such experts; or the court may authorize the expenditure of state funds to pay for the retainer of expert consultants of defense counsel's own choosing. An indigent defendant who "is able to make an *ex parte* threshold showing to the trial court that his sanity is likely to be a significant factor in his defense" has a federal constitutional right at least to an examination by a neutral expert who will thereafter be available to "assist in evaluation, preparation, and presentation of the defense," *Ake v. Oklahoma*, 470 U.S. 68, 82-83 (1985), and perhaps to a partisan defense expert. See paragraphs [181] (C), [299] *infra*.

(C) Often, motions seeking the defendant's commitment or examination by neutral experts or the appointment or allowance of payment of defense psychiatric experts will not be entertained by the court until after the filing of the charging paper. But by the time the paper is filed or very soon thereafter, counsel should have decided whether to seek examination of the defendant by any of these means. It is ordinarily desirable to invoke procedures for examination at the earliest possible stage of the proceedings, since counsel with a mentally disordered defendant will be considering raising the defenses of lack of criminal responsibility (that is, insanity within *M'Naghten* or the prevailing nonresponsibility test) or diminished capacity (where recognized) or both. An examination to determine the defendant's fitness to stand trial will also provide expert psychiatric information and opinion on the issues of criminal responsibility and diminished capacity, and the information or opinion will be more persuasive if it is acquired closer in time to the date of the offense.

(D) Indeed, when the defendant is indigent, often the only ways in which defense counsel can amass evidence to sustain any sort of psychiatric defense are either:

(i)   to move for the appointment or compensation of an expert consultant, or

(ii) to question the defendant's competency for arraignment and trial and to request that the defendant be committed or examined in connection with that issue.

Nevertheless, these are risky procedures. Before deciding to pursue them, counsel should consider:

(1) The mental state of the defendant as counsel is able to judge it from counsel's interviews with the defendant and counsel's investigation of the defendant's history (see paragraphs [82], [90] *supra*);

(2) The availablity of private psychiatric examinations of the defendant arranged by counsel without court process, hence without alerting the prosecution to the psychiatric aspect of the case (see paragraphs [120]-[122] *supra*) or, if the examinations have been made, their results;

(3) The defendant's attitude toward the raising of questions relating to his or her psychiatric balance;

(4) The nature of the psychiatrists at the institution to which the defendant will be committed or of those whom the court is likely to appoint (see paragraph [122] *supra*);

(5) The delay of other proceedings occasioned by the commitment or examination;

(6) In the case of commitment, the effect upon the defendant of a 30-day or 90-day pretrial incarceration in a mental institution;

(7) The potential harm to the defense if the prosecutor and the court are advised of possible psychiatric disorder in the client, including the risks of:

(a) Initiation by the prosecutor or the court of proceedings to have the defendant declared incompetent to be tried even though defense counsel eventually decides not to raise this issue—proceedings which may result in protracted involuntary commitment to a mental institution (see paragraph [181] *infra*);

(b) Rescission of the allowance of bail on the ground of the defendant's supposed dangerousness (see paragraph [57] *supra*), or increase of bail to a prohibitive figure by a judge who prefers not to have a mentally questionable defendant released from custody prior to trial;

(c) Obtaining of psychiatric evaluations by the prosecutor (who will always have access to the psychiatric report in the event of a statutory commitment or examination and may obtain a court order allowing a prosecution psychiatrist to examine the defendant in the event examination by an appointed defense psychiatrist is allowed), which the prosecutor can use to combat a defense of criminal nonresponsibility or diminished capacity at trial;

(d) Discouragement of the prosecutor's willingness to negotiate for a noncourt disposition (see paragraphs [206]-[218] *infra*) in the case of a potentially incompetent or "dangerous" defendant;

(e) Stimulation of damaging psychiatric inquiry, or the use of previously acquired psychiatric information, at the sentencing stage in the event of trial and conviction; and

(8) Disclosure by the defendant, in the course of the psychiatric examination, of information on the issue of guilt, to the extent that the prosecutor is likely to obtain the information and is permitted to use it to prove guilt at trial.

(E) This last point is a particularly complicated one:

(1) The courts are increasingly coming to hold that information disclosed by a defendant during a court-ordered psychiatric examination may not be used by the prosecution at trial on the issue of guilt, but the scope of this prohibition varies from jurisdiction to jurisdiction and may depend, within any given jurisdiction, on the nature of the examination (that is, whether it was ordered to determine the defendant's present competency or to determine the defendant's sanity at the time of the offense); whether the examination was ordered on defense motion or on motion by the prosecution or by the court *sua sponte*; whether it was ordered before or after the defendant tendered a claim of incompetency or plea raising some psychiatric defense, such as not guilty by reason of insanity; whether the defendant raises some such defense at trial; and whether if s/he does, s/he calls defense psychiatric experts to support it. Compare the approaches taken in *People v. Spencer*, 60 Cal. 2d 64, 383 P.2d 134, 31 Cal. Rptr. 782 (1963); *In re Spencer*, 63 Cal. 2d 400, 406 P.2d 33, 46 Cal. Rptr. 753 (1965); *People v. Arcega*, 32 Cal. 3d 504, 651 P.2d 338, 186 Cal. Rptr. 94 (1982); *Parkin v. State*, 238 So. 2d 817, 820 (Fla. 1970); *People v. Stevens*, 386 Mich. 579, 194 N.W.2d 370 (1972); *State v. Whitlow*, 45 N.J. 3, 210 A.2d 763 (1965); *Lee v. County Court*, 27 N.Y.2d 432, 267 N.E.2d 452, 318 N.Y.S.2d 705 (1971); *State ex rel. La Follette v. Raskin*, 34 Wis. 607, 150 N.W.2d 318 (1967); Fed. R. Crim. P. 12.2 (c), (d).

(2) A ground for federal constitutional exclusion of prosecution-tendered evidence obtained through pretrial court-ordered psychiatric examination of the defendant is established by *Estelle v. Smith*, 451 U.S. 454 (1981), which holds the Fifth Amendment privilege against self-incrimination (see paragraph [232] *infra*) applicable to a criminal defendant's "statements . . . uttered in the context of a psychiatric examination," *id.* at 465. *Accord, Satterwhite v. Texas*, 56 U.S.L.W. 4470 (U.S., May 31, 1988). Specifically, *Smith* decided that a state defendant's Fifth Amendment rights were violated by the admission of opinion testimony of a psychiatrist called by the prosecution to prove the defendant's probable future dangerousness as the basis for a death sentence at the penalty stage of the defendant's capital trial, when the psychiatrist's opinion

was based upon his questioning of the defendant during a pretrial competency examination ordered *sua sponte* by the trial court, without notice to the defendant and waiver by the defendant of his privilege against self-incrimination. There is no doubt that *Smith* also applies to prosecution evidence offered on the issue of guilt; the Court could "discern no basis to distinguish between the guilt and penalty phases of [a] . . . capital murder trial so far as the protection of the Fifth Amendment privilege is concerned." 451 U.S. at 462-63. However, Smith had "neither initiate[d] a psychiatric evaluation nor attempt[ed] to introduce any psychiatric evidence, " *id.* at 468; and in *Buchanan v. Kentucky*, 107 S. Ct. 2906 (1987), the Court held that when a defendant had *both* "joined in a motion for [a pretrial psychiatric] . . . examination" (*id.* at 2918) *and* presented an expert witness at trial "to establish . . . a mental-status defense" (*id.* at 2908), the prosecutor could constitutionally use the results of the examination to impeach this witness. The principal questions left after *Buchanan* are (a) whether *Smith*'s prohibition of prosecutorial use of pretrial psychiatric examination results continues to govern cases in which the examination was ordered at the defendant's request or in response to the defendant's raising of a claim of incompetency or a psychiatric defense before trial *but the defendant abandons or presents no evidence in support of the defense at trial*, and (b) whether the exception to the *Smith* prohibition recognized by *Buchanan* is limited to the use of pretrial examination materials *to rebut expert psychiatric evidence presented by the defendant at trial* or whether the defendant's raising of a psychiatric issue at trial opens the door to the prosecutor's use of the materials generally:

(a) The argument appears substantial that, unless and until the defendant actually presents evidence in support of a psychiatric plea or defense, *Smith* prohibits the prosecutor's incriminating use of any information produced by a pretrial psychiatric examination of the defendant, even one requested or invited by the defense. This is so because the logic of *Smith* was not that Smith's Fifth Amendment rights were violated by the competency examination conducted in that case—to the contrary, the Supreme Court acknowledged that the competency examination had been "validly ordered" by the trial judge *sua sponte*, 451 U.S. at 468—but rather that the Fifth Amendment came into play "[w]hen [the psychiatrist] . . . went beyond simply reporting to the court on the issue of competence and testified for the prosecution at the penalty phase on the crucial issue of . . . future dangerousness, [so that] his role changed and became essentially like that of an agent of the State recounting unwarned statements made in a postarrest custodial setting," *id.* at 467; *see also id.* at 465. *Compare Allen v. Illinois*, 106 S. Ct. 2988 (1986), upholding compulsory psychiatric examination of an individual subject to civil commitment proceedings as long as that individual "is protected from use of his [or her] compelled answers in any subsequent criminal case in which [s/]he is the defendant," *id.* at 2992. Under this logic it should make no difference that the defendant originally moves for the examination or triggers it by a pretrial plea of incompetency, unless such a motion or plea can properly be treated as a waiver of the Fifth Amendment privilege. But it cannot. Under *Pate v. Robinson*, 383 U.S. 375 (1966), and *Drope v. Missouri*, 420 U.S. 162 (1975), a state criminal defendant has a federal constitutional right to an adequate psychiatric evaluation and judicial determination of competency to stand trial; and it would impermissibly place the defendant "'between the rock and the whirlpool' " (*Garrity v. New Jersey*, 385 U.S. 493, 498 (1967)) to treat the defendant's invocation of this right as a waiver of the Fifth Amendment privilege. *See Simmons v. United States*, 390 U.S. 377, 389-94 (1968), described in paragraph [253] (B) *infra* and reaffirmed in *United States v. Salvucci*, 448 U.S. 83, 89-90 (1980); *Brooks v. Tennessee*, 406 U.S. 605, 607-12 (1972), described in paragraph [274] (B) *infra*; *Lefkowitz v. Cunningham*, 431 U.S. 801, 807-8 (1977); *cf. Jeffers v. United States*, 432 U.S. 137, 153 n. 21 (1977) (plurality opinion); *United States v. Goodwin*, 457 U.S. 368, 372 (1982) (dictum); *Spaziano v. Florida*, 468 U.S. 447, 455 (1984) (dictum); *and compare United States v. Jackson*, 390 U.S. 570, 581-83 (1968), *with Middendorf v. Henry*, 425 U.S. 25, 47-48 (1976), *and Corbitt v. New Jersey*, 439 U.S. 212, 218-20 & n.8 (1978); *compare Jackson v. Denno*, 378 U.S. 368, 389 n.16 (1964), *with Spencer v. Texas*, 385 U.S. 554, 565 (1967), *and Jenkins v. An-*

derson, 447 U.S. 231, 236-37 (1980). To treat the defendant's request for a psychiatric examination as a waiver of the Fifth Amendment privilege is the more impermissible because the very purpose of the examination is to obtain information that is necessary to an intelligent judgment regarding the merit of potential psychiatric defenses and regarding the defendant's capability to participate in that judgment: A forced choice between forgoing such information and forgoing a constitutional right has none of the qualities of a valid waiver. *Compare Brooks v. Tennessee, supra, with Town of Newton v. Rumery*, 107 S. Ct. 1187, 1192-93 (1987). Thus *Smith's* ban upon the use of evidence obtained from a pretrial psychiatric examination of the defendant, for the purpose of proving the defendant's guilt, should apply "whether the defendant or the prosecutor requested the examination and whether it was had for the purpose of determining competence to stand trial or sanity," *Gibson v. Zahradnick*, 581 F.2d 75, 80 (4th Cir. 1978). *See Battie v. Estelle*, 655 F. 2d 692, 700-3 (5th Cir. 1981); *and see Collins v. Auger*, 577 F. 2d 1107, 1109-10 (8th Cir. 1978).

(b) *Buchanan* describes the "narrow" issue it decides as "whether the admission of findings from a psychiatric examination . . . proffered solely to rebut other psychological evidence presented by . . . [the defendant] violated his . . . [constitutional] rights," 107 S. Ct. at 2908; *see also id.* at 2917-18. It treats this issue as "one of the situations that we distinguished from the facts in *Smith.*" *Id.* at 2918. The *Smith* opinion itself, in noting that the prosecution might be permitted to use evidence obtained by a pretrial psychiatric examination of the defendant in rebuttal, appeared to limit this possibility to cases in which the defense (i) presents expert psychiatric evidence and (ii) addresses the evidence to the specific issue on which the prosecution offers its rebuttal evidence. *Estelle v. Smith, supra*, 451 U.S. at 466 n.10; *see also id.* at 465-66; *Gholson v. Estelle*, 675 F. 2d 734, 741 & n.6 (5th Cir. 1982); *Battie v. Estelle, supra*, 655 F. 2d at 701-2. There are pre-*Smith* cases allowing the prosecution greater latitude in rebuttal—for example, permitting the prosecution to use the defendant's statements made during the psychiatric examination to impeach the defendant's trial testimony, by analogy to *Harris v. New York*,

401 U.S. 222 (1971), paragraph [390] (H) *infra. People v. Brown*, 399 Mich. 350, 249 N.W.2d 693 (1976); *People v. White*, 401 Mich. 482, 257 N.W.2d 912 (1977). But these decisions are assailable under Supreme Court holdings that a defendant's statements obtained in disregard of the Fifth Amendment may not be used even to impeach the defendant's inconsistent testimony at trial. *Mincey v. Arizona*, 437 U.S. 385, 397-98 (1978); *New Jersey v. Portash*, 440 U.S. 450, 458-60 (1979); *see also United States v. Leonard*, 609 F.2d 1163 (5th Cir. 1980).

(3) Obviously the law in this area is thorny, and the interjection of psychiatric issues into any criminal case involves substantial dangers that may offset its contemplated benefits. Its possibly harmful consequences to the defendant should caution counsel ordinarily not to bring psychiatric inquiries to the attention of the prosecution and the court unless the charges against the defendant are serious ones, carrying heavy penalties, and the prosecutor's evidence of guilt appears strong. Even in these cases, counsel who is seeking a psychiatric examination of the defendant for the purpose of exploring possible claims of incompetency to stand trial or possible defenses based on mental disorder is advised:

- *first*, to attempt to arrange such an examination privately, without court process (see paragraph [121] *supra*); then, if this cannot be done,

- *second*, to move the court (*ex parte*, if *ex parte* motions for state-paid assistance to the defense are authorized in counsel's jurisdiction) for funds to retain, or for court appointment of, a psychiatric expert *as a defense consultant, to examine the defendant and advise counsel regarding the defendant's mental state for purposes of assisting counsel to prepare the defense* (see paragraphs [298]-[301] *infra*), since information conveyed to such a defense consultant by either the defendant or counsel is shielded by attorney-client privilege (*see, e.g., People v. Lines*, 13 Cal. 3d 500, 507-16, 531 P.2d 793, 797-804, 119 Cal Rptr. 225, 229-36 (1975); *United States v. Alvarez*, 519 F.2d 1036, 1045-47 (3rd Cir. 1975)); then, if the motion is denied,

- *third*, to file whatever objections may be necessary to preserve a claim of error, including federal constitutional error (see paragraphs [299]-[300] *infra*), in its denial; and, only after weighing the various risks described earlier in this paragraph,

- *fourth*, to decide whether to make a motion for, or to enter a plea that will result in, the defendant's examination by court-appointed "neutral and impartial" psychiatric experts.

(F) Consideration of the same risks should dictate whether counsel chooses to oppose a prosecutor-initiated or court-initiated proceeding to commit the defendant for psychiatric examination or to order the defendant to submit to examination by court-appointed "neutral and impartial" experts. Legal grounds for opposition vary from state to state. The relevant statutes or common law rules may permit pretrial commitment of the defendant for mental examination only upon medical affidavits or upon a *prima facie* showing of the defendant's incompentency or when "there is reason to believe" that the defendant is incompetent or when "it appears" or "it is stated to the court" that s/he is incompetent. Even if the applicable standard is satisfied, the statutes and rules ordinarily authorize but do not require commitment. They confer discretion on the court, and counsel may urge, for example, that it is an inappropriate exercise of discretion to commit a defendant involuntarily to a mental hospital as long as there exist community mental health facilities available for the defendant's diagnosis on an out-patient basis. *Cf. State v. Page*, 11 Ohio Misc. 31, 228 N.E. 2d 686 (C.P., Cuyahoga Cty. 1967). For the most part, the constitutionality of defendants' involuntary commitment for competency examinations has been upheld. *See Annotation*, 32 A.L.R.2d 434 (1953). The commitment hearing must, however, satisfy the requirements of procedural due process (*cf. Vitek v. Jones*, 445 U.S. 480, 491-94 (1980); *Jones v. United States*, 463 U.S. 354, 361 (1983) (dictum)), which would appear to include both a full adversary hearing on whatever issues of fact are decisive of the propriety of a commitment order under state law (*Vitek v. Jones, supra*, 445 U.S. at 494-96) and a right to challenge the findings supporting such an order on the ground that there is "no basis" for them in fact (*see Schware v. Board of Bar Examiners*,

353 U.S. 232, 239 (1957), and cases cited together with *Schware* in paragraph [57-A] (B) (3) *supra*). In addition, there are a number of decisions holding that the privilege against self-incrimination precludes any judicial order that the defendant cooperate in the examination by talking to psychiatrists or answering psychiatrists' questions, at least when the defendant has not previously pleaded insanity or incompetency to be tried. *State v. Obstein*, 52 N.J. 516, 247 A.2d 5 (1968); *State v. Olson*, 274 Minn. 225, 143 N.W.2d 69 (1966); *cf. State ex rel. La Follete v. Raskin*, subparagraph (E) *supra*. (*Estelle v. Smith*, subparagraph (E) *supra*, does not forbid the compulsion of the defendant to undergo examination that includes potentially incriminating questions; it merely forbids the use of any resulting information for other purposes than determining competency.) Whether defense pleas of insanity or incompetency constitute a waiver of the privilege when it would otherwise be recognized as a bar to incriminating inquiries by a psychiatrist during a court-ordered examination is a disputed point. *Compare French v. District Court*, 153 Colo. 10, 384 P.2d 268 (1963); *State v. Hoskins*, 292 Minn. 111, 193 N.W.2d 802 (1972); *and Shepard v. Bowe*, 250 Ore. 288, 442 P.2d 238 (1968), reaffirmed in *State ex rel. Johnson v. Woodrich*, 279 Ore. 31, 566 P.2d 859 (1977), *and State ex rel. Ott v. Cushing*, 291 Ore. 355, 630 P.2d 861 (1981), *with Parkin v. State*, subparagraph (E) *supra*; *People v. Martin*, 386 Mich. 407, 192 N.W. 2d 215 (1971); *and Lee v. County Court*, subparagraph (E) *supra*, which collects the authorities in 267 N.E. 2d at 457. *See also United States v. Bohle*, 445 F.2d 54, 66-67 (7th Cir. 1971), and the federal cases collected in *United States v. Handy*, 454 F.2d 885, 888-89 (9th Cir. 1972); *United States v. Madrid*, 673 F.2d 1114, 1118-21 (10th Cir. 1982); and *United States v. Hinckley*, 525 F. Supp. 1342, 1345-51 (D.D.C. 1981), *rulings on other issues aff'd*, 672 F.2d 115 (D.C. Cir. 1982). *Cf. Williams v. Florida*, 399 U.S. 78 (1970), paragraph [193] (H) *infra*. (Most of these cases involve attempts by the prosecution to procure examinations of the defendant with regard to sanity at the time of the crime, as bearing on the issue of criminal responsibility. Examinations limited to the question of competency to be tried present a distinguishable question that has been little litigated. Presum-

ably, in the wake of *Estelle v. Smith*, subparagraph (E) *supra*, most courts will deal with the latter question by requiring the defendant to submit to the examination and to answer all questions asked "upon the condition that the results [will] . . . be applied solely for [the] . . . purpose" of adjudicating present competency. *See id.*, 451 U.S. at 468.)

(G) Judicial orders committing the defendant for examination or refusing defense requests for a commitment or examination or for appointment of a defense psychiatrist are commonly unappealable as interlocutory. When this is so, they may nevertheless be challenged by prerogative writs, such as prohibition or mandamus, as local practice makes appropriate. See paragraphs [312]-[314] *infra*. The committing court should be requested to stay its commitment order pending review by the writs. If it refuses to do so, a stay should be sought from the appellate court in which the application for the writ is filed. When no other form of review of commitment orders is recognized by local practice, *habeas corpus* should be used (see paragraphs [70]-[71] *supra*), and the *habeas* court should be asked to stay the defendant's commitment *pendente lite*.

[181] **Same.** (A) In addition to the considerations involved in deciding whether to have the defendant psychiatrically examined by way of court process, counsel will want to consider the following concerns before finally determining whether to challenge the defendant's competency to plead or to be tried:

(1) The advantages to the defense of conducting a hearing on the issue of the defendant's competency, including:

(a) The possibility of putting into the record, in a form that may make it admissible at a subsequent trial, evidence favorable to psychiatric defenses, such as insanity and diminished capacity;

(b) The possibility of early disclosure to the judge, who may preside at trial and sentencing, of evidence of mental illness that may attract the judge's sympathy; and

(c) The possibility of using the hearing for discovery of some portion of the prosecution's case;

(2) The disadvantages of such a hearing, including:

(a) Advance disclosure to the prosecutor of evidence that may subsequently be used by the defense to support psychiatric defenses at trial, with an opportunity for the prosecutor to cross-examine defense psychiatric experts, learn their weaknesses, and make a record for their subsequent impeachment;

(b) Disclosure to the court and to the prosecutor of evidence that incriminates the defendant on the guilt issue;

(c) Disclosure to the court and to the prosecutor of matters respecting the defendant's character and psychic makeup that may be prejudicial at the stage of sentencing in the event of conviction or on such other matters as the allowance or amount of bail pending trial or appeal;

(d) The possibility that if counsel decides not to present psychiatric defenses at trial, the jury may nevertheless learn from allusions to the pretrial hearing at trial—or from newspaper accounts of the hearing or from courthouse gossip— that there is some question whether the defendant may be mentally ill; and

(e) The delay of other proceedings occasioned by the hearing;

(3) The likelihood of success in convincing the court that the defendant is not competent to stand trial;

(4) The benefits of success, including:

(a) The possibility of avoiding a trial on the merits of the charges against the defendant either because the defendant is unlikely ever to recover competency to be tried or because the prosecution is likely to drop the charges rather than try a "stale" case after the defendant finally recovers competency;

(b) Other advantages of delaying the trial, including the abatement of prejudicial publicity or community sentiment that may make it difficult for the defendant to get a fair trial or a reasonable plea bargain at the present time;

(c) The potential advantages of a pretrial finding of incompetency for the defendant's presentation of psychiatric defenses at trial if the finding can be brought to the attention of the trial jury, for example, by calling as defense witnesses any hospital personnel who may examine or treat the defendant following his or her commitment upon such a finding; and

(d) The acquisition of additional evidence supporting psychiatric defenses at trial, which may emerge from post-commitment examination, observation, and treatment of the defendant, particularly since the hospital personnel who encounter the defendant in this setting *begin* with the assumption that s/he is mentally disordered and may interpret their observations in this light;

(5) The costs of success, including:

(a) Delay of the trial until the defendant is subsequently found competent;

(b) Possible incarceration of the defendant in a mental institution during the period of this delay (an incarceration that, under the constitutional standards announced in *Jackson v. Indiana*, 406 U.S. 715 (1972), "cannot be . . . [for] more than the reasonable period of time necessary to determine whether there is a substantial probability that he will attain . . . capacity [to stand trial] in the foreseeable future"; then, "[i]f it is determined that this is not the case, . . . the State must either institute the customary civil commitment proceeding . . . or release the defendant," whereas "even if it is determined that the defendant probably soon will be able to stand trial, his continued commitment must be justified by progress toward that goal," *id.* at 738; *and see Miller v. Gomez*, 412 U.S. 914 (1973) (per curiam), *aff'g*, 341 F. Supp. 323 (S.D.N.Y. 1972) (three-judge court); *Jones v. United States*, 463 U.S. 354, 364 n.12 (1983) (dictum); *cf. O'Connor v. Donaldson*, 422 U.S. 563, 575 (1975) ("even if . . . involuntary confinement was initially permissible, it could not constitutionally continue after [its initial] . . . basis no longer existed")); and

(c) The effect upon the defendant's record of a formal adjudication of incompetency; and

(6) The defendant's attitude toward taking the position that s/he is incompetent.

As the preceding summary suggests, some of the consequences of raising a claim of incompetency (for example, delay and the exposure of the judge to the defendant's psychiatric background) may be advantageous or disadvantageous, depending on all the circumstances. These require a particularized analysis on the facts of each individual case.

(B) On the legal issue of competency to plead or to be tried (which must be distinguished from the defense of non-responsibility on account of insanity at the time of the crime), the prevailing test in most jurisdictions is the relatively simple one whether the defendant:

(1) Has a mental disease or disorder

(2) That causes him or her

(3) To be unable, at the time of the plea or the trial, to

(a) Understand the nature and purpose of the proceedings, or

(b) Consult and cooperate with counsel in preparing and presenting the defense.

E.g., Dusky v. United States, 362 U.S. 402 (1960). This is probably the federal constitutional test as well. *See Pate v. Robinson*, 383 U.S. 375 (1966); *Drope v. Missouri*, 420 U.S. 162, 171-72 (1975). The test is generally applied by the courts to include only active psychotics, but it clearly should cover many other defendants as well, for example:

(i) Defendants whose mental disorder affects their ability to recall the events of the period when the offense is alleged to have been committed, *see Wilson v. United States*, 391 F. 2d 460 (D.C. Cir. 1968);

(ii) Defendants whose mental disorder impairs their ability to testify intelligibly in their own defense or makes them distasteful to the jury or court; and

(iii) Defendants whose mental disorder precludes their participation in a rational fashion in certain crucial decisions, such as whether to plead guilty in return for a bargained disposition or whether to invoke the defense of nonresponsibility.

(C) Concerning the selection of a psychiatric expert by the defense, see paragraph [122] *supra*. The right of an indigent defendant to state-paid expert psychiatric assistance is established by *Ake v. Oklahoma*, 470 U.S. 68 (1985), and the cases cited together with *Ake* in paragraph [299] *infra*.

(D) Orders sustaining or overruling defense objections to the defendant's competence to be tried and orders committing the defendant on a finding of incompetency may be appealable or unappealable by local practice. If unappealable, they may be reviewable by mandamus or prohibition or (in the case of commitment orders) by *habeas corpus*.

[182] **Defensive investigation.** At arraignment the defendant will have to enter a plea to the charge. (See paragraphs [188], [192]-[199] *infra*.) Although the plea may later be changed under some circumstances (see paragraphs [194], [195], [218], [220] (A) *infra*), leave to change it is ordinarily within the court's discretion. The initial plea entered at arraignment can be quite important, both for this reason and because the arraignment judge may be a particularly favorable one before whom to enter a guilty plea if the defendant is eventually going to plead guilty (see paragraph [218] *infra*). Consequently, counsel's factual investigation of the case should be completed before the initial choice of plea at arraignment, if at all practicable. The plea decision will usually be preceded by negotiations with the prosecutor (paragraph [179] *supra*), in which the bargaining position of the defense will depend in major part upon defense counsel's grasp of the facts of the case. See paragraphs [202]-[212] *infra*. The need to be knowledgeable in bargaining puts a premium on pushing defense factual investigation as far and fast as possible after the filing of the charging paper. See paragraphs [89]-[119] *supra*. New investigative leads may be provided by the charging paper itself, by a bill of particulars, by a witness list, or through initial discovery proceedings. See paragraphs [183]-[184] *infra*.

[183] **Defensive discovery: motion for a bill of particulars, motion for a list of witnesses, and other devices.** (A) Upon the filing of a charging paper that is insufficiently detailed to inform the defendant of the vital statistics of the offense charged, s/he may move for a bill of particulars, setting out in the motion the additional information that s/he seeks. S/he is ordinarily entitled to:
   (1) The specific date and time of the offense;
   (2) Its street location;
   (3) The name of the complainant or victim; and

(4) The means by which it is asserted that the defendant committed the offense.

Allowance of a bill of particulars is generally said to rest in the discretion of the court, and the standard jargon is that the bill does not lie to discover prosecution "evidence" (that is, means of proving facts, as distinguished from the operative facts of the offense themselves). But counsel should note the more liberal practice recognized in *Will v. United States*, 389 U.S. 90, 99 (1967). In most jurisdictions the defendant may not demur to the facts stated in the bill or move to dismiss it on the ground of failure to state an offense (see paragraph [173] *supra*); and in the event that the prosecution's proof at trial varies from the particulars contained in the bill, the defendant is usually given nothing more in the way of relief than a continuance (or mistrial and continuance if continuance without a mistrial is not feasible); only very rarely will a court dismiss a prosecution for variance of the proof from a bill of particulars. The bill is therefore a device of limited utility.

(B) More significant is the defendant's right to a list of witnesses. The right is given by statute or rule in most jurisdictions and may entail (depending upon statutory phraseology) a right to the names of all witnesses who appeared before the grand jury or at the preliminary hearing or a right to the names of all witnesses whom the prosecution plans to use at trial. (The latter right is generally held not to include prosecution rebuttal witnesses; it is enforced at trial, during the prosecution's case in chief, by defense objection to any witness not named in the list. The court may exclude the testimony of the witness, or it may allow the witness to testify and may grant a defense continuance to meet the testimony, in the discretion of the judge.) The right to a witness list is given by statutes or rules of two sorts: those which require that the names of witnesses be endorsed on the charging paper and those which authorize the defense to demand the names from the prosecutor. Even under statutes of the former sort, it is often common for prosecutors to withhold a witness list unless defense counsel ask them for it. After checking local practice, counsel should demand the list from the prosecutor, move to dismiss the charging paper by reason of the absence of witnesses' names on it, or move the court for an order requiring the prosecutor to produce a list, as occasion warrants.

(C) In addition to the motion for a bill of particulars and the demand for a witness list, defense counsel may, in some jurisdictions, proceed before arraignment with the various discovery devices discussed in paragraphs [265]-[275] *infra*.

[184] **Motions for the suppression of illegally obtained evidence.** Substantive and procedural matters relating to these motions are discussed in paragraphs [223]-[253] (A) *infra*. The motions may ordinarily be made during a part or all of the period after arraignment and prior to trial. But when they are also authorized before arraignment, there may be good reason to make them at that time. *First,* the motions are often a valuable informal discovery technique. Hearings on suppression motions can provide considerable information about the prosecutor's case. Any investigative leads unearthed in this manner are most useful if they come sufficiently early so that the defense has ample time to follow them up thoroughly. *Second,* many defensive cases (particularly in the possession crimes) stand or fall entirely on the motion to suppress. If this is lost, the defendant is advised to plead guilty. Of course, s/he usually may plead not guilty at arraignment, move to suppress thereafter, and, in the event the motion is lost, change the plea to guilty. But there are some advantages to having the decks cleared for an initial guilty plea at arraignment if counsel thinks this advised (for example, when the arraignment judge turns out to be a favorable sentencer). For this reason, it is often sensible to make the suppression motion before arraignment and, if necessary, move to continue arraignment pending disposition of the motion.

[185] **Motion for a change of venue.** These motions, discussed in paragraphs [254]-[257] *infra*, are ordinarily made following arraignment. In some jurisdictions, however, they may or must be made before arraignment. Local practice should be checked.

[186] Challenges to the venire of trial jurors. Matters relating to the selection of trial jurors (sometimes called petit jurors or traverse jurors) are discussed in paragraphs [315]-[340] *infra*. It is sufficient to note here that challenges to the venire or to the array of trial jurors, raising contentions of improper selection methods or standards or of the disqualification of the jurors on a ground common to all of them, are required in some jursidictions to be made within a designated time after the filing of the charging paper. Local practice must be consulted.

[187] The matter of delay. Questions of the timing of the various stages of the criminal proceeding following filing of the charging paper are discussed generally in paragraphs [302]-[311] *infra*. These paragraphs deal with procedures and grounds for defensive efforts to speed the proceeding up or to slow it down. Several matters, particularly, require consideration by defense counsel at the prearraignment stage:

(A) Counsel will sometimes have grounds to move to dismiss the charging paper because it was not filed within a period of time limited by statute or rule following bind-over or commitment. See paragraph [166] *supra*. The motion ordinarily must be made prior to plea.

(B) Counsel may wish to expedite trial or to lay a foundation for a motion to dismiss the prosecution because of lack of expedition of the trial. State statutes or rules frequently limit the time within which a defendant must be tried following bind-over or "commitment" or the filing of the charging paper. (In some jurisdictions, more than one of these periods is limited.) The statutes and rules, however, are usually qualified (explicitly or by judicial construction) by a principle known as the "demand rule," which obliges a defendant to invoke the statutory rights by a motion to compel trial. In the absence of such a motion, no motion to dismiss the prosecution for delay beyond the statutory periods prescribed for trial will subsequently lie. See paragraph [309] *infra*. In some jurisdictions, the period nominally prescribed by statute as running from bind-over or commitment or the filing of the charging paper is held by judicial construction to be tolled during the period of a defendant's failure to demand trial, with the result that the period actually runs from the date of demand. This version of the demand rule obviously requires counsel's attention in the days immediately following indictment or information.

(C) Counsel may, on the other hand, want to consider a motion for continuance of the arraignment in order to allow time for preparation for matters that will arise at arraignment. See paragraphs [188]-[219], [304] *infra*.

XII. ARRAIGNMENT AND DEFENSIVE PLEAS

[188] Arraignment procedure generally. Arraignment is the stage of proceedings when a misdemeanor or felony defendant ordinarily first appears before the court that has jurisdiction to try the case. The defendant has been notified of the arraignment date as indicated in paragraph [168] *supra*. A judge of the court presides at arraignment. The charging paper (indictment or information) is handed to the defendant and is usually read to the defendant by the clerk. The defendant is then asked to enter a plea to the charging paper. S/he may enter one or more of a variety of pleas. See paragraphs [192]-[199] *infra*. If s/he pleads not guilty, a trial date is set. If s/he enters a special plea requiring a hearing or an argument before trial on the merits, a date is ordinarily set for that purpose. If s/he indicates a wish to plead guilty, s/he is ordinarily advised by the judge that s/he has the right to have a trial, the rights to be represented by counsel, call witnesses, and cross-examine the prosecution's witnesses at trial, and the right to jury trial (if applicable), that a plea of guilty waives all these rights, and that upon the plea the defendant will be convicted and may be sentenced by the court in its discretion to a term of imprisonment of as much as x years (specifying the maximum) and to a fine of as much as y dollars (specifying the maximum). If mandatory minimum sentences or other special sentencing consequences apply to pleas of guilty to particular offenses, local law or practice may require the judge to inform the defendant of these. The defendant will be asked whether s/he understands the judge's warnings. Most judges will then proceed to interrogate the defendant to determine whether his or her plea is voluntary. The defendant will be asked whether s/he is pleading guilty of his or her own free will, because s/he is guilty, and for no other reason, and whether anyone has made any threats or any promises to the defendant to induce the guilty plea or has promised that the defendant will receive any sentence less than the maximum in this case. Some judges will reiterate that it is the judge's duty to decide what the sentence should be and that the judge will not be a party to, and will not honor, any promises on sentence but will sentence the defendant solely in light of his or her background and the nature of the offense. Some judges also will ask the defendant whether s/he is guilty of the charge of *x* (reading each charge) and then ask the defendant to describe briefly in his or her own words what s/he did (that is, to confess in factual detail in open court). Judges will ask whether the defendant has consulted his or her lawyer, whether the lawyer has advised the defendant concerning the consequences of the guilty plea, and whether the defendant is satisfied with the services of the lawyer. This interrogation is sometimes conducted by the prosecuting attorney instead of the judge; in other courts defense counsel is expected to conduct it. Courts differ considerably regarding the extent of the inquiry that they conduct or require: Some ask a few perfunctory questions of the defendant or defense counsel; others cross-examine the defendant at length. Judicial questioning of defendants has generally become more searching in the wake of *Boykin v. Alabama*, 395 U.S. 238 (1969), paragraph [195] *infra*, and *Blackledge v. Allison*, 431 U.S. 63 (1977), paragraph [216] *infra*. (In federal practice, FED. R. CRIM. P. 11 now requires the judge to address the defendant personally and to make specified inquiries.) If the defendant gives satisfactory answers, his or her formal plea of guilty is taken. S/he may then be sentenced at once, or a sentencing date may be set, with or without presentence investigation by the probation officer of the court and with or without a subsequent evidentiary hearing on sentence.

[189] **Rushed proceedings; making the record clear; continuances.** Counsel should expect that arraignment will be a hectic proceeding. Especially in metropolitan courts dozens of cases are scheduled for arraignment in a morning. Defendants and their lawyers are moving back and forth from the bench. The judge is frequently impatient. Sometimes the prosecution will request a continuance to continue its investigation, and this will be granted before the defendant or counsel reaches the bench. Counsel will have to keep composure in this con-

fusion. When s/he does not understand what the judge is doing, or has done, with counsel's case, s/he should respectfully ask the court for an explanation. The record should be clear on whether the arraignment has been held or continued and, if continued, on whose motion. Defense objections to a prosecution-sought continuance should be noted. If defense counsel is confronted by something unexpected, s/he should ask for time to withdraw and confer with the client or for a continuance to a later hour or date. S/he should resist being harried or pressured into snap judgments on previously unconsidered matters.

[190] Appointment of counsel at arraignment. When a defendant is called for arraignment and appears without counsel, s/he is generally advised by the judge of the right to counsel and to have counsel appointed if s/he is indigent. If s/he says s/he wants a lawyer and swears under oath that s/he cannot afford one (or executes a form pauper's affidavit), the court will appoint a lawyer. Sometimes a lawyer is appointed from among the members of the bar who are in the courtroom on other matters. The judge may say something like: "Counselor, will you talk with this defendant and advise the defendant on arraignment?" Such a request leaves it unclear whether the lawyer is being asked to represent the client and, if so, whether for the arraignment only or for the whole case. Counsel's first job is to clarify his or her own role. S/he should ask the court whether s/he is being appointed to represent the defendant as the defendant's attorney. Counsel should not accept an appointment to "talk to this defendant." Either s/he represents the defendant or s/he does not. Further, s/he should ask the court whether the appointment is to represent the defendant generally in the matter, at this and later stages, or only for the arraignment. If the latter, counsel should express the understanding that this means that the court will appoint other counsel to represent the defendant at subsequent stages if subsequent proceedings are advised. Counsel should make a clear request on behalf of the client for the assurance of adequate representation throughout the case. As an attorney s/he has an obligation to accept appointment, but s/he has neither the obligation nor the right to be used to create the appearance of representation without its reality. Counsel's second job, therefore, is to request adequate time to interview the defendant privately and to prepare for the arraignment. This is as important as at a preliminary arraignment, and counsel's position should be the same. See paragraphs [45]-[47], [53] *supra*. Ample opportunity for lawyer-client consultation is guaranteed by the Sixth Amendment to the federal Constitution, *see Geders v. United States*, 425 U.S. 80 (1976), and counsel must insist on it. Ordinarily a continuance of the arraignment to a later day should be requested. If the request is denied and counsel is forced to proceed, s/he should make an objection for the record on the ground that s/he is unprepared, has just been appointed, is being allowed insufficient time to acquaint himself or herself with the case, and that thereby the defendant's Sixth Amendment right to counsel at the arraignment (*Hamilton v. Alabama*, 368 U.S. 52 (1961)) is being denied. See paragraph [53] *supra*. If the defendant is nevertheless compelled to plead, counsel should advise the defendant to stand mute, whereupon the court will enter a not guilty plea. See paragraph [198] *infra*. After counsel has had time to investigate the case further, s/he may want to move to withdraw that plea, again claiming the Sixth Amendment right, in order to make other pleas or to raise defenses or objections customarily waived by a not guilty plea. See paragraphs [192]-[193], [220] (A) (2) *infra*. Should counsel be relieved from representing the defendant after entry of the plea and the appointment of another lawyer, counsel should inform that lawyer of the circumstances under which the plea was taken.

[191] **Continuances.** Arraignment may be continued, in the discretion of the presiding judge, on motion of either the prosecution or the defense. Defense counsel should request a continuance whenever s/he is unprepared to proceed (see paragraphs [189]-[190] *supra*) or needs additional time for some purpose (for example, to complete negotiations with the prosecutor, see paragraphs [206]-[219] *infra*). Whenever a defense motion is pending (see paragraphs [169]-[187] *supra*)

that, if granted, would terminate the proceedings or affect the choice of a defensive plea (see paragraphs [192]-[205] *infra*), counsel should either move to continue the arraignment or ask leave to withhold entry of a plea until the motion is decided. Local practice varies with regard to whether motions for continuances of arraignment are made (a) in writing prior to the arraignment date; (b) by telephone, more or less informally, to the judge or clerk prior to the arraignment date; or (c) in open court when the case is called for arraignment. In localities in which more than one of these procedures is permitted, counsel should nevertheless ordinarily try to give the court at least some advance notice of a request for continuance. The court will appreciate this courtesy and may be more sympathetic to the request. It is also important to attempt to obtain the prosecutor's agreement to, or acquiescence in, a defense motion for continuance, if possible. If an application for a continuance is denied, counsel should object and then have the client stand mute (see paragraph [198] *infra*) or plead not guilty. Of course, if counsel is prepared to enter special pleas prior to a plea of not guilty, s/he should do so. See paragraphs [192]-[193] *infra*. But standing mute or entering a not guilty plea is the safest course if counsel is unprepared and is forced, over objection, to plead. Should subsequent developments suggest a guilty plea, the plea of not guilty entered at arraignment can ordinarily be withdrawn and a guilty plea can be entered, with leave of court, at a later stage. This leave is usually very easy to obtain. Should special pleas later appear advised, a motion to withdraw the not guilty plea for the purpose of pleading specially is in order. See paragraph [220] (A) *infra*.

[192] **Special pleas.** In some jurisdictions, particularly those that maintain the old common-law forms of criminal procedure, certain defensive contentions must be raised by special pleas at arraignment. In other jurisdictions these contentions are raised by motion, before or at arraignment or a specified time prior to trial on the merits, as prescribed by statue or rule of court. Where special pleas are used, they must ordinarily be made prior to the entry of a general plea (guilty or not

guilty). Usually a defendant may plead both generally and specially at arraignment, but s/he must enter the special pleas *first*. Several states are quite strict in holding that a general plea waives the right to present any defensive contention raisable but not raised by a prior special plea. Except where the grounds for the special plea are not then available or discoverable, *cf. O'Connor v. Ohio*, 385 U.S. 92, 93 (1966); *Smith v. Yeager*, 393 U.S. 122, 126 (1968); *Reed v. Ross*, 468 U.S. 1 (1984); *Amadeo v. Zant*, 56 U.S.L.W. 4460 (U.S. May 31, 1988), it is probable that these sorts of enforced waivers can be made to stick. *See Davis v. United States*, 411 U.S. 233 (1973); *Francis v. Henderson*, 425 U.S. 536 (1976); *cf. Wainwright v. Sykes*, 433 U.S. 72 (1977); *Engle v. Isaac*, 456 U.S. 107 (1982); *but see Humphrey v. Cady*, 405 U.S. 504, 517 (1972); *Blackledge v. Perry*, 417 U.S. 21 (1974); *cf. Menna v. New York*, 423 U.S. 61 (1975) (per curiam), discussed in *Abney v. United States*, 431 U.S. 651, 659-62 (1977). On the other hand, where—as is common— the arraignment or trial judge is given broad discretion to permit the withdrawal of a general plea in order to allow the belated entry of special pleas, the unfavorable exercise of that discretion in particular cases may not foreclose federal constitutional claims against subsequent appeal or collateral attack. *Barr v. City of Columbia*, 378 U.S. 146, 149-50 (1964); *James v. Kentucky*, 466 U.S. 341, 345-49 (1984); *Williams v. Georgia*, 349 U.S. 375, 382-89 (1955); *Shuttlesworth v. City of Birmingham*, 376 U.S. 339 (1964) (per curiam); *compare Engle v. Isaac, supra*, 456 U.S. at 135 n.44. Counsel who seeks and is denied leave to enter an untimely special plea under these discretionary practices should therefore be sure that the special plea and the grounds for it are preserved in the record for appeal. See paragraph [419] *infra*.

[193] Checklist of special pleas and other matters that must be presented at arraignment. In the various jurisdictions counsel may find that one or more of the following special pleas is used. Local practice should be consulted.

A. *Plea to the jurisdiction*. (This plea challenges the jurisdiction of the court over the subject matter or the person of the defendant.)

B. *Pleas in abatement*. (These pleas are used to attack the face of the charging paper for substantive or technical inadequacy. They raise points like those that are considered in connection with the motions discussed in paragraphs [173]-[176], [178] *supra*.)

C. *Plea of limitations.* (The contention that prosecution is barred by the statute of limitations is sometimes raised by a special plea. In other localities it is raised by a plea in abatement, by pretrial motion, or by demurrer or motion at trial. See paragraph [176] *supra*.)

D. *Special pleas in bar.* These include:

    1. Pardon (that is, executive pardon).

    2. Double jeopardy (technically, *autrefois convict, autrefois acquit,* or former jeopardy; see paragraph [177] *supra*).

    3. Immunity (see paragraph [161] *supra*).

E. *Plea of not guilty by reason of insanity* (that is, lack of criminal responsibility by reason of mental disease under *M'Naghten* or cognate standards *at the time of the offense charged*). In some jurisdictions the defendant is automatically committed for pretrial mental examination upon the entry of this plea. See paragraphs [180]-[181] *supra*.

F. *Plea of incompetency to be tried* (that is, *present* mental disorder rendering the defendant incapable of appreciating the nature of the proceedings or of consulting with counsel in his or her defense). In some jurisdictions the defendant is automatically committed for pretrial mental examination upon the entry of this plea. See paragraphs [180]-[181] *supra*. The contention is sometimes made by an objection to pleading on the ground that the defendant is mentally incompetent to plead.

In addition to these special pleas, some jurisdictions require the filing of certain notices or motions at arraignment. The principal ones are:

G. *Notice of intention to present the defense of insanity* (that is, lack of criminal responsibility) *or other psychiatric defenses.* In a number of jurisdictions the notice procedure is used in lieu of, or in addition to, a special plea of not guilty by reason of insanity (subparagraph (E) *supra*). Unlike the traditional special plea the notice is frequently required to state the names and addresses of the witnesses whom the defendant intends to call in support of the insanity defense. A few jurisdictions require similar notice of intention to present expert testimony in support of other mental defenses, such as diminished capacity. (In federal practice, *see* FED. R. CRIM. P. 12.2(b).) The constitutionality of these several requirements is governed by the principles discussed in the following subparagraph.

H. *Notice of intention to present the defense of alibi.* This notice also is ordinarily required to contain specified details: the names and addresses of alibi witnesses and the place where the defendant contends that s/he was at the time of the offense. State courts have generally sustained the constitutionality of notice-of-alibi statutes against attacks based upon the state privileges against self-incrimination; and in *Williams v. Florida,* 399 U.S. 78 (1970), the Supreme Court upheld a notice-of-alibi provision challenged under the Fifth and Fourteenth Amendments. However, *Wardius v. Oregon,* 412 U.S. 470 (1973), holds "that the Due Process Clause . . . forbids enforcement of alibi rules unless reciprocal discovery rights are given to criminal defendants," *id.* at 472; and a strong argument can be based on *Brooks v. Tennessee,* 406 U.S. 605 (1972), that the Fifth Amendment also forbids enforcement of alibi rules unless local practice provides the defendant with sufficient discovery, *prior* to the time when the alibi notice is required to be filed, to permit defense counsel to make an advised decision whether or not to rely upon an alibi defense. See paragraph [274] (B) *infra.* Both *Williams* and *Wardius* reserve the question of the constitutionality of the sanction commonly prescribed by notice-of-alibi statutes: exclusion of the defendant's alibi evidence at trial if s/he fails to file timely notice. *See* 399 U.S. at 83 n. 14; 412 U.S. at 472 n. 4. The treatment of similar issues in *United States v. Nobles,* 422 U.S. 225, 241 (1975), and *Taylor v. Illinois,* 108 S. Ct. 646 (1988), strongly suggests that the exclusionary sanction will be sustained, *see also Estelle v. Smith,* 451 U.S. 454, 466 n.10 (1981). But where, as is usual, the statutes give the trial judge discretion to relieve defendants of this sanction, a failure to allow relief in particular cases may be challenged under the principle of *Williams v. Georgia,* 349 U.S. 375 (1955), paragraph [192] *supra,* since the right to present alibi evidence is unquestionably protected by the Sixth Amendment against arbitrary or unreasonable restriction by the states. *See Chambers v. Mississippi*, 410 U.S. 284, 302 (1973), paragraph [270] (D) *infra*; *Rock v. Arkansas*, 107 S. Ct. 2704, 2709-10 (1987); *Taylor v. Illinois, supra*, 108 S. Ct. at 651-53 (dictum).

I. *Motions to suppress illegally obtained evidence* (see paragraph [184] *supra*; paragraphs [223]-[253] *infra*).

J. *Election or waiver of jury trial* (see paragraphs [316]-[318] *infra*.

K. *Motions to dismiss or to quash the indictment or the information.* As noted in paragraph [192] *supra*, many jurisdictions have abolished or limited special pleas and now provide that some or all of the contentions discussed in paragraphs [171]-[178] *supra* should be raised by motions to dismiss or to quash the charging paper. Like the special pleas these motions may be required to be filed prior to the entry of a general plea; or some other deadline for their filing, before or shortly after arraignment, may be fixed by statute or rule of court.

In some jurisdictions there are rather strict technical rules governing the order in which special pleas and motions must be made. Local practice should be consulted.

[194] General pleas—the plea of not guilty. The general pleas are not guilty, guilty, and *nolo contendere* (or *non vult*). The plea of not guilty (at common law, a general plea in bar) raises what is known in the jargon as "the general issue." That is, it requires the prosecution to prove its case on the facts beyond a reasonable doubt and permits the defendant to show any defense to the charge that is not required to be set up by special plea, motion, or notice. As noted in paragraphs [192]-[193] *supra*, these latter matters must ordinarily be pleaded *before* the entry of a general plea of not guilty, or they are waived. A not guilty plea at arraignment may later be withdrawn by leave of court to permit the defendant to enter a guilty plea, and courts are very liberal to grant leave at any time prior to the close of trial. Therefore, unless a case presents some issue that must be raised by special plea, motion, or notice, a not guilty plea may ordinarily be safely entered at arraignment as a holding operation, leaving the defendant the option of pleading guilty later at some more advantageous time. See paragraph [218] *infra* on considerations of timing in entering a guilty plea.

[195] **Same—the guilty plea.** A plea of guilty is an admission by the defendant that s/he is legally guilty of the charges to which the plea is entered. The consequence is that a judgment of conviction may be entered on the plea and the defendant sentenced to the penalties provided by law for the offense. The plea ordinarily waives all rights to make any defense against conviction and thus forecloses an appeal raising even claims that error was committed in judicial proceedings prior to the entry of the plea (for example, preplea rulings on motions attacking the composition or procedure of the grand jury, motions to suppress evidence, and so forth). In some jurisdictions a limited number of fundamental contentions may be raised on appeal or by *certiorari* or on collateral attack (see paragraph [472] (C) *infra*) following a guilty plea: the facial constitutionality of the criminal statute charged; the jurisdiction of the court; the question whether the charging paper charges an offense (paragraph [173](1) *supra*). By recent statutes a few jurisdictions also permit the appeal of preplea rulings on suppression motions and similar matters, notwithstanding a guilty plea. But counsel should make very sure that postplea review is expressly authorized by statute or authoritative judicial decision in the particular jurisdiction before s/he advises a guilty plea in the expectation that any ground of legal defense will survive it, for the Supreme Court of the United States has gone extremely far in according finality to guilty pleas and in holding them effective waivers of all defensive claims. *Brady v. United States*, 397 U.S. 742 (1970); *McMann v. Richardson*, 397 U.S. 759 (1970); *Parker v. North Carolina*, 397 U.S. 790 (1970); *North Carolina v. Alford*, 400 U.S. 25 (1970); *Tollett v. Henderson*, 411 U.S. 258 (1973); *see also Corbitt v. New Jersey*, 439 U.S. 212, 218-25 (1978); *United States v. Goodwin*, 457 U.S. 368, 377-80 & n.10 (1982); *Mabry v. Johnson*, 467 U.S. 504, 508-9 (1984). The upshot of these decisions is that a voluntary and understanding guilty plea entered by an adequately counseled defendant is conclusive upon the issue of guilt unless the

applicable state law provides otherwise, *see Lefkowitz v. Newsome*, 420 U.S. 283 (1975); *Lo-Ji Sales, Inc. v. New York*, 442 U.S. 319, 324-25 (1979); *Shea v. Louisiana*, 470 U.S. 51, 53 (1985); *cf. Berkemer v. McCarty*, 468 U.S. 420, 424-25 & n.2 (1984). (In federal practice a 1983 amendment to Rule 11 permits defendants to enter a conditional plea of guilty or *nolo contendere*, with the assent of the court and prosecutor, reserving the right to appellate review of specified rulings on pretrial motions. FED. R. CRIM. P. 11(a)(2). This resolves the previously open question (*see United States v. Morrison*, 449 U.S. 361, 363 n.1 (1981)) of the propriety of conditional guilty pleas in the federal courts.) In the absence of a controlling statute authorizing appellate review of preplea issues despite a guilty plea, most state courts will not consider these issues, with the result that the only issues that survive a plea of guilty are (a) whether the plea itself was voluntary, *e.g.*, *Machibroda v. United States*, 368 U.S. 487 (1962); *Fontaine v. United States*, 411 U.S. 213 (1973), and made with an understanding of the charge, *e.g. Marshall v. Lonberger*, 459 U.S. 422, 436 (1983) (dictum); *Smith v. United States*, 309 F.2d 165 (9th Cir. 1962), including all of its critical elements, *see Henderson v. Morgan*, 426 U.S. 637, 647 n. 18 (1976), and with an understanding of the possible penalty, *Marvel v. United States*, 380 U.S. 262 (1965); *Chapin v. United States*, 341 F.2d 900 (10th Cir. 1965); *cf. Lane v. Williams*, 455 U.S. 624, 630 & n.9 (1982) (reserving the question whether and under what circumstances a failure to inform a defendant of a mandatory parole term will invalidate a guilty plea); *Hill v. Lockhart*, 106 S. Ct. 366, 369 (1985) (dictum that failure to inform a defendant that his eligibility for parole is restricted because of a prior conviction would not invalidate a guilty plea); (b) whether an adequate inquiry into voluntariness and understanding was conducted on the record before the plea was accepted, *McCarthy v. United States*, 394 U.S. 459 (1969) (held nonretroactive in *Halliday v. United States*, 394 U.S. 831 (1969)); *Boykin v. Alabama*, 395 U.S. 238 (1969) (whose retroactivity was reserved in *Brady v. United States, supra*, 397 U.S. at 747-48 n. 4)); *see also United States v. Timmreck*, 441 U.S. 780, 784 (1979) (stating in dictum that a violation of FED. R. CRIM. P. 11 would be raisable on direct appeal, while holding that such a violation is not raisable in collateral attack proceedings in the absence of a showing of prejudice resulting in a miscarriage of justice); (c) whether any promise made to the defendant as a part of a plea bargain has been violated, *Santobello v. New York*, 404 U.S. 257 (1971); *Blackledge v. Allison*, 431 U.S. 63 (1977); *Mabry v. Johnson, supra*, 467 U.S. at 509 (dictum); *compare United States v. Benchimol*, 471 U.S. 453 (1985) (per curiam); (d) whether the defendant was mentally competent to plead, *e.g.*, *Taylor v. United States*, 282 F.2d 16 (8th Cir. 1960); (e) whether s/he was adequately represented by counsel in connection with the plea or validly waived counsel, *e.g.*, *Williams v. Kaiser*, 323 U.S. 471 (1945); *Tollett v. Henderson, supra*; *United States ex rel. Durocher v. LaVallee*, 330 F.2d 303 (2d Cir. 1964); *Fields v. Peyton*, 375 F.2d 624 (4th Cir. 1967), considering the standards for effective assistance of counsel articulated in *United States v. Cronic*, 466 U.S. 648 (1984); *Strickland v. Washington*, 466 U.S. 668 (1984); and *Hill v. Lockhart, supra*; *see also Evitts v. Lucey*, 469 U.S. 387, 395-96 (1985); (f) whether the court had jurisdiction of the offense; (g) whether some constitutional right precluded the defendant's *prosecution* for the offense to which s/he pleaded guilty (as distinguished from the procedures used in the prosecution or in the investigation of the offense underlying it), *see Blackledge v. Perry*, 417 U.S. 21 (1974); *Menna v. New York*, 423 U.S. 61 (1975) (per curiam); *Haring v. Prosise*, 462 U.S. 306, 320 (1983) (dictum); and (h) whether there are any issues relating to sentence. Courts frequently have discretion to permit the withdrawal of a valid guilty plea (that is, a voluntary and understanding plea made by a competent, adequately counseled defendant), but most are reluctant to do so. See paragraph [220] (A)(3) *infra*. The entry of a guilty plea at arraignment may, therefore, be irrevocable.

[196] **Same.** A plea of guilty may be entered to the offense charged in the charging paper or, upon agreement of the prosecutor, to any lesser included offense. See paragraph [437] *infra*. Sometimes leave of court is required for a plea to a lesser offense, and in a few jurisdictions the prosecutor is required to file a statement of reasons for agreeing to a guilty

plea to a lesser offense. A number of jurisdictions disallow a plea of guilty to a specific degree of homicide: the defendant may plead guilty to homicide (or to murder) "generally," leaving to the court the determination of the degree of the offense. Other jurisdictions forbid a plea of guilty to a capital charge; if an offense is punishable capitally, the defendant's guilty plea to it may be taken (with agreement of the prosecutor), but the defendant may thereupon be sentenced only to some punishment less than death. (This practice is plainly unconstitutional under *United States v. Jackson*, 390 U.S. 570 (1968). *See Funicello v. New Jersey*, 403 U.S. 948 (1971) (per curiam); *Atkinson v. North Carolina*, 403 U.S. 948 (1971) (per curiam); *compare Corbitt v. New Jersey*, 439 U.S. 212 (1978).) In jurisdictions where sentencing is done by a jury following trial and conviction on a not guilty plea, the effect of a guilty plea may be to waive jury sentencing and authorize sentencing by the court. Considerations involved in the decision to plead guilty and in guilty plea negotiation are discussed in paragraphs [201]-[219] *infra*.

[197] Same—nolo contendere or non vult. The pleas of *nolo contendere* or *non vult contendere* mean that the defendant does not contest the charge. They have the same effect as a guilty plea for the purpose of the criminal proceeding; that is, they authorize conviction and sentence without more ado. They differ from the guilty plea in that they do not constitute an admission of guilt and are, therefore, inadmissible in any collateral proceedings (other than collateral proceedings challenging conviction on the plea). Hence they are used principally in cases in which there are, or may be, civil proceedings arising out of the same set of facts on which the criminal prosecution is grounded, such as vehicular homicide, fraud, and antitrust cases. The *nolo* plea usually may be entered only with leave of court and agreement by the prosecutor, and neither leave nor agreement is likely to be given unless defense counsel can point to the pendency or probability of a related civil action.

[198] Standing mute. In some jurisdictions the defendant is permitted to stand mute at arraignment. Defense counsel announces that the defendant is standing mute, and the judge thereupon enters a plea of not guilty. The device is most useful in cases in which defense counsel is unprepared to plead and when counsel's motion for a continuance has been overruled and counsel's objection to proceeding has been noted for the record. See paragraphs [190], [191] *supra*. Standing mute in this situation dramatizes the point that defendant waives nothing and particularly does not waive the special pleas and defenses that a not guilty plea might forfeit. See paragraphs [192]-[193] *supra*.

[199] Pleading to priors. In most jurisdictions recidivist sentencing statutes authorize more severe penalties for a second or subsequent conviction of some or all offenses. See paragraph [205] (A) *infra*. In many jurisdictions the previous offenses upon which the prosecutor will rely to support invocation of the stiffer recidivist penalties are not charged at the initial stages of a criminal prosecution but are made the subject of a supplemental information filed after verdict of guilty. See paragraph [469] *infra*. In other jurisdictions, however, the previous offenses (called in the jargon "the priors") are charged in the initial charging paper, and the defendant is required to plead to them, as well as to the offense presently charged, at the time of arraignment. By pleading guilty to the priors, s/he admits that s/he was, in fact, previously convicted, as alleged. By pleading not guilty, s/he contests that issue, which is then submitted to the jury on the proof of the previous convictions by the prosecutor and any proof the defendant may offer (mistaken identity, and so forth). The result of pleading not guilty to the priors is, therefore, that the jury which is trying the defendant's guilt on the present charge learns in the prosecution's case in chief about the defendant's prior convictions. Since there is ordinarily no real contest to be made about the defendant's record, it is usually wise to plead guilty to the priors (or to stipulate the priors, as local practice may have it). This generally obviates the need for proof of the priors at trial and precludes the prosecutor from presenting evidence of prejudicial priors to the jury. A different procedure for contesting priors should be used when the defendant admits their factual accuracy but disputes their legal validity or the legal propriety of their use as the basis for enhanced penalties under the recidivist statute. This sort of collateral attack on previous convictions must be entertained by all courts if a prior is challenged as being invalid on federal constitutional grounds. *Burgett v. Texas*, 389 U.S. 109 (1967); *see Baldasar v. Illinois*, 446 U.S. 222 (1980); *United States v. Addonizio*, 442 U.S. 178, 187 (1979) (dictum); *Lewis v. United States*, 445 U.S. 55, 60 (1980) (dictum); *cf. United States v. Mendoza-Lopez*, 107 S. Ct. 2148 (1987). If its invalidity is asserted to rest on state-law grounds, the state's practice may, or may not, permit such an attack. But in any case in which the attack is permitted, it raises issues of law for the court, not the jury, and so it would appear to be appropriately presented either by a motion to quash or strike the particular allegations of priors that are contested or by a simple objection to presenting that portion of the charging paper to the jury or to the court for purposes of sentencing. When collateral attack in this form is not permitted, counsel will have to use some sort of postconviction remedy to vacate the earlier convictions (see paragraph [472] (C), (D) *infra*), and s/he should undertake to do so before arraignment on the present charge, if possible. Sometimes a continuance of the arraignment will be advised, but ordinarily the postconviction proceeding against the previous convictions will be protracted and therefore render continuance of arraignment on the present charge impracticable. In this situation counsel should explain that s/he is asking the court to entertain a collateral attack on the priors; that the attack presents only a question of law; that counsel does not want the priors to go to the jury because they will prejudice the defendant on the guilt issue; and that the defendant will stipulate to the priors or enter a guilty plea to them, with the reservation of all rights subsequently to challenge their legal validity and the validity of their use in this proceeding.

[200] Dismissal of charges on motion of the prosecution.
The prosecutor may move at arraignment to dismiss charges
in the interest of justice or for want of evidence or because
the defendant has agreed to cooperate and testify against others. This is another stage at which discussion with the prosecutor may invoke a favorable exercise of the prosecutorial
discretion. See paragraphs [99]-[100], [103], [150], [179]
supra. Prosecutors will frequently insist that the defendant sign
a stipulation of the validity of his or her arrest (or that there
was probable cause for the arrest) or a waiver of any legal
claims in connection with the arrest as the condition of an
"interest of justice" dismissal. If the prosecution's case is
known to be very weak, defense counsel can afford to resist
the execution of such a stipulation or waiver, and the prosecutor will often back down. But if the prosecution has any
strength, the signing of a stipulation or a waiver is usually a
small price to pay for dismissal, since the client is unlikely to
persist in any desire to sue the police (a desire usually voiced
very loudly when the prosecutor offers to drop charges but
soon forgotten), and even more unlikely to win a suit if s/he
sues. Local law should, however, be carefully consulted in
regard to the form of the stipulation or waiver, and consideration must be given to which of the client's various possible
concerns with the arrest is paramount. A stipulation that there
was probable cause for the arrest, for example, may preclude
the client from subsequently having the arrest record expunged, but it may not bar a damage action for false arrest
on grounds other than lack of probable cause. A waiver of
claims in connection with the arrest may bar the damage action
(*see Town of Newton v. Rumery*, 107 S. Ct. 1187 (1987)) but not
preclude expungement. Other sorts of consideration for the
dismissal of charges may be exacted by the prosecutor in some
cases, see paragraphs [104]-[105] *supra*; paragraph [219] *infra*;
and these should be thoroughly discussed with the client, with
due appreciation for the truism that what looks like a good
deal now (such as an agreement to make restitution to a complainant in installments over a period of time) may begin to
gall the client seriously as time passes. Plea bargaining is considered in the immediately following paragraphs.

XIII. THE DECISION TO PLEAD GUILTY; PLEA NEGOTIATION

[201] Responsibility for the guilty plea. The decision whether to plead guilty or to contest a criminal charge is ordinarily the most important single decision in any criminal case. This decision must ultimately be left to the client's wishes. Counsel cannot plead a client guilty, or not guilty, against the client's will. *See Jones v. Barnes*, 463 U.S. 745, 751, 753 n.6 (1983) (dictum). But counsel may and must give the client the benefit of counsel's professional advice on this crucial decision; and often counsel can protect the client from disaster only by using a considerable amount of persuasion to convince the client that a plea which the client instinctively disfavors is, in fact, in his or her best interest. This persuasion is most often needed to convince the client that s/he should plead guilty in a case in which a not guilty plea would be destructive. The limits of allowable persuasion are fixed by the lawyer's conscience. Of course, s/he must make absolutely clear to the client that if the client insists on pleading not guilty when the lawyer thinks a guilty plea wise, the lawyer will nevertheless defend the client vigorously and will raise every defense that the client legitimately has. The lawyer must also make clear the limits of his or her own predictive capacities: In describing both the likely favorable consequences of a guilty plea and the likely unfavorable consequences of a not guilty plea, s/he must not make probabilities sound like certainties. Although s/he may emphasize the risks of going to trial in a way that accurately portrays the danger involved, s/he should avoid language that makes it seem as though *counsel* is threatening the client. And it goes without saying that counsel must scrupulously stick to the facts and probabilities as s/he sees them, without exaggeration. Beyond this, the question of how much s/he should bend a particular client's ear in a particular case must rest on counsel's judgment. Counsel's appraisal of the case is probably far better than the defendant's, and counsel's difficult and painful responsibilities include making every reasonable effort to save the defendant from the defendant's ill-informed or ill-estimated choices.

[202] Factors affecting the choice to plead guilty. Putting aside for the present the subject of plea negotiation (paragraphs [206]-[218] *infra*), a number of factors may militate in favor of a guilty plea to the offense charged. These include:

(A) *A strong prosecution case and the absence of a good defense, legal or factual.* Of course, the decision to plead guilty depends in large part on the defendant's chances of being convicted at trial upon a not guilty plea. But a plea is particularly strongly advised when the prosecution's evidence of guilt is overwhelming, since the trial judge will often reflect in the sentence considerable irritation at a defendant who has wasted court time (in the judge's opinion) by demanding a trial of a frivolous case. In appraising the relative strengths of the case for the prosecution and for the defense, counsel must consider:

(1) The legal merit of the prosecutor's theory and the convincing power of the prosecutor's legally admissible evidence to prove the facts on which that theory rests;

(2) The likely availability of the prosecutor's evidence at the time of trial;

(3) Factors that may tend to impeach or discredit the prosecutor's witnesses or evidence (for example, a witness's criminal record or prior inconsistent statements);

(4) The legal merit of each possible defensive theory and the convincing power of the evidence to support it;

(5) The likely availability of the defensive evidence at the time of trial;

(6) Factors that may tend to impeach or discredit defense witnesses or evidence.

(B) *Circumstances that will tend to prejudice the trier of fact against the defendant,* including:

(1) The nature of the offense. (Hard drug offenses, violent sex crimes, crimes involving torturous or gruesome injuries to the victim, crimes against children, and certain other offenses are peculiarly abhorrent to jurors and, to a slightly lesser extent, to judges. Sometimes the inflammatory character

of these offenses is so great that it overwhelms the judge's or jury's capacity to appraise the defendant's case objectively, so that s/he may be convicted even on weak proof of identity and strong alibi testimony.)

(2) The sympathetic or abrasive character of the complainant, the defendant, and the witnesses for the prosecution and defense. (In addition to their appearances, personal characteristices, and social positions, counsel must keep in mind probable jury reactions to interracial crimes and crimes committed upon victims who differ greatly in age from the defendant.)

(3) The defendant's criminal record if s/he has one. (If s/he does, it may be used for impeachment, and the jury will therefore most likely learn of the record if s/he testifies. See paragraphs [381], [390] (F) *infra*. If s/he does not testify, the jury will ordinarily bclicvc that to be a telling circumstance against the defendant. See paragraph [390] (A) *infra*. Counsel must also consider the likelihood, in view of various evidentiary doctrines (see paragraphs [368]-[369] *infra*) and courthouse leaks, that the judge or jury will learn of the record, even if the defendant does not take the stand.)

(4) News media and other publicity surrounding the case.

(C) *Circumstances that make it difficult to obtain a favorably disposed trier of fact.* Counsel must consider:

(1) Jury attitudes in the locality, as demonstrated in similar previous cases;

(2) The judge before whom the case is likely to come in the event of jury waiver, in light of counsel's ability to steer the case in front of particular judges, and the judge's demonstrated attitude in similar previous cases.

(D) *Superior ability, experience, or personableness on the part of the prosecutor who will try the case.*

(E) *The absence of debatable or dubious legal points relating to substantive or evidentiary matters on which the trial judge might commit reversible error.*

(F) *The absence of likely reversible error in prearraignment rulings that counsel has saved for appeal.*

(G) *Circumstances that may make a trial disadvantageous to the defendant, at the sentencing stage, in the event of conviction,* including:

(1) The defendant's insistence on taking the stand and telling a story that the judge will believe is perjurious and will punish covertly by increasing the sentence;

(2) Exposure at trial of facts that will not otherwise likely be disclosed to (or as immediately brought home to) the judge and that will prejudice the defendant at sentencing (for example, the extent of a victim's injuries).

(H) *Circumstances that make trial disadvantageous to the defendant, regardless of its outcome,* including:

(1) Delay in disposition, particularly if the defendant is in jail;

(2) Embarrassment or adverse publicity;

(3) Nervous stress.

(I) *Circumstances that will tend to give the defendant an advantage in sentencing if s/he pleads guilty,* including:

(1) The opportunity to steer a case before a judge who is a favorable sentencer (see paragraph [218] *infra*);

(2) Local judicial practices of "giving consideration" in sentencing for a guilty plea or similar demonstrated attitudes of a particular sentencing judge. (Judges generally do tend to give lighter sentences to defendants who plead guilty. Some judges regard the plea as a sign of contrition and a first step toward reform. Others want, consciously or unconsciously, to express appreciation for the defendant's contribution to alleviating docket congestion. And often the presentence report or other sentencing record alone makes the defendant's crime less vivid than a trial would do.)

(J) *Circumstances indicating that the offense charged is not the most serious charge that could be made against the defendant on the facts of the case, with the result that a quick plea of guilty may bar the subsequent filing of aggravated charges.* The constitutional prohibition against double jeopardy (see paragraph [177] *supra*) bars a defendant's prosecution upon greater charges following his or her conviction of a lesser included offense, *Brown v. Ohio,* 432 U.S. 161 (1977); *Illinois v. Vitale,* 447 U.S. 410, 419-21 (1980); *Morris v. Mathews,* 106 S. Ct. 1032, 1037 (1986) (dictum); *see also Jeffers v. United States,* 432 U.S. 137, 150-51

(1977) (plurality opinion) (dictum), except when the State files all of the charges in the alternative at the outset, *Ohio v. Johnson*, 467 U.S. 493 (1984), or when "the State is unable to proceed on the more serious charge at the outset because the additional facts necessary to sustain that charge have not occurred or have not been discovered *despite the exercise of due diligence*," *Brown v. Ohio, supra*, 432 U.S. at 169 n.7 (dictum) (emphasis added); *Garrett v. United States*, 471 U.S. 773, 789-92 (1985).

The converse aspects of these concerns militate against a guilty plea. Also bearing against a plea are the considerations that, in an appropriate case:

(K) *The nature of the evidence or of the law or the character of the parties to the alleged offense is sufficiently controversial* to set a jury at loggerheads, with the result that the jury may hang or bring in a compromise verdict of guilty on a lesser included charge.

(L) *The trial, even in the event of conviction, will tend to bring out extenuating or sympathetic circumstances likely to affect the judge on sentencing.*

(M) *The defendant does not "feel" guilty and will enter a plea only with considerable reluctance*, with the result that:

(1) S/he will be unhappy if the plea is accepted;

(2) His or her unhappiness will be sufficiently apparent at arraignment that the judge will not accept the plea. As indicated in paragraph [188] *supra*, the judge may interrogate the defendant extensively before a guilty plea is taken.

[203] Same—options in addition to the guilty plea or trial. The considerations just enumerated, of course, suppose a simple choice between entering a guilty plea and going to trial. There may be other available options, and these have to be considered. For the most part, they depend on agreement with the prosecutor, and they are, therefore, considered in paragraphs [206]-[218] *infra*.

[204] Same—consequences of conviction. No intelligent plea decision can be made by either lawyer or client without full understanding of the possible consequences of a conviction. These consequences describe the defendant's potential exposure if s/he goes to trial and is convicted of the offense charged or if s/he pleads guilty to the offense charged with no plea bargain. They are the baseline for measuring the worth of any bargain that can be negotiated; and if the prosecutor will not negotiate, they measure the worth of the defendant's chances of acquittal or of conviction only of a lesser included offense (see paragraph [437] *infra*) at a trial. In some defendants' cases the consequences of conviction may be so devastating that even the faintest ray of hope offered by a trial is magnified in significance. If, for example, a conviction of the offense charged will result in the automatic revocation of the defendant's parole from a prior prison sentence on which s/he owes long years of back time or will result in the automatic application of a draconian recidivist-sentencing provision or mandatory minimum-term provision to the new conviction, then the defendant has little to lose by denying guilt and going to trial, even with a weak defense.

[205] **Same—checklist of possible consequences of conviction.** The possible consequences of a conviction require research in each case concerning:

(A) *The maximum penalties authorized by law upon the conviction,* including:

    (1) Imprisonment.

    (2) Fine.

    (3) Restitution.

    (4) Subjection to liability for enhanced punishment under statutes such as:

        (a) Recidivist sentencing provisions.

        (b) "Sexual psychopath" and similar laws.

        (c) "Defective delinquent" and similar laws.

        (d) Special indeterminate sentencing legislation applicable to the defendant, like "Youthful Offender" or "Youth Corrections" legislation.

(B) *Any applicable mandatory minimum penalties under the same statutes.*

(C) *Applicable statutes, rules, and regulations governing probation, relating to eligibility for probation, duration of the probationary period, conditions that may be permissibly imposed upon the allowance of probation, and grounds for revocation.* These must be considered with regard both to the offense presently charged and to any offense or offenses for which the defendant was on probation at the time of this offense. Conviction on the present offense may result in revocation of a prior probation and in a prison sentence for the prior offense that exceeds the maximum for the present offense. *See Black v. Romano,* 471 U.S. 606, 616 (1985). If probation on the present offense is a possibility, counsel should review the rules governing administration of probationary supervision, which are often oppressive and galling. (The courts are showing no disposition to curb them. *See, e.g., Griffin v. Wisconsin,* 107 S. Ct. 3164 (1987); *Minnesota v. Murphy,* 465 U.S. 420 (1984).)

(D) *Applicable statutes, rules, and regulations governing parole, relating to these same factors, with an eye particularly to the minimum term in prison required to be served before parole eligibility, and the requirements of the "parole plan" demanded by the parole authorities as a condition of admission to parole.* (In some jurisdictions six months must be added to the professed minimum prison time because it invariably requires six months or more for the prisoner to work out a satisfactory parole plan—job, acceptable living quarters, community "sponsor"—demanded as the precondition of release. Owing to parole eligibility standards or parole plan requirements, it is also possible to predict that for some defendants the possibility of parole is illusory. A frequently encountered example is the policy of some parole boards to deny parole to any prisoner who has a detainer lodged against him or her for trial on other charges or for service of sentence on other convictions in any jurisdiction.) Parole issues also must be considered with regard both to the present offense and to any offense or offenses for which the defendant was on parole at the time of this offense.

(E) *Forfeiture statutes condemning automobiles and other paraphernalia used to commit liquor, gambling, drug, and like offenses.*

(F) *Civil disabilities imposed by state law,* including:

(1) Loss of any outstanding occupational license (hack license, professional license, license to operate a bar, and so forth) and ineligibility for future licensing.

(2) Loss of a driver's license (frequent under traffic and drug legislation) and ineligibility for future licensing.

(3) Loss of public office or employment and ineligibility for future public office or employment.

(4) Loss of voting rights (*see Richardson v. Ramirez*, 418 U.S. 24 (1974); *compare Hunter v. Underwood*, 471 U.S. 222 (1985)).

(5) Criminal registration requirements.

(G) *Liabilities under federal law or regulations*, including:

(1) Ineligibility for military service (including National Guard service, which, in turn, is the precondition for certain employments).

(2) Ineligibility for public office or employment.

(3) Liability to deportation if the defendant is an alien.

(H) *Privately imposed sanctions*:

(1) Higher insurance rates (particularly in traffic cases).

(2) Restrictions on employment, residence, admission to professions, admission to educational institutions, and so forth.

Of course, in addition to knowing each of the consequences that *may* follow conviction, counsel must undertake to calculate the likelihood of actual occurence of each.

[206] **Plea negotiation—counsel's obligation.** "Plea bargaining" conjures up sleazy images in many minds, ranging from a commercialized, incompetent, or craven practice of criminal law ("bleed 'em and plead 'em") to outright graft. Undoubtedly, there are some corruptions in plea bargaining. But the negotiated disposition of criminal charges is no more to be scorned for that reason than are all contracts because some of them are fraudulent. It is just as appropriate for counsel to settle a criminal case as a civil case. What is involved in negotiating a criminal settlement is trying to find a basis for agreement on a disposition that reconciles the legitimate interests of the prosecution and the defendant, without subjecting either to the risks and costs of trial. When the risks or costs are substantial, effective plea bargaining is part of effective representation of one's client. For many clients, indeed, the only realistic service that a defense attorney can provide

is to work out with the prosecutor the least damaging deal that can be made in a case in which there is no serious prospect of acquittal. Thus not only may defense counsel explore the possibility of settlement with a clear conscience; s/he violates the obligation to adequately represent the client if s/he does not.

[207] **Opening discussions with the prosecutor.** Beginning early in the proceedings, counsel will have been discussing the case with the prosecutor. See paragraph [91]-[105], [150], [179] *supra*. Initial discussions should have focused principally on learning what the prosecution was willing to disclose about its evidence. But counsel should also have learned something about the prosecutor's attitude; counsel should have tried to mold that attitude in favor of the client; and in the course of urging a favorable exercise of the prosecutor's charging discretion, counsel should have asked what the prosecutor regards as a satisfactory outcome of the case. Counsel can ordinarily do this much without making any offer to plead the client guilty or even intimating that the client might be receptive to a noncourt disposition; counsel can, therefore, do this much without specific authorization by the client.

[208] **When negotiation should begin.** Exactly when negotiation in a stricter sense should begin—that is, when defense counsel should begin to raise the possibility of a guilty plea if some mutually satisfactory terms of settlement can be agreed upon—depends on a variety of circumstances. In many cases there are pressures for counsel to begin very early. When several defendants have been arrested in connection with an offense, the one who first cooperates to "break" the case and implicate the others will very likely receive the most consideration from the prosecution. In their immediate postarrest interrogation the police frequently stress the value of cooperation (whether or not the defendant has been arrested with others), partly to obtain a confession of the offense for which the arrest was made but more often to encourage an arrestee to confess to, and hence to "clear," other unsolved crimes. (Police efficiency is judged by clearance rates.) These sug-

gestions by the police set a tone that may make the defendant quite anxious to "clinch" a quick deal; and particularly if the client is rap-wise, s/he will expect counsel to jump into bargaining with both feet. From counsel's own point of view, plea negotiation is one of the most profitable methods of informal discovery. Most prosecutors will disclose their case to some extent to persuade defense counsel that a guilty plea is advised; some will disclose *only* if a guilty plea is being discussed. And counsel wants to begin discovery early. See paragraph [108] *supra*. On the other hand, counsel is frequently in no position to negotiate at the outset of the case. Adequate factual investigation and legal research are the necessary preconditions of intelligent negotiation, lest counsel make bad bargains. Furthermore, negotiation involves offering something, even if the something is only a possibility. Offering something *does* require authorization of the client, and so counsel often has nothing to offer at this early time. The plea decision will ultimately be the client's, and although some clients are of the sort just described—anxious to discuss a deal—others persist long after arrest in vigorously protesting innocence and spouting plausible tales (some true, some not) that, if true, render the suggestion of a guilty plea inconceivable. Counsel cannot broach the subject of a possible guilty plea to these clients, for the purpose of obtaining their authority to negotiate, without appearing to call the client a liar; and counsel has not yet established the rapport needed to probe the client's position tactfully yet skeptically to see whether the client will stick to it in the face of all of the hard questions and hard facts that counsel will eventually have to put to the client. (See paragraphs [83], [89] *supra*.)

[209] **Same.** Probably the best approach is to be guided by the client's outlook in the initial interview. If the client admits guilt and obviously feels that s/he has been caught redhanded, counsel may raise the question of a possible guilty plea and suggest that—if the client wishes—counsel will explore the prosecutor's attitude toward some sort of a plea bargain at the same time that counsel checks further into the facts of the case. Counsel should explain that, of course, s/he will make no

commitments and will not indicate to the prosecutor that the client has any interest in pleading guilty, nor has s/he any idea of the prosecutor's position at this time. But counsel will undertake to find out what the prosecutor might be willing to accept in the way of a reduced sentence; and after counsel has thoroughly investigated the facts, s/he and the client will talk further about all the possibilities. The client should be assured that in absolutely no event will counsel discuss a guilty plea with the prosecutor or even consider one unless it appears that the prosecution's case is strong and likely to result in a conviction at trial. S/he should also be assured that counsel is starting out with the attitude that "if this case can be fought, we are going to fight it" and that counsel's only reason for bringing up the possibility of a plea is that s/he does not want to overlook any opportunity of getting the most favorable deal for the client if the client later decides that s/he would do better with a plea than with a trial. Even with a client who acknowledges guilt, counsel is wise not to seem too attracted by a possible guilty-plea disposition at the outset, lest the client get the impression that counsel is anxious to sell the client out in order to save counsel work. (See paragraph [79] *supra*.) But if counsel's mention of talking to the prosecutor elicits a positive reaction from the client, counsel might as well start talking early. On the other hand, if the client denies involvement in the offense or speaks of contesting guilt and there appear no pressing reasons to begin negotiation, counsel can let the matter go over until the initial phases of defense investigation have made counsel more familiar with the case. After s/he has investigated the facts, has had a chance to study and make some tentative evaluation of the matters suggested in paragraphs [202] and [205] *supra*, and has also considered the matters enumerated in paragraphs [210]-[211] *infra*, s/he should raise with the client the question of a possible guilty plea. At this stage counsel is still not prepared to tell the client with any certainty what the advantages of a guilty plea will be, but s/he is in a position to suggest that there may be some advantages, depending on the prosecutor's attitude toward negotiation. Even though counsel may have come to the unilateral conclusion that the case is plainly one for a not guilty

plea and trial, s/he owes it to the client to give the client the
option of having negotiation with the prosecutor explored as
an alternative. Of course, if counsel and the client are agreed
at this stage that the case should be fought out on the guilt
issue, no matter what sort of disposition the prosecutor might
agree to—or if the client is adamant against any thought of a
guilty plea notwithstanding counsel's belief that negotiations
looking to a plea might profitably be considered—the matter
is ended. There remains nothing for counsel to do but prepare
for trial and perhaps raise the issue with the client again later
in light of subsequent developments. If, however, the client is
willing to have the possibilities of negotiation explored, counsel should proceed to discuss them with the prosecutor.

**[210] The conditions precedent of effective defense ne-
gotiation—things to know.** Thorough investigation must pre-
cede any serious negotiation. Counsel must know enough
about the prosecutive and defensive cases—that is, about the
facts, their likely provability in court, and the likely responses
of a judge or jury to them—to make, at least provisionally,
the sort of evaluation suggested in paragraph [202] *supra*.
S/he must know the consequences of conviction on the offense
charged. Paragraph [205] *supra*. S/he should also have a comprehensive working knowledge of:

(1) *The identity of every lesser offense included within the offense
charged against the defendant* (see paragraph [437] *infra*) and the
consequences of conviction on each of these offenses (see
paragraph [205] *supra*);

(2) *The identity of every other offense that might be charged against
the defendant on the basis of the facts of the case*, or on the basis of
some of those facts, and the consequences of conviction on
each of these offenses (see paragraph [205] *supra*);

(3) *Legal doctrines relating to*:

(a) *The authority of the court to suspend sentence and the consequences of different forms of suspended sentences* (see paragraph [464] (E) *infra*);

(b) *The potential applicability of specialized sentencing provisions, such as "Youthful Offender" laws, and the procedures
for, and consequences of, sentencing the defendant under*

those laws (see paragraph [464] (B) *infra*), which may be more favorable to the defendant than the ordinary sentencing provisions in some aspects or circumstances and less favorable in others;

(c) *Merger of offenses and concurrent or consecutive sentencing in the event of conviction of more than one offense* (see paragraph [464] (G) *infra*);

(4) *The defendant's previous criminal record, including probation or parole status at the time of the present offense, and all other charges presently pending or contemplated against the defendant in any jurisdiction;*

(5) *The identity of, and conditions at, the various places of confinement to which the defendant might be committed at the court's discretion* (or assigned by state correctional officials at the court's recommendation) *in the event of an incarcerative disposition* (see paragraph [464] (C) *infra*), including specialized rehabilitative and training programs available at these various institutions;

(6) *The defendant's family resources and local community resources available to the defendant,* which may offer assistance in making some nonincarcerative disposition of the case that has affirmative rehabilitative or restitutive potential, including:

(a) Employment opportunities for the defendant,
(b) Educational and job-training opportunities for the defendant,
(c) In-patient or out-patient medical or psychiatric treatment facilities for the defendant,
(d) Alternative places of residence for the defendant, including places out of the locality,
(e) Present or potential financial resources of the defendant to make restitution to the complainant, in an appropriate case.

S/he should know, in addition, whether the client is able and willing to cooperate with the prosecution in:

(7) *Incriminating other persons or turning state's evidence;*

(8) *Confessing guilt of uncleared offenses and thereby assisting in their clearance by the police.*

It is also helpful, if possible, for counsel to know:

(9) *Any more or less formally articulated policies of the prosecutor's office bearing on the sort of case involved;*

(10) *Previous similar cases in which plea negotiations favorable to the defense have been worked out.* (Argument from precedent is often quite effective in negotiation.)

[211] Same—plans for alternative disposition. Armed with this information, counsel is prepared to draft a set of possible settlements of the case that entail less onerous consequences or more rehabilitative promise than does conviction on the offense charged. S/he should consider what the defendant can offer the prosecutor, including:

(A) A plea of guilty to some offense[s];

(B) Voluntary submission to treatment programs, changes of residence, and so forth, that could not be compelled by law;

(C) Voluntary contribution of resources for restitutive or rehabilitative purposes;

(D) Cooperation to incriminate or convict other persons;

(E) Cooperation to clear uncleared crimes.

(F) A waiver of claims to damages for unlawful arrest and other violations of the defendant's rights in the initial stages of the criminal proceeding.

S/he should also make a complete inventory of potential dispositions that are preferable to conviction and a maximum sentence on the offense[s] charged, for example:

(1) *The defendant's plea of guilty to some lesser offense[s] included within the offense[s] charged.* A guilty plea to a lesser offense is the classic form of "copping a plea" and the one that most defendants think of first. It produces a guaranteed reduction of the statutory maximum sentence to which the defendant is exposed, limiting the "max" to the penalty authorized by law for the lesser offense. It also usually—but not invariably—lessens the sentence that the defendant will actually receive. Approval of the court for a plea of guilty to a lesser included offense is not often required and, where required, is ordinarily routinely given. There is little or no way the prosecutor can renege once the plea is entered. This sort of an agreed disposition is therefore less risky than some others. However, its value to the defendant varies greatly, depending upon judicial sentencing patterns—and, in particular, upon the relationship

between the maximum sentence authorized by law and the actual sentences customarily given for both the greater and the lesser included offenses. Assume, for example, the common phenomenon of a judge who (a) never sentences first offenders to more than a third of the statutory maximum term for armed robbery and (b) assumes that any defendant who pleads guilty to simple robbery is really guilty of armed robbery and is copping a plea. Counsel representing a first offender before this judge is not likely to see a great difference in the sentence if the client pleads to armed robbery rather than simple robbery. If counsel wants to make a deal that means much in terms of time served, s/he will have to consider other possible forms of plea bargaining.

(2) *The defendant's plea of guilty to less than all of the offenses charged, with dismissal of the others on a nolle prosequi.* "Knocking off" indictments or counts also ordinarily produces a guaranteed reduction of the maximum sentencing power of the court. But this is so only when state law or the constitutional law of double jeopardy (see paragraph [464] (A) *infra*) does not bar cumulative punishment for the several offenses. Counsel, therefore, must research this issue. Counsel should also be aware of local judicial practice with regard to consecutive or concurrent sentencing for convictions on related offenses. Some courts invariably give concurrent sentences for these offenses, so counsel has gained nothing by a dropping of some charges. It is also significant that the *nolle prosequi* often requires leave of court, and leave is not always routinely given. Furthermore, the prosecutor may sometimes renege on a *nol pros*; local law and the prosecutor's habits should be checked out.

(3) *The defendant's plea of guilty to the offense[s] charged or to some lesser offense[s], on the prosecutor's promise of a sentencing recommendation.* Sentencing recommendations may include:

    (a) The recommendation of a specific sentence.

    (b) The recommendation of a sentence not more than x.

    (c) The recommendation of a suspended sentence, with or without probation. The suspension may be unconditional or may be conditioned on the defendant's doing or refraining from doing specified things. This is a point at which the defendant's ability and willingness to submit to voluntary community-based treatment programs or to make various changes in his or her lifestyle become significant.

(d) The recommendation that sentences on several present charges be concurrent or that they be made concurrent with sentences on previous convictions, including sentences on which the defendant's probation or parole will be revoked by reason of the present conviction.

(e) The recommendation that a term of imprisonment be served in a specialized facility (minimum security prison, drug farm, and so forth). /

(f) The recommendation that the defendant be sentenced under specialized sentencing provisions ("Youth Corrections" Act, and so forth).

(g) A general recommendation of leniency or announcement to the court that the defendant is "cooperating."

Sentencing recommendations are only recommendations. They are the riskiest form of agreements because the judge may not go along with them. Some judges invariably do; some never do; some do or do not, depending on the case. Negotiating for a sentencing recommendation is effective only if counsel has sufficient information about the judge who will be—or about all of the judges who may be—the sentencing judge. In some cases it may be possible to meet with the judge in chambers, in a formal or informal pretrial conference, to sound out his or her reaction to a proposed sentencing recommendation by the prosecutor. See paragraph [275] (A) *infra*. Defense counsel may wish to suggest such a conference when the judge's attitude toward sentencing recommendations is uncertain.

In some localities a formal or informal practice of "conditional" plea bargaining has developed. Under this practice the prosecution and defense negotiate (i) the terms of the sentence that the defendant will receive if s/he pleads guilty (an "on the nose" bargain) or (ii) the rules that will be followed in sentencing the defendant if s/he pleads guilty (for example, that the sentence will be no more than x [nor less than y]; that the prosecution will inform the court that the defendant is cooperating with the authorities and will ask the court to consider this circumstance in mitigation, or any other arrangement among those described in subparagraphs (c) through (g) *supra* or in paragraphs (4), (6), or (7) *infra*). The parties' agreement is then submitted to the sentencing judge for approval. If the judge agrees (i) to impose the bargained sentence or (ii) to observe the bargained sentencing rules, the defendant pleads guilty and the judge performs as agreed. If the judge does not agree, then the deal is off, and the case goes to trial (or to renegotiation). (The practice in federal criminal cases is codified in FED. R. CRIM. P. 11(e).) If this procedure is customary in counsel's jurisdiction, counsel should ordinarily follow it; if it is not, counsel should consider suggesting it to the prosecutor and the judge for use on an *ad hoc* basis.

(4) *The defendant's plea of guilty to the offense[s] charged or to some lesser offense[s], on the prosecutor's agreement to make no recommendation on sentence and to take no position on the question, leaving defense counsel free to argue the matter to the court.* This sort of agreement is usefully made to break the stalemate in negotiation that occurs when the prosecutor and defense counsel are agreed that the defendant should receive some consideration for a guilty plea but are far apart on the sort of sentence that should be imposed.

(5) *The defendant's plea of guilty to the offense[s] charged or to some lesser offense[s], on the prosecutor's promise that the case will be brought before a particular judge (or will not be brought before a particular judge) for sentencing.* The prosecutor often has power to control the identity of the sentencing judge. See paragraphs [217]-[218] *infra*. Again, the value of this sort of agreement depends on the judges and on counsel's knowledge about them.

(6) *The defendant's plea of guilty to the offense[s] charged or to some lesser offense[s], on the prosecutor's agreement not to "press the priors,"* that is, not to invoke the provisions of recidivist sentencing legislation of various sorts (including habitual-criminal, sexual-psychopath and defective-delinquent provisions). The prosecutor may or may not have authority under local practice to decide unilaterally whether the stiffer penalties of

recidivist law will be invoked. Counsel should determine whether the judge has any power to invoke the priors *sua sponte*.

(7) *The defendant's plea of guilty to offenses charged in a new indictment or information that are less serious than the offense[s] presently charged but are not lesser included offenses.* See paragraph [210] (2) *supra*. On this plea the prosecutor *nol prosses* the original indictment or information. Although the *nol pros* requires leave of court, the court may have no choice but to grant it if the new offenses selected for the plea bar prosecution of the original charges under the principles of double jeopardy. See paragraph [177] *supra*.

(8) *The defendant's plea of guilty to the offense[s] charged or to a lesser offense, on the prosecutor's agreement to secure the dropping of other charges against the defendant in other jurisdictions, federal or state.* The prosecutor may or may not be able to deliver on this agreement. Counsel should ordinarily get personal assurances from the other prosecutors involved. S/he should also be familiar with prosecutorial policies, or s/he may be making a bad deal. The federal government very infrequently prosecutes for a federal offense following state conviction on a charge based upon the same incident (see paragraph [177] *supra*); the agreement to have federal charges dropped is therefore often worth little.

Plea negotiation may also include consideration of such interim matters as the speed with which the case will be brought on for disposition (a matter of significance to a jailed defendant, particularly in a case in which a sentence of imprisonment is unlikely), favorable terms of bail, release on recognizance, and so forth. As a part of the package, the defendant may agree to forgo damage claims based upon asserted violations of his or her rights in the course of the criminal proceedings to date. *Cf. Town of Newton v. Rumery*, 107 S. Ct. 1187 (1987).

[212] **Negotiation.** (A) The process of negotiation with the prosecutor is in some ways like negotiation looking to settlement of a civil case. The prosecutor must generally be impressed with the discrepancy between what s/he wants and what s/he is likely to get or with the inconvenience involved

in getting what s/he wants before s/he will settle for less than what s/he wants. The major difference in criminal negotiation is that it is the prosecutor alone, not a client, who decides what the prosecutor wants. Considerations of justice affect this calculus, and the prosecutor may be appealed to on all of the grounds suggested in paragraph [100] *supra*, dealing with the prosecutorial discretion. In negotiating with the prosecutor, defense counsel must also bear in mind that, unlike most civil litigation, criminal trials are of public interest, that journalistic coverage is sometimes extensive, and that the prosecutor must be able to justify any "deals" to the public. An additional problem is that the prosecutor relies heavily on the police and needs their cooperation. When the police have done a good job in building a case, they may be chagrined to see the prosecutor dismiss or compromise it. This latter consideration may suggest the desirability of counsel's doing a bit of lobbying with the investigating officer after s/he has begun plea negotiations with the prosecutor. In a case in which the complainant's wishes are likely to be significant to the prosecutor, a discussion with the complainant may also be advised. In both cases, of course, extreme caution must be observed in counsel's decision to involve these parties in the affair. Often the prosecutor will not consult them, and their involvement may stir up trouble for the defense.

(B) Like any negotiation, plea negotiation involves the art of agreeing with the other side's position on all points that are not essential to counsel as a means of getting the other side to agree with counsel's position on essential points. This means, analytically, that counsel must figure out what the prosecutor really wants (for example, a prosecutor who says that s/he thinks "this defendant ought to be taken off the streets" does not necessarily want jail time; s/he may be saying that s/he wants the defendant out of the community so as not to give the complainant, the police, and this prosecutor any further trouble; s/he may be quite satisfied with a suspended sentence and probation if probationary supervision can be shifted to another county) and how to give the prosecutor what s/he wants without sacrificing what counsel wants (for example, the prosecutor who *does* want to give the defendant a "taste of jail" may agree to a probationary disposition if counsel suggests deferring arraignment for a week and not bailing the defendant out). The multitude of possible offenses that could be charged in any factual situation (including offenses of which the defendant is not technically guilty) and the large range of sentencing alternatives available for those offenses under the laws of most jurisdictions (see paragraphs [205], [210] *supra*) ordinarily give counsel plenty of possibilities for effective compromise if s/he reviews them thoroughly and uses imagination. See paragraph [211] *supra*. Similarly, the range of practical possibilities must be viewed with imagination. A prosecutor who adamantly refuses to make a formal sentencing recommendation to the court, for instance, may be willing to make an informal recommendation to the probation officer who is writing up the presentence report on the case— and the latter recommendation may be just as valuable to the defense as the former. See paragraphs [460]-[461] *infra*. At the personal level it is clearly desirable to minimize the extent of counsel's disagreements with the prosecutor without giving in to the prosecutor on substantive matters, and it is particularly important for counsel to appear not to be standing in personal opposition to the prosecutor, even when counsel's position is opposed to the prosecutor's position. One way for defense counsel to avoid a clash of personalities with the prosecutor is for counsel to establish a personal posture that is not completely identified with counsel's bargaining position, by associating the bargaining position with the client and appearing to play the role of an honest broker between the client's interests and the prosecutor's. Thus the "I-really-see-the-case-the-way-you-do-because-any-sensible-lawyer-would-know-that-what-you-say-makes-sense-but-you've-got-to-help-me-to-sell-it-to-my-client-by-giving-me-something-more-to-take-to-the-client-that-s/he-can-live-with" approach is frequently productive. This use of the absent client as a third force in negotiation allows defense counsel to hold firm to his or her position while establishing a broad base of personal and professional agreement with the prosecutor. It also avoids arousing any instincts that the prosecutor may have toward combative gamesmanship—that is, the game of "beating" defense counsel in fleamarket haggling. However, when possible, counsel should not say that the client *does not* or *will not* accept the prosecutor's position, since this may simply redirect the prosecutor's combativeness toward the client. The better formulation is an "I-just-don't-think-I-can-sell-that-to-my-client-unless- . . ." approach or its equivalent. Keeping on the prosecutor's good side and avoiding clashes that may arouse the prosecutor's ire at either the defendant or defense counsel is indispensable because, as a practical matter, the prosecutor ordinarily has the upper hand in the bargaining process. Although defense counsel may be able to appeal to some judges to lean on a prosecutor who stands adamant on an outrageous bargaining position (see paragraph [275] (A) *infra*), the prosecutor can usually get away with either stonewalling or playing very rough at the bargaining table. *See, e.g., Weatherford v. Bursey*, 429 U.S. 545, 561 (1977) ("there is no constitutional right to plea bargain; the prosecutor need not do so if he prefers to go to trial"); *Ricketts v. Adamson*, 107 S. Ct. 2680, 2685 n.5 (1987), citing *Mabry v. Johnson*, 467 U.S. 504 (1984) (same); *Bordenkircher v. Hayes*, 434 U.S. 357 (1978) (finding no constitutional objection to a prosecutor's filing a recidivist charge, carrying a mandatory life sentence, for the admitted purpose of inducing the defendant to accept the prosecutor's offer of a plea bargain involving a five-year sentencing recommendation); *United States v. Goodwin*, 457 U.S. 368, 377-80 (1982) (reaffirming *Bordenkircher*). The prosecutor is under heavy pressure to settle most cases in order to reduce the prosecution's trial docket to manageable proportions, and that pressure is defense counsel's greatest asset as long as counsel does nothing to give the prosecutor the impression that this case deserves "special treatment." But if the prosecutor gets riled, s/he usually has sufficient resources to make any particular case unpleasantly "special" for the defendant.

[213] Agreement with the prosecutor. (A) In most jurisdictions, agreements between defense counsel and the prosecutor are not reduced to writing. The reputation and integrity of each attorney are the only guarantees that each will keep his or her word. *See Mabry v. Johnson*, 467 U.S. 504 (1984). In theory, of course, a guilty plea entered in consideration of a prosecutorial promise that is not fulfilled must be set aside. *E.g., Santobello v. New York*, 404 U.S. 257 (1971); *Blackledge v. Allison*, 431 U.S. 63 (1977). But proof of the facts necessary to bring the theory into play is not easy; postconviction litigation over broken plea bargains can consume years; and the relief, if any, that the client ultimately gets may be nothing more than the right to stand trial. Therefore, if counsel does not know the particular prosecutor, s/he should inquire about the prosecutor's reputation among knowledgeable members of the bar *before* a plea is entered.

(B) In some states or localities the practice of setting down the terms of plea bargains in writing and filing them with the court has developed. *See, e.g., People v. West*, 3 Cal. 3d 595, 477 P.2d 409, 91 Cal. Rptr. 385 (1970). (This practice is often but not always incidental to the "conditional" plea bargaining procedure described in paragraph [211] *supra*.) The practice should ordinarily be followed if the prosecutor and the court can be persuaded to accept it. Defense counsel should always offer to draft the written instrument for the prosecutor's review rather than *vice versa*, since the drafter of a document has the advantages of initiative, inertia, and a working familiarity with the draft during any negotiations that may be required to secure its approval or arrange for its revision into final form.

(C) A plea agreement which contemplates that the defendant will serve as an informer or a witness against accomplices or will otherwise assist the prosecution in any way other than the mere entry of a plea of guilty should be detailed and unambiguous regarding (1) the specific actions that the defendant is to take, (2) the investigations or cases in which (or the persons against whom) s/he is to take those actions, (3) the circumstances under which s/he is to take the actions, and (4) the duration of the defendant's obligation to act. See paragraph [105] *supra*. Ambiguity in the scope of the defendant's responsibilities to assist the prosecution has to be avoided, since a defendant who subsequently disagrees with the prosecutor's interpretation of those responsibilities does so at the risk that the entire plea bargain will be set aside and s/he will then be prosecuted for the most serious offenses originally charged if the courts prefer the prosecutor's interpretation to the defendant's. *Ricketts v. Adamson*, 107 S. Ct. 2680 (1987).

(D) The agreement should include the provision that the defendant's plea and any admissions, statements, evidence, information, or leads of any sort which incriminate the defendant in the present offense or any other offense and which are given to the prosecutor, any law enforcement authority, the court, or its probation department by the defendant or defense counsel during the negotiation of the agreement or following its negotiation but before the agreement is fully executed by the defendant's sentencing according to its terms are expressly understood to have been given in consideration of the agreement and shall not be used against the defendant in any way by the prosecutor or by any party in privity with the prosecutor except (1) with defendant's express consent, in the course of proceedings undertaken to secure the defendant's conviction and sentencing pursuant to the agreement or (2) if, and after, the defendant has been convicted and sentenced according to the terms of the agreement and so long as that conviction and sentence have not been vacated; but in no event shall any of these matters be used against the defendant in connection with any criminal charge other than the charge[s] to which the defendant is presently agreeing to plead guilty.

(E) Except when terms of the sort described in the preceding subparagraph have been embodied in a written agreement or explicitly included in an oral agreement with a prosecutor whom counsel trusts, counsel should not divulge, or permit the defendant to divulge, any incriminating information to anyone during or after plea bargaining. *See Hutto v. Ross*, 429 U.S. 28 (1976) (per curiam).

[214] Advice to the client and the client's agreement. (A) If counsel has determined to advise a client to plead guilty either on a negotiated plea or without any *quid pro quo* from the prosecutor, counsel should thoroughly explain his or her reasoning to the client. S/he should discuss the evidence in the case and make as clear to the client as possible the considerations that lead counsel to believe a guilty plea is advised.

See paragraph [202] *supra*. S/he must also explain to the client all of the consequences of the plea, see paragraph [195] *supra*, and of conviction, see paragraph [205] *supra*. The terms of any plea bargain that counsel has managed to work out with the prosecutor should be described in detail; counsel should give the client written instructions regarding all obligations that the client will assume under this agreement; and counsel should emphasize the importance of the client's scrupulous performance of those obligations, together with the risks that face the client if s/he fails to perform. See paragraph [213] (C) *supra*. The benefits of the agreement to the client should, of course, be stressed as well; and counsel may properly express the forceful conclusion that the client's best interests call for taking a plea bargain offered by the prosecutor or for pleading guilty. See paragraph [201] *supra*.

(B) The client should be given adequate time to think about the decision and, in an appropriate case, may be urged to talk to his or her family, religious counselor, or other trusted personal adviser about it. When the client has reached a decision, this decision should be clearly understood by both counsel and client, and it should be further understood that this is the *client's* decision.

(C) Counsel should make file notes of all conversations with the client leading up to a decision by the client to plead guilty and should specifically note having given the client all of the advice and explanations mentioned in this paragraph. These notes will protect the attorney from unwarranted allegations — all too common in postconviction petitions in guilty plea cases — that counsel coerced the defendant to plead or gave the defendant inadequate advice concerning the significance and consequences of the plea, the defendant's rights, and so forth. See paragraph [392] *infra*.

(D) Counsel should also advise the client about what the client should expect, the client's rights and duties, and ways in which the client can best cope with unfamiliar circumstances, in whatever jail, prison, or probationary setting the client will be entering as a result of his or her plea and conviction. It is particularly important to counsel the client regarding the conditions of probationary supervision, including the visitational powers of probation officers, *see Griffin v. Wisconsin*, 107 S. Ct. 3164 (1987), and how the client should behave in dealing with his or her probation officer, *see Minnesota v. Murphy*, 465 U.S. 420 (1984).

[215] The guilty plea and the "innocent" client. Views differ on whether a lawyer may properly advise (or even permit) a client to plead guilty who protests his or her innocence. Fortunately, the moral problem seldom need arise. If the case is such that a guilty plea is advised, the client probably (although not invariably) *is* guilty; and if counsel discusses the evidence critically with the client and subjects the client to the sort of cross-examination that in every case will be necessary to prepare adequately for trial (see paragraphs [89], [151] *supra*; paragraphs [279]-[280] *infra*), the client will most commonly admit guilt. Should the client continue to assert innocence, a guilty plea will not be accepted by the court unless it is entered before a judge who makes little or no inquiry of defendants pleading guilty or a judge who is willing to take a plea from an adequately informed and counseled defendant professing innocence but recognizing that his or her best tactical choice is a guilty plea. Such a judge is often hard to find. The propriety of judicial acceptance of a plea of guilty from a defendant who denies factual guilt is unsettled in many jurisdictions, although the Supreme Court's toleration of the practice in *North Carolina v. Alford*, 400 U.S. 25 (1970), has given it somewhat greater currency. Many judges prefer not to accept such a plea even when they recognize that they are legally free to do so. When there is a judge available who will either advisedly or inadvertently take the plea, then the question of counsel's own responsibility must be resolved at the level of counsel's individual conscience. Obviously, a client who believes and asserts that s/he is innocent should not be advised to plead guilty unless the client, as well as counsel, is very strongly convinced that a plea is distinctly to the client's best advantage. This condition met, the hard decision follows.

[216] **Preparing the defendant for arraignment.** The client who is pleading guilty must be informed in advance and in considerable detail what to expect in court at arraignment. S/he must be told that s/he is going to be interrogated by the judge or by the prosecutor or by counsel, if this is so, and what questions will be asked. See paragraph [188] *supra*. This preparation has two functions. First, it helps to set the client at ease, so that s/he will be less traumatized by the experience and will make a better impression in court. Second, it helps to reduce the likelihood that the client will say something that renders the guilty plea unacceptable. There are some clients who will admit guilt to their lawyers and will agree to a plea of guilty, negotiated or unnegotiated, but who never really accept the notion of their guilt as anything but a highly private affair—a secret between themselves and counsel—not for public announcement. Thus when the judge questions them about their version of the offense, they deny guilt. This, of course, will prove embarrassing to all concerned, and it may well cause the judge to refuse to take the guilty plea. Avoidance of the situation is possible if counsel advises the client before arraignment that a public admission of guilt in court will be required, that the client will be asked by the judge to describe his or her version of the facts of the offense (which counsel and the client should rehearse carefully), and that if the client enters a plea of guilty, this is an admission of guilt in fact which cannot be denied in court without causing the judge to reject the plea. (An exception to this advice is in order, of course, in the situation discussed in the preceding paragraph, in which counsel has decided to go ahead with a guilty plea on behalf of a client who is resolved to enter the plea on tactical grounds while continuing to assert innocence even in his or her private discussions with counsel. Here, since counsel cannot countenance the client's lying to the court, it becomes counsel's job to bring the case on for pleading before a judge who will either accept the plea notwithstanding the client's protestations of innocence or forbear to inquire into the client's factual guilt or the reasons for the plea. If such a judge can be found in the locality, the prosecutor will ordinarily know who s/he is.) Before most judges, the client will be required to answer the

question whether anyone has made any promises to the client in exchange for his or her plea or any representations to the client about the sentence that will be imposed or about the disposition of any other charges against the client. Some judges expect a "no" answer to this question, even though they know that a plea has been negotiated, apparently on the theory that such matters as sentencing recommendations and *nol prosses* (when subject to judicial approval) are not binding on the court and hence not firm *promises* of the consequences of the plea. A more candid response for the client is that the prosecutor has said s/he would recommend such-and-such a disposition but that the client understands that this is not a promise of the sentence s/he is going to get and understands that it is up to the judge to decide what the sentence will be. Plea bargaining has "recently . . . become a visible practice accepted as a legitimate component in the administration of criminal justice," *Blackledge v. Allison*, 431 U.S. 63, 76 (1977); and this development will doubtless cause an increasing number of judges to be willing to accept avowedly bargained pleas and to spread the terms of the bargain on the record (see paragraphs [211], [213] (B) *supra*). But old attitudes spawned by "decades [when bargaining] . . . was a *sub rosa* process shrouded in secrecy and deliberately concealed by participating defendants, defense lawyers, prosecutors, and even judges" (*Blackledge v. Allison, supra*, 431 U.S. at 76) have not vanished overnight; and some judges remain less willing than others to tolerate the fact (or at least the visible appearance) of "bargain justice." Counsel must therefore know the attitudes of the sitting judge in order to prepare the client properly for the proceedings at which a guilty plea will be tendered.

[217] **Selecting the sentencing judge.** Despite recent attempts to achieve judicial uniformity in sentencing, individual judges continue to differ enormously in their sentencing patterns and attitudes. Often the most significant thing that counsel can do to affect a client's sentence is to have the sentence imposed by the right judge or not imposed by the wrong judge. Experienced criminal lawyers in a locality (and the prosecutor

if s/he is trustworthy and cooperative) will always know a good deal about who are the right and wrong judges in particular sorts of cases.

[218] **Same—the timing of the guilty plea.** The judge before whom a plea of guilty is entered ordinarily assumes jurisdiction over future stages of the case and becomes the sentencing judge. For this reason plea negotiation with the prosecutor may profitably include consideration of bringing the case on for arraignment at a time when the arraignment judge is a favorable one. If this cannot be done at the initial arraignment (as it can in localities where the prosecutor controls the calendar call at arraignments), a continuance by agreement may be in order. Alternatively, the defendant may plead not guilty at the arraignment, with an eye to changing the plea at a later time. See paragraph [194] *supra*. Sometimes judges will receive a plea at other than regular arraignment sessions, and this possibly should be explored with the prosecutor. Or the prosecutor may have sufficient control over calendaring for trial so that the case can be listed before a favorable judge, with the understanding that the defendant will withdraw his or her initial not guilty plea and will plead guilty on the trial date. In the absence of a negotiated plea, counsel whose client is pleading guilty will have to make such decisions concerning timing as counsel can unilaterally effectuate. Whether or not the plea should be entered at arraignment will depend on whether there is a chance that a more lenient judge will sit on postarraignment motions or at trial. Similar sentencing considerations may determine whether to ask for a jury trial or to waive a jury; different judges will likely be sitting in jury and nonjury courts. Knowledge of individual judicial predilections and of court calendars is indispensable.

[219] **Disposition when the defendant turns state's evidence.** Generally, when a defendant has agreed to plead guilty and testify against an accomplice, there is some reluctance on the part of the prosecution to proceed to make a final disposition of the case before the defendant has, in fact, testified. Defense counsel sometimes can, and should try to, overcome

this reluctance by urging the prosecutor that the defendant has no love for the accomplice and can be counted on to testify against the accomplice without the coercion applied by keeping the defendant's own charges pending. Furthermore, defense counsel can point out that the defendant will be more impeachable as a prosecution witness if those charges are still pending than if they have already been disposed of. If this persuasion fails and if the delay in disposition of the charges will not prejudice the defendant, then the defendant's arraignment should be continued until after s/he has testified; most judges will readily agree to a continuance once the situation is described to them. However, if prejudice may result from the delay—as when the defendant is jailed in default of bail or when there is a risk that the prosecutor's understanding of the testimony which the defendant has agreed to give is not the same as the defendant's understanding—counsel should attempt to bring the case on for arraignment before a judge who will appreciate the prejudice and do something about it: for example, release the defendant on nominal bail or accept the plea, impose sentence, and suspend its execution in whole or in part upon condition only that the defendant testify (without regard to the content of the testimony) in the event that the accomplice goes to trial. If the state's-evidence arrangement contemplates dismissal of the charges against the defendant, rather than the defendant's pleading guilty to them, a final disposition before the defendant testifies will ordinarily be far more difficult to obtain. Nevertheless, it may be possible for counsel to convince a sympathetic arraignment judge to dismiss the charges "in the interest of justice" (when local practice allows judicial discretion to order a dismissal on this ground without the prosecutor's assent), subject to refiling if the defendant subsequently balks at testifying. Or if an applicable immunity statue can be found to apply (see paragraphs [105], [161] *supra*), the arraignment judge might be persuaded to enter an order immunizing the defendant pursuant to the statute and thereupon dismiss the charges.

TABLE OF CASES AND AUTHORITIES

(References are to section numbers)

CASES

A

B

H

I

J

K

P

R

S

U

Y

Z

Statutes And Rules

United States Code

D.C. Code

Federal Rules of Criminal Procedure

Federal Rules of Evidence

Other Authorities

INDEX OF SUBJECTS

(References are to section numbers)